Real-Time 3D Graphics with WebGL 2
WebGL 2
Second Edition

Build interactive 3D applications with JavaScript and WebGL 2 (OpenGL ES 3.0)

Farhad Ghayour
Diego Cantor

BIRMINGHAM - MUMBAI

Real-Time 3D Graphics with WebGL 2
Second Edition

Commissioning Editor: Kunal Chaudhari
Acquisition Editor: Divya Poojari
Content Development Editor: Francis Carneiro
Technical Editor: Sachin Sunilkumar
Copy Editor: Safis Editing
Project Coordinator: Sheejal Shah
Proofreader: Safis Editing
Indexer: Aishwarya Gangawane
Graphics: Jason Monteiro
Production Coordinator: Shraddha Falebhai

First published: June 2012
Second edition: October 2018

Production reference: 1311018

Published by Packt Publishing Ltd.
Livery Place
35 Livery Street
Birmingham
B3 2PB, UK.

ISBN 978-1-78862-969-0

www.packtpub.com

To God, for His many blessings, and to my caring family, friends, and colleagues, who have always been there for me.

– Farhad Ghayour

To my family: Luis, Cecy, Jonathan, and Fredy.

– Diego Cantor

`mapt.io`

Mapt is an online digital library that gives you full access to over 5,000 books and videos, as well as industry leading tools to help you plan your personal development and advance your career. For more information, please visit our website.

Why Subscribe?

- Spend less time learning and more time coding with practical eBooks and Videos from over 4,000 industry professionals

- Improve your learning with Skill Plans built especially for you

- Get a free eBook or video every month

- Mapt is fully searchable

- Copy and paste, print, and bookmark content

Packt.com

Did you know that Packt offers eBook versions of every book published, with PDF and ePub files available? You can upgrade to the eBook version at `www.packt.com` and as a print book customer, you are entitled to a discount on the eBook copy. Get in touch with us at `customercare@packtpub.com` for more details.

At `www.packt.com`, you can also read a collection of free technical articles, sign up for a range of free newsletters, and receive exclusive discounts and offers on Packt books and eBooks.

Foreword

Having worked with Farhad Ghayour for over 10 years, I can assure you that he prioritizes practicality and innovation above all. With years of experiences in building businesses from the ground up, Farhad will help you filter what is useful from what is unnecessary in guiding you towards success.

WebGL is a technology that will change the way we interact with our digital devices. As a UI/UX thought leader, Farhad will walk you through a systematic process for how to deliver and optimize compelling user experiences with WebGL. This book will show you what can be done with practical examples and what we can look forward to in the near future.

Jonathan Melo

Lead Engineer and Serial Entrepreneur

Contributors

About the Authors

Farhad Ghayour is a technology consultant based out of San Francisco, California, where he helps transform Fortune 500 companies worldwide.

Currently, he is focused on technology solutions at the intersection of computer graphics, vision, and machine learning. Previously, he was a core contributor to a leading open source WebGL engine, lead engineer at various start-ups around the world, a philosophy teacher, a serial entrepreneur, and an investment banker.

He is passionate about all things philosophy, math, code, and design. When he is not working, you can either find him racing cars or trying out new Chinese hotpot restaurants—most likely, hotpot.

I'd like to thank my colleagues at Famo.us, who ignited my enduring passion for graphics; my philosophy professors, who provided me with tools and rigor; my collaborators, Diego and Brandon, for offering me a solid foundation; my close friends for continually helping me grow; and the Packt editorial, especially Francis Savio Carneiro, for their patience and continual support.

Most importantly, I'd like to express my deepest appreciation and special gratitude to my loving and supporting family.

About the Authors

Diego Cantor received his M.Eng. in Systems and Computer Engineering from Universidad de Los Andes (Colombia), and his Ph.D. in Biomedical Engineering from Western University (Canada). He published the first-ever online beating heart and brain cortex map using WebGL. He is also the author of the WebGL Beginner's Guide which sold internationally in English, Korean and Chinese. Diego is passionate about open source and web technologies, and he has worked extensively in medical imaging technologies. In his free time, he enjoys working out, classical music and learning new languages.

I wish to express my most sincere gratitude and appreciation to Farhad Ghayour for his commitment to this project. Farhad's enthusiasm and knowledge about WebGL are both abundant and compelling. Without him, this book would not have been a reality. Farhad: I look forward to future collaborations! Also, I would like to recognize the amazing work of the technical reviewers and the Packt editorial team and, in particular, to Divya Poojari for her infinite patience and willingness to collaborate across oceans, and time zones.

About the Reviewers

Sebastian Hack is an R&D software engineer who specializes in computer vision, machine learning, and robotics. After graduating from the University of California, Berkeley, with a bachelor's degree in Electrical Engineering and Computer Science, he moved to work on Microsoft's HoloLens. Outside of work, he enjoys playing tennis, watching classic films, and racing quadcopter drones.

> *I would like to acknowledge Maggie Miller-Hack for supporting my interest in engineering, and Farhad Ghayour for spearheading this project.*

Brian Foster grew up as a traditional artist and, over time, became fascinated by technology and its applied advances. He has a diverse background in visual design, programming, and information security, and has always been fascinated in identifying efficiency gaps, automating scalable solutions, and integrating various mediums for the sake of establishing innovation and new discoveries. Brian believes WebGL 2 represents the dawn of a new age for an internet-based experience.

> *I would like to acknowledge Farhad Ghayour for taking me with him in his charismatic approach to truly understanding WebGL 2 and its practical uses. The true value of this book is that it will allow newcomers to grow and accomplish relevant projects that require a more dynamic web-based experience.*

Joseph Sample is a graphics engineer with a particular focus on WebGL. When he is not working, he is a touring musician in the band *Ice Cream*, and is particularly interested in the intersection of sound and graphics.

Alexander Gugel is a software engineer working at Facebook. He previously worked on the platform team at Famo.us building a 3D rendering engine.

Packt Is Searching for Authors like You

If you're interested in becoming an author for Packt, please visit `authors.packtpub.com` and apply today. We have worked with thousands of developers and tech professionals, just like you, to help them share their insight with the global tech community. You can make a general application, apply for a specific hot topic that we are recruiting an author for, or submit your own idea.

Table of Contents

Preface

WebGL is a powerful web technology that brings hardware-accelerated 3D graphics to the browser without requiring the user to install additional software. Given that WebGL is based on OpenGL and introduces 3D graphics programming to web development, it may seem unfamiliar to even experienced web developers. On the other hand, for those with experience in traditional computer graphics, building 3D applications with JavaScript takes some getting use to. A common view is that JavaScript is not as fast as other traditional languages used in computer graphics; although this is a concern in comparing CPU-bound algorithms, it is not an issue in comparing GPU-bound work. This is where WebGL shines! The powerful capabilities that WebGL offers, coupled with the ubiquity and accessibility of browsers, positions the technology in a unique and attractive position to power the future of immersive experiences on the web.

Packed with many examples, this book shows how WebGL can be easy to learn despite its unfriendly appearance. Each chapter addresses one of the important aspects of 3D graphics programming and presents different alternatives for its implementation. The topics are always associated with exercises that will allow the reader to put the concepts to the test.

Real-Time 3D Graphics with WebGL 2 presents a clear roadmap to learning WebGL 2. While WebGL1 is based on the OpenGL ES 2.0 specification, WebGL 2 is derived from OpenGL ES 3.0, which guarantees the availability of many WebGL1 extensions along with new features. Each chapter starts with a summary of the learning goals for the chapter, followed by a detailed description of each topic. The book offers example-rich, up-to-date introductions to a wide range of essential WebGL topics, including drawing, color, texture, transformations, frame buffers, light, surfaces, geometry, and more. Each chapter is packed with useful and practical examples that demonstrate the implementation of these topics in a WebGL scene. With each chapter, you will "level up" your 3D graphics programming skills. This book will become your trustworthy companion, filled with the information required to develop compelling 3D web applications with JavaScript and WebGL 2.

Who This Book Is For

This book is written for developers who are interested in building 3D applications for the web. A basic understanding of JavaScript and Linear Algebra is ideal, but not mandatory. No prior WebGL knowledge is expected.

What This Book Covers

Chapter 1, *Getting Started*, introduces the HTML5 `canvas` element and describes how to obtain a WebGL 2 context for it. After that, it discusses the basic structure of a WebGL application. The virtual car showroom application is presented as a demo of the capabilities of WebGL. This application also showcases the different components of a WebGL application.

Chapter 2, *Rendering*, presents the WebGL API to define, process, and render objects. This chapter also demonstrates how to perform asynchronous geometry loading using AJAX and JSON.

Chapter 3, *Lights*, introduces ESSL, the shading language for WebGL. This chapter shows how to implement a lighting strategy for the WebGL scene using ESSL shaders. The theory behind shading and reflective lighting models is covered and put into practice through a variety of examples.

Chapter 4, *Cameras*, illustrates the use of matrix algebra to create and operate cameras in WebGL. The Perspective and Normal matrices that are used in a WebGL scene are also described here. The chapter also shows how to pass these matrices to ESSL shaders so that they can be applied to every vertex. The chapter contains several examples that show how to set up a camera in WebGL.

Chapter 5, *Animations*, extends the use of matrices to perform geometrical transformations (move, rotate, scale) on scene elements. In this chapter, the concept of matrix stacks is discussed. It is shown how to maintain isolated transformations for every object in the scene using matrix stacks. Also, the chapter describes several animation techniques using matrix stacks and JavaScript timers. A practical demonstration is provided of each technique.

Chapter 6, *Colors, Depth Testing, and Alpha Blending*, goes into detail about the use of colors in ESSL shaders. This chapter shows how to define and operate with more than one light source in a WebGL scene. It also explains the concepts of depth testing and alpha blending, and shows how these features can be used to create translucent objects. The chapter contains several practical exercises that put these concepts into practice.

Chapter 7, *Textures*, shows how to create, manage, and map textures in a WebGL scene. The concepts of texture coordinates and texture mapping are presented here. This chapter discusses different mapping techniques that are presented through practical examples. The chapter also shows how to use multiple textures and cube maps.

Chapter 8, *Picking*, describes a simple implementation of picking, which is the technical term that describes the selection and interaction of the user with objects in the scene. The method described in this chapter calculates mouse-click coordinates and determines whether the user is clicking on any of the objects being rendered in the canvas. The architecture of the solution is presented with several callback hooks that can be used to implement logic-specific application. A couple of examples of picking are given.

Chapter 9, *Putting It All Together*, ties in the concepts discussed throughout the book. In this chapter, the architecture of the demos is reviewed and the virtual car showroom application outlined in Chapter 1, *Getting Started*, is revisited and expanded. Using the virtual car showroom as the case study, this chapter shows how to import Blender models into WebGL scenes and how to create ESSL shaders that support the materials used in Blender.

Chapter 10, *Advanced Techniques*, provides a sample of a number of advanced techniques, including post-processing effects, point sprites, normal mapping, and ray tracing. Each technique is provided with a practical example. After reading this chapter, you will be able to take on more advanced techniques on your own.

Chapter 11, *WebGL 2 Highlights*, outlines some of the major features and updates to the WebGL 2 specification. This chapter also provides a migration strategy for converting applications based on WebGL1 to WebGL 2.

Chapter 12, *Journey Ahead*, concludes *Real-Time 3D Graphics with WebGL 2* with recommendations regarding techniques, concepts, tools, and communities that readers can leverage on their journey in mastering real-time 3D graphics.

To Get the Most out of This Book

You need a browser that implements WebGL 2. WebGL 2 is supported by all major browser vendors with the exception of Microsoft Internet Explorer:

- Firefox 51 or above
- Google Chrome 56 or above
- Chrome for Android 64 or above

An updated list of WebGL-enabled browsers can be found here: http://www.khronos.org/webgl/wiki/Getting_a_WebGL_Implementation.

You also need a source code editor that recognizes and highlights JavaScript syntax.

And you need a web server, such as Apache, Lighttpd, or Python, to load remote assets.

Download the Example Code Files

You can download the example code files for this book from your account at www.packt.com. If you purchased this book elsewhere, you can visit www.packt.com/support and register to have the files emailed directly to you.

You can download the code files by following these steps:

1. Log in or register at www.packt.com.
2. Select the Support tab.
3. Click on **Code Downloads & Errata**.
4. Enter the name of the book in the **Search** box and follow the onscreen instructions.

Once the file is downloaded, please make sure that you unzip or extract the folder using the latest version of:

- WinRAR/7-Zip for Windows
- Zipeg/iZip/UnRarX for Mac
- 7-Zip/PeaZip for Linux

The code bundle for the book is also hosted on GitHub at https://github.com/ PacktPublishing/Real-Time-3D-Graphics-with-WebGL-2. In case there's an update to the code, it will be updated on the existing GitHub repository.

We also have other code bundles from our rich catalog of books and videos available at https://github.com/PacktPublishing/. Check them out!

Running Examples Locally

If you do *not* have a web server, we recommend that you install a lightweight web server from the following options:

- **Serve:** https://github.com/zeit/serve
- **Lighttpd:** http://www.lighttpd.net
- **Python server:** https://developer.mozilla.org/en-US/docs/Learn/Common_ questions/set_up_a_local_testing_server

That being said, to run the examples locally on your machine, be sure to run your server from the root of the examples directory, since the common directory is a shared dependency across chapters.

Download the Color Images

We also provide a PDF file that has color images of the screenshots/diagrams used in this book. You can download it here: `https://www.packtpub.com/sites/default/files/downloads/9781788629690_ColorImages.pdf`.

Conventions Used

There are a number of text conventions used throughout this book.

`CodeInText`: Indicates code words in text, folder names, filenames, file extensions, pathnames, dummy URLs, user input, and so forth. Here is an example: "Open the `ch01_01_demo.html` file in your editor."

A block of code is set as follows:

```html
<html>
<head>
  <title>Real-Time 3D Graphics with WebGL 2</title>

  <style type="text/css">
    canvas {
      border: 5px dotted blue;
    }
  </style>
</head>
<body>

  <canvas id="webgl-canvas" width="800" height="600">
    Your browser does not support the HTML5 canvas element.
  </canvas>

</body>
</html>
```

When we wish to draw your attention to a particular part of a code block, the relevant lines or items are set in bold:

```html
<canvas id="webgl-canvas" width="800" height="600">
  Your browser does not support the HTML5 canvas element.
</canvas>
```

Any command-line input or output is written as follows:

```
$ mkdir webgl-demo
$ cd webgl-demo
```

Bold: Indicates a new term, an important word, or words that you see on screen. For example, words in menus or dialog boxes appear in the text like this. Here is an example: "Select **System info** from the **Administration** panel."

 Warnings or important notes appear like this.

 Tips and tricks appear like this.

Sections

In this book, you will find several headings that appear frequently (Time for Action, What just happened?, and Have a Go).

To give clear instructions on how to complete a procedure or task, we use these sections as follows:

Time for Action

1. Action 1
2. Action 2
3. Action 3

Instructions often require some extra explanation to ensure they make sense, so they are followed by these sections:

What just happened?

This section explains the working of the tasks or instructions that you have just completed.

Have a Go

These are practical challenges that give you ideas on how to experiment using what you have learned.

Get in Touch

Feedback from our readers is always welcome.

General feedback: If you have questions about any aspect of this book, mention the book title in the subject of your message and email us at customercare@packtpub.com.

Errata: Although we have taken every care to ensure the accuracy of our content, mistakes do happen. If you have found a mistake in this book, we would be grateful if you would report this to us. Please visit www.packt.com/submit-errata, selecting your book, clicking on the Errata Submission Form link, and entering the details.

Piracy: If you come across any illegal copies of our works in any form on the Internet, we would be grateful if you would provide us with the location address or website name. Please contact us at copyright@packt.com with a link to the material.

If you are interested in becoming an author: If there is a topic that you have expertise in and you are interested in either writing or contributing to a book, please visit authors.packtpub.com.

Reviews

Please leave a review. Once you have read and used this book, why not leave a review on the site that you purchased it from? Potential readers can then see and use your unbiased opinion to make purchase decisions, we at Packt can understand what you think about our products, and our authors can see your feedback on their book. Thank you!

For more information about Packt, please visit packt.com.

Getting Started

1

There was a time when most of the web comprised pages with static content—the only graphics were embedded images. Over time, however, application requirements became more ambitious and began running into limitations. As highly interactive applications became an increasingly important part of the user experience, there was, eventually, enough demand for a fully programmable graphics **Application Programming Interface** (**API**) to address these requirements. In 2006, Vladimir Vukicevic, an American-Serbian software engineer, began working on an OpenGL prototype for a then-upcoming HTML `<canvas>` element that he called Canvas 3D. In March 2011, his work would lead to the Kronos Group, the nonprofit organization behind OpenGL, to create **WebGL**, a specification to grant internet browsers access to **Graphics Processing Units** (**GPUs**).

All of the browser engines collaborated to create WebGL, the standard for rendering 3D graphics on the web. It was based on OpenGL **Embedded Systems** (**ES**), a cross-platform API for graphics targeted at embedded systems. This was the right starting place, because it made it possible to easily implement the same API in all browsers, especially since most browser engines were running on systems that had support for OpenGL.

WebGL was originally based on OpenGL ES 2.0, the OpenGL specification version for devices such as Apple's iPhone and iPad. But, as the specification evolved, it became independent with the goal of providing portability across various operating systems and devices. The idea of web-based, real-time rendering opened a new world of possibilities for web-based 3D environments. Due to the pervasiveness of web browsers, these and other kinds of 3D applications could now be rendered on desktop and mobile devices such as smartphones and tablets. According to the Khronos Group, the ability for Web developers to directly access OpenGL-class graphics directly from JavaScript, and freely mix 3D with other HTML content, will enable a new wave of innovation in Web gaming, educational and training applications.

Even though WebGL was vastly adopted for many years after it matured into a stable release—shipping inside Firefox, Chrome, Opera, IE11, and Android's mobile web browsers—Apple still lacked official WebGL support. Neither OS X Safari nor Safari Mobile supported WebGL. In fact, it wasn't until 2014, at June's **Worldwide Developers Conference** (**WWDC**), that Apple announced that both OS X Yosemite and iOS 8 would ship with WebGL support. This became a turning point for 3D graphics on the web. With official support from all major browsers, the entire range of 3D graphics—at native speeds—could be delivered to billions of desktop and mobile devices. WebGL unleashed the power of graphics processors to developers on an open platform, allowing console-quality application to be built for the web.

In this chapter, we will do the following:

- Understand the necessary system requirements to run WebGL.
- Cover the common high-level components of a WebGL application.
- Set up a drawing area (`canvas`).
- Test your browser's WebGL capabilities.
- Understand that WebGL acts as a state machine.
- Modify WebGL variables that affect your scene.
- Load and examine a fully-functional scene.

System Requirements

WebGL is a web-based 3D Graphics API. As such, there is *no* installation needed. While WebGL 1 is based on the OpenGL ES 2.0 specification, WebGL 2 is based on OpenGL ES 3.0, which guarantees the availability of many WebGL 1 extensions along with new features.

WebGL 2 Versus WebGL 1

Given this book covers WebGL 2, all WebGL and WebGL 2 terms reference the WebGL 2 (OpenGL ES 3.0) specification. Any references to WebGL 1 (OpenGL ES 2.0) will be done so explicitly.

As of January 27, 2016, WebGL 2 is available by default in Firefox and Chrome. You will automatically have access to WebGL 2, provided you have one of the following web browsers:

- Firefox 51 or above
- Google Chrome 56 or above
- Chrome for Android 64 or above

For an updated list of the web browsers that support WebGL, please visit the Khronos Group web page: `http://www.khronos.org/webgl/wiki/Getting_a_WebGL_Implementation`.

Or visit the well-known **CanIUse.com** resource: `https://caniuse.com/#search=WebGL 2`.

Modern Standards

Since we will be using modern browsers to run WebGL 2, we will also leverage HTML5, CSS3, and JavaScript ES6 throughout this book. For more information on these modern standards, please refer to the following link: `https://developer.mozilla.org/en-US/docs/Web`.

At the time of this book's publication, WebGL 2 remains a specification that's in flux. Some parts of the specification are considered stable and have been implemented in modern browsers; other parts should be considered experimental and have been partially implemented to varying degrees. Therefore, you should be familiar with how the standardization process works and the levels of implementation for each new property. That being said, WebGL 2 is nearly 100% backward compatible with WebGL 1. All exceptions to backward compatibility are recorded in the following link: `https://www.khronos.org/registry/webgl/specs/latest/2.0/#BACKWARDS_INCOMPATIBILITY`.

Migrating to WebGL 2

If you have prior experience with WebGL 1 or are curious about migration strategies to WebGL 2, you can refer to `Chapter 11`, *WebGL 2 Highlights*, where key differences between WebGL 1 and WebGL 2 are highlighted.

Lastly, you will need to make sure that your computer has an approved graphics card. To quickly validate your current configuration for WebGL 2, please visit the following link: `https://get.webgl.org/WebGL 2/`.

WebGL Rendering

WebGL is a 3D graphics library that enables modern web browsers to render 3D scenes in a standard and efficient manner. According to Wikipedia, **rendering** is the process of generating an image from a model by means of computer programs. Since this is a process executed by a computer, there are different ways to produce such images. There are three main distinctions to make when discussing rendering: software-based and hardware-based rendering, server-based and client-based rendering, and retained-mode and immediate-mode rendering. As we will see, WebGL offers a unique approach to hardware and client based rendering with an immediate-mode API on the web.

Software and Hardware Based Rendering

The first distinction we should make is whether we are using any special graphics hardware. On one hand, we can talk about **software-based rendering** for cases where all required calculations to render 3D scenes are performed using the computer's **Central Processing Unit** (**CPU**). On the other hand, as is the case with WebGL, we use the term **hardware-based rendering** for scenarios where there is a GPU performing 3D graphics computations. From a technical standpoint, hardware-based rendering is much more efficient than software-based rendering, because the former involves dedicated hardware handling the necessary operations. In contrast, a software-based rendering solution can be more common due to the lack of hardware dependencies.

Server and Client Based Rendering

The second distinction to make is whether the rendering process is happening locally or remotely. When the image that needs to be rendered is too complex, the render will most likely occur remotely. This is the case for 3D animated movies where dedicated servers with lots of hardware resources render intricate scenes. We call this **server-based rendering**. The opposite of this approach takes place when rendering occurs locally. We call this **client-based rendering**. WebGL offers a client-based rendering approach: the elements that are a part of the 3D scene are usually downloaded from a server. However, the processing required to obtain an image is all performed locally using the client's graphics hardware. Although this is not a unique solution, compared to other technologies (such as Java 3D, Flash, and the Unity Web Player Plugin), WebGL presents several advantages:

- **JavaScript programming**: JavaScript is a language that is natural to both web developers and browsers. Working with JavaScript allows you to access all parts of the DOM and easily integrate WebGL applications with other JavaScript libraries such as jQuery, React, and Angular.

- **Automatic memory management**: WebGL—unlike other technologies, such as OpenGL, where memory allocation and deallocation are handled manually—follows the rules for JavaScript variable scoping and automatic memory management. This simplifies programming tremendously while reducing the code footprint. Ultimately, this simplification makes it easier to understand the application logic.

- **Pervasiveness**: Web browsers with JavaScript capabilities are installed in smartphones and tablet devices by default. This means you can leverage WebGL across a vast ecosystem of desktop and mobile devices.

- **Performance**: Performance of WebGL applications is comparable to equivalent standalone applications (with some exceptions). This is possible due to WebGL's ability to access the local graphics hardware. Until recently, many 3D web rendering technologies used software-based rendering.

- **Zero compilation**: WebGL is written in JavaScript; therefore, there is no need to compile your code before executing it on the web browser. This empowers you to make changes in real-time and see how those changes affect your 3D web application. Nevertheless, when we cover shader programs, we will understand that some compilation is needed. However, this occurs in your graphics hardware and not in your browser.

Retained and Immediate Mode Rendering

The third distinction to make is that WebGL is an immediate mode 3D rendering API designed for the web. Graphics APIs can be divided into retained-mode APIs and immediate-mode APIs.

Retained-Mode Rendering

A **retained-mode** API is declarative. The application builds a scene from primitives, such as shapes and lines, and then the graphics library maintains a scene model in memory. To change what is rendered, the application issues a command to update the scene, which could include, for example, adding or removing a shape; the library is then responsible for managing and redrawing the scene:

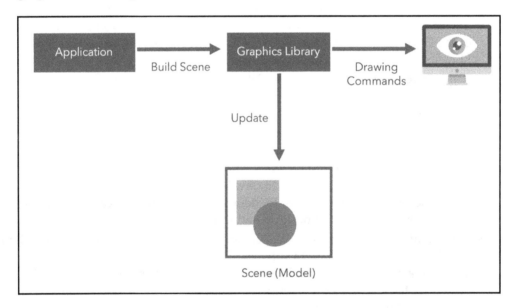

Immediate-Mode Rendering

An **immediate-mode** API is procedural. Immediate mode rendering requires the application to directly manage rendering. In this case, the graphics library does not maintain a scene model. Each time a new frame is drawn, the application issues all drawing commands required to describe the entire scene, regardless of actual changes. This method provides the maximum amount of control and flexibility to the application program:

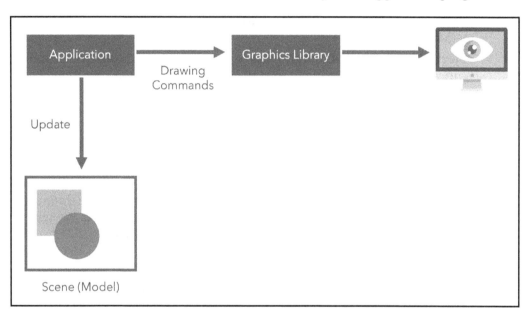

Retained Versus Immediate Mode Rendering

Retained-mode rendering can be simpler to use, because the API does more of the work for you, such as initialization, state maintenance, and cleanup. However, it is often less flexible since the API forces its own particular scene model; it can also have higher memory prerequisites because it needs to provide a general-purpose scene model. Immediate-mode rendering, on the other hand, as offered with WebGL, is much more flexible and can implement targeted optimizations.

Elements in a WebGL Application

WebGL, like other 3D graphics libraries, comprises many common 3D elements. These fundamental elements will be covered, chapter-by-chapter, throughout this book.

Some of these common elements include the following:

- `canvas`: It is the placeholder where our scene is rendered. It is a standard HTML5 element and as such, can be accessed using the **Document Object Model (DOM)**.
- **Objects**: These are the 3D entities that make up the scene. These entities are composed of triangles. In the following chapters, we will see how WebGL handles and renders geometries using **buffers**.
- **Lights**: Nothing in a 3D world can be seen without lights. In later chapters, we will learn that WebGL uses **shaders** to model lights in the scene. We will see how 3D objects reflect or absorb light according to the laws of physics. We will also discuss different light models to visualize our objects.
- **Camera**: `canvas` acts as the viewport to the 3D world. We see and explore a 3D scene through it. In the following chapters, we will understand the different matrix operations that are required to produce a view perspective. We will understand how these operations can be modeled as a camera.

This chapter will cover the first element of our list: `canvas`. The following sections will help us understand how to create a `canvas` element and how to set up a WebGL context.

Time for Action: Creating an HTML5 Canvas Element

A `canvas` is a rectangular element in your web page where your 3D scene will be rendered. Let's create a web page and add a HTML5 `canvas` element:

1. Using your favorite editor, create a web page with the following code:

```html
<html>
<head>
  <title>Real-Time 3D Graphics with WebGL2</title>
  <link rel="shortcut icon" type="image/png"
  href="/common/images/favicon.png" />

  <style type="text/css">
```

```
   canvas {
     border: 5px dotted blue;
   }
 </style>
</head>
<body>

  <canvas id="webgl-canvas" width="800" height="600">
    Your browser does not support the HTML5 canvas element.
  </canvas>

</body>
</html>
```

2. Save the file as ch01_01_canvas.html.
3. Open it with a supported browser.
4. You should see something similar to the following screenshot:

What just happened?

We created a simple web page containing a canvas element. This canvas will contain our 3D application. Let's go very quickly over some relevant elements presented in this example.

Defining a CSS Style

This is the piece of code that determines the `canvas` style:

```
<style type="text/css">
  canvas {
    border: 5px dotted blue;
  }
</style>
```

This code is not fundamental to build a WebGL application. Given that the `canvas` element is initially empty, a blue-dotted border is a simple way to verify the location of the `canvas`.

Understanding Canvas Attributes

There are three attributes in our previous example:

- `id`: This is the `canvas` identifier in the DOM.
- `width` and `height`: These two attributes determine the size of our `canvas` element. When these two attributes are missing, Firefox, Chrome, and WebKit will default to using `300px` by `150px`.

What If Canvas Is Not Supported?

If you see the following message on your screen, **Your browser does not support the HTML5 canvas element** (which is the message between the `<canvas>` tags), you need to make sure that you're using one of the supported web browsers described earlier.

If you're using Firefox and you still see this message, you may want to check whether WebGL is enabled (it is by *default*). To do so, go to Firefox and type `about:config` in the address bar. Then, look for the `webgl.disabled` property. If it is set to `true`, change it to `false`. When you restart Firefox and load `ch01_01_canvas.html`, you should be able to see the dotted border of the `canvas` element.

In the remote case that you still do not see `canvas`, it could be because your browser has blacklisted your GPU. If this is the case, please use a system with the appropriate hardware.

Time for Action: Accessing the WebGL Context

A WebGL context is a handle (more strictly a JavaScript object) through which we can access WebGL functions and attributes. These available features constitute the WebGL API.

We are going to create a JavaScript function that will check whether a WebGL context can be obtained. Unlike other technologies that need to be downloaded into your project, WebGL is *already in your browser*. In other words, if you are using one of the supported browsers, you don't need to install or include any library.

Let's modify the previous example to add a JavaScript function to check the WebGL availability in your browser. This function is going to be called when the page has loaded. For this, we will use the standard DOM `onload` event:

1. Open the `ch01_01_canvas.html` file in your favorite text editor.
2. Add the following code right below the closing `<style>` tag:

```
<script type="text/javascript">
  'use strict';
  function init() {
    const canvas = document.getElementById('webgl-canvas');

    // Ensure we have a canvas
    if (!canvas) {
      console.error('Sorry! No HTML5 Canvas was found on
       this page');
      return;
    }

    const gl = canvas.getContext('webgl2');

    // Ensure we have a context
    const message = gl
      ? 'Hooray! You got a WebGL2 context'
      : 'Sorry! WebGL is not available';

    alert(message);
  }

  // Call init once the document has loaded
  window.onload = init;
</script>
```

3. Save the file as `ch01_02_context.html`.

4. Open the `ch01_02_context.html` file using one of the WebGL 2 supported browsers.

5. If you can run WebGL 2, you will see a dialog similar to the following:

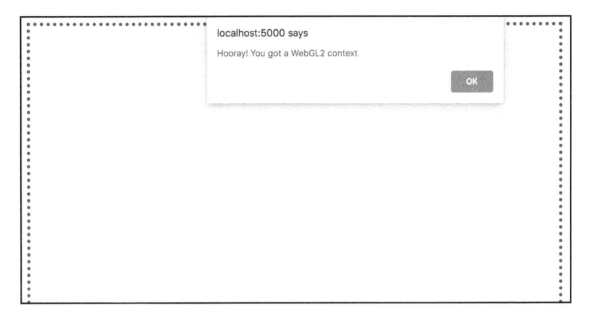

Strict Mode

The Strict Mode, declared by `'use strict';`, is a feature that allows you to place a program, or a function, in a "strict" operating context. This strict context prevents certain actions from being taken and throws more exceptions. For more information, please visit the following link: `https://developer.mozilla.org/en-US/docs/Web/JavaScript/Reference/Strict_mode`.

What just happened?

Assigning a JavaScript variable (`gl`), we obtained a reference to a WebGL context. Let's go back and check the code that allows accessing WebGL:

```
const gl = canvas.getContext('webgl2');
```

The `canvas.getContext` method gives us access to WebGL. `getContext` also provides access to the HTML5 2D graphics library when using `2D` as the context name. The HTML5 2D graphics API is completely independent from WebGL and is beyond the scope of this book.

State Machine

A WebGL context can be understood as a state machine: once you modify attributes, the modifications persist until later modifications. At any point, you can query the state of these attributes to determine the current state of your WebGL context. Let's analyze this behavior with an example.

Time for Action: Setting up WebGL Context Attributes

In this example, we are going to learn to modify the color we use to clear the `canvas` element:

1. Using your favorite text editor, open the `ch01_03_attributes.html` file:

```html
<html>
<head>
  <title>Real-Time 3D Graphics with WebGL2</title>
  <link rel="shortcut icon" type="image/png"
   href="/common/images/favicon.png" />

  <style>
    canvas {
      border: 5px dotted blue;
    }
  </style>

  <script type="text/javascript">
    'use strict';

    let gl;

    function updateClearColor(...color) {
      // The ES6 spread operator (...) allows for us to
      // use elements of an array as arguments to a function
      gl.clearColor(...color);
```

```
      gl.clear(gl.COLOR_BUFFER_BIT);
      gl.viewport(0, 0, 0, 0);
    }

    function checkKey(event) {
      switch (event.keyCode) {
        // number 1 => green
        case 49: {
          updateClearColor(0.2, 0.8, 0.2, 1.0);
          break;
        }
        // number 2 => blue
        case 50: {
          updateClearColor(0.2, 0.2, 0.8, 1.0);
          break;
        }
        // number 3 => random color
        case 51: {
          updateClearColor(Math.random(), Math.random(),
           Math.random(), 1.0);
          break;
        }
        // number 4 => get color
        case 52: {
          const color = gl.getParameter(gl.COLOR_CLEAR_VALUE);
          // Don't let the following line confuse you.
          // It basically rounds up the numbers to one
          // decimal cipher for visualization purposes.

          // TIP: Given that WebGL's color space ranges
          // from 0 to 1 you can multiply these values by 255
          // to display in their RGB values.
          alert(`clearColor = (
            ${color[0].toFixed(1)},
            ${color[1].toFixed(1)},
            ${color[2].toFixed(1)}
          )`);
          window.focus();
          break;
        }
      }
    }

    function init() {
      const canvas = document.getElementById('webgl-canvas');

      if (!canvas) {
        console.error('Sorry! No HTML5 Canvas was found on this
```

```
page');
        return;
    }

    gl = canvas.getContext('webgl2');

    const message = gl
      ? 'Hooray! You got a WebGL2 context'
      : 'Sorry! WebGL is not available';

    alert(message);

    // Call checkKey whenever a key is pressed
    window.onkeydown = checkKey;
    }

    window.onload = init;
  </script>
</head>
<body>

  <canvas id="webgl-canvas" width="800" height="600">
    Your browser does not support the HTML5 canvas element.
  </canvas>

</body>
</html>
```

2. You will see that this file is similar to our previous example. However, there are new code constructs that we will explain briefly. This file contains three JavaScript functions:

Function	Description
updateClearColor	Updates clearColor and then sets the canvas element clear color, which is one of the WebGL context attributes. As previously mentioned, WebGL works as a state machine. Therefore, it will maintain this color until it's changed using the gl.clearColor WebGL function (see the checkKey source code).
checkKey	This is an auxiliary function that has been attached to the window onkeydown event. It captures the keyboard input and executes code depending on the key entered.
init	This function gets called on the document onload event. It obtains a WebGL context and sets it to the global gl variable.

3. Open the ch01_03_attributes.html file in your browser.

4. Press *1*. You will see how the `canvas` changes its color to green. If you want to query the exact color used, press *4*.

5. The `canvas` element will maintain the green color until we change it by calling `gl.clearColor`. Let's change it by pressing 2. If you look at the source code, this will change the `canvas` clear color to blue. If you want to know the exact color, press 4.

6. You can press *3* to set the clear color to a random color. As before, you can get the color by pressing *4*:

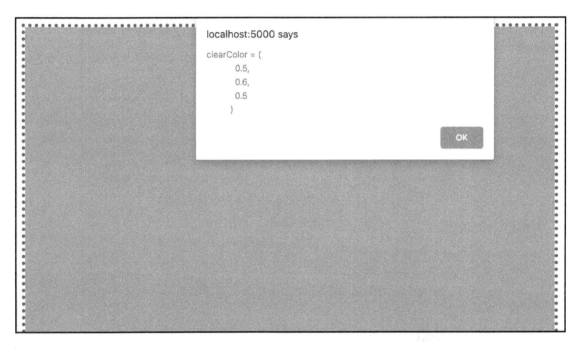

What just happened?

In this example, we saw that we can change the color that WebGL uses to clear the `canvas` element by calling the `clearColor` function. Correspondingly, we used `getParameter(gl.COLOR_CLEAR_VALUE)` to obtain the current value of the `canvas` clear color.

Throughout this book, we will encounter similar constructs where specific functions establish attributes of the WebGL context while the `getParameter` function retrieves the current values for such attributes whenever the respective argument (in our example, `COLOR_CLEAR_VALUE`) is used.

Using the Context to Access the WebGL API

It is essential to note that all of the WebGL functions are accessed through the WebGL context. In our examples, the context is being held by the `gl` variable. Therefore, any call to the WebGL API will be performed using this variable.

Loading a 3D Scene

So far, we have seen how to set up a `canvas` element and how to obtain a WebGL context; the next step is to discuss objects, lights, and cameras. But why wait to see what WebGL can do? In this section, we will take a quick peek at a simplified version of the final WebGL application that we'll be building in this book.

Virtual Car Showroom

Through this book, we will develop a virtual car showroom application using WebGL. At this point, we will load one simple scene into the `canvas` element. This scene will contain a car, some lights, and a camera.

Time for Action: Visualizing a 3D Showroom

Once you finish reading this book, you will be able to create compelling 3D scenes such as the one we are going to play with next. This scene showcases one of the cars from this book's virtual car showroom:

1. Open the `ch01_04_showroom.html` file in your browser.

2. You will see a WebGL scene with a car in it, as shown in the following screenshot. In the following chapters, we will cover geometry rendering and will see how to load and render various 3D models:

3. Use the sliders to interactively update the four light sources that have been defined for this scene. Each light source has two elements: diffuse and specular elements. We have Chapter 3, *Lights*, dedicated entirely to lights in a 3D scene.

4. Click and drag on canvas to rotate the car and visualize it from different perspectives. You can zoom by pressing the *Alt* key while dragging the mouse on the canvas. You can also use the *arrow* keys to rotate the camera around the car. Make sure that canvas is in focus by clicking on it before using the *arrow* keys. In Chapter 4, *Cameras*, we will discuss how to create and operate our own custom cameras in WebGL.

5. Use the color selector widget to change the color of the car. The use of colors in the scene will be discussed in detail later in this book.

What just happened?

We have loaded a simple scene in a browser using WebGL. This scene consists of the following:

- A `canvas` element through which we see the scene.
- A series of polygonal meshes (**objects**) that constitute the car: roof, windows, headlights, fenders, doors, wheels, spoiler, bumpers, and so on.
- **Light** sources, otherwise everything would appear black.
- A **camera** that determines where our viewpoint is in the 3D world. This camera is interactive where the viewpoint can change, depending on user input. For example, we used various keys and the mouse to move the camera around the car.

There are many other elements in this scene such as textures, colors, and special light effects (specularity). Do not panic! We will explain each element throughout this book. The point here is to identify that the four basic elements we discussed previously are present in the scene. That said, feel free to examine the source code to get a sense of what's to come.

Architecture Updates

As we progress through chapters, we will encounter common functionality (for example, design patterns, utility functions, helpers, and data structures) that we can build upon. Not only this will serve us in writing **DRY** code, but it will also provide a useful architecture to support an advanced 3D WebGL application by the end of this book.

DRY

 Don't Repeat Yourself (**DRY**) is a software development principle, the main aim of which is to reduce repetition of code. **Write Everything Twice** (**WET**) is a cheeky abbreviation to mean the opposite— code that doesn't adhere to the DRY principle.

Let's cover some changes that we will use in future chapters:

1. Open `common/js/utils.js` in your editor to see the following code.
2. We will use `utils` to include many of the utility functions to serve us in building our 3D application. The two methods, `getCanvas` and `getGLContent`, inside of `utils` are similar to the code we've implemented earlier in this chapter:

```
'use strict';

// A set of utility functions for /common operations across our
// application
const utils = {

  // Find and return a DOM element given an ID
  getCanvas(id) {
    const canvas = document.getElementById(id);

    if (!canvas) {
      console.error(`There is no canvas with id ${id} on this
        page.`);
      return null;
    }

    return canvas;
  },

  // Given a canvas element, return the WebGL2 context
  getGLContext(canvas) {
    return canvas.getContext('webgl2') || console.error('WebGL2 is
      not available in your browser.');
  }

};
```

3. `getCanvas` returns the `canvas` element with the provided `id` as the argument.
4. `getGLContext` returns a WebGL 2 context for a given `canvas` element.
5. Open up `ch01_05_attributes-final.html` in your editor to see the following changes.
6. We've included `<link rel="stylesheet" href="/common/lib/normalize.css">` in the `<head>` of our document that resets many of the inconsistencies across browsers. This is an external library to help us normalize CSS styling across browsers.
7. We've included `<script type="text/javascript" src="/common/js/utils.js"></script>`.

8. Scroll to the `init` function where the necessary changes were made to use the `utils.getCanvas` and `utils.getGLContext` functions:

```
function init() {
  const canvas = utils.getCanvas('webgl-canvas');
  gl = utils.getGLContext(canvas);
  window.onkeydown = checkKey;
}
```

9. Open up `ch01_05_attributes-final.html` in a browser to see these changes in action.

Example Code Structure

All example code has been structured so that common functionality is at the root of the directory (`common/`), while examples for each chapter are categorized under chapter directories (for example, `ch01/`, `ch02/`, and `ch03/`). That being said, to view these examples in your browser, you will need to start a server at the root of the directory to load all required assets for each example. Please refer to the `Preface` of this book for more details.

Summary

Let's summarize what we've learned in this chapter:

- We covered the history of WebGL and how it came to fruition.
- We learned about common elements—`canvas`, objects, lights, and camera—that are, generally, present in WebGL applications.
- We learned how to add a HTML5 `canvas` element to our web page and how to set its `id`, `width`, and `height`.
- We implemented the code to obtain a WebGL context.
- We covered how WebGL works as a state machine and, as such, we can query any of its variables using the `getParameter` function.
- We got a glimpse of the interactive 3D application that we'll build by the end of this book.

In the next chapter, we will learn how to define, load, and render objects into a WebGL scene.

2
Rendering

In the previous chapter, we covered the history of WebGL, along with its evolution. We discussed the fundamental elements in a 3D application and how to set up a WebGL context. In this chapter, we will investigate how geometric entities are defined in WebGL.

WebGL renders objects following a "divide and conquer" approach. Complex polygons are decomposed into triangles, lines, and point primitives. Then, each geometric primitive is processed in parallel by the GPU in order to create the final scene.

In this chapter, you will:

- Understand how WebGL defines and processes geometric information
- Discuss the relevant API methods that relate to geometry manipulation
- Examine why and how to use **JavaScript Object Notation** (**JSON**) to define, store, and load complex geometries
- Continue our analysis of WebGL as a state machine to describe the attributes that are relevant to geometry manipulation that can be set and retrieved
- Experiment with creating and loading different geometry models

WebGL Rendering Pipeline

Although WebGL is often thought of as a comprehensive 3D API, it is, in reality, just a rasterization engine. It draws points, lines, and triangles based on the code you supply. Getting WebGL to do anything else requires you to provide code to use points, lines, and triangles to accomplish your task.

WebGL runs on the GPU on your computer. As such, you need to provide code that runs on that GPU. The code should be provided in the form of pairs of functions. Those two functions are known as the **vertex shader** and **fragment shader**, and they are each written in a very strictly-typed C/C++-like language called GLSL (GL Shader Language). Together, they are called a **program**.

GLSL

GLSL is an acronym for the official OpenGL Shading Language. GLSL is a C/C++-like, high-level programming language for several parts of the graphic card. With GLSL, you can code short programs, called shaders, which are executed on the GPU. For more information, please check out `https://en.wikipedia.org/wiki/OpenGL_Shading_Language`.

A vertex shader's job is to compute vertex attributes. Based on various positions, the function outputs values that can be used to rasterize various kinds of primitives, including points, lines, and triangles. When rasterizing these primitives, it calls a second user-supplied function known as a fragment shader. A fragment shader's job is to compute a color for each pixel of the primitive currently being drawn.

Nearly all of the WebGL API is about setting up state for these pairs of functions to execute. For each thing you want to draw, you need to set up state to run these functions by invoking `gl.drawArrays` or `gl.drawElements`, which executes your shaders on the GPU.

Before going any further, let's examine what WebGL's rendering pipeline looks like. In subsequent chapters, we will discuss the pipeline in more detail. The following is a diagram of a simplified version of WebGL's rendering pipeline:

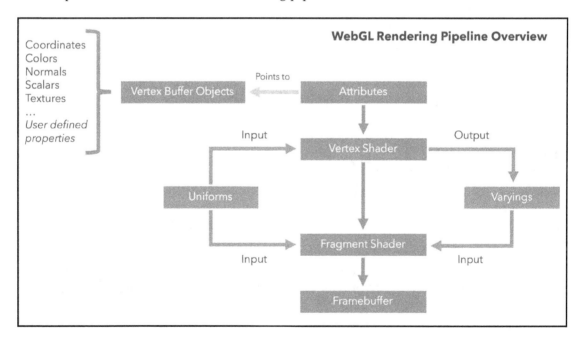

Let's take a moment to describe each element.

Vertex Buffer Objects (VBOs)

VBOs contain the data that is used to describe the geometry to be rendered. Vertex coordinates, which are points that define the vertices of 3D objects, are usually stored and processed in WebGL as VBOs. Additionally, there are several data elements, such as vertex normals, colors, and texture coordinates, that can be modeled as VBOs.

Index Buffer Objects (IBOs)

While VBOs contain vertices describing a geometry, **IBOs** contain information about the relationship of the vertices as the rendering pipeline constructs the drawing type primitives. It uses the index of each vertex in the vertex buffer as a value.

Vertex Shader

The **vertex shader** is called on each vertex. The shader manipulates *per-vertex* data, such as vertex coordinates, normals, colors, and texture coordinates. This data is represented by attributes inside the vertex shader. Each attribute points to a VBO from where it reads vertex data.

Fragment Shader

Every set of three vertices defines a triangle. Each element on the surface of that triangle needs to be assigned a color. Without this, our surfaces wouldn't have a color. Each surface element is called a **fragment**. Since we are dealing with surfaces that will be displayed on your screen, these elements are more commonly known as **pixels**.

The main goal of the **fragment shader** is to calculate the color of *individual pixels*. The following diagram illustrates this idea:

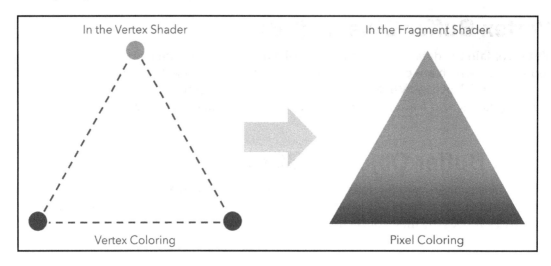

Framebuffer

A two-dimensional buffer contains the fragments that have been processed by the fragment shader. Once all of the fragments have been processed, a 2D image is formed and displayed on screen. The **framebuffer** is the final destination of the rendering pipeline.

Attributes

Attributes are input variables that are used in the vertex shader. Attributes are used to specify how to pull data out of buffers and provide them to the vertex shader. For example, you may put positions in a buffer as three 32-bit floats per position. You would tell a particular attribute which buffer to pull the positions out of, what type of data it should pull out (3-component, 32-bit floating point numbers), what offset in the buffer the positions start at, and how many bytes to get from one position to the next. Since the vertex shader is called on each vertex, the attributes will be different every time the vertex shader is invoked.

Uniforms

Uniforms are input variables that are available to both the vertex shader and the fragment shader. Unlike attributes, uniforms are constant during a rendering cycle. For example, the position of a light is often modeled as a uniform. Uniforms are effectively global variables that you set before executing your shader program.

Textures

Textures are arrays of data that can be accessed in your shader program. Image data is the most common thing to put in a texture, but textures are simply data and can just as easily contain something other than an array of colors describing an image.

Varyings

Varyings are used to *pass data* from the vertex shader to the fragment shader. Depending on what is being rendered – points, lines, or triangles – the values set on a varying by a vertex shader will be interpolated while executing the fragment shader.

Now, let's cover the principles of creating a simple geometric object.

Rendering in WebGL

WebGL handles geometry in a standard way, independent of the complexity and number of points that surfaces can have. There are two data types that are fundamental to represent the geometry of any 3D object: *vertices* and *indices*.

Vertices

Vertices are the points that define the corners of 3D objects. Each vertex is represented by three floating-point numbers that correspond to the x, y, and z coordinates of the vertex. Unlike its cousin, OpenGL, WebGL does not provide API methods to pass independent vertices to the rendering pipeline; therefore, all of our vertices need to be written in a **JavaScript array**, which can then be used to construct a WebGL vertex buffer.

Indices

Indices are numeric labels for the vertices in a given 3D scene. Indices allow us to tell WebGL how to connect vertices in order to produce a surface. As with vertices, indices are stored in a JavaScript array and are then passed along to WebGL's rendering pipeline using a WebGL index buffer.

VBOs Versus IBOs

There are two kinds of WebGL buffers used to describe and process geometry. Buffers that contain vertex data are known as **VBOs**, and buffers that contain index data are known as **IBOs**.

In this section, we will use the following steps to render an object in WebGL:

1. Define a geometry using JavaScript arrays
2. Create the respective WebGL buffers
3. Point a vertex shader attribute to a VBO from the previous step to store vertex coordinates
4. Use the IBO to render the geometry

Defining a Geometry Using JavaScript Arrays

To practice using the preceding steps, let's use a trapezoid to see how we can define its vertices and indices. We need two JavaScript arrays – one for the vertices and one for the indices:

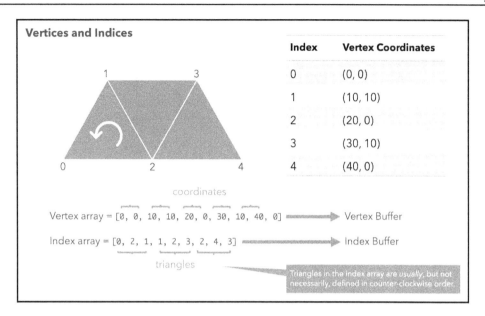

As you can see from the preceding illustration, we have placed the coordinates sequentially in the vertex array and then indicated how these coordinates are used to draw the trapezoid in the index array. So, the first triangle is formed with the vertices having the indices 0, 2, and 1; the second, with the vertices having the indices 1, 2, and 3; and finally, the third, with the vertices having the indices 2, 4, and 3. We will follow the same procedure for all possible geometries.

Index Array Order

Triangles in the index array are usually, but not necessarily, defined in counter-clockwise order. It's important to pick one approach and keep it consistent to help you determine the front and back sides of geometry primitives. Consistency is important, because programs may use the clockwise/counter-clockwise order to determine whether a face is facing forward or backward for **culling** and rendering purposes.

Culling

In computer graphics, back-face culling determines whether a polygon of a graphical object is visible. It is a step in the graphical pipeline that tests whether the points in the polygon appear in clockwise or counter-clockwise order when projected onto the screen. For more information, visit https://en.wikipedia.org/wiki/Back-face_culling.

Creating WebGL Buffers

Now that we understand how to define a geometry using vertices and indices, let's render a square. Once we have created the JavaScript arrays that define the vertices and indices for our geometry, the next step is to create the respective buffers. In this case, we have a simple square on the x-y plane with the z values set as 0:

```
const vertices = [
   -0.5,  0.5, 0,
   -0.5, -0.5, 0,
    0.5, -0.5, 0,
    0.5,  0.5, 0
];

const positionBuffer = gl.createBuffer();
```

Clipspace Coordinates

These vertices are defined in clipspace coordinates, because WebGL only deals with clipspace coordinates. Clipspace coordinates always go from −1 to +1, regardless of the size of the canvas. In later chapters, we will cover coordinates in more detail and learn how to convert between different coordinate systems.

In Chapter 1, *Getting Started*, you may remember learning that WebGL operates as a state machine. Now, when positionBuffer is made the currently-bound WebGL buffer, any subsequent buffer operation will be executed on this buffer until it is unbound, or another buffer is made the current one with a bound call. We can bind a buffer with the following instruction:

```
gl.bindBuffer(gl.ARRAY_BUFFER, positionBuffer);
```

The first parameter is the type of buffer we are creating. We have two options for this parameter:

- gl.ARRAY_BUFFER: Vertex data
- gl.ELEMENT_ARRAY_BUFFER: Index data

In the previous example, we created the buffer for vertex coordinates; therefore, we use ARRAY_BUFFER. For indices, the ELEMENT_ARRAY_BUFFER type is used.

Bound Buffer Operations

WebGL will always access the currently-bound buffer looking for the data. This means that we need to ensure that we always have bound a buffer before calling any other operation for geometry processing. If there is no buffer bound, you will obtain the INVALID_OPERATION error.

Remember that drawArrays uses VBOs. Once we have bound a buffer, we need to pass along its contents. We do this with the bufferData function:

```
gl.bufferData(gl.ARRAY_BUFFER, new Float32Array(vertices), gl.STATIC_DRAW);
```

In this example, the vertices variable is a normal JavaScript array that contains the vertex coordinates. WebGL does not accept JavaScript arrays as a parameter for the bufferData method. Instead, WebGL requires JavaScript typed array so that the buffer data can be processed in its native binary form with the objective of speeding up geometry-processing performance.

The typed arrays used by WebGL include Int8Array, Uint8Array, Int16Array, Uint16Array, Int32Array, Uint32Array, Float32Array, and Float64Array.

It's important to note that vertex coordinates can be float, but indices are *always* integers. Therefore, we will use Float32Array for VBOs and Uint16Array for IBOs in this book. These two types represent the largest typed arrays that you can use in WebGL *per rendering call*. Other types may or may not be present in your browser, as this specification is not yet final at the time of this book's publication.

Since the indices support in WebGL is restricted to 16-bit integers, an index array can only be 65,535 elements in length. If you have a geometry that requires more indices, you will need to use several rendering calls. More about rendering calls will be presented later in this chapter.

JavaScript Typed arrays

Specifications for typed arrays can be found at http://www.khronos.org/registry/typedarray/specs/latest/.

Finally, it is a good practice to unbind the buffer. We can achieve this by calling the following instruction:

```
gl.bindBuffer(gl.ARRAY_BUFFER, null);
```

We will repeat the same calls described here for every WebGL buffer (VBO or IBO) that we will use.

Let's review what we have just learned with an example. We are going to look at an example from `ch02_01_square.html` to see the definition of VBOs and IBOs for a square:

```
// Set up the buffers for the square
function initBuffers() {
  /*
    V0                      V3
    (-0.5, 0.5, 0)          (0.5, 0.5, 0)
    X--------------------X
    |                    |
    |                    |
    |         (0, 0)     |
    |                    |
    |                    |
    X--------------------X
    V1                      V2
    (-0.5, -0.5, 0)         (0.5, -0.5, 0)
  */
  const vertices = [
    -0.5, 0.5, 0,
    -0.5, -0.5, 0,
    0.5, -0.5, 0,
    0.5, 0.5, 0
  ];

  // Indices defined in counter-clockwise order
  indices = [0, 1, 2, 0, 2, 3];

  // Setting up the VBO
  squareVertexBuffer = gl.createBuffer();
  gl.bindBuffer(gl.ARRAY_BUFFER, squareVertexBuffer);
  gl.bufferData(gl.ARRAY_BUFFER, new Float32Array(vertices),
   gl.STATIC_DRAW);

  // Setting up the IBO
  squareIndexBuffer = gl.createBuffer();
  gl.bindBuffer(gl.ELEMENT_ARRAY_BUFFER, squareIndexBuffer);
  gl.bufferData(gl.ELEMENT_ARRAY_BUFFER, new Uint16Array(indices),
   gl.STATIC_DRAW);

  // Clean
  gl.bindBuffer(gl.ARRAY_BUFFER, null);
  gl.bindBuffer(gl.ELEMENT_ARRAY_BUFFER, null);
}
```

If you want to see this scene in action, launch the `ch02_01_square.html` file in your browser.

To summarize, for every buffer, we want to do the following:

- Create a new buffer
- Bind it to make it the current buffer
- Pass the buffer data using one of the typed arrays
- Unbind the buffer

Operations to Manipulate WebGL Buffers

The operations to manipulate WebGL buffers are summarized in the following table:

Method	Description
`createBuffer()`	Creates a new buffer.
`deleteBuffer(buffer)`	Deletes the supplied buffer.
`bindBuffer(target, buffer)`	Binds a buffer object. The accepted values for target are as follows: • ARRAY_BUFFER (for vertices) • ELEMENT_ARRAY_BUFFER (for indices)
`bufferData(target, data, type)`	Provides the buffer data. The accepted values for target are as follows: • ARRAY_BUFFER (for vertices) • ELEMENT_ARRAY_BUFFER (for indices) As mentioned earlier, WebGL only accepts JavaScript typed arrays for the data. The parameter type is a performance hint for WebGL. The accepted values for type are as follows: • STATIC_DRAW: Data in the buffer will not be changed (specified once and used many times) • DYNAMIC_DRAW: Data will be changed frequently (specified many times and used many times) • STREAM_DRAW: Data will change on every rendering cycle (specified once and used once)

Associating Attributes to VBOs

Once we have created the VBOs, we need to associate these buffers to vertex shader attributes. Each vertex shader attribute will refer to *one* and *only one* buffer, depending on the correspondence that is established, as shown in the following diagram:

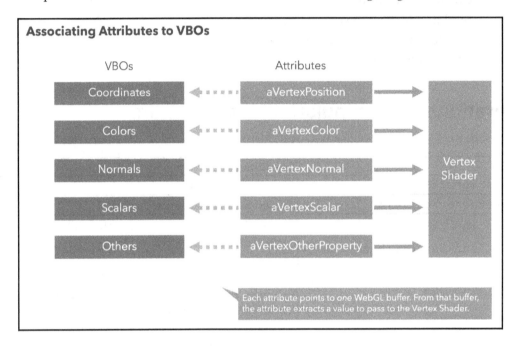

We can achieve this by following these steps:

1. Bind a VBO
2. Point an attribute to the currently-bound VBO
3. Enable the attribute
4. Unbind

Let's take a look at the first step.

Binding a VBO

We already know how to do this:

```
gl.bindBuffer(gl.ARRAY_BUFFER, myBuffer);
```

Where `myBuffer` is the buffer we want to map.

Pointing an Attribute to the Currently-Bound VBO

The majority of the WebGL API is about setting up state to supply data to our GLSL programs. In this case, the only input to our GLSL program is `aVertexPosition`, which is an attribute. In `Chapter 3`, *Lights*, we will learn how to define and reference vertex and fragment shader attributes. For now, let's assume that we have the `aVertexPosition` attribute, which describes the vertex coordinates in the shader.

The WebGL function that allows pointing attributes to the currently-bound VBOs is `vertexAttribPointer`. The following is its signature:

```
gl.vertexAttribPointer(index, size, type, normalize, stride, offset);
```

Let's describe each parameter individually:

- **Index**: An attribute's index that we are going to map the currently-bound buffer to.
- **Size**: Indicates the number of values per vertex that are stored in the currently-bound buffer.
- **Type**: Specifies the data type of the values stored in the current buffer. It is one of the following constants: `FIXED`, `BYTE`, `UNSIGNED_BYTE`, `FLOAT`, `SHORT`, or `UNSIGNED_SHORT`.
- **Normalize**: This parameter can be set to `true` or `false`. It handles numeric conversions that are beyond the scope of this introductory guide. For our purposes, we will set this parameter to `false`.
- **Stride**: If stride is `0`, then we are indicating that elements are stored sequentially in the buffer.
- **Offset**: The position in the buffer from which we will start reading values for the corresponding attribute. It is usually set to `0` to indicate that we will start reading values from the first element of the buffer.

Buffer Pointer

`vertexAttribPointer` defines a pointer for reading information *from the currently-bound buffer*. Remember that an error will be generated if there is no VBO currently bound.

Enabling the Attribute

Finally, we need to activate the vertex shader attribute. Following our example, we just need to add `gl.enableVertexAttribArray(positionAttributeLocation);`.

The following diagram summarizes the mapping procedure:

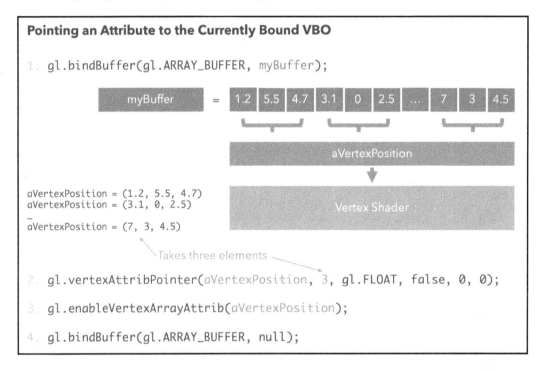

Pointing an Attribute to the Currently Bound VBO

1. `gl.bindBuffer(gl.ARRAY_BUFFER, myBuffer);`

    myBuffer = | 1.2 | 5.5 | 4.7 | 3.1 | 0 | 2.5 | ... | 7 | 3 | 4.5 |

    aVertexPosition

    Vertex Shader

    aVertexPosition = (1.2, 5.5, 4.7)
    aVertexPosition = (3.1, 0, 2.5)
    ...
    aVertexPosition = (7, 3, 4.5)

    Takes three elements

2. `gl.vertexAttribPointer(aVertexPosition, 3, gl.FLOAT, false, 0, 0);`

3. `gl.enableVertexArrayAttrib(aVertexPosition);`

4. `gl.bindBuffer(gl.ARRAY_BUFFER, null);`

Unbinding a VBO

As a rule of thumb, we should unbind our buffers after we're done using them. We can do so with:

`gl.bindBuffer(gl.ARRAY_BUFFER, null);`.

Rendering

Once we have defined our VBOs and we have mapped them to the corresponding vertex shader attributes, we are ready to render! To do this, we can use one of the two API functions: `drawArrays` or `drawElements`.

Drawing Functions

The `drawArrays` and `drawElements` functions are used for writing to the framebuffer. `drawArrays` uses vertex data in the order in which it is defined in the buffer to create the geometry. In contrast, `drawElements` uses indices to access the vertex data buffers and create the geometry. Both `drawArrays` and `drawElements` will only use **enabled arrays**. These are the vertex buffer objects that are mapped to active vertex shader attributes.

In our example, the buffer that contains the vertex coordinates is the only enabled array. However, in a more general scenario, there may be several enabled arrays at our disposal.

For instance, we can have arrays with information about vertex colors, vertex normals, texture coordinates, and any other per-vertex data required by the application. In this case, each one of them would be mapped to an active vertex shader attribute.

Using Multiple VBOs

In `Chapter 3`, *Lights*, we will learn how to use a vertex normal buffer and vertex coordinates to create a lighting model for our geometry. In that scenario, we will have two active arrays: vertex coordinates and vertex normals.

Using drawArrays

We will call `drawArrays` when information about indices is not available. In most cases, `drawArrays` is used when the geometry is simple enough that defining indices is overkill – for instance, when we want to render a triangle or a rectangle. In that case, WebGL will create the geometry in the order in which the vertex coordinates are defined in the VBO. If you have contiguous triangles (as we did in the trapezoid example), you will have to *repeat* these coordinates in the VBO.

If you need to repeat many vertices to create the geometry, `drawArrays` is not the optimal method, because the more vertex data you duplicate, the more calls you will have on the vertex shader. This can reduce the overall performance, since the same vertices must go through the pipeline several times, one for each time that they are repeated in the respective VBO:

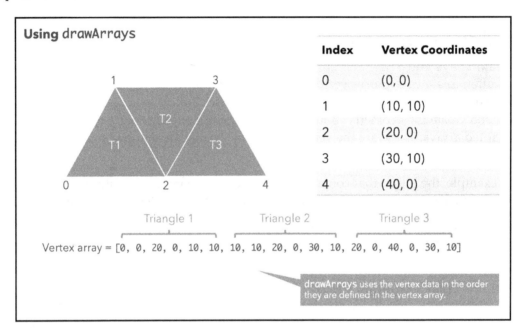

The signature for `drawArrays` is as follows:

```
gl.drawArrays(mode, first, count)
```

Where:

- `mode`: Represents the type of primitive that we are going to render. The possible values for mode
  are `gl.POINTS`, `gl.LINE_STRIP`, `gl.LINE_LOOP`, `gl.LINES`, `gl.TRIANGLE_ST RIP`, `gl.TRIANGLE_FAN`, and `gl.TRIANGLES`.
- `first`: Specifies the starting element in the enabled arrays.
- `count`: The number of elements to be rendered.

WebGL drawArrays **Specification**

When drawArrays is called, it uses count sequential elements from each enabled array to construct a sequence of geometric primitives, beginning with the element *first*. Mode specifies what kinds of primitives are constructed and how the array elements construct those primitives.

Using drawElements

Unlike the previous case where no IBO was defined, drawElements allows us to use the IBO to tell WebGL how to render the geometry. Remember that drawArrays uses VBOs, which means that the vertex shader will process the repeated vertices as many times as they appear in the VBO. On the other hand, drawElements uses indices. Therefore, vertices are only processed once, and can be used as many times as they are defined in the IBO. This feature reduces both the memory and processing required on the GPU.

Let's revisit the following diagram:

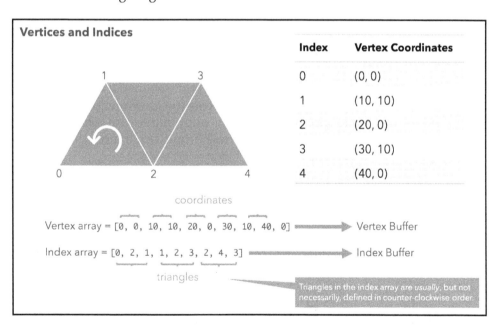

When we use drawElements, we need at least two buffers: a VBO and an IBO. As the vertex shader gets executed on each vertex, the rendering pipeline assembles the geometry into triangles using the IBO.

Binding the IBO with drawElements

When using `drawElements`, you need to make sure that the corresponding IBO is currently bound.

The signature for `drawElements` is as follows:

```
gl.drawElements(mode, count, type, offset)
```

Where:

- `mode`: Represents the type of primitive we are going to render. The possible values for mode are `POINTS`, `LINE_STRIP`, `LINE_LOOP`, `LINES`, `TRIANGLE_STRIP`, `TRIANGLE_FAN`, and `TRIANGLES`.
- `count`: Specifies the number of elements to be rendered.
- `type`: Specifies the type of the values in indices. Must be `UNSIGNED_BYTE` or `UNSIGNED_SHORT`, as we are handling indices (integer numbers).
- `offset`: Indicates which element in the buffer will be the starting point for rendering. It is usually the first element (zero value).

WebGL drawElements Specification

When `drawElements` is called, it uses count sequential elements from an enabled array, starting at the offset to construct a sequence of geometric primitives. Mode specifies what kinds of primitives are constructed and how the array elements construct these primitives. If more than one array is enabled, each is used.

Putting Everything Together

Since you've probably been waiting to see how everything works together, let's go over a simple WebGL program that renders a square.

Time for Action: Rendering a Square

Follow the given steps:

1. Open the `ch02_01_square.html` file in a code editor (ideally one that supports syntax highlighting).

2. Examine the structure of this file with the help of the following diagram:

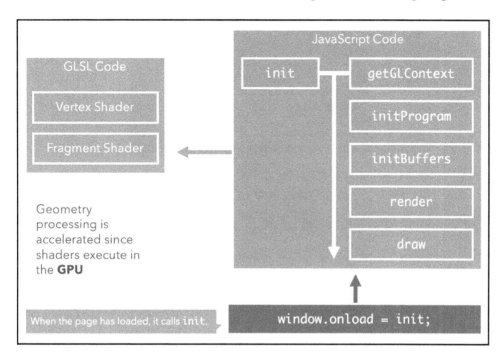

3. The web page contains the following:

- The `<script id="vertex-shader" type="x-shader/x-vertex">` script contains the vertex shader code.
- The `<script id="fragment-shader" type="x-shader/x-fragment">` script contains the fragment shader code. We won't pay attention to these two scripts as they will be the main point of study in the next chapter. For now, simply notice that we have a fragment shader and a vertex shader.
- The next script on our web page, `<script type="text/javascript">`, contains all the JavaScript WebGL code that we will need. This script is divided into the following functions:

```
// Global variables that are set and used
// across the application
let gl,
  program,
  squareVertexBuffer,
  squareIndexBuffer,
  indices;
```

- We list a few global variables that we use throughout our application:

```
// Given an id, extract the content's of a shader script
// from the DOM and return the compiled shader
function getShader(id) {
  const script = document.getElementById(id);
  const shaderString = script.text.trim();

  // Assign shader depending on the type of shader
  let shader;
  if (script.type === 'x-shader/x-vertex') {
    shader = gl.createShader(gl.VERTEX_SHADER);
  }
  else if (script.type === 'x-shader/x-fragment') {
    shader = gl.createShader(gl.FRAGMENT_SHADER);
  }
  else {
    return null;
  }

  // Compile the shader using the supplied shader code
  gl.shaderSource(shader, shaderString);
  gl.compileShader(shader);

  // Ensure the shader is valid
  if (!gl.getShaderParameter(shader, gl.COMPILE_STATUS)) {
    console.error(gl.getShaderInfoLog(shader));
    return null;
  }

  return shader;
}
```

- getShader extracts the contents of a shader present in the HTML web page given its id:

```
// Create a program with the appropriate vertex and fragment
shaders
function initProgram() {
  const vertexShader = getShader('vertex-shader');
  const fragmentShader = getShader('fragment-shader');

  // Create a program
  program = gl.createProgram();
  // Attach the shaders to this program
  gl.attachShader(program, vertexShader);
  gl.attachShader(program, fragmentShader);
  gl.linkProgram(program);
```

```
if (!gl.getProgramParameter(program, gl.LINK_STATUS)) {
  console.error('Could not initialize shaders');
}

// Use this program instance
gl.useProgram(program);
// We attach the location of these shader values to the program
// instance for easy access later in the code
program.aVertexPosition = gl.getAttribLocation(program,
'aVertexPosition');
}
```

- initProgram obtains a reference for the vertex shader and the fragment shader
  present in the web page (that is, the first two scripts that we discussed) and
  passes them along to the GPU to be compiled. Lastly, we attach the location of
  the aVertexPosition attribute to the program object so that it can be easily
  referenced later. Looking up attribute and uniform locations is expensive;
  therefore, such operations should happen once during initialization. We will
  cover these techniques in later chapters:

```
// Set up the buffers for the square
function initBuffers() {
  /*
    V0                      V3
    (-0.5, 0.5, 0)          (0.5, 0.5, 0)
    X--------------------X
    |                    |
    |                    |
    |        (0, 0)      |
    |                    |
    |                    |
    X--------------------X
    V1                      V2
    (-0.5, -0.5, 0)         (0.5, -0.5, 0)
  */
  const vertices = [
    -0.5, 0.5, 0,
    -0.5, -0.5, 0,
    0.5, -0.5, 0,
    0.5, 0.5, 0
  ];

  // Indices defined in counter-clockwise order
  indices = [0, 1, 2, 0, 2, 3];

  // Setting up the VBO
  squareVertexBuffer = gl.createBuffer();
```

```
gl.bindBuffer(gl.ARRAY_BUFFER, squareVertexBuffer);
gl.bufferData(gl.ARRAY_BUFFER, new Float32Array(vertices),
 gl.STATIC_DRAW);

// Setting up the IBO
squareIndexBuffer = gl.createBuffer();
gl.bindBuffer(gl.ELEMENT_ARRAY_BUFFER, squareIndexBuffer);
gl.bufferData(gl.ELEMENT_ARRAY_BUFFER, new Uint16Array(indices),
 gl.STATIC_DRAW);

// Clean
gl.bindBuffer(gl.ARRAY_BUFFER, null);
gl.bindBuffer(gl.ELEMENT_ARRAY_BUFFER, null);
}
```

- initBuffers contains the API calls to create and initialize buffers, as we discussed earlier in this chapter. In this example, we create a VBO to store coordinates for the square and an IBO to store the indices of the square:

```
// We call draw to render to our canvas
function draw() {
  // Clear the scene
  gl.clear(gl.COLOR_BUFFER_BIT | gl.DEPTH_BUFFER_BIT);
  gl.viewport(0, 0, gl.canvas.width, gl.canvas.height);

  // Use the buffers we've constructed
  gl.bindBuffer(gl.ARRAY_BUFFER, squareVertexBuffer);
  gl.vertexAttribPointer(program.aVertexPosition, 3, gl.FLOAT,
   false, 0, 0);
  gl.enableVertexAttribArray(program.aVertexPosition);

  // Bind IBO
  gl.bindBuffer(gl.ELEMENT_ARRAY_BUFFER, squareIndexBuffer);

  // Draw to the scene using triangle primitives
  gl.drawElements(gl.TRIANGLES, indices.length, gl.UNSIGNED_SHORT,
   0);

  // Clean
  gl.bindBuffer(gl.ARRAY_BUFFER, null);
  gl.bindBuffer(gl.ELEMENT_ARRAY_BUFFER, null);
}
```

- draw maps the VBO to the respective vertex buffer attribute, program.aVertexPosition, and enables it by calling enableVertexAttribArray. It then binds the IBO and calls the drawElements function. We will cover this in more detail in later chapters:

```
// Entry point to our application
function init() {
  // Retrieve the canvas
  const canvas = utils.getCanvas('webgl-canvas');

  // Set the canvas to the size of the screen
  canvas.width = window.innerWidth;
  canvas.height = window.innerHeight;

  // Retrieve a WebGL context
  gl = utils.getGLContext(canvas);
  // Set the clear color to be black
  gl.clearColor(0, 0, 0, 1);

  // Call the functions in an appropriate order
  initProgram();
  initBuffers();
  draw();
}
```

- init is the entry point for the entire application. When the page has loaded, init is invoked via window.onload = init. It's important to note that the order of functions invoked inside of init are important to set up and render the geometry. We also set the canvas dimension to take the size of the entire window (fullscreen). As mentioned previously, in the draw function, we are using canvas.width and canvas.height as the source of truth for our drawing dimensions.

4. Open the `ch02_01_square.html` file in the HTML5 browser of your preference (Firefox, Safari, Chrome, or Opera), and you should see the following:

5. Open up the code for `ch02_01_square.html` and scroll down to the `initBuffers` function. Please pay attention to the diagram that appears as a comment inside of the function. This diagram describes how the vertices and indices are organized. You should see something like the following:

```
/*
  V0                          V3
  (-0.5,  0.5,  0)            (0.5,  0.5,  0)
  X----------------------X
  |                      |
  |                      |
  |          (0,  0)     |
  |                      |
  |                      |
  X----------------------X
  V1                          V2
  (-0.5,  -0.5,  0)          (0.5,  -0.5,  0)
*/
```

6. Try to modify the existing buffers to turn the square into a pentagon. How would you do this?

Updating the Geometry Definition

Modify the vertex buffer array and index array so that the resulting figure is a pentagon instead of a square. To do this, you need to add one vertex to the vertex array and define one more triangle in the index array.

7. Save the file with a different name and open it in the HTML5 browser of your preference to test it.

What just happened?

You have learned about the different code elements that conform to a WebGL app. The `initBuffers` function has been examined closely and modified to render a different geometry.

Have a Go: Changing the Square Color

Go to the fragment shader and change the color of your geometry.

Four-Component Color Vector

The format is (red, green, blue, alpha). Alpha is always `1.0` (for now), and the first three arguments are float numbers in the range of `0.0` to `1.0`.

Remember to save the file after making the changes in your text editor before opening it in your browser.

Have a Go: Rendering Using drawArrays

Our square was defined using `drawElements` via vertices and indices. Go ahead and render the same square using `drawArrays`.

Hint

Given that you don't use indices with `drawArrays`, you won't need an `IBO`. So, you will need to duplicate vertices to construct this geometry.

Hint

For reference, you can find the source code for this exercise in `ch02_02_square-arrays.html`.

Vertex Array Objects

Vertex array objects (VAOs) allow you to store all of the vertex/index binding information for a set of buffers in a single, easy to manage object. That is, the state of attributes, which buffers to use for each attribute, and how to pull data out from those buffers, is collected into a VAO. Although we can implement VAOs in WebGL 1 by using extensions, they are available by default in WebGL 2.

This is an important feature that should *always* be used, since it significantly reduces rendering times. When not using VAOs, all attributes data is in global WebGL state, which means that calling functions such as `gl.vertexAttribPointer`, `gl.enableVertexAttribArray`, and `gl.bindBuffer(gl.ELEMENT_ARRAY_BUFFER, buffer)` manipulates the global state. This leads to performance loss, because before any draw call, we would need to set up all vertex attributes and set the `ELEMENT_ARRAY_BUFFER` where indexed data is being used. On the other hand, with VAOs, we would set up all attributes during our application's initialization and simply bind the data at render, yielding much better performance.

Let's see how we can start using VAOs from here on out!

Time for Action: Rendering a Square Using a VAO

Let's refactor a previous example using VAOs:

1. Open up `ch02_01_square.html` in your editor.
2. First, we update our global variables:

```
// Global variables that are set and used
// across the application
let gl,
  program,
  squareVAO,
  squareIndexBuffer,
  indices;
```

3. We've replaced `squareVertexBuffer` with `squareVAO`, as we no longer need to reference the vertex buffer directly.

4. Next, we update the `initBuffers` functions as follows:

```
// Set up the buffers for the square
function initBuffers() {
  /*
    V0                       V3
    (-0.5, 0.5, 0)           (0.5, 0.5, 0)
    X--------------------X
    |                    |
    |                    |
    |          (0, 0)    |
    |                    |
    |                    |
    X--------------------X
    V1                       V2
    (-0.5, -0.5, 0)          (0.5, -0.5, 0)
  */
  const vertices = [
    -0.5, 0.5, 0,
    -0.5, -0.5, 0,
    0.5, -0.5, 0,
    0.5, 0.5, 0
  ];

  // Indices defined in counter-clockwise order
  indices = [0, 1, 2, 0, 2, 3];

  // Create VAO instance
  squareVAO = gl.createVertexArray();

  // Bind it so we can work on it
  gl.bindVertexArray(squareVAO);

  const squareVertexBuffer = gl.createBuffer();
  gl.bindBuffer(gl.ARRAY_BUFFER, squareVertexBuffer);
  gl.bufferData(gl.ARRAY_BUFFER, new Float32Array(vertices),
   gl.STATIC_DRAW);

  // Provide instructions for VAO to use data later in draw
  gl.enableVertexAttribArray(program.aVertexPosition);
  gl.vertexAttribPointer(program.aVertexPosition, 3, gl.FLOAT,
   false, 0, 0);

  // Setting up the IBO
  squareIndexBuffer = gl.createBuffer();
  gl.bindBuffer(gl.ELEMENT_ARRAY_BUFFER, squareIndexBuffer);
  gl.bufferData(gl.ELEMENT_ARRAY_BUFFER, new Uint16Array(indices),
   gl.STATIC_DRAW);
```

```
      // Clean
      gl.bindVertexArray(null);
      gl.bindBuffer(gl.ARRAY_BUFFER, null);
      gl.bindBuffer(gl.ELEMENT_ARRAY_BUFFER, null);
   }
```

5. We create a new VAO instance using `gl.createVertexArray();` and assign it to `squareVAO`.

6. Then, we bind `squareVAO` with `gl.bindVertexArray(squareVAO);` so that all of our attribute settings will apply to that set of attribute state.

7. After the `squareVertexBuffer` has been configured, we instruct the currently bound VAO (i.e. `squareVAO`) on how to extract data given the instructions for `aVertexPosition`. These instructions are the same ones that previously sat inside of the `draw` function; but now, they happen *once* during initialization.

8. Lastly, we need to use this VAO in our `draw` function:

```
   // We call draw to render to our canvas
   function draw() {
     // Clear the scene
     gl.clear(gl.COLOR_BUFFER_BIT | gl.DEPTH_BUFFER_BIT);
     gl.viewport(0, 0, gl.canvas.width, gl.canvas.height);

     // Bind the VAO
     gl.bindVertexArray(squareVAO);

     gl.bindBuffer(gl.ELEMENT_ARRAY_BUFFER, squareIndexBuffer);

     // Draw to the scene using triangle primitives
     gl.drawElements(gl.TRIANGLES, indices.length, gl.UNSIGNED_SHORT,
      0);

     // Clean
     gl.bindVertexArray(null);
     gl.bindBuffer(gl.ARRAY_BUFFER, null);
     gl.bindBuffer(gl.ELEMENT_ARRAY_BUFFER, null);
   }
```

9. The updated `draw` function is far simpler! We simply bind the VAO (i.e. `squareVAO`) and allow for it to handle the instructions we provided it inside of `initBuffers`.

10. Lastly, it's good practice to unbind buffers and VAOs after usage by providing `null` values.

11. Save the file and open it in your browser. You should see the same square being rendered using a VAO:

12. The source code for this exercise can be found in `ch02_03_square-vao.html`.

Given that we're currently rendering a single geometry, using a VAO may seem unnecessarily complex. That is a reasonable assessment! However, as the complexity of our application grows, using VAOs becomes a foundational feature.

Time for Action: Rendering Modes

Let's revisit the signature of the `drawElements` function:

```
gl.drawElements(mode, count, type, offset)
```

The first parameter determines the type of primitives that we are rendering. In the following section, we will see the different rendering modes with examples.

Follow the given steps:

1. Open the `ch02_04_rendering-modes.html` file in your browser. This example follows the same structure as in the previous section.

2. Open `ch02_04_rendering-modes.html` in your editor and scroll down to the `initBuffers` function:

```
function initBuffers() {
  const vertices = [
    -0.5, -0.5, 0,
```

```
    -0.25, 0.5, 0,
    0.0, -0.5, 0,
    0.25, 0.5, 0,
    0.5, -0.5, 0
];

indices = [0, 1, 2, 0, 2, 3, 2, 3, 4];

// Create VAO
trapezoidVAO = gl.createVertexArray();

// Bind VAO
gl.bindVertexArray(trapezoidVAO);

const trapezoidVertexBuffer = gl.createBuffer();
gl.bindBuffer(gl.ARRAY_BUFFER, trapezoidVertexBuffer);
gl.bufferData(gl.ARRAY_BUFFER, new Float32Array(vertices),
 gl.STATIC_DRAW);
// Provide instructions to VAO
gl.vertexAttribPointer(program.aVertexPosition, 3, gl.FLOAT,
 false, 0, 0);
gl.enableVertexAttribArray(program.aVertexPosition);

trapezoidIndexBuffer = gl.createBuffer();
gl.bindBuffer(gl.ELEMENT_ARRAY_BUFFER, trapezoidIndexBuffer);
gl.bufferData(gl.ELEMENT_ARRAY_BUFFER, new Uint16Array(indices),
 gl.STATIC_DRAW);

// Clean
gl.bindVertexArray(null);
gl.bindBuffer(gl.ARRAY_BUFFER, null);
gl.bindBuffer(gl.ELEMENT_ARRAY_BUFFER, null);
}
```

3. Here, you will see that we are drawing a trapezoid. However, on screen, you will see two triangles! Later, we'll see how this happened.

4. At the top of the page, there is a settings controller that allows you to select the different rendering modes that WebGL provides:

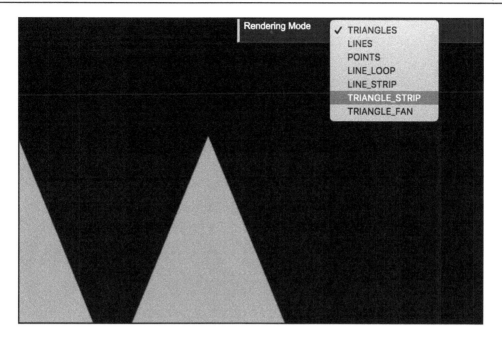

```
let gl,
  canvas,
  program,
  indices,
  trapezoidVAO,
  trapezoidIndexBuffer,
  // Global variable that captures the current rendering mode type
  renderingMode = 'TRIANGLES';
```

5. When you select any option from the settings, you are changing the value of the renderingMode variable defined at the top of the code (scroll up if you want to see where it is defined). The code that sets up the settings controller is inside the initControls function. We will cover this functionality later.

6. To see how each option modifies the rendering, scroll to the draw function:

```
function draw() {
  gl.clear(gl.COLOR_BUFFER_BIT | gl.DEPTH_BUFFER_BIT);
  gl.viewport(0, 0, gl.canvas.width, gl.canvas.height);

  // Bind VAO
  gl.bindVertexArray(trapezoidVAO);

  gl.bindBuffer(gl.ELEMENT_ARRAY_BUFFER, trapezoidIndexBuffer);

  // Depending on the rendering mode type, we will draw differently
```

```
switch (renderingMode) {
  case 'TRIANGLES': {
    indices = [0, 1, 2, 2, 3, 4];
    gl.bufferData(gl.ELEMENT_ARRAY_BUFFER, new
     Uint16Array(indices), gl.STATIC_DRAW);
    gl.drawElements(gl.TRIANGLES, indices.length,
     gl.UNSIGNED_SHORT,
     0);
    break;
  }
  case 'LINES': {
    indices = [1, 3, 0, 4, 1, 2, 2, 3];
    gl.bufferData(gl.ELEMENT_ARRAY_BUFFER, new
     Uint16Array(indices), gl.STATIC_DRAW);
    gl.drawElements(gl.LINES, indices.length, gl.UNSIGNED_SHORT,
     0);
    break;
  }
  case 'POINTS': {
    indices = [1, 2, 3];
    gl.bufferData(gl.ELEMENT_ARRAY_BUFFER, new
     Uint16Array(indices), gl.STATIC_DRAW);
    gl.drawElements(gl.POINTS, indices.length, gl.UNSIGNED_SHORT,
     0);
    break;
  }
  case 'LINE_LOOP': {
    indices = [2, 3, 4, 1, 0];
    gl.bufferData(gl.ELEMENT_ARRAY_BUFFER, new
     Uint16Array(indices), gl.STATIC_DRAW);
    gl.drawElements(gl.LINE_LOOP, indices.length,
     gl.UNSIGNED_SHORT, 0);
    break;
  }
  case 'LINE_STRIP': {
    indices = [2, 3, 4, 1, 0];
    gl.bufferData(gl.ELEMENT_ARRAY_BUFFER, new
     Uint16Array(indices), gl.STATIC_DRAW);
    gl.drawElements(gl.LINE_STRIP, indices.length,
     gl.UNSIGNED_SHORT, 0);
    break;
  }
  case 'TRIANGLE_STRIP': {
    indices = [0, 1, 2, 3, 4];
    gl.bufferData(gl.ELEMENT_ARRAY_BUFFER, new
     Uint16Array(indices), gl.STATIC_DRAW);
    gl.drawElements(gl.TRIANGLE_STRIP, indices.length,
     gl.UNSIGNED_SHORT, 0);
```

```
      break;
    }
    case 'TRIANGLE_FAN': {
      indices = [0, 1, 2, 3, 4];
      gl.bufferData(gl.ELEMENT_ARRAY_BUFFER, new
       Uint16Array(indices), gl.STATIC_DRAW);
      gl.drawElements(gl.TRIANGLE_FAN, indices.length,
       gl.UNSIGNED_SHORT, 0);
      break;
    }
  }

  // Clean
  gl.bindVertexArray(null);
  gl.bindBuffer(gl.ARRAY_BUFFER, null);
  gl.bindBuffer(gl.ELEMENT_ARRAY_BUFFER, null);
}
```

7. You will see that after binding the IBO `trapezoidIndexBuffer` with the following instruction:

```
gl.bindBuffer(gl.ELEMENT_ARRAY_BUFFER, trapezoidIndexBuffer);
```

8. You also have a switch statement where there is some code that executes, depending on the value of the `renderingMode` variable.

9. For each mode, we define the contents of the JavaScript array indices. Then, we pass this array to the currently-bound buffer, `trapezoidIndexBuffer`, by using the `bufferData` function. Finally, we call the `drawElements` function.

10. Let's see what each mode does:

Mode	Description
TRIANGLES	When you use the TRIANGLES mode, WebGL will use the first three indices defined in your IBO to construct the first triangle, the next three to construct the second triangle, and so on. In this example, we are drawing two triangles, which can be verified by examining the JavaScript indices array that populates the IBO: `indices = [0, 1, 2, 2, 3, 4];`.

LINES	The LINES mode will instruct WebGL to take each consecutive pair of indices defined in the IBO and draw lines by taking the coordinates of the corresponding vertices. For instance, indices = [1, 3, 0, 4, 1, 2, 2, 3]; will draw four lines: from vertex number 1 to vertex number 3, from vertex number 0 to vertex number 4, from vertex number 1 to vertex number 2, and from vertex number 2 to vertex number 3.
POINTS	When we use the POINTS mode, WebGL will not generate surfaces. Instead, it will render the vertices that we had defined using the index array. In this example, we will only render vertices number 1, 2, and 3 with indices = [1, 2, 3];.
LINE_LOOP	LINE_LOOP draws a closed loop connecting the vertices defined in the IBO to the next one. In our case, it will be indices = [2, 3, 4, 1, 0];.
LINE_STRIP	LINE_STRIP is similar to LINE_LOOP. The difference is that WebGL does not connect the last vertex to the first one (not a closed loop). The indices JavaScript array will be indices = [2, 3, 4, 1, 0];.
TRIANGLE_STRIP	TRIANGLE_STRIP draws connected triangles. Every vertex is specified after the first three. In our example, vertices number 0, number 1, and number 2 create a new triangle. If we have indices = [0, 1, 2, 3, 4];, then we will generate the triangles *(0, 1, 2)*, *(1, 2, 3)*, and *(2, 3, 4)*.
TRIANGLE_FAN	TRIANGLE_FAN creates triangles in a similar way to TRIANGLE_STRIP. However, the first vertex defined in the IBO is taken as the origin of the fan (the only shared vertex among consecutive triangles). In our example, indices = [0, 1, 2, 3, 4]; will create the triangles *(0, 1, 2)* and *(0, 3, 4)*.

11. The following diagram can be useful in visualizing these various rendering modes. That being said, it's easiest to see these modes in action by changing the setting's drop-down values and seeing the various results:

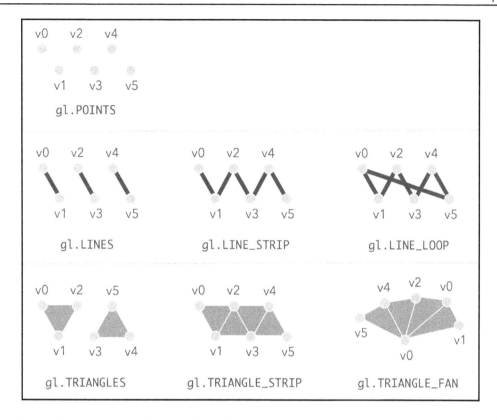

12. Let's make some changes by editing `ch02_04_rendering-modes.html` so that when you select the `TRIANGLES` option, you render the trapezoid instead of two triangles.

Hint

You need one extra triangle in the indices array.

13. Save the file and test it in your browser.
14. Edit the web page so that you draw the letter **M** using the `LINES` option.

Hint

You need to define four lines in the indices array.

15. Just like before, save your changes and test them in your browser.
16. Using the LINE_LOOP mode, draw only the boundary of the trapezoid.

What just happened?

This simple exercise helped us see the different rendering modes supported by WebGL. These different modes determine how to interpret vertex and index data to render an object.

WebGL as a State Machine: Buffer Manipulation

When dealing with buffers for the getParameter, getBufferParameter, and isBuffer functions, new information about the state of the rendering pipeline becomes available to us.

Similar to Chapter 1, *Getting Started*, we will use getParameter(parameter), where parameter can have the following values:

- ARRAY_BUFFER_BINDING: Retrieves a reference to the currently-bound VBO
- ELEMENT_ARRAY_BUFFER_BINDING: Retrieves a reference to the currently-bound IBO

We can also query the size and the usage of the currently-bound VBO and IBO using getBufferParameter(type, parameter), where type can have the following values:

- ARRAY_BUFFER: To refer to the currently-bound VBO
- ELEMENT_ARRAY_BUFFER: To refer to the currently-bound IBO

And parameter can have the following values:

- BUFFER_SIZE: Returns the size of the requested buffer
- BUFFER_USAGE: Returns the usage of the requested buffer

Binding Buffers

Your VBO and/or IBO needs to be bound when you inspect the state of the currently-bound VBO and/or IBO
with `getParameter` and `getBufferParameter`.

Finally, `isBuffer(object)` will return `true` if the object is a WebGL buffer, or `false` with an error when the buffer is invalid.

Unlike `getParameter` and `getBufferParameter`, `isBuffer` does not require any VBO or IBO to be bound.

Time for Action: Querying the State of Buffers

Follow the given steps:

1. Open the `ch02_05_state-machine.html` file in your browser. You should see the following:

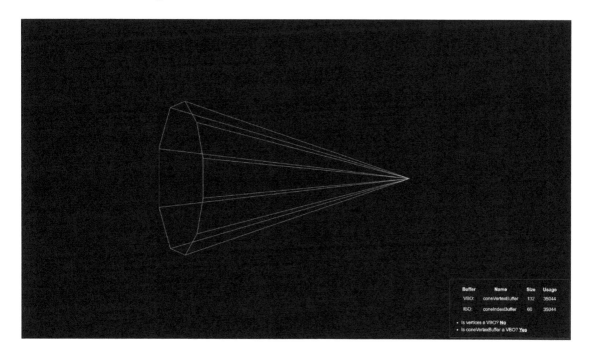

2. Open `ch02_05_state-machine.html` in your editor and scroll down to the `initBuffers` method:

```
function initBuffers() {
  const vertices = [
    1.5, 0, 0,
    -1.5, 1, 0,
    -1.5, 0.809017, 0.587785,
    -1.5, 0.309017, 0.951057,
    -1.5, -0.309017, 0.951057,
    -1.5, -0.809017, 0.587785,
    -1.5, -1, 0,
    -1.5, -0.809017, -0.587785,
    -1.5, -0.309017, -0.951057,
    -1.5, 0.309017, -0.951057,
    -1.5, 0.809017, -0.587785
  ];

  indices = [
    0, 1, 2,
    0, 2, 3,
    0, 3, 4,
    0, 4, 5,
    0, 5, 6,
    0, 6, 7,
    0, 7, 8,
    0, 8, 9,
    0, 9, 10,
    0, 10, 1
  ];

  // Create VAO
  coneVAO = gl.createVertexArray();

  // Bind VAO
  gl.bindVertexArray(coneVAO);

  const coneVertexBuffer = gl.createBuffer();
  gl.bindBuffer(gl.ARRAY_BUFFER, coneVertexBuffer);
  gl.bufferData(gl.ARRAY_BUFFER, new Float32Array(vertices),
   gl.STATIC_DRAW);

  // Configure instructions
  gl.vertexAttribPointer(program.aVertexPosition, 3, gl.FLOAT,
   false, 0, 0);
  gl.enableVertexAttribArray(program.aVertexPosition);

  coneIndexBuffer = gl.createBuffer();
```

```
gl.bindBuffer(gl.ELEMENT_ARRAY_BUFFER, coneIndexBuffer);
gl.bufferData(gl.ELEMENT_ARRAY_BUFFER, new Uint16Array(indices),
 gl.STATIC_DRAW);

// Set the global variables based on the parameter type
if (coneVertexBuffer ===
  gl.getParameter(gl.ARRAY_BUFFER_BINDING)) {
  vboName = 'coneVertexBuffer';
}
if (coneIndexBuffer ===
  gl.getParameter(gl.ELEMENT_ARRAY_BUFFER_BINDING)) {
  iboName = 'coneIndexBuffer';
}

vboSize = gl.getBufferParameter(gl.ARRAY_BUFFER, gl.BUFFER_SIZE);
vboUsage = gl.getBufferParameter(gl.ARRAY_BUFFER,
 gl.BUFFER_USAGE);

iboSize = gl.getBufferParameter(gl.ELEMENT_ARRAY_BUFFER,
 gl.BUFFER_SIZE);
iboUsage = gl.getBufferParameter(gl.ELEMENT_ARRAY_BUFFER,
 gl.BUFFER_USAGE);

try {
  isVerticesVbo = gl.isBuffer(vertices);
}
catch (e) {
  isVerticesVbo = false;
}

isConeVertexBufferVbo = gl.isBuffer(coneVertexBuffer);

// Clean
gl.bindVertexArray(null);
gl.bindBuffer(gl.ARRAY_BUFFER, null);
gl.bindBuffer(gl.ELEMENT_ARRAY_BUFFER, null);
}
```

3. Pay attention to how we use the methods discussed in this section to retrieve and display information about the current state of the buffers.

4. The information queried by the `initBuffers` function is shown in the settings section of the web page when we use `updateInfo`.

5. In the settings section of the web page, you will see the following result:

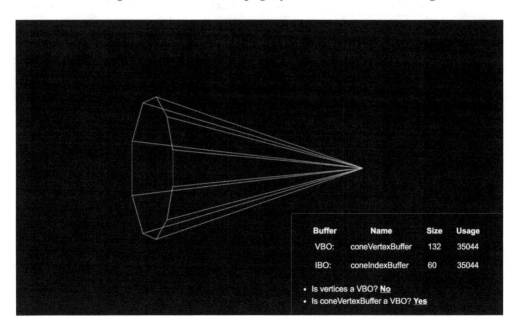

6. Copy the following line, `gl.bindBuffer(gl.ARRAY_BUFFER, null);`, and paste it right before the following line inside of the `initBuffers` function: `coneIndexBuffer = gl.createBuffer();`.

7. What happens when you launch the page in your browser again?

8. Why do you think this behavior occurs?

What just happened?

You have learned that the currently-bound buffer is a state variable in WebGL. The buffer is bound until you unbind it by calling `bindBuffer` again with the corresponding type (`ARRAY_BUFFER` or `ELEMENT_ARRAY_BUFFER`) as the first parameter and with `null` as the second argument (that is, no buffer to bind). You have also learned that you can only query the state of the currently-bound buffer. Therefore, if you want to query a different buffer, you need to bind it first.

Have a Go: Add One Validation

Modify the file so that you can validate and show on screen whether the indices array and the `coneIndexBuffer` are WebGL buffers.

Hint

In order to display the values, you will have to modify the table in the HTML body and modify the `updateInfo` function accordingly.

Advanced Geometry-Loading Techniques

So far, we've rendered very simple objects. Now, let's investigate how to load a geometry (vertices and indices) from a file instead of declaring the vertices and indices every time we call `initBuffers`. To do this, we will make asynchronous calls to the web server using AJAX. We will retrieve the file with our geometry from the web server and then use the built-in JSON parser to convert the context of our files into JavaScript objects. In our case, these objects will be the vertices and indices arrays.

Introduction to JavaScript Object Notation (JSON)

JSON stands for **JavaScript Object Notation**. It is a lightweight, text-based, open format used for data interchange. JSON is commonly used as an alternative to XML.

The power of JSON is that it's language-agnostic. This means that there are parsers in many languages to read and interpret JSON objects. Also, JSON is a subset of the object literal notation of JavaScript. Therefore, we can define JavaScript objects using JSON.

Defining JSON-Based 3D Models

Let's assume, for example, that we have a model object with two arrays: vertices and indices. Say that these arrays contain the information described in the cone example (`ch02_06_cone.html`), as follows:

```
function initBuffers() {
  const vertices = [
    1.5, 0, 0,
    -1.5, 1, 0,
    -1.5, 0.809017, 0.587785,
    -1.5, 0.309017, 0.951057,
    -1.5, -0.309017, 0.951057,
    -1.5, -0.809017, 0.587785,
    -1.5, -1, 0,
```

```
        -1.5, -0.809017, -0.587785,
        -1.5, -0.309017, -0.951057,
        -1.5, 0.309017, -0.951057,
        -1.5, 0.809017, -0.587785
    ];

    indices = [
        0, 1, 2,
        0, 2, 3,
        0, 3, 4,
        0, 4, 5,
        0, 5, 6,
        0, 6, 7,
        0, 7, 8,
        0, 8, 9,
        0, 9, 10,
        0, 10, 1
    ];

    // ...
}
```

Following the JSON notation, we would represent these two arrays as an object, as follows:

```
{
  "vertices": [
    1.5, 0, 0,
    -1.5, 1, 0,
    -1.5, 0.809017, 0.587785,
    -1.5, 0.309017, 0.951057,
    -1.5, -0.309017, 0.951057,
    -1.5, -0.809017, 0.587785,
    -1.5, -1, 0,
    -1.5, -0.809017, -0.587785,
    -1.5, -0.309017, -0.951057,
    -1.5, 0.309017, -0.951057,
    -1.5, 0.809017, -0.587785
  ],
  "indices": [
    0, 1, 2,
    0, 2, 3,
    0, 3, 4,
    0, 4, 5,
    0, 5, 6,
    0, 6, 7,
    0, 7, 8,
    0, 8, 9,
    0, 9, 10,
```

```
    0, 10, 1
  ]
}
```

Based on this example, we can infer the following syntax rules:

- The extent of a JSON object is defined by curly brackets ({ }).
- Attributes in a JSON object are separated by commas (,).
- There is no comma after the last attribute.
- Each attribute of a JSON object has two parts: a **key** and a **value.**
- The name of an attribute is enclosed by quotation marks (" ").
- Each attribute key is separated from its corresponding value with a colon (:).
- Attributes of the array are defined in the same way you would define them in JavaScript.

Time for Action: Encoding and Decoding JSON

Most modern web browsers support native JSON encoding and decoding. Let's examine the methods available inside this object:

Method	Description
JSON.stringify(object)	We use JSON.stringify to convert JavaScript objects to JSON-formatted text.
JSON.parse(string)	We use JSON.parse to convert text into JavaScript objects.

Let's learn how to encode and decode with the JSON notation by creating a simple model—a 3D line. Here, we will be focusing on how we do JSON encoding and decoding. Follow the given steps:

1. In your browser, open the interactive JavaScript console. Use the following table for assistance:

Browser	Shortcut keys (PC/Mac)
Firefox	*Ctrl + Shift + K/Command + Alt + K*
Safari	*Ctrl + Shift + C/Command + Alt + C*
Chrome	*Ctrl + Shift + J/Command + Alt + J*

2. Create a JSON object by typing the following:

```
const model = { vertices: [0, 0, 0, 1, 1, 1], indices: [0, 1] };
```

3. Verify that the model is an object by writing the following:

```
typeof(model); // outputs "object"
```

JavaScript Type-Checking

Since many things in JavaScript are *objects*, it is recommended that you are more rigorous with type-checking. We will just use `typeof` for demonstration purposes. Additionally, there are many utility libraries, such as Lodash (`https://lodash.com`), that extend JavaScript features to provide these operations and more.

4. Let's print the model attributes. Write this in the console (press *Enter* at the end of each line):

```
model.vertices // outputs the vertices
model.indices // outputs the indices
```

5. Let's create a JSON text:

```
const text = JSON.stringify(model);
alert(text);
```

6. What happens when you type `text.vertices`?

7. As you can see, you get a message saying that `text.vertices` is `undefined`. This happens because text is not a JavaScript object, but a `string` with the peculiarity of being written according to JSON notation to describe an `object`. Everything in it is text, and so it does not have any fields.

8. Let's convert the JSON text back into an object. Type the following:

```
const model2 = JSON.parse(text);
typeof(model2); // outputs "object"
model2.vertices; // outputs vertices
```

What just happened?

We have learned to encode and decode JSON objects. These exercises are relevant because we will use the same process to define our geometry to be loaded from external files. In the next section, we will see how to download geometric models specified with JSON from a web server.

Asynchronous Loading with AJAX

The following diagram summarizes the asynchronous loading of files by the web browser using AJAX:

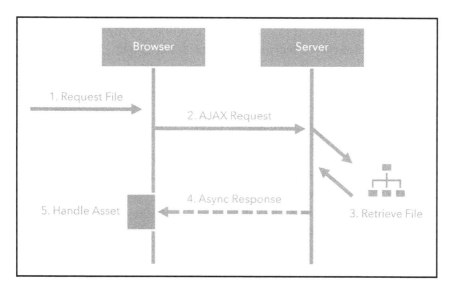

Let's analyze this more closely:

- **Request File**: Indicates the path to the file you want to load. Remember that this file contains the geometry that we will be loading from the web server instead of coding the JavaScript arrays (vertices and indices) directly into the web page.
- **AJAX Request**: We need to write a function that will perform the AJAX request. Let's call this function `load`. The code looks like this:

```
// Given a path to a file, load the assets asynchronously
function load(filePath) {
  // We return the promise so that, if needed, you can know when
  // `load` has resolved
  return fetch(filePath)
```

```
// Convert to a valid json
.then(res => res.json())
// Handle the parsed JSON data
.then(data => {
  // Handle data
})
.catch(error => {
  // Handle error
});
}
```

AJAX Requests with fetch

We are leveraging `fetch`, an AJAX API provided in modern browsers, for fetching resources. It is very convenient with a **Promise**-based implementation. To learn more about `fetch`, visit `https://developer.mozilla.org/en-US/docs/Web/API/Fetch_API`.

For now, let's say that this function will perform the AJAX request.

- **Retrieving the file**: The web server will receive and treat our request as a regular HTTP request. In fact, the server does not know that this request is *asynchronous* (it is asynchronous for the web browser since it does not wait for the answer). The server will look for our file and generate a response, regardless of whether it finds the request.
- **Asynchronous response**: Once a response is sent to the web browser, the `fetch` promise is resolved and the provided callback is invoked. This callback corresponds to the `then` request method. If the request is successful, we invoke the `then` callback; if it fails, we invoke the `catch` callback.
- **Handling the loaded model**: After our data is received and parsed, we attach a new callback to process the file retrieved from the server. Please notice that in the previous segment of code, we used the promise-based JSON parser to create a JavaScript object from the file before passing it to the next function. The code for the `load` function looks like this:

```
// Given a path to a file, load the assets asynchronously
function load(filePath) {
  // We return the promise so that, if needed, you can know when
  // `load` has resolved
  return fetch(filePath)
  // Convert to a valid json
  .then(res => res.json())
  // Handle the parsed JSON data
```

```
  .then(data => {
    model = data;

    // Create VAO
    vao = gl.createVertexArray();

    // Bind VAO
    gl.bindVertexArray(coneVAO);

    const modelVertexBuffer = gl.createBuffer();
    gl.bindBuffer(gl.ARRAY_BUFFER, modelVertexBuffer);
    gl.bufferData(gl.ARRAY_BUFFER, new
     Float32Array(model.vertices), gl.STATIC_DRAW);

    // Configure instructions
    gl.enableVertexAttribArray(program.aVertexPosition);
    gl.vertexAttribPointer(program.aVertexPosition, 3, gl.FLOAT,
     false, 0, 0);

    modelIndexBuffer = gl.createBuffer();
    gl.bindBuffer(gl.ELEMENT_ARRAY_BUFFER, modelIndexBuffer);
    gl.bufferData(gl.ELEMENT_ARRAY_BUFFER, new
     Uint16Array(model.indices), gl.STATIC_DRAW);

    // Clean
    gl.bindVertexArray(null);
    gl.bindBuffer(gl.ARRAY_BUFFER, null);
    gl.bindBuffer(gl.ELEMENT_ARRAY_BUFFER, null);
  })
  // Display into the console if there are any errors
  .catch(console.error);
}
```

If you look closely, you'll realize that this function is very similar to one of the functions we saw previously: the initBuffers function. This is reasonable, given that we cannot initialize the buffers until we retrieve the geometry data from the server. Just like initBuffers, we configure our VAO, VBO, and IBO and pass them the information contained in the JavaScript arrays of our model object.

Setting up a Web Server

Now that we're fetching assets from a server, we need to serve our application by using a server. If you do *not* have a web server, we recommend that you install a lightweight web server from the following options:

- **Serve:** https://github.com/zeit/serve
- **Lighttpd:** http://www.lighttpd.net
- **Python Server:** https://developer.mozilla.org/en-US/docs/Learn/Common_questions/set_up_a_local_testing_server

Hosting Examples

Although any web server will be able to serve these examples, serve provides simplicity and great functionality. That being said, be sure to run your server from the root of the examples directory, since the common directory is a shared dependency across chapters.

Working Around the Web Server Requirement

If you have Firefox and do not want to install a web server, you can change strict_origin_policy to false in about:config.

If you are using Chrome and do not want to install a web server, make sure that you run it from the command line with the following modifier:

```
--allow-file-access-from-files
```

Let's use AJAX and JSON to load a cone from our web server.

Time for Action: Loading a Cone with AJAX

Follow the given steps:

1. Make sure that your web server is running and access the ch02_07_ajax-cone.html file using your web server.

Web Server Address

You know that you are using the web server if the URL in the address bar starts with localhost/ or 127.0.0.1/ instead of file://.

2. The folder containing the code for this chapter should look like this:

Index of **webgl2-book/ch02/**

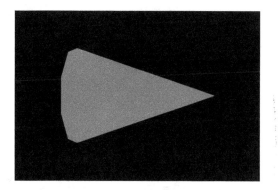

3. Click on `ch02_07_ajax-cone.html`.

4. The example will load in your browser and you will see something similar to this:

5. Please review the `load` functions to better understand the use of AJAX and JSON in the application.

6. How is the global `model` variable used? *(Check the source code.)*

7. Check what happens when you change the color in the `common/models/geometries/cone.json` file and reload the page.

8. Modify the coordinates of the cone in the `common/models/geometries/cone.json` file and reload the page. Here, you can verify that WebGL reads and renders the coordinates from the file. If you modify them in the file, the geometry will be updated on the screen.

What just happened?

You learned how to use AJAX and JSON to load geometries from a remote location (web server) instead of specifying these geometries (using JavaScript arrays) inside the web page.

Have a Go: Loading a Nissan GTR

Follow the given steps:

1. Open the `ch02_08_ajax-car.html` file using your web server.
2. You should see something like this:

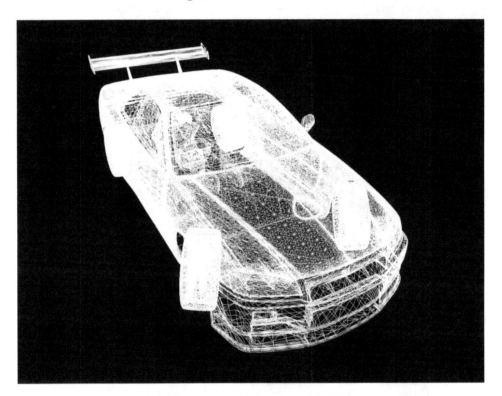

3. The reason we selected the `LINES` model instead of the `TRIANGLES` model is to easily visualize the structure of the car.
4. Find the line where the rendering mode is being selected and make sure that you understand what the code does.
5. Go to the `draw` function.
6. In the `drawElements` instruction, change the mode from `gl.LINES` to `gl.TRIANGLES`.
7. Refresh the page in the web browser.
8. What do you see? Can you guess why the visuals are different? What is your rationale?

Lights

Illumination helps us visualize complex geometries more clearly. Without lights, all of our volumes will look opaque, and it will be difficult to distinguish their parts when changing from LINES to TRIANGLES.

Architecture Updates

Let's cover some useful functions that we can refactor for use in later chapters:

1. Open common/js/utils.js in your editor to see the following changes.
2. We have added two additional methods, autoResizeCanvas and getShader, to utils.js that look very similar to the code we implemented earlier in this chapter:

```
'use strict';

// A set of utility functions for /common operations across our
// application
const utils = {

  // Find and return a DOM element given an ID
  getCanvas(id) {
    // ...
  },

  // Given a canvas element, return the WebGL2 context
  getGLContext(canvas) {
    // ...
  },

  // Given a canvas element, expand it to the size of the window
  // and ensure that it automatically resizes as the window changes
  autoResizeCanvas(canvas) {
    const expandFullScreen = () => {
      canvas.width = window.innerWidth;
      canvas.height = window.innerHeight;
    };
    expandFullScreen();
    window.addEventListener('resize', expandFullScreen);
  },

  // Given a WebGL context and an id for a shader script,
  // return a compiled shader
```

```
getShader(gl, id) {
  const script = document.getElementById(id);
  if (!script) {
    return null;
  }

  const shaderString = script.text.trim();

  let shader;
  if (script.type === 'x-shader/x-vertex') {
    shader = gl.createShader(gl.VERTEX_SHADER);
  }
  else if (script.type === 'x-shader/x-fragment') {
    shader = gl.createShader(gl.FRAGMENT_SHADER);
  }
  else {
    return null;
  }

  gl.shaderSource(shader, shaderString);
  gl.compileShader(shader);

  if (!gl.getShaderParameter(shader, gl.COMPILE_STATUS)) {
    console.error(gl.getShaderInfoLog(shader));
    return null;
  }

  return shader;
}

};
```

3. The autoResizeCanvas method takes a canvas element and dynamically resizes it to be fullscreen by watching browser-resizing events.

4. The getShader function takes a gl instance and an id script to compile and return the shader source. Internally, getShader reads the source code of the script and stores it in a local variable. Then, it creates a new shader by using the WebGL createShader function. After that, it will add the source code to it using the shaderSource function. Finally, it will try to compile the shader using the compileShader function.

5. Open ch02_09_ajax-car-final.html in your editor to see the following changes.

6. Scroll to the `init` function where the necessary changes were made to use the `utils.autoResizeCanvas` method:

```
function init() {
  const canvas = utils.getCanvas('webgl-canvas');
  // Handle automatic resizing
  utils.autoResizeCanvas(canvas);

  // Retrieve a valid WebGL2 context
  gl = utils.getGLContext(canvas);
  gl.clearColor(0, 0, 0, 1);
  gl.enable(gl.DEPTH_TEST);

  initProgram();
  // We are no longer blocking the render until `load` has
  // resolved, as we're not returning a Promise.
  load();
  render();
}
```

7. Scroll to the `initProgram` function inside of `ch02_09_ajax-car-final.html`, where the necessary changes were made to use the `utils.getShader` method:

```
function initProgram() {
  // Retrieve shaders based on the shader script IDs
  const vertexShader = utils.getShader(gl, 'vertex-shader');
  const fragmentShader = utils.getShader(gl, 'fragment-shader');

  program = gl.createProgram();
  gl.attachShader(program, vertexShader);
  gl.attachShader(program, fragmentShader);
  gl.linkProgram(program);

  if (!gl.getProgramParameter(program, gl.LINK_STATUS)) {
    console.error('Could not initialize shaders');
  }

  gl.useProgram(program);

  program.aVertexPosition = gl.getAttribLocation(program,
   'aVertexPosition');
  program.uProjectionMatrix = gl.getUniformLocation(program,
   'uProjectionMatrix');
  program.uModelViewMatrix = gl.getUniformLocation(program,
   'uModelViewMatrix');
}
```

8. Open `ch02_09_ajax-car-final.html` in a browser to see these changes in action.

Summary

Let's summarize what we've learned in this chapter:

- The WebGL API itself is just a rasterizer and, conceptually, is fairly simple.
- WebGL's rendering pipeline describes how the WebGL buffers are used and passed in the form of attributes to be processed by the vertex shader. The vertex shader parallelizes vertex processing in the GPU. Vertices define the surface of the geometry that is going to be rendered. Every element on this surface is known as a fragment. These fragments are processed by the fragment shader.
- Fragment processing also occurs in parallel in the GPU. When all fragments have been processed, the framebuffer, a two-dimensional array, contains the image that is then displayed on your screen.
- WebGL is actually a pretty simple API. Its job is to execute two user-supplied functions, a vertex shader and fragment shader, and draw triangles, lines, or points. While it can get more complicated to do 3D, that complication is added by you, the programmer, in the form of more complex shaders.
- The fine details of how WebGL renders geometry. Remember that there are two kinds of WebGL buffers that deal with geometry rendering: VBOs and IBOs.
- WebGL works as a state machine. As such, properties referring to buffers are available and their values depend on the currently-bound buffer.
- JSON and AJAX are two JavaScript technologies that integrate well with WebGL by enabling us to load large and complex assets.

In the next chapter, we will learn more about shaders and use them to implement light sources in our WebGL scene by passing information back and forth between the WebGL JavaScript API and the attributes, uniforms, and varyings.

3
Lights

In the previous chapter, we covered WebGL's rendering pipeline, defining geometries, passing data to the GPU, drawing types, and leveraging AJAX to asynchronously load external assets. Although we briefly covered shaders and their role in creating a WebGL application, we will go into more detail in this chapter and leverage the vertex and fragment shaders to create a lighting model for our scene.

Shaders allow us to define a mathematical model that governs how our scene is lit. To learn how to implement shaders, we will study different algorithms and see examples of their application. A basic knowledge of linear algebra will be really useful to help you understand the contents of this chapter. We will use a JavaScript library that handles most of the vector and matrix operations, so you do not need to worry about the mathematical operations. Nonetheless, your overall success depends on a strong conceptual understanding of the linear algebra operations that we will discuss.

In this chapter, we will:

- Learn about light sources, normals, and materials.
- Learn the difference between shading and lighting.
- Use the Goraud and Phong shading methods.
- Use the Lambertian and Phong lighting models.
- Define and use uniforms, attributes, and varyings.
- Work with ESSL, the shading language for WebGL.
- Discuss relevant WebGL API methods that relate to shaders.
- Continue our analysis of WebGL as a state machine and describe the attributes relevant to shaders that can be set and retrieved from the state machine.

Lights, Normals, and Materials

In the real world, we see objects because they reflect light. The illumination of an object depends on its position relative to the light source, surface orientation, and its material composition. In this chapter, we will learn how to combine these three elements in WebGL to model different illumination schemes:

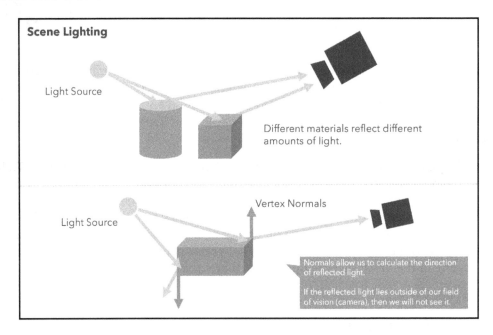

Positional Versus Directional Lights

Light sources can be **positional** or **directional**. A light source is called positional when its location will affect how the scene is lit. For instance, a lamp inside a room is a positional light source. Objects far from the lamp will receive very little light and may even appear obscure. In contrast, directional lights are lights that produce the same luminous result, regardless of their position. For example, the light from the sun will illuminate all objects in a terrestrial scene, regardless of their distance from the sun. This is because the sun is so far away that all light rays are considered parallel when they intersect the surface of an object. Directional lighting assumes that the light is coming uniformly from one direction:

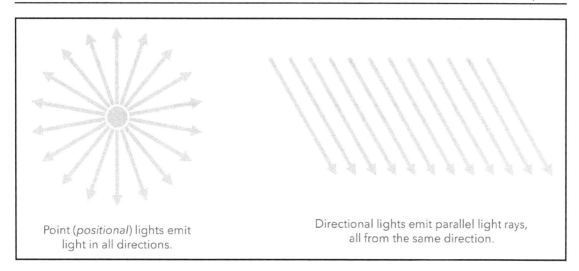

Point (*positional*) lights emit
light in all directions.

Directional lights emit parallel light rays,
all from the same direction.

A positional light is modeled by a point in space, while a directional light is modeled with a vector that indicates its direction. It is common to use a normalized vector for this purpose, given that this simplifies mathematical operations. Also, it is generally the case that computing directional lighting is actually simpler and less computationally expensive than positional lighting.

Normals

Normals are vectors that are perpendicular to the surface we want to illuminate. Normals represent the orientation of the surface and are therefore critical to modeling the interaction between a light source and the object. Given that each vertex has an associated normal vector, we can use the cross product to calculate normals.

Cross-Product

By definition, the cross-product of vectors A and B will be a vector perpendicular to both vectors A and B.

Let's break this down. If we have the triangle conformed by vertices p0, p1, and p2, we can define the v1 vector as p1 – p0 and the v2 vector as p2 – p0. The normal is then obtained by calculating the v1 x v2 cross-product. Graphically, this procedure looks something like the following:

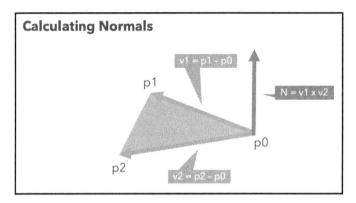

We then repeat the same calculation for each vertex on each triangle. But, what about the vertices that are shared by more than one triangle? Each shared vertex normal will receive a contribution from each of the triangles in which the vertex appears.

For example, say that the p1 vertex is shared by the #1 and #2 triangles, and that we have already calculated the normals for the vertices of the #1 triangle. Then, we need to update the p1 normal by adding up the calculated normal for p1 on the #2 triangle. This is a **vector sum**. Graphically, this looks similar to the following:

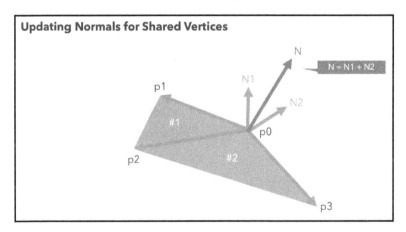

Similar to lights, normals are generally normalized to facilitate mathematical operations.

Materials

In WebGL, the material of an object can be modeled by several parameters, including its color and texture. Material colors are usually modeled as triplets in the RGB (red, green, blue) space. Textures, on the other hand, correspond to images that are mapped onto the surface of the object. This process is usually called **texture mapping**. We will cover texture mapping in later chapters.

Using Lights, Normals, and Materials in the Pipeline

In Chapter 2, *Rendering*, we discussed that WebGL buffers, attributes, and uniforms are used as input variables to the shaders, and that varyings are used to pass information between the vertex shader and the fragment shader. Let's revisit the pipeline and see where lights, normals, and materials fit in:

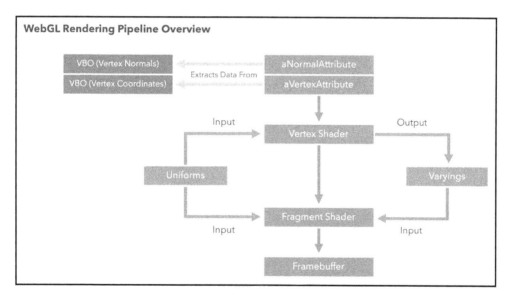

Normals are defined on a vertex-per-vertex basis; therefore, normals are modeled as a VBO and are mapped using an attribute, as shown in the preceding diagram. Note that attributes cannot be directly passed to the fragment shader. To pass information from the vertex shader to the fragment shader, we must use varyings.

Lights and materials are passed as uniforms. Uniforms are available to both the vertex shader and the fragment shader. This gives us a lot of flexibility to calculate our lighting model, because we can calculate how the light is reflected on a vertex-by-vertex basis (vertex shader) or on a fragment-per-fragment basis (fragment shader).

Program

Remember that the vertex shader and fragment shader together are referred to as a **program**.

Parallelism and the Difference Between Attributes and Uniforms

There is an important distinction to make between attributes and uniforms. When a draw call is invoked (using `drawArrays` or `drawElements`), the GPU will launch several copies of the vertex shader in parallel. Each copy will receive a different set of attributes. These attributes are drawn from the VBOs that are mapped onto the respective attributes.

On the other hand, all of the copies of the vertex shaders will receive the same uniforms – hence the name: uniform. In other words, uniforms can be seen as constants *per draw call*:

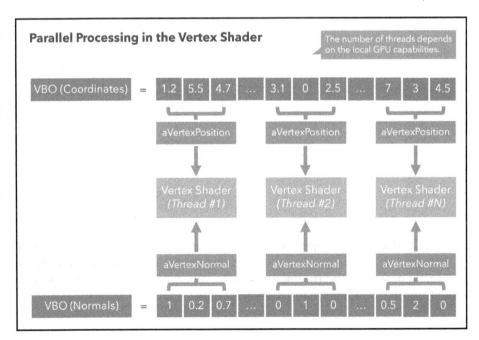

Once lights, normals, and materials are passed to the program, the next step is to determine which *shading* and *lighting* models we will implement. Let's investigate what this involves.

Shading Methods and Light-Reflection Models

Although the terms *shading* and *lighting* are often ambiguously interchanged, they refer to two different concepts.

Shading refers to the type of *interpolation* that is performed to obtain the final color for every fragment in the scene. Later, we will explain how the type of shading determines where the final color is calculated – in the vertex shader or in the fragment shader.

Once the shading model is established, the lighting model determines *how* the normals, materials, and lights need to be combined to produce the final color. Since the equations for lighting models use the physical principles of light reflection, lighting models are also referred to as *reflection models*.

Shading/Interpolation Methods

In this section, we will analyze two basic types of interpolation methods: **Goraud** and **Phong** shading.

Goraud Interpolation

The **Goraud** interpolation method calculates the final color in the *vertex shader*. The vertex normals are used to perform this calculation. Then, using a varying variable, the final color for the vertex is passed to the fragment shader. Due to the automatic interpolation of varyings provided by the rendering pipeline, each fragment will have a color that is the result of interpolating the colors of the enclosing triangle for each fragment.

 Varying Interpolation

The interpolation of varyings is automatic in the rendering pipeline. No programming is required.

Phong Interpolation

The **Phong** method calculates the final color in the *fragment shader*. To do so, each vertex normal is passed from the vertex shader to the fragment shader using a varying. Because of the interpolation mechanism of varyings included in the pipeline, each fragment will have its own normal. Fragment normals are then used to calculate the final color in the fragment shader.

The following diagram summarizes the two interpolation models:

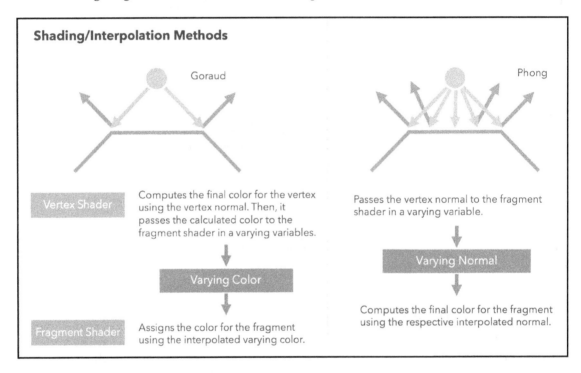

The shading method does not specify how the final color for each fragment is calculated. It only specifies *where* (vertex or fragment shader) and the *type of interpolation* (vertex colors or vertex normals) to be used.

Goraud Versus Phong Shading

We now understand that Goraud shading performs the calculations inside the vertex shader and leverages the built-in rendering pipeline's interpolation. Phong shading, on the other hand, performs all of the calculations inside the fragment shader – that is, per fragment (or pixel). With these two details in mind, can you guess some of the advantages and disadvantages of these two shading techniques?

Goraud shading is considered to be faster since the performed calculations are computed per vertex, whereas Phong shading is calculated per fragment. The speed in performance does come at the cost of accurate or more realistic interpolation. This is most noticeable in cases where a light's intensity does not linearly degrade between two vertices. Later in this chapter, we will cover these two techniques in more detail.

Light-Reflection Models

As we mentioned previously, the lighting model is independent from the shading/interpolation model. The shading model only determines where the final color is calculated. Now, it's time to talk about how to perform such calculations.

The Lambertian Reflection Model

Lambertian reflections are commonly used in computer graphics as a model for *diffuse reflections*, which are the kinds of reflections where an incident light ray is reflected in many angles instead of just *one* angle, as is the case for *specular reflections*:

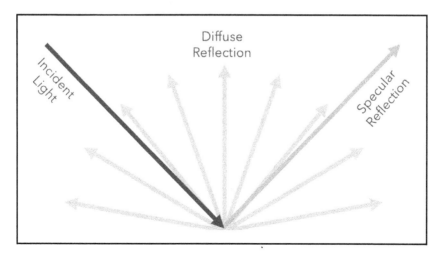

This lighting model is based on the **cosine emission law**, or **Lambert's emission law**. It is named after Johann Heinrich Lambert, from his *Photometria*, published in 1760.

The Lambertian reflection is usually calculated as the dot product between the surface normal (vertex or fragment normal, depending on the interpolation method used) and the negative of the light-direction vector. Then, the number is multiplied by the material and light source colors.

Light-Direction Vector

The light-direction vector is the vector that starts on the surface and ends on the light source position. It is essentially the vector that maps the light's position to the surface of the geometry.

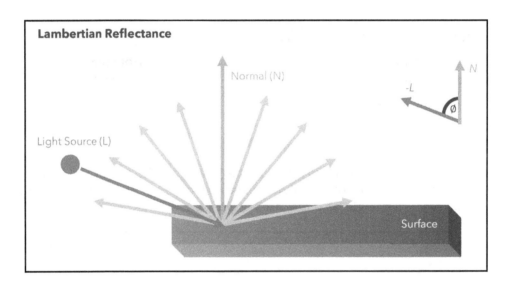

Where:

$$F = C_l C_m (-L \bullet N)$$

F is the final diffuse color, C_l is the light diffuse color, and C_l is the material diffuse color.

That being said, we'd derive the final diffuse color with the following:

$$-L \bullet N = |-L||N| cos \varnothing$$

If L and N are normalized, then:

$$-L \bullet N = cos\varnothing$$

$$-L \bullet N = cos\varnothing$$
$$F = C_l C_m cos\varnothing$$

Phong Reflection Model

The Phong reflection model describes the way a surface reflects the light as the sum of three types of reflection: ambient, diffuse, and specular. It was developed by Bui Tuong Phong, who published it in his 1973 PhD dissertation:

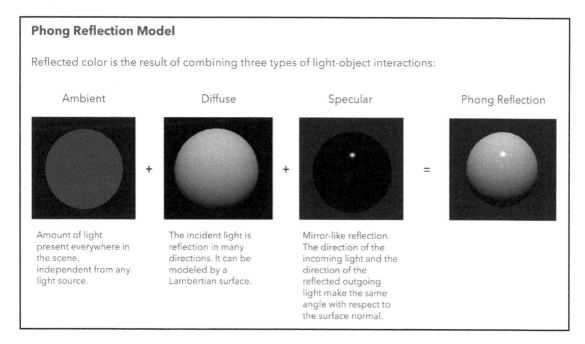

Phong Reflection Model

Reflected color is the result of combining three types of light-object interactions:

Ambient	Diffuse	Specular	Phong Reflection

Amount of light present everywhere in the scene, independent from any light source.

The incident light is reflection in many directions. It can be modeled by a Lambertian surface.

Mirror-like reflection. The direction of the incoming light and the direction of the reflected outgoing light make the same angle with respect to the surface normal.

Let's cover these concepts individually.

Ambient

The **ambient** term accounts for the scattered light present in the scene. This term is independent from any light source and is the same for all fragments.

Diffuse

The **diffuse** term corresponds to diffuse reflections. A Lambertian model is typically used for this component.

Specular

The **specular** term provides mirror-like reflections. Conceptually, the specular reflection reaches its maximum when we look at the object at an angle that is equal to the reflected light-direction vector.

The specular term is modeled by the dot product of two vectors, namely, the eye vector and the reflected light-direction vector. The eye vector originates in the fragment and terminates in the view position (camera). The reflected light-direction vector is obtained by reflecting the light-direction vector upon the surface normal vector. When this dot product equals 1 (by working with normalized vectors), our camera will capture the maximum specular reflection.

The dot product is then exponentiated by a number that represents the shininess of the surface. After that, the result is multiplied by the light and material specular components:

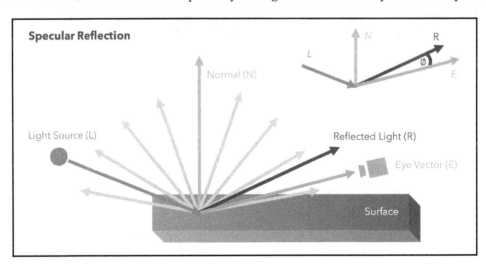

Where:

$$F_s = C_l C_m (R \bullet E)^n$$

F_s is the final specular color, C_l is the light specular color, C_l is the material specular color, and n is the shininess factor.

That being said, we'd derive the final specular color with the following:

$$R \bullet E = |R||E|cos\varnothing$$

If R and E are normalized, then:

$$R \bullet E = cos\varnothing$$
$$F = C_l C_m cos^n \varnothing$$

It's important to note that the specular reflection reaches its maximum when R and E have the same direction.

Once we have the ambient, diffuse, and specular terms, we add them to find the final color of the fragment, which provides us with the Phong reflection model.

Now, it's time to learn about the language that will allow us to implement the shading and lighting strategies inside the vertex and fragment shaders. This language is called ESSL.

OpenGL ES Shading Language (ESSL)

The OpenGL ES Shading Language (ESSL) is the language we'll use to write our shaders. Its syntax and semantics are very similar to C/C++. However, it has types and built-in functions that make it easier to manipulate vectors and matrices. In this section, we will cover the basics of ESSL so that we can start using it right away.

GLSL and ESSL

It's quite common for developers to refer to the shading language used in WebGL as GLSL. However, it is technically ESSL. WebGl2 is built on the OpenGL ES 3.0 spec and therefore uses ESSL, which is a subset of GLSL (the shading language for OpenGL).

This section summarizes the official GLSL ES specifications. You can find the complete reference at https://www.khronos.org/registry/OpenGL/ specs/es/3.0/GLSL_ES_Specification_3.00.pdf.

Storage Qualifier

Variable declarations may have a storage qualifier specified in front of the type:

- attribute: Data pulled from buffers that serve as the link between a vertex shader and a WebGL application for per-vertex data. This storage qualifier is only legal inside the vertex shader.
- uniform: Value does not change across the object being processed. Uniforms form the link between a shader and a WebGL application. Uniforms are legal in both the vertex and fragment shaders. If a uniform is shared by the vertex and fragment shader, the respective declarations must match. Uniform values stay the same for all vertices of a single draw call.
- varying: This is the link between a vertex shader and a fragment shader for interpolated data. By definition, varyings must be shared by the vertex shader and fragment shader. The declaration of varyings needs to match between the vertex and fragment shaders.
- const: A compile-time constant, or a function parameter that is read-only. They can be used anywhere in the code of an ESSL program.

Types

Here is a non-exhaustive list of the most common ESSL types:

- void: For functions that do not return a value or for an empty parameter list
- bool: A conditional type, taking on values of true or false
- int: A signed integer
- float: A single floating-point scalar

- `vec2`: A two-component floating-point vector
- `vec3`: A three-component floating-point vector
- `vec4`: A four-component floating-point vector
- `bvec2`: A two-component Boolean vector
- `bvec3`: A three-component Boolean vector
- `bvec4`: A four-component Boolean vector
- `ivec2`: A two-component integer vector
- `ivec3`: A three-component integer vector
- `ivec4`: A four-component integer vector
- `mat2`: A 2×2 floating-point matrix
- `mat3`: A 3×3 floating-point matrix
- `mat4`: A 4×4 floating-point matrix
- `sampler2D`: A handle for accessing a 2D texture
- `sampler3D`: A handle for accessing a 3D texture
- `samplerCube`: A handle for accessing a cube-mapped texture
- `struct`: Used to declare custom data structures based on standard types

ESSL

There are many other types and features that the OpenGL ES 3.0 shading language provides. Here is a useful guide that covers many of its core features: `https://www.khronos.org/files/opengles3-quick-reference-card.pdf`.

An input variable will have one of the qualifiers followed by one type. For example, we will declare our `uLightColor` variable as follows:

```
uniform vec4 uLightColor;
```

This means that the `uLightColor` variable is a `uniform` vector with four components.

The GLSL and ESSL Naming Convention

Convention dictates that we prefix shader variables with their type. This makes for clear and readable shader code. For example, for a given color uniform, you would name the variable `uLightColor`. For a position varying, `vNormal`. For a normal attribute, `aVertexNormal`.

Vector Components

We can refer to each one of the components of an ESSL vector by its index. For example, uLightColor[3] will refer to the fourth element of the vector (zero-based vectors). However, we can also refer to each component by a letter, as demonstrated in the following table:

{ x, y, z, w }	Useful when accessing vectors that represent points or vectors.
{ r, g, b, a }	Useful when accessing vectors that represent colors.
{ s, t, p, q }	Useful when accessing vectors that represent texture coordinates.

For example, if we want to set the *alpha channel* (fourth component) of our uLightColor variable to 1.0, we can do so by writing in any of the following formats:

```
uLightColor[3] = 1.0;
uLightColor.w = 1.0;
uLightColor.a = 1.0;
uLightColor.q = 1.0;
```

In all these of cases, we are referring to the same fourth component. However, given that uLightColor represents a color, it makes more sense to use the r, g, b, a notation.

It's also possible to use the vector component notation to refer to subsets inside a vector. For example (*taken from GLSL ES specification*):

```
vec4 v4;

v4.rgba;   // is a vec4 and the same as just using v4
v4.rgb;    // is a vec3
v4.b;      // is a float
v4.xy;     // is a vec2
v4.xgba;   // is illegal - the component names do not come from the same set
```

Operators and Functions

One of the major advantages of GLSL and ESSL are the powerful built-in mathematical operators. ESSL provides many useful operators and functions that simplify vector and matrix operations. According to the specifications, the arithmetic binary operators add (+), subtract (−), multiply (*), and divide (/) operate on integer and floating-point typed expressions, including vectors and matrices. The two operands must be the same type, or one can be a scalar float and the other a float vector or matrix, or one can be a scalar integer and the other an integer vector. Additionally, for multiply (*), one can be a vector and the other a matrix with the same dimensional size as the vector. These result in the same fundamental types (integer or float) as the expressions they operate on. If one operand is a scalar and the other is a vector or a matrix, the scalar is applied component-wise to the vector or the matrix, with the final result being of the same type as the vector or the matrix. It's important to note that dividing by zero does not cause an exception, but it does result in an unspecified value. Let's see a few examples of these operations:

- −x: The negative of the x vector. It produces the same vector in the exact opposite direction.
- x + y: Sum of the x and y vectors. Both vectors need to have the same number of components.
- x − y: Subtraction of the x and y vectors. Both vectors need to have the same number of components.
- x * y: If x and y are both vectors, this operator yields a component-wise multiplication. Multiplication applied to two matrices returns a linear algebraic matrix multiplication, not a component-wise multiplication.
- matrixCompMult(matX, matY): Component-wise multiplication of matrices. They need to have the same dimensions (mat2, mat3, or mat4).
- x / y: The division operator behaves similarly to the multiplication operator.
- dot(x, y): Returns the dot product (scalar) of two vectors. They need to have the same dimensions.
- cross(vecX, vecY): Returns the cross product (vector) of two vectors. They must both be vec3.
- normalize(x): Returns a vector in the same direction but with a length of 1.
- reflect(t, n): Reflects the t vector along the n vector.

Shaders offer many more functions, including trigonometric and exponential functions. We will refer to them as needed in the development of different lighting models.

Let's see a quick example of the shader's ESSL code for a scene with the following properties:

- **Goraud shading**: We will interpolate vertex colors to obtain fragment colors. Therefore, we need one `varying` to pass the vertex color information from the vertex shader to the fragment shader.
- **Lambertian reflection model**: We account for the diffuse interaction between one light source and our scene. This means that we will use uniforms to define the light properties that is, the material properties. We will follow *Lambert's Emission Law* to calculate the final color for every vertex.

First, let's dissect what the attributes, uniforms, and varyings will be.

Vertex Attributes

We will start by defining two attributes in the vertex shader. Every vertex will have the following code:

```
in vec3 aVertexPosition;
in vec3 aVertexNormal;
```

Attributes

Remember that attributes are only available to use inside the vertex shader.

If you're curious as to why `in` is used instead of the `attribute` qualifier, we will cover this shortly. Right after the `in` keyword, we find the type of the variable. In this case, it is `vec3`, as each vertex position is determined by three elements (x, y, z). Similarly, the normals are also determined by three elements (x, y, z). Please note that a position is a *point* in three-dimensional space that tells us where the vertex is, while a normal is a *vector* that gives us information about the orientation of the surface that passes along that vertex.

Uniforms

Uniforms are available to both the vertex shader and the fragment shader. While attributes differ every time the vertex shader is invoked, uniforms are constant throughout a rendering cycle – that is, during the `drawArrays` or `drawElements` WebGL call.

Parallel Processing

We process vertices in parallel; therefore, each copy/thread of the vertex shader processes a different vertex.

We can use uniforms to pass along information about lights (such as diffuse color and direction), and materials (diffuse color):

```
uniform vec3 uLightDirection;  // incoming light source direction
uniform vec4 uLightDiffuse;    // light diffuse component
uniform vec4 uMaterialDiffuse; // material diffuse color
```

Again, the `uniform` keyword tells us that these variables are uniforms, and the `vec3` and `vec4` ESSL types tell us that these variables have three or four components. For the colors, these components are the red, blue, green, and alpha channels (RGBA), and for the light direction, these components are the x, y, and z coordinates that define the vector in which the light source is directed in the scene.

Varyings

As described earlier, varyings allow for the vertex shader to pass information to the fragment shader. For example, if we want to carry the vertex color from the vertex shader to the fragment shader, we would first update our vertex shader:

```
#version 300 es

out vec4 vVertexColor;

void main(void) {
  vVertexColor = vec4(1.0, 1.0, 1.0, 1.0);
}
```

And we would reference that varying inside of our fragment shader as follows:

```
in vec4 vVertexColor;
```

Keep in the mind that the *Storage Qualifier*, the declaration of varyings, needs to match between the vertex and fragment shaders.

The in and out variables

These keywords describe the direction of the *input* and *output*. As seen with the *attribute* and *varying* declarations, when we use in, that variable is supplied to the shader. When we use out, the shader exposes that variable. Let's see how these keywords are used in earlier versions of WebGL within the vertex and fragment shader.

Changing attribute to in

In WebGL 1 with *ESSL 100*, you might have this:

```
attribute vec4 aVertexPosition;
attribute vec3 aVertexNormal;
```

In WebGL 2 with *ESSL 300*, this becomes the following:

```
in vec4 aVertexPosition;
in vec3 aVertexNormal;
```

Changing varying to in / out

WebGL 1 with *ESSL 100*, you declare a varying in both the vertex and fragment shaders, like so:

```
varying vec4 vVertexPosition;
varying vec3 vVertexNormal;
```

In WebGL 2 with *ESSL 300*, in the vertex shader, the varyings become this:

```
out vec4 vVertexPosition;
out vec3 vVertexNormal;
```

And in the fragment shader, they become this:

```
in vec4 vVertexPosition;
in vec3 vVertexNormal;
```

Now, let's plug the attributes, uniforms, and varyings into the code and see what the vertex shader and fragment shader look like.

Vertex Shader

Let's cover a sample vertex shader:

```
#version 300 es

uniform mat4 uModelViewMatrix;
uniform mat4 uProjectionMatrix;
uniform mat4 uNormalMatrix;
uniform vec3 uLightDirection;
uniform vec3 uLightDiffuse;
uniform vec3 uMaterialDiffuse;

in vec3 aVertexPosition;
in vec3 aVertexNormal;

out vec4 vVertexColor;

void main(void) {
  vec3 normal = normalize(vec3(uNormalMatrix * vec4(aVertexNormal, 1.0)));
  vec3 lightDirection = normalize(uLightDirection);

  float LambertianTerm = dot(normal, -lightDirection);

  vVertexColor = vec4(uMaterialDiffuse * uLightDiffuse * LambertianTerm,
    1.0);

  gl_Position = uProjectionMatrix * uModelViewMatrix *
    vec4(aVertexPosition, 1.0);
}
```

On first inspection, we can identify the attributes, uniforms, and varyings that we will use, along with some matrices that we will discuss later. We can also see that the vertex shader has a `main` function that does not accept parameters and instead returns `void`. Inside, we can see some ESSL functions, such as `normalize` and `dot`, along with some arithmetical operators.

```
#version 300 es
```

This string must be the very first line of your shader. No comments or blank lines are allowed before it! `#version 300 es` tells WebGL that you want to use WebGL 2's shader language (GLSL ES 3.00). If that isn't written as the first line, the shader language defaults to WebGL 1.0's GLSL ES 1.00, which has fewer features.

There are three uniforms that we haven't discussed yet:

```
uniform mat4 uModelViewMatrix;
uniform mat4 uProjectionMatrix;
uniform mat4 uNormalMatrix;
```

We can see that these three uniforms are 4x4 matrices. These matrices are required in the vertex shader to calculate the location for vertices and normals whenever we move the camera. There are a couple of operations here that involve using these matrices:

```
vec3 normal = normalize(vec3(uNormalMatrix * vec4(aVertexNormal, 1.0)));
```

The previous line of code calculates the *transformed normal*:

```
gl_Position = uProjectionMatrix * uModelViewMatrix * vec4(aVertexPosition,
1.0);
```

This line calculates the *transformed vertex position*. `gl_Position` is a special output variable that stores the transformed vertex position.

We will come back to these operations in Chapter 4, *Cameras*. For now, we should acknowledge that these uniforms and operations deal with camera and world transformations (rotation, scale, and translation).

Returning to the main function's code, we can clearly see that the Lambertian reflection model is being implemented. The `dot` product of the normalized normal and light direction vector is obtained and then multiplied by the light and material diffuse components. Finally, this result is passed into the `vVertexColor` varying to be used in the fragment shader, as follows:

```
vVertexColor = vec4(uMaterialDiffuse * uLightDiffuse * LambertianTerm,
1.0);
```

Also, as we are calculating the color in the vertex shader and then automatically interpolating it for the fragments of every triangle, we are using the Goraud interpolation method.

Fragment Shader

The fragment shader is very simple. The first three lines define the precision of the shader. This is mandatory according to the ESSL specification. Similarly, for the vertex shader, we define our input; in this case, just one varying variable, and then we have the main function:

```
#version 300 es

// Fragment shaders don't have a default precision so we need
// to pick one. mediump is a good default. It means "medium precision"
precision mediump float;

in vec4 vVertexColor;
// we need to declare an output for the fragment shader
out vec4 fragColor;

void main() {
   fragColor = vVertexColor;
}
```

We just need to assign the `vVertexColor` varying to the `fragColor` output variable.

No More `gl_FragColor`

In WebGL 1, your fragment shader would set the `gl_FragColor` special variable to compute the output of the shader: `gl_FragColor = vec4(1.0, 0.0, 0.0, 1.0);`.

In WebGL 2, *ESSL 300* forces you to declare your own output variable and then set it. You can pick any name you want, but names cannot begin with `gl_`.

Remember that the value of the `vVertexColor` varying will be different from the one calculated in the vertex shader since WebGL will interpolate it by taking the corresponding calculated colors for the vertices surrounding the correspondent fragment (pixel).

Writing ESSL Programs

Now, let's take a moment to step back and look at the big picture. ESSL allows us to implement a lighting strategy, provided that we define a shading method and a light reflection model. In this section, we will take a sphere as the object that we want to illuminate, and we will see how the selection of a lighting strategy changes the scene:

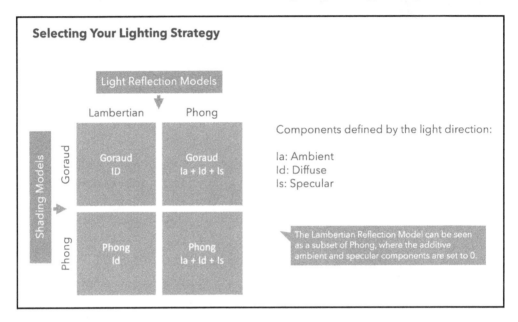

We will see two scenarios for Goraud interpolation: one with Lambertian and one with Phong reflections. We will only see one case for Phong interpolation; under Phong shading, the Lambertian reflection model is no different from a Phong reflection model where the ambient and specular components are set to 0.

Goraud Shading with Lambertian Reflections

The Lambertian reflection model only considers the interaction of diffuse material and diffuse light properties. In short, we assign the final color as follows:

```
aVertexColor = Id;
```

The following value is seen:

```
Id = lightDiffuseProperty * materialDiffuseProperty * lambertCoefficient;
```

Under Goraud shading, the **Lambert coefficient** is obtained by calculating the dot product of the vertex normal and the inverse of the light-direction vector. Both vectors are normalized before finding the dot product.

Let's take a look at the vertex shader and the fragment shader from the provided example, ch03_01_goraud_lambert.html:

Here's the vertex shader:

```
#version 300 es
precision mediump float;

uniform mat4 uModelViewMatrix;
uniform mat4 uProjectionMatrix;
uniform mat4 uNormalMatrix;
uniform vec3 uLightDirection;
uniform vec3 uLightDiffuse;
uniform vec3 uMaterialDiffuse;

in vec3 aVertexPosition;
```

```
in vec3 aVertexNormal;

out vec4 vVertexColor;

void main(void) {
    // Calculate the normal vector
    vec3 N = normalize(vec3(uNormalMatrix * vec4(aVertexNormal, 1.0)));
    // Normalized light direction
    vec3 L = normalize(uLightDirection);
    // Dot product of the normal product and negative light direction vector
    float lambertTerm = dot(N, -L);
    // Calculating the diffuse color based on the Lambertian reflection model
    vec3 Id = uMaterialDiffuse * uLightDiffuse * lambertTerm;
    vVertexColor = vec4(Id, 1.0);
    // Setting the vertex position
    gl_Position = uProjectionMatrix * uModelViewMatrix *
vec4(aVertexPosition, 1.0);
}
```

Here's the fragment shader:

```
#version 300 es
precision mediump float;

// Expect the interpolated value fro, the vertex shader
in vec4 vVertexColor;

// Return the final color as fragColor
out vec4 fragColor;

void main(void)   {
    // Simply set the value passed in from the vertex shader
    fragColor = vVertexColor;
}
```

We can see that the final vertex color that we processed in the vertex shader is carried into a varying variable to the fragment shader. Remember that the value that arrives to the fragment shader is *not* the original value that we calculated in the vertex shader. The fragment shader interpolates the vVertexColor variable to generate a final color for the respective fragment. This interpolation takes into account the vertices that enclose the current fragment.

Time for Action: Updating Uniforms in Real Time

Let's cover an example of how we'd update shader uniforms interactively:

1. Open the ch03_01_goraud_lambert.html file in your browser:

2. Notice that in this example, the controls widget is at the top right of the page. If you're curious about how it works, you can check the initControls function inside of the example code.

The Settings Widget

The settings widget was created using **DatGui**, an open source library. While we won't cover the intuitive DatGui API, it may be useful to read the documentation and the code in the provided examples to see how it works. For more information, you can check out https://github.com/dataarts/dat.gui.

3. **Translate X, Y, Z**: These control the direction of the light. By changing these sliders, you will modify the `uLightDirection` uniform:

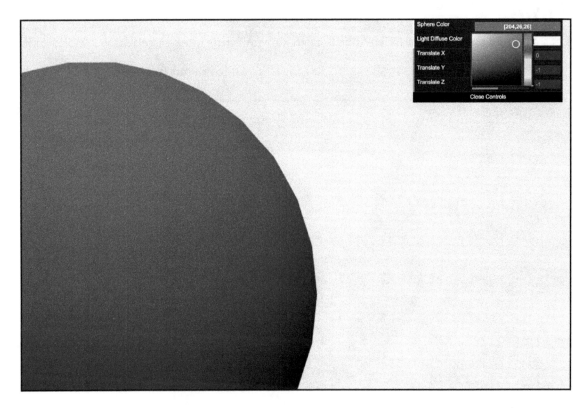

4. **Sphere Color**: This changes the `uMaterialDiffuse` uniform, which represents the diffuse color of the sphere. Here, you use the color selection widget, which allows you to try different colors. `onChange` of `Sphere Color` in the `initControls` function receives the updates from the widget and updates the `uMaterialDiffuse` uniform.

5. **Light Diffuse Color**: This changes the `uLightDiffuse` uniform, which represents the diffuse color of the light source. There is no reason why the light color must be white. We achieve this by assigning the slider value to the RGB components of `uLightDiffuse` while we keep the alpha channel set to `1.0`. We do this inside the `onChange` function under the lights settings, which receives the slider updates.

6. Try different settings for the light source position, the diffuse material, and light properties.

What just happened?

We've seen an example of a simple scene illuminated using Goraud interpolation and a Lambertian reflection model. We have also seen the immediate effects of changing uniform values for the Lambertian lighting model.

Have a Go: Moving Light

We mentioned before that we use matrices to move the camera around the scene. We can also use matrices to move lights. To do this, perform the following steps:

1. Open ch03_02_moving-light.html in your editor. The vertex shader is very similar to the previous diffuse model example. However, there is one extra line:

   ```
   vec3 light = vec3(uModelViewMatrix * vec4(uLightDirection, 0.0));
   ```

2. Here, we are transforming the uLightDirection vector and assigning it to the light variable. Notice that the uLightDirection uniform is a vector with three components (vec3) and that the uModelViewMatrix is a 4x4 matrix. In order to complete the multiplication, we need to transform this uniform into a four-component vector (vec4). We achieve this with the following construct:

   ```
   vec4(uLightDirection, 0.0);
   ```

3. The uModelViewMatrix matrix contains the *Model-View transformation matrix*. We will see how all this works in Chapter 4, *Cameras*. For now, suffice to say that this matrix allows us to update vertices' positions, and in this example, the light's position as well.

4. Take another look at the vertex shader. In this example, we are rotating the sphere and the light. Every time the draw function is invoked, we rotate the modelViewMatrix matrix a little bit on the y-axis:

   ```
   mat4.rotate(modelViewMatrix, angle * Math.PI / 180, [0, 1, 0]);
   ```

5. If you examine the code more closely, you will notice that the modelViewMatrix matrix is mapped to the uModelViewMatrix uniform:

   ```
   gl.uniformMatrix4fv(program.uModelViewMatrix, false,
   modelViewMatrix);
   ```

6. Run the example in your browser. You will see a sphere and a light source rotating on the y-axis:

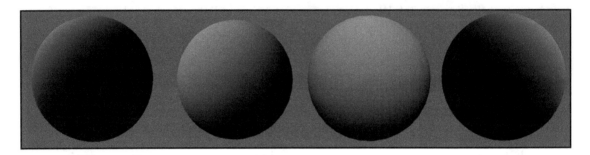

7. Look for the `initLights` function and change the light orientation so that the light is pointing in the negative z-axis direction:

```
gl.uniform3f(program.uLightDirection, 0, -1, -1);
```

8. Save the file and run it again. What happened? Change the light direction uniform so that it points to `[-1, 0, 0]`. Save the file and run it again on your browser. What happened? You should see that changing these values manipulates the light's orientation.

9. Set the light back to the 45-degree angle by changing the `uLightDirection` uniform so that it returns to its initial value:

```
gl.uniform3f(program.uLightDirection, 0, -1, -1);
```

10. Go to `draw` and find the following line:

```
mat4.rotate(modelViewMatrix, angle * Math.PI / 180, [0, 1, 0]);
```

11. Change it to this:

```
mat4.rotate(modelViewMatrix, angle * Math.PI / 180, [1, 0, 0]);
```

12. Save the file and launch it again in your browser. What happens? You should notice that the light moves on a different axis.

What just happened?

As you can see, the vector that is passed as the third argument to `mat4.rotate` determines the axis of the rotation. The first component corresponds to the x-axis, the second to the y-axis, and the third to the z-axis.

Goraud Shading with Phong Reflections

Different from the Lambertian reflection model, the Phong reflection model considers three properties: the ambient, diffuse, and specular, and ultimately yields a more realistic reflection. Following the same analogy that we used in the previous section, consider the following example:

```
finalVertexColor = Ia + Id + Is;
```

Where:

```
Ia = lightAmbient * materialAmbient;
Id = lightDiffuse * materialDiffuse * lambertCoefficient;
Is = lightSpecular * materialSpecular * specularCoefficient;
```

Notice that:

- As we use Goraud interpolation, we still use vertex normals to calculate the diffuse term. This will change when using Phong interpolation, where we will use fragment normals.
- Both light and material have three properties: the ambient, diffuse, and specular colors.
- On these equations, we can see that `Ia`, `Id`, and `Is` receive contributions from their respective light and material properties.

Based on our knowledge of the Phong reflection model, let's see how to calculate the specular coefficient in ESSL:

```
float specular = pow(max(dot(lightReflection, eyeVector), 0.0), shininess);
```

Where:

- `eyeVector` is the view vector or camera vector
- `lightReflection` is the reflected light vector
- `shininess` is the specular exponential factor or shininess
- `lightReflection` is calculated as `lightReflection = reflect(lightDirection, normal);`
- `normal` is the vertex normal, and `lightDirection` is the light direction that we have been using to calculate the Lambert coefficient

Let's take a look at the ESSL implementation for the vertex and fragment shaders. Here's the vertex shader:

```
#version 300 es
precision mediump float;

uniform mat4 uModelViewMatrix;
uniform mat4 uProjectionMatrix;
uniform mat4 uNormalMatrix;
uniform vec3 uLightDirection;
uniform vec4 uLightAmbient;
uniform vec4 uLightDiffuse;
uniform vec4 uMaterialDiffuse;

in vec3 aVertexPosition;
in vec3 aVertexNormal;

out vec4 vVertexColor;

void main(void) {
  vec3 N = vec3(uNormalMatrix * vec4(aVertexNormal, 1.0));
  vec3 light = vec3(uModelViewMatrix * vec4(uLightDirection, 0.0));
  vec3 L = normalize(light);
  float lambertTerm = dot(N,-L);
  vec4 Ia = uMaterialDiffuse * uLightAmbient;
  vec4 Id =  uMaterialDiffuse * uLightDiffuse * lambertTerm;
  vVertexColor = vec4(vec3(Ia + Id), 1.0);
  gl_Position = uProjectionMatrix * uModelViewMatrix *
vec4(aVertexPosition, 1.0);
}
```

We can obtain negative dot products for the Lambert term when the geometry of our objects is concave or when the object is in the way between the light source and our point of view. In either case, the negative of the light-direction vector and the normals will form an obtuse angle, producing a negative dot product, as shown in the following diagram:

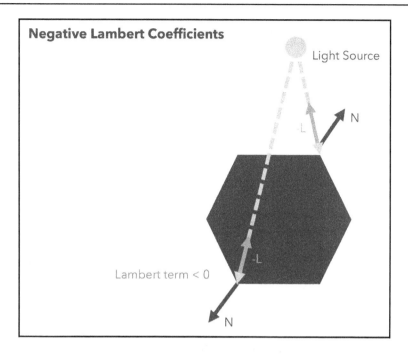

For that reason, we are using the ESSL built-in clamp function to restrict the dot product to the positive range. If we obtain a negative dot product, the clamp function will set the lambert term to zero and the respective diffuse contribution will be discarded, generating the correct result.

Given that we are still using Goraud interpolation, the fragment shader is the same as before:

```
#version 300 es
precision mediump float;

in vec4 vVertexColor;

out vec4 fragColor;

void main(void)   {
    fragColor = vVertexColor;
}
```

In the next section, we will explore the scene to see what it looks like when we have negative Lambert coefficients that have been clamped to the [0,1] range.

Time for Action: Goraud Shading

Let's cover an example where we implement lighting with Goraud shading:

1. Open the ch03_03_goraud_phong.html file in your browser. You will see something similar to the following screenshot:

2. The interface looks a little bit more elaborate than the diffuse lighting example. Let's stop here for a moment to explain these widgets:

   - **Light Color** (light diffuse term): As mentioned at the beginning of this chapter, we can have an example where our light is not white. We have included a color selector widget here for the light color so that you can experiment with different combinations.

   - **Light Ambient Term**: The light ambient property. In this example, this is a gray value: r = g = b.

   - **Light Specular Term**: The light specular property. This is a gray value: r = g = b.

- **Translate X,Y,Z**: The coordinates that define the light's orientation.
- **Sphere Color** (material diffuse term): The material diffuse property. We have included a color selector so that you can try different combinations for the r, g, and b channels.
- **Material Ambient Term**: The material ambient property. We have included it just for the sake of it. But as you might have noticed in the diffuse example, this vector is not always used.
- **Material Specular Term**: The material specular property. This is a gray value : r = g = b.
- **Shininess**: The specular exponential factor for the Goraud model.
- **Background Color** (gl.clearColor): This widget simply allows us to change the background color.

3. The specular reflection in the Phong reflection model depends on the shininess, the specular property of the material, and the specular property of the light. When the specular property of the material is close to 0, the material *loses* its specular property. Check this behavior with the widget provided:
   - What happens when the specularity of the material is low and the shininess is high?
   - What happens when the specularity of the material is high and the shininess is low?
   - Using the widgets, try different combinations for the light and material properties.

What just happened?

- We saw how the different parameters of the Phong lighting model interact with each other.
- We modified the light orientation, the properties of the light, and the material to observe different behaviors of the Phong lighting model.
- Unlike the Lambertian reflection model, the Goraud lighting model has two extra terms: the ambient and specular components. We saw how these parameters affect the scene.

Just like the Lambertian reflection model, the Phong reflection model obtains the vertex color in the vertex shader. This color is interpolated in the fragment shader to obtain the final pixel color. This is because, in both cases, we are using Goraud interpolation. Let's now move the heavy processing to the fragment shader and study how we implement the Phong interpolation method.

Phong Shading

Unlike the Goraud interpolation, where we calculated the final color for each vertex, the Phong interpolation calculates the final color for every fragment. This means that the calculation of the ambient, diffuse, and specular terms in the Phong model are performed in the fragment shader instead of the vertex shader. As you can imagine, this is computationally more intensive than performing a simple interpolation like in the two previous scenarios where we were using Goraud interpolation. However, we obtain a scene that seems more realistic.

After this translation, you may be wondering what is left for the vertex shader to do. Well, in this case, we will create varyings that will allow us to do all of the calculations in the fragment shader. For example, the vertex normals are a great fit.

Whereas before we had a normal per vertex, now we need to generate a normal for every pixel so that we can calculate the Lambert coefficient for each fragment. We do so by interpolating the normals that we pass to the fragment shader. Nevertheless, the code is very simple. All we need to know is how to create a varying that stores the normal for the vertex we are processing in the vertex shader and to obtain the interpolated value in the fragment shader (courtesy of ESSL). That's all! Conceptually, this is represented in the following diagram:

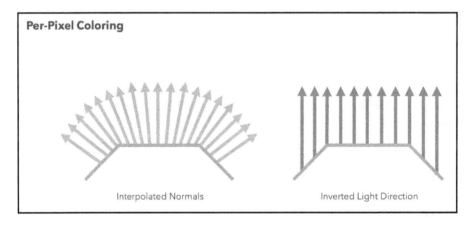

Now, let's take a look at the vertex shader under Phong shading:

```
#version 300 es
precision mediump float;

uniform mat4 uModelViewMatrix;
uniform mat4 uProjectionMatrix;
uniform mat4 uNormalMatrix;
```

```
in vec3 aVertexPosition;
in vec3 aVertexNormal;

out vec3 vNormal;
out vec3 vEyeVector;

void main(void) {
  vec4 vertex = uModelViewMatrix * vec4(aVertexPosition, 1.0);
  vNormal = vec3(uNormalMatrix * vec4(aVertexNormal, 1.0));
  vEyeVector = -vec3(vertex.xyz);
  gl_Position = uProjectionMatrix * uModelViewMatrix *
vec4(aVertexPosition, 1.0);
}
```

Unlike our examples with the Goraud interpolation, the vertex shader looks really simple. There is no final color calculation and we are using two varyings to pass information to the fragment shader. The fragment shader will now look like the following:

```
#version 300 es
precision mediump float;

uniform float uShininess;
uniform vec3 uLightDirection;
uniform vec4 uLightAmbient;
uniform vec4 uLightDiffuse;
uniform vec4 uLightSpecular;
uniform vec4 uMaterialAmbient;
uniform vec4 uMaterialDiffuse;
uniform vec4 uMaterialSpecular;

in vec3 vNormal;
in vec3 vEyeVector;

out vec4 fragColor;

void main(void) {
  vec3 L = normalize(uLightDirection);
  vec3 N = normalize(vNormal);
  float lambertTerm = dot(N, -L);
  vec4 Ia = uLightAmbient * uMaterialAmbient;
  vec4 Id = vec4(0.0, 0.0, 0.0, 1.0);
  vec4 Is = vec4(0.0, 0.0, 0.0, 1.0);

  if (lambertTerm > 0.0) {
    Id = uLightDiffuse * uMaterialDiffuse * lambertTerm;
    vec3 E = normalize(vEyeVector);
    vec3 R = reflect(L, N);
    float specular = pow( max(dot(R, E), 0.0), uShininess);
```

```
    Is = uLightSpecular * uMaterialSpecular * specular;
  }

  fragColor = vec4(vec3(Ia + Id + Is), 1.0);
}
```

When we pass vectors as varyings, it is possible that they denormalize in the interpolation step. Therefore, you may have noticed that both `vNormal` and `vEyeVector` are normalized again in the fragment shader.

As we mentioned before, under Phong lighting, the Lambertian reflection model can be seen as a Phong reflection model where the ambient and specular components are set to 0. Therefore, we will only cover the general case in the next section where we will see what the sphere scene looks like when using Phong shading and Phong lighting combined.

Time for Action: Phong Shading with Phong Lighting

Let's cover an example of implementing lighting using Phong shading:

1. Open the `ch03_04_sphere_Phong.html` file in your browser. The page will look similar to the following screenshot:

2. The interface is very similar to the Goraud example's interface. As previously described, it is quite evident how the Phong shading combined with Phong lighting delivers a more realistic scene. Experiment with the controls widget to see the immediate result of this new lighting model.

What just happened?

We have seen Phong shading and Phong lighting in action. We explored the source code for the vertex and fragment shaders. We also modified the different parameters of the model and observed the immediate effect of the changes on the scene.

Back to WebGL

It's time to go back to our JavaScript code, but we now need to consider how to close the gap between our JavaScript code and our ESSL code. First, we need to take a look at how we create a **program** using our WebGL context. Please remember that we refer to both the vertex shader and fragment shader as the program. Second, we need to know how to initialize attributes and uniforms.

Let's take a look at the structure of the web apps we have developed so far:

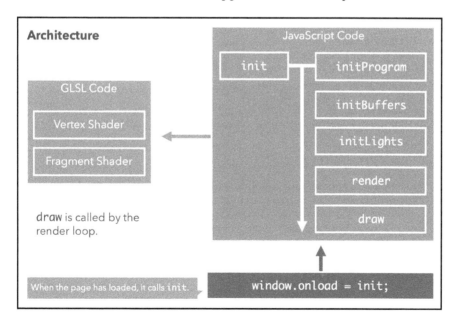

Each application has a vertex shader and a fragment shader embedded in the web page. In addition, there is a script section where we write all of our WebGL code. Finally, we have the HTML code that defines the page components, such as titles and the location of the widgets and the `canvas`.

In the JavaScript code, we are calling the `init` function on the `onload` event of the web page. This is the entry point for our application. The first thing that `init` does is obtain a WebGL context for the `canvas` within `initProgram`, and then calls a series of functions that initialize the program, the WebGL buffers, and the lights. Finally, it gets into a render loop where every time that the loop goes off, the `draw` function is invoked.

In this section, we will take a closer look at the `initProgram` and `initLights` functions. `initProgram` allows us to create and compile an ESSL program while `initLights` allows us to initialize and pass values to the uniforms defined in the programs. It is inside `initLights` where we will define the light's position, direction, and color components (ambient, diffuse, and specular) as well as default values for material properties.

Creating a Program

To start, open up `ch03_05_wall.html` in an editor. Let's take a step-by-step look at `initProgram`:

```
function initProgram() {
  const canvas = utils.getCanvas('webgl-canvas');
  utils.autoResizeCanvas(canvas);

  gl = utils.getGLContext(canvas);
  gl.clearColor(0.9, 0.9, 0.9, 1);
  gl.clearDepth(100);
  gl.enable(gl.DEPTH_TEST);
  gl.depthFunc(gl.LEQUAL);

  const vertexShader = utils.getShader(gl, 'vertex-shader');
  const fragmentShader = utils.getShader(gl, 'fragment-shader');

  program = gl.createProgram();
  gl.attachShader(program, vertexShader);
  gl.attachShader(program, fragmentShader);
  gl.linkProgram(program);

  if (!gl.getProgramParameter(program, gl.LINK_STATUS)) {
    console.error('Could not initialize shaders');
  }
```

```
gl.useProgram(program);

program.aVertexPosition = gl.getAttribLocation(program,
  'aVertexPosition');
program.aVertexNormal = gl.getAttribLocation(program, 'aVertexNormal');

program.uProjectionMatrix = gl.getUniformLocation(program,
  'uProjectionMatrix');
program.uModelViewMatrix = gl.getUniformLocation(program,
  'uModelViewMatrix');
program.uNormalMatrix = gl.getUniformLocation(program,
  'uNormalMatrix');
program.uLightDirection = gl.getUniformLocation(program,
  'uLightDirection');
program.uLightAmbient = gl.getUniformLocation(program, 'uLightAmbient');
program.uLightDiffuse = gl.getUniformLocation(program, 'uLightDiffuse');
program.uMaterialDiffuse = gl.getUniformLocation(program,
  'uMaterialDiffuse');
}
```

First, we retrieve a WebGL context, as we've seen in previous chapters. Then, we use the `utils.getShader` utility function to retrieve the contents of the vertex shader and the fragment shader:

```
const canvas = utils.getCanvas('webgl-canvas');
utils.autoResizeCanvas(canvas);

gl = utils.getGLContext(canvas);
gl.clearColor(0.9, 0.9, 0.9, 1);
gl.clearDepth(100);
gl.enable(gl.DEPTH_TEST);
gl.depthFunc(gl.LEQUAL);

const vertexShader = utils.getShader(gl, 'vertex-shader');
 const fragmentShader = utils.getShader(gl, 'fragment-shader');
```

The program's creation occurs in the following lines:

```
program = gl.createProgram();
gl.attachShader(program, vertexShader);
gl.attachShader(program, fragmentShader);
gl.linkProgram(program);

if (!gl.getProgramParameter(program, gl.LINK_STATUS)) {
  alert('Could not initialize shaders');
}

gl.useProgram(program);
```

Here, we have used several functions provided by the WebGL context. These include the ones shown in the following table:

WebGL Function	Description
`createProgram()`	Creates a new program (*program*).
`attachShader(program, shader)`	Attaches a shader to the current program.
`linkProgram(program)`	Creates executable versions of the vertex and fragment shaders that are passed to the GPU.
`getProgramParameter(program, parameter)`	This is part of the WebGL state-machine query mechanism. It allows you to query the program parameters. We use this function to verify whether the program has been successfully linked.
`useProgram(program)`	It will load the program onto the GPU if the program contains valid code (that is, it has been successfully linked).

Finally, we create a **mapping** between JavaScript variables and the program attributes and uniforms:

```
program.aVertexPosition = gl.getAttribLocation(program, 'aVertexPosition');
program.aVertexNormal = gl.getAttribLocation(program, 'aVertexNormal');

program.uProjectionMatrix = gl.getUniformLocation(program,
'uProjectionMatrix');
program.uModelViewMatrix = gl.getUniformLocation(program,
'uModelViewMatrix');
program.uNormalMatrix = gl.getUniformLocation(program, 'uNormalMatrix');
program.uLightDirection = gl.getUniformLocation(program,
'uLightDirection');
program.uLightAmbient = gl.getUniformLocation(program, 'uLightAmbient');
program.uLightDiffuse = gl.getUniformLocation(program, 'uLightDiffuse');
program.uMaterialDiffuse = gl.getUniformLocation(program,
'uMaterialDiffuse');
```

Instead of creating several JavaScript variables here (one per program `attribute` or `uniform`), we are attaching properties to the `program` object. This does not have anything to do with WebGL. It is just a convenience step to keep all of our JavaScript variables as part of the program object.

WebGL Programs

Since we are attaching many of the important variables to our WebGL program, you may be wondering why we don't attach it to our WebGL context rather than the program. In our example, we're using a single **program** because our example is small. As WebGL applications grow, you may find that you have several programs that you switch throughout your application with the `gl.useProgram` function.

All of this information pertains to `initProgram`. Here, we have used the following WebGL API functions:

WebGL Function	Description
`getAttribLocation(program, name)`	This function receives the current program object and a string that contains the name of the attribute that needs to be retrieved. This function then returns a **reference** to the respective **attribute**.
`getUniformLocation(program, name)`	This function receives the current program object and a string that contains the name of the uniform that needs to be retrieved. This function then returns a **reference** to the respective **uniform**.

Using this mapping, we can initialize the uniforms and attributes from our JavaScript code, as we will see in the next section.

Another addition to WebGL 2 is an increasingly optimized approach for getting item locations from the vertex shader. In our example, we use `getAttribLocation` and `getUniformLocation` for getting the locations of these items. If you inspect their return values, you'll see that they return *whole numbers*.

Whole numbers are simply the numbers 0, 1, 2, 3, 4, 5, ... (and so on).

Convention dictates that with large 3D applications, you can leverage tested design patterns and data structures to organize your code, which may include organizing shader resources in a predetermined or programmatic order.

One example would be to leverage the **layout qualifier** to look up resource locations. Here's a simplified example from Chapter 2, *Rendering,* where we looked up and enabled both aVertexPosition and aVertexColor using getAttribLocation:

```
const vertexPosition = gl.getAttribLocation(program, 'aVertexPosition');
gl.enableVertexAttribArray(vertexPosition);

const colorLocation = gl.getAttribLocation(program, 'aVertexColor');
gl.enableVertexAttribArray(colorLocation);
```

And here is the associated vertex shader:

```
#version 300 es

in vec4 aVertexPosition;
in vec3 aVertexColor;

out vec3 vVertexColor;

void main() {
  vVertexColor = aVertexColor;
  gl_Position = aVertexPosition;
}
```

These would turn into the following:

```
const vertexPosition = 0;
gl.enableVertexAttribArray(vertexPosition);

const colorLocation = 1;
gl.enableVertexAttribArray(colorLocation);
```

And here is the updated vertex shader:

```
#version 300 es

layout (location=0) in vec4 aVertexPosition;
layout (location=1) in vec3 aVertexColor;

out vec3 vVertexColor;

void main() {
  vVertexColor = aVertexColor;
  gl_Position = aVertexPosition;
}
```

As you can see, it's a subtle change where we define the locations using indices within the vertex shader and simply enable the items using those indices.

Performance Hits

Every time we need to look up or set shader values from the JavaScript context, it comes at a performance cost. Because of this, we should always be careful of how often we perform such operations.

Although the layout qualifier is optimal, we will continue leveraging the traditional variable and definition lookup throughout this book, given that it's more readable and requires less overhead.

Layout Qualifiers

For more information on layout and other qualifiers, please visit `https://www.khronos.org/opengl/wiki/Layout_Qualifier_(GLSL)`.

Initializing Attributes and Uniforms

Once we have compiled and installed the program, the next step is to initialize the attributes and variables. We will initialize our uniforms using the `initLights` function:

```
function initLights() {
  gl.uniform3fv(program.uLightDirection, [0, 0, -1]);
  gl.uniform4fv(program.uLightAmbient, [0.01, 0.01, 0.01, 1]);
  gl.uniform4fv(program.uLightDiffuse, [0.5, 0.5, 0.5, 1]);
  gl.uniform4f(program.uMaterialDiffuse, 0.1, 0.5, 0.8, 1);
}
```

In this example, you can see that we're using the references obtained with `getUniformLocation` (we did this in `initProgram`).

These are the functions that the WebGL API provides to set and get uniform values:

WebGL Function	Description
`uniform[1234][fi]`	Specifies 1-4 `float` or `int` values of a uniform variable.
`uniform[1234][fi]v`	Specifies the value of a uniform variable as an array of 1-4 `float` or `int` values.
`getUniform(program)`	Retrieves the contents of a uniform variable. The reference parameter has been previously obtained with `getUniformLocation`.

In Chapter 2, *Rendering*, we learned that a four-step process is required to initialize and use attributes. Recall that we do the following:

1. Bind a VBO.
2. Point an attribute to the currently-bound VBO.
3. Enable the attribute.
4. Unbind the VBO.

The key piece here is step 2. We do this with the following instruction:

```
gl.vertexAttribPointer(index, size, type, normalize, stride, offset);
```

If you check out the ch03_05_wall.html example, you will see that we do this inside the draw function:

```
gl.bindBuffer(gl.ARRAY_BUFFER, verticesBuffer);
gl.vertexAttribPointer(program.aVertexPosition, 3, gl.FLOAT, false, 0, 0);

gl.bindBuffer(gl.ARRAY_BUFFER, normalsBuffer);
gl.vertexAttribPointer(program.aVertexNormal, 3, gl.FLOAT, false, 0, 0);
```

Bridging the Gap Between WebGL and ESSL

It's now useful to test out how we integrate our ESSL program with our WebGL code by taking the code from ch03_05_wall.html and making some modifications.

Imagine a wall composed of the sections A, B, and C, and you are facing section B with a flashlight in your hand (frontal view). Intuitively, you know that section A and section C will be darker than section B. This fact can be modeled by starting at the color of the center of section B and darkening the color of the surrounding pixels as we move away from the center:

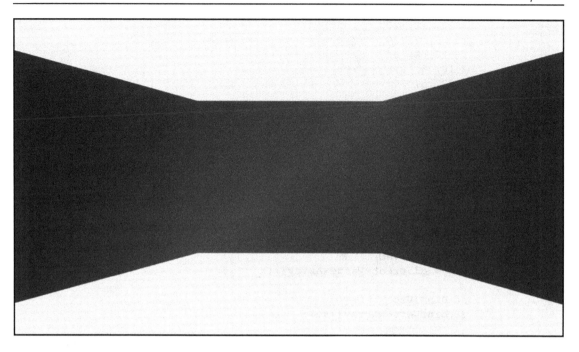

Let's summarize the code we need to cover:

- The ESSL program containing the vertex and fragment shaders. For the wall, we will select Goraud shading with a Diffuse/Lambertian reflection model.
- The `initProgram` function. We need to make sure that we map all of the attributes and uniforms that we defined in the ESSL code, including the normals:

  ```
  program.aVertexNormal= gl.getAttribLocation(program,
  'aVertexNormal');
  ```

- The `initBuffers` function. Here, we need to create our geometry. We can represent the wall with eight vertices that define six triangles, such as the ones shown in the previous diagram. In `initBuffers`, we will apply what we learned in the previous chapters to set up the appropriate VAOs and buffers. This time, we need to set up an additional buffer: the VBO that contains information about normals. The code to set up the normals VBO looks like this:

  ```
  function initBuffers() {
    const vertices = [
      -20, -8, 20, // 0
      -10, -8, 0,  // 1
      10, -8, 0,   // 2
  ```

```
     20, -8, 20,   // 3
    -20, 8, 20,    // 4
    -10, 8, 0,     // 5
     10, 8, 0,     // 6
     20, 8, 20     // 7
];

indices = [
  0, 5, 4,
  1, 5, 0,
  1, 6, 5,
  2, 6, 1,
  2, 7, 6,
  3, 7, 2
];

// Create VAO
vao = gl.createVertexArray();

// Bind Vao
gl.bindVertexArray(vao);

const normals = utils.calculateNormals(vertices, indices);

const verticesBuffer = gl.createBuffer();
gl.bindBuffer(gl.ARRAY_BUFFER, verticesBuffer);
gl.bufferData(gl.ARRAY_BUFFER, new Float32Array(vertices),
 gl.STATIC_DRAW);
// Configure instructions
gl.enableVertexAttribArray(program.aVertexPosition);
gl.vertexAttribPointer(program.aVertexPosition, 3, gl.FLOAT,
 false, 0, 0);

const normalsBuffer = gl.createBuffer();
gl.bindBuffer(gl.ARRAY_BUFFER, normalsBuffer);
gl.bufferData(gl.ARRAY_BUFFER, new Float32Array(normals),
 gl.STATIC_DRAW);
// Configure instructions
gl.enableVertexAttribArray(program.aVertexNormal);
gl.vertexAttribPointer(program.aVertexNormal, 3, gl.FLOAT, false,
 0, 0);

indicesBuffer = gl.createBuffer();
gl.bindBuffer(gl.ELEMENT_ARRAY_BUFFER, indicesBuffer);
gl.bufferData(gl.ELEMENT_ARRAY_BUFFER, new Uint16Array(indices),
 gl.STATIC_DRAW);

// Clean
```

```
      gl.bindVertexArray(null);
      gl.bindBuffer(gl.ARRAY_BUFFER, null);
      gl.bindBuffer(gl.ELEMENT_ARRAY_BUFFER, null);
    }
```

- To calculate the normals, we use the `calculateNormals(vertices, indices)` helper function. You can find this method in the `common/js/utils.js` file.
- `initLights`: We covered this function already and know how to do that.
- There's only one minor but important change to make inside the `draw` function. We need to make sure that the VBOs are bound before we use `drawElements`. The code to do that looks like this:

```
function draw() {
  gl.viewport(0, 0, gl.canvas.width, gl.canvas.height);
  gl.clear(gl.COLOR_BUFFER_BIT | gl.DEPTH_BUFFER_BIT);

  mat4.perspective(projectionMatrix, 45, gl.canvas.width /
   gl.canvas.height, 0.1, 10000);
  mat4.identity(modelViewMatrix);
  mat4.translate(modelViewMatrix, modelViewMatrix, [0, 0, -40]);

  gl.uniformMatrix4fv(program.uModelViewMatrix, false,
   modelViewMatrix);
  gl.uniformMatrix4fv(program.uProjectionMatrix, false,
   projectionMatrix);

  mat4.copy(normalMatrix, modelViewMatrix);
  mat4.invert(normalMatrix, normalMatrix);
  mat4.transpose(normalMatrix, normalMatrix);

  gl.uniformMatrix4fv(program.uNormalMatrix, false, normalMatrix);

  try {
    // Bind VAO
    gl.bindVertexArray(vao);

    gl.bindBuffer(gl.ELEMENT_ARRAY_BUFFER, indicesBuffer);
    gl.drawElements(gl.TRIANGLES, indices.length,
     gl.UNSIGNED_SHORT, 0);

    // Clean
    gl.bindVertexArray(null);
    gl.bindBuffer(gl.ARRAY_BUFFER, null);
    gl.bindBuffer(gl.ELEMENT_ARRAY_BUFFER, null);
  }
```

```
catch (error) {
  console.error(error);
}
}
```

In the following section, we will explore the functions that we just described for building and illuminating the wall.

Time for Action: Working on the Wall

Let's cover an example showcasing the preceding concepts in action:

1. Open the ch03_05_wall.html file in your browser. You will see something similar to the following screenshot:

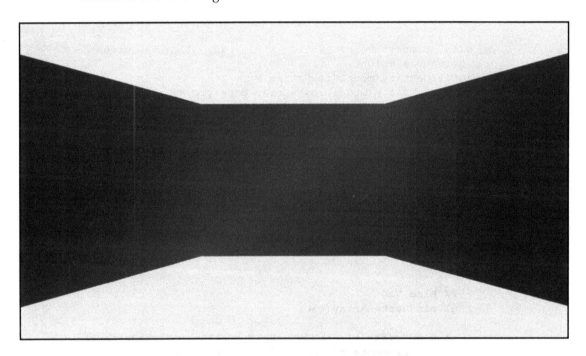

2. Open the ch03_05_wall.html file in a code editor.
3. Go to the vertex shader. Make sure that you identify the attributes, uniforms, and varyings that are declared there.
4. Go to the fragment shader. Notice that there are no attributes here, because attributes are exclusive to the vertex shader.

Vertex and Fragment Shaders

TIP

You can find these shaders inside the script tags with the appropriate ID names. For example, the vertex shader can be found inside `<script id="vertex-shader" type="x-shader/x-vertex">`.

5. Go to the `init` function. Verify that we are calling `initProgram` and `initLights` there.

6. Go to `initProgram`. Make sure that you understand how the program is built and how we obtain references to attributes and uniforms.

7. Go to `initLights`. Update the values of the uniforms, as shown here:

```
function initLights() {
  gl.uniform3fv(program.uLightDirection, [0, 0, -1]);
  gl.uniform4fv(program.uLightAmbient, [0.01, 0.01, 0.01, 1]);
  gl.uniform4fv(program.uLightDiffuse, [0.5, 0.5, 0.5, 1]);
  gl.uniform4f(program.uMaterialDiffuse, 0.1, 0.5, 0.8, 1);
}
```

8. Notice that one of the updates consists of changing from `uniform4f` to `uniform4fv` for the `uMaterialDiffuse` uniform.

9. Save the file.

10. Open it again (or reload it) in your browser. What happened?

11. Let's do something a bit more interesting. We are going to create a key listener so that every time we hit a key, the light orientation changes.

12. Right after the `initLights` function, write the following code:

```
function processKey(ev) {
  const lightDirection = gl.getUniform(program,
program.uLightDirection);
  const incrementValue = 10;

  switch (ev.keyCode) {
    // left arrow
    case 37: {
      azimuth -= incrementValue;
      break;
    }
    // up arrow
    case 38: {
      elevation += incrementValue;
      break;
    }
```

```
      // right arrow
      case 39: {
        azimuth += incrementValue;
        break;
      }
      // down arrow
      case 40: {
        elevation -= incrementValue;
        break;
      }
    }

    azimuth %= 360;
    elevation %= 360;

    const theta = elevation * Math.PI / 180;
    const phi = azimuth * Math.PI / 180;

    // Spherical to cartesian coordinate transformation
    lightDirection[0] = Math.cos(theta) * Math.sin(phi);
    lightDirection[1] = Math.sin(theta);
    lightDirection[2] = Math.cos(theta) * -Math.cos(phi);

    gl.uniform3fv(program.uLightDirection, lightDirection);
  }
```

13. This function processes the arrow keys and changes the light direction accordingly. There's a bit of trigonometry (`Math.cos`, `Math.sin`) involved, but we are simply converting the angles (azimuth and elevation) into Cartesian coordinates.

14. Please note that we get the current light direction by using the following function:

```
const lightDirection = gl.getUniform(program,
program.uLightDirection);
```

15. After processing the key strokes, we can save the updated light direction with the following code:

```
gl.uniform3fv(program.uLightDirection, lightDirection);
```

16. Save the work and reload the web page:

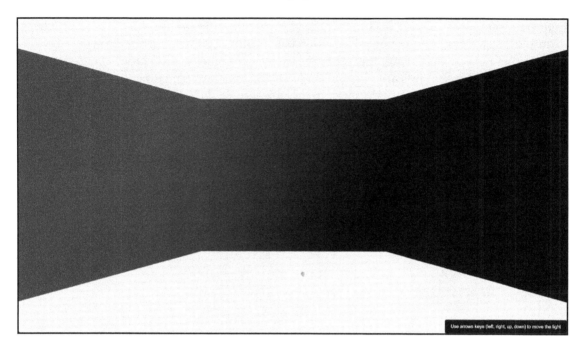

17. Use the arrow keys to change the light direction.
18. If you have any problems during the development of this exercise or just want to verify the final result, please check the ch03_06_wall_final.html file, which contains the completed exercise.

What just happened?

In this exercise, we created a keyboard listener that allows us to update the light's orientation so that we can move it around the wall and see how it reacts to surface normals. We also saw how the vertex shader and fragment shader input variables are declared and used. We learned how to build a program by reviewing the initProgram function. We also learned about initializing uniforms in the initLights function. Finally, we studied the getUniform function to retrieve the current value of a uniform. Although we haven't covered the examples entirely, this exercise was intended to familiarize you with vertex and fragment shaders so that you can implement various light-shading and reflection models.

More on Lights: Positional Lights

Before finishing this chapter, let's revisit the topic of lights. So far, for the purpose of our examples, we've assumed that our light source is infinitely far away from the scene. This assumption allows us to model the light rays as being parallel to each other. An example of this is sunlight. These lights are *directional lights*. Now, we are going to consider a case where the light source is relatively close to the object it needs to illuminate. Think, for example, of a desk lamp illuminating the document you're reading. These lights are *positional lights*:

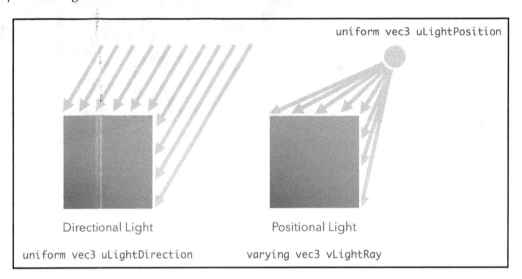

As we experienced before, when working with directional lights, only one variable is required. This is the light direction we represented in the uLightDirection uniform.

In contrast, when working with positional lights, we need to know the location of the light. We can represent it by using a uniform that we will name uLightPosition. As is the case when using positional lights, the light rays here are not parallel to each other; as a result, we need to calculate each light ray separately. We will do this by using a varying that we will name vLightRay.

In the next section, we will investigate how a positional light interacts with a scene.

Time for Action: Positional Lights in Action

Let's cover an example of positional lights in action:

1. Open the `ch03_07_positional_lighting.html` file in your browser. The page will look similar to the following screenshot:

2. The interface of this exercise is very simple. You can use the controls widget to interact with the scene. Unlike in previous exercises, the **Translate X**, **Y**, and **Z** sliders do not represent light direction here. Instead, they allow us to set the light source position. Go ahead and play with them.

3. For clarity, a little sphere representing the position of the light source has been added to the scene to visualize the light source, but this is not generally required.

4. What happens when the light source is located on the surface of the cone versus on the surface of the sphere?

5. What happens when the light source is inside the sphere?

6. Let's take a look at the way we calculate the light rays by inspecting the vertex shader in the source code. The light ray calculation is performed in the following two lines of code:

```
vec4 light = uModelViewMatrix * vec4(uLightPosition, 1.0);
vLightRay = vertex.xyz - light.xyz;
```

7. The first line allows us to obtain a transformed light position by multiplying the Model-View matrix by the `uLightPosition` uniform. If you review the code in the vertex shader, you'll note that we also use this matrix for calculating transformed vertices and normals. We will discuss these matrix operations in `Chapter 4`, *Cameras*. For now, we can just assume that this is necessary to obtain transformed vertices, normals, and light positions whenever we move the camera. To test this, modify this line by removing the matrix from the equation so that the line looks like the following:

```
vec4 light = vec4(uLightPosition, 1.0);
```

8. Save the file and launch it in your browser. What is the effect of not transforming the light position? What you can see is that the camera is moving, but the light source position is not being updated!

9. We can see that the light ray is calculated as the vector that reaches from the transformed light position (light) to the vertex position.

Thanks to the interpolation of varyings that is provided by ESSL, we automatically obtain all the light rays per pixel in the fragment shader:

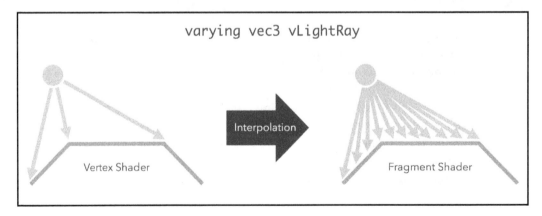

What just happened?

We studied the difference between directional lights and positional lights. We also investigated the importance of the Model-View matrix for the correct calculation of positional lights when the camera is moving. Finally, we modeled the procedure to obtain per-vertex light rays.

Virtual Showroom Example

In this chapter, we've included an example of the Nissan GTR exercise we saw in Chapter 2, *Rendering*. This time, we've used a Phong lighting model with a positional light to illuminate the scene. You can find this example in ch03_08_showroom.html:

Here, you can experiment with different light positions. Pay special attention to the nice specular reflections you obtain thanks to the specularity property of the car and the shininess of the light.

Architecture Updates

Let's cover some useful functions that we can refactor to use in later chapters:

1. We've seen how to create and compile a program using shaders. We've also covered how to load and reference attributes and uniforms. Let's include a module that abstracts away this low-level functionality with a simpler API:

   ```
   <script type="text/javascript"
   src="/common/js/Program.js"></script>
   ```

2. Like we did previously, we will include this script tag in the <head> of the HTML document. Be sure to include it after the other module scripts, since they may use the libraries and earlier modules we've covered.

3. Let's update our initProgram function inside of ch03_08_showroom.html so that we can use this module:

   ```
   function initProgram() {
     const canvas = document.getElementById('webgl-canvas');
     utils.autoResizeCanvas(canvas);

     gl = utils.getGLContext(canvas);
     gl.clearColor(...clearColor, 1);
     gl.enable(gl.DEPTH_TEST);
     gl.depthFunc(gl.LEQUAL);

     program = new Program(gl, 'vertex-shader', 'fragment-shader');

     const attributes = [
       'aVertexPosition',
       'aVertexNormal'
     ];

     const uniforms = [
       'uProjectionMatrix',
       'uModelViewMatrix',
       'uNormalMatrix',
       'uLightAmbient',
       'uLightPosition',
       'uMaterialSpecular',
       'uMaterialDiffuse',
       'uShininess'
     ];

     program.load(attributes, uniforms);
   }
   ```

4. All of the heavy lifting of creating a program, compiling shaders, and attaching uniforms and attributes to our program is done for us.

5. Let's inspect the `Program` class source code. Most of the operations should look familiar to you:

```
'use strict';

/*
 * Program constructor that takes a WebGL context and script tag IDs
 * to extract vertex and fragment shader source code from the page
 */
class Program {

  constructor(gl, vertexShaderId, fragmentShaderId) {
    this.gl = gl;
    this.program = gl.createProgram();

    if (!(vertexShaderId && fragmentShaderId)) {
      return console.error('No shader IDs were provided');
    }

    gl.attachShader(this.program, utils.getShader(gl,
      vertexShaderId));
    gl.attachShader(this.program, utils.getShader(gl,
      fragmentShaderId));
    gl.linkProgram(this.program);

    if (!this.gl.getProgramParameter(this.program,
      this.gl.LINK_STATUS)) {
      return console.error('Could not initialize shaders.');
    }

    this.useProgram();
  }

  // Sets the WebGL context to use current program
  useProgram() {
    this.gl.useProgram(this.program);
  }

  // Load up the given attributes and uniforms from the given
values
  load(attributes, uniforms) {
    this.useProgram();
    this.setAttributeLocations(attributes);
    this.setUniformLocations(uniforms);
  }
```

```
// Set references to attributes onto the program instance
setAttributeLocations(attributes) {
  attributes.forEach(attribute => {
    this[attribute] = this.gl.getAttribLocation(this.program,
      attribute);
  });
}

// Set references to uniforms onto the program instance
setUniformLocations(uniforms) {
  uniforms.forEach(uniform => {
    this[uniform] = this.gl.getUniformLocation(this.program,
      uniform);
  });
}

// Get the uniform location from the program
getUniform(uniformLocation) {
  return this.gl.getUniform(this.program, uniformLocation);
}

}
```

6. We initialize `Program` by passing in a reference to the `gl` context, the vertex, and the fragment shader `id`.
7. We load and reference the `attributes` and `uniforms` programs by supplying the `program` instance with the array of attributes and uniforms.
8. The other methods are helper functions that we'll use in later chapters.
9. You can find an example of these changes in `ch03_09_showroom-final.html`.
10. You may have caught two additional utils methods used throughout this chapter: `normalizeColor` and `denormalizeColor`. These two methods simply normalize colors from range `[0-255]` to `[0-1]` or denormalize from `[0-1]` to `[0-255]`:

```
const utils = {

  // Normalize colors from 0-255 to 0-1
  normalizeColor(color) {
    return color.map(c => c / 255);
  },

  // De-normalize colors from 0-1 to 0-255
  denormalizeColor(color) {
    return color.map(c => c * 255);
  },
```

```
    // ...
};
```

Summary

Let's summarize what we learned in this chapter:

- We learned in detail what light sources, materials, and normals are, and how these elements interact to illuminate a WebGL scene.
- We covered the differences between a shading method and a lighting model.
- We studied the basics of the Goraud and Phong shading methods, along with the Lambertian and Phong lighting models. With the help of several examples, we also covered how to implement these shading and lighting models in code using ESSL, and how to communicate between the WebGL code and the ESSL code through attributes and uniforms.
- We can use the vertex shader and the fragment shader to define a lighting model for our 3D scene.
- We covered many of these operations through the lens of the latest and greatest techniques provided to us in WebGL 2's updated shading language.

In the next chapter, we will expand on using matrices in ESSL so that we can learn how to use them to represent and move our viewpoint in a 3D scene.

4
Cameras

In the previous chapter, we covered the vertex shader, fragment shader, and ESSL to a define a lighting model in our 3D scene. In this chapter, we will leverage these concepts to learn more about the matrices that we have seen in the source code. These matrices represent transformations that, when applied to our scene, allow us to display and move things around. In one case, we've already used them to set the camera to a distance to see all the objects in our scene, and in another case, we've used them to spin our 3D car model.

Even though we have a camera within our 3D application, there is no camera object in the WebGL API—only matrices. That is because having matrices instead of a camera object gives WebGL the flexibility to represent complex projections and animations. In this chapter, we will learn what these matrix transformations mean and how we can use them to define and operate a virtual camera.

In this chapter, we will look at the following topics:

- Understanding the transformations that the scene undergoes from a 3D world to a 2D screen.
- Learning about affine transformations.
- Mapping matrices to ESSL uniforms.
- Working with the Model-View and Projection matrix.
- Appreciating the value of the Normal matrix.
- Creating a camera and using it to move around a 3D scene.

WebGL Does Not Have Cameras

How is it that there are no cameras in a 3D computer-graphics technology? Well, let's rephrase this: WebGL does not have a camera object that you can manipulate. However, we can assume that what we render in the `canvas` is what our camera captures. In this chapter, we are going to solve the problem of how to represent a camera in WebGL. The short answer is that we need 4x4 matrices.

Every time we move our camera around, we will need to update the objects according to the new camera position. To do this, we need to systematically process each vertex and apply a transformation that produces the new viewing position. Similarly, we need to make sure that the object normals and light directions are still consistent after the camera has moved. In summary, we need to analyze two different types of transformations: vertex (points) and normal (vectors).

Vertex Transformations

Objects in a WebGL scene go through different transformations before we see them on our screen. Each transformation is encoded by a 4x4 matrix. How do we multiply vertices that have three components, (x, y, z), by a 4x4 matrix? The short answer is that we need to augment the cardinality of our tuples by one dimension. Each vertex will then have a fourth component called the Homogeneous coordinate. Let's see what they are and why they are useful.

Homogeneous Coordinates

Homogeneous coordinates are a key component of any computer-graphics program. These coordinates make it possible to represent *affine* transformations (such as rotation, scaling, shear, and translation) and *projective* transformations as 4x4 matrices.

In Homogeneous coordinates, vertices have four components: x, y, z, and w. The first three components are the vertex coordinates in **Euclidian Space**. The fourth is the perspective component. The four-tuple (x, y, z, w) take us to a new space: the **Projective Space**.

Homogeneous coordinates make it possible to solve a system of linear equations where each equation represents a line that is parallel with all the others in the system. Remember that in Euclidian Space, a system like that does not have solutions, because there are no intersections. However, in Projective Space, this system has a solution—the lines will intersect at infinity. This fact is represented by the perspective component having a value of 0. A good analogy of this idea is the image of train tracks: parallel lines that converge at the vanishing point when you look at them in the distance:

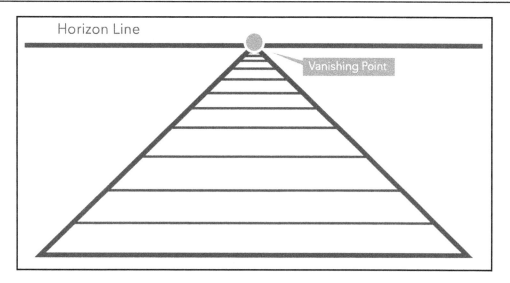

It's easy to convert from Homogeneous coordinates to non-Homogeneous, old-fashioned, Euclidean coordinates. All you need to do is divide the coordinate by `w`:

$$h(x, y, z, w) = v(x/w, y/w, z/w)$$

Consequently, if you want to go from Euclidean to Projective space, you add the fourth component, `w`, and make it `1`:

$$v(x, y, z) = h(x, y, z, 1)$$

In fact, this is what we've been doing throughout the first three chapters of this book! Let's go back to one of the shaders we discussed in the last chapter: the Phong vertex shader. The code looks as follows:

```
#version 300 es
precision mediump float;

uniform mat4 uModelViewMatrix;
uniform mat4 uProjectionMatrix;
uniform mat4 uNormalMatrix;

in vec3 aVertexPosition;
in vec3 aVertexNormal;

out vec3 vVertexNormal;
out vec3 vEyeVector;

void main(void) {
```

```
    // Transformed vertex position
    vec4 vertex = uModelViewMatrix * vec4(aVertexPosition, 1.0);

    // Transformed normal position
    vVertexNormal = vec3(uNormalMatrix * vec4(aVertexNormal, 0.0));

    // Eye vector
    vEyeVector = -vec3(vertex.xyz);

    // Final vertex position
    gl_Position = uProjectionMatrix * uModelViewMatrix *
vec4(aVertexPosition, 1.0);
}
```

Please note that for the `aVertexPosition` attribute, which contains a vertex of our geometry, we create a four-tuple from the three-tuple that we receive. We do this with the ESSL construct, `vec4()`. ESSL knows that `aVertexPosition` is a `vec3` and therefore, we only need the fourth component to create a `vec4`.

Coordinates Transformations

To pass from Homogeneous coordinates to Euclidean coordinates, we divide by `w`.

To pass from Euclidean coordinates to Homogeneous coordinates, we add `w = 1`.

Homogeneous coordinates with `w = 0` represent a point at infinity.

There is one more thing to note about Homogeneous coordinates: while vertices have a Homogeneous coordinate, `w = 1`, vectors have a Homogeneous coordinate, `w = 0`. This is because in the Phong vertex shader, the line that processes the normals looks like this:

```
    vVertexNormal = vec3(uNormalMatrix * vec4(aVertexNormal, 0.0));
```

To code vertex transformations, we will use Homogeneous coordinates unless indicated otherwise. Now, let's see the different transformations that our geometry undergoes to be displayed on screen.

Model Transform

We start our analysis from the object-coordinate system. This is the space where vertex coordinates are specified. If we want to translate or move objects around, we use a matrix that encodes these transformations. This matrix is known as the **Model matrix**. Once we multiply the vertices of our object by the Model matrix, we obtain new vertex coordinates. These new vertices will determine the position of the object in our 3D world.

In object coordinates, each object is free to define where its origin is and to specify where its vertices are with respect to this origin. In world coordinates, the origin is shared by all of the objects. World coordinates allow us to know where objects are located with respect to each other. It is with the model transform that we determine where the objects are in the 3D world:

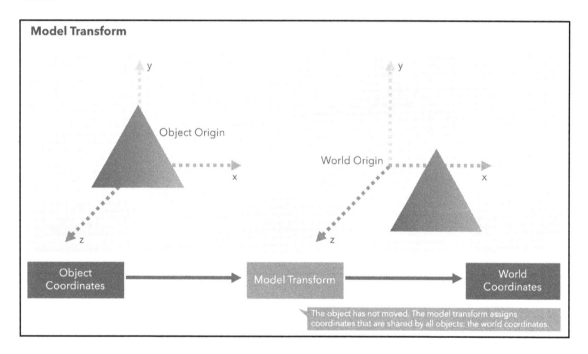

View Transform

The next transformation, the view transform, shifts the origin of the coordinate system to the view origin. The view origin is where our *eye* or *camera* is located with respect to the world origin. In other words, the view transform switches world coordinates by view coordinates. This transformation is encoded in the **View matrix**. We multiply this matrix by the vertex coordinates obtained by the model transform. The result of this operation is a new set of vertex coordinates whose origin is the view origin. It is in this coordinate system that our camera is going to operate.

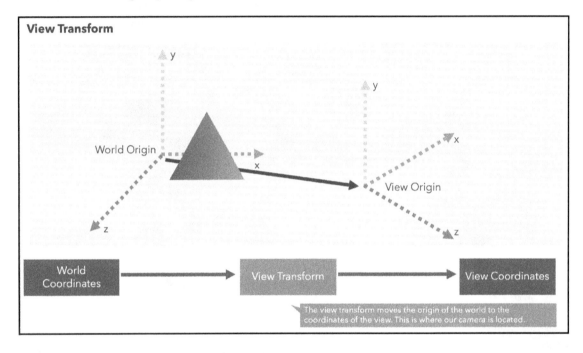

We will return to this later in the chapter!

Projection Transform

The next operation is called the **projection transform**. This operation determines how much of the view space will be rendered and how it will be mapped onto the computer screen. This region is known as the **frustum** and it is defined by six planes (near, far, top, bottom, right, and left planes), as shown in the following diagram:

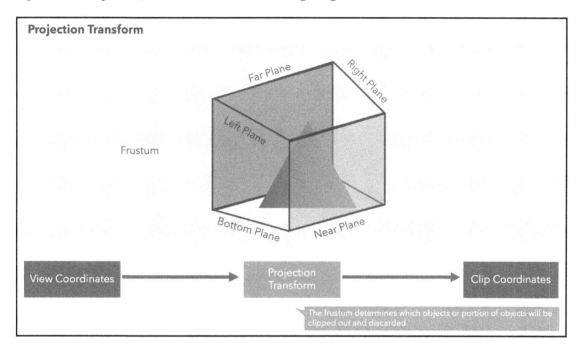

These six planes are encoded in the **Projection matrix**. Any vertices lying outside the frustum after applying the transformation are *clipped out* and discarded from further processing. Therefore, the frustum *defines* clipping coordinates, and the Projection matrix that encodes the frustum *produces* clipping coordinates.

The shape and extent of the frustum determines the type of projection from the 3D viewing space to the 2D screen. If the far and near planes have the same dimensions, the frustum will then determine an *orthographic* projection. Otherwise, it will be a *perspective* projection, as shown in the following diagram:

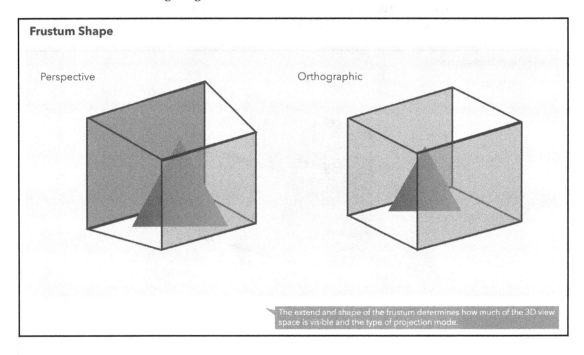

Frustum Shape

Perspective

Orthographic

The extend and shape of the frustum determines how much of the 3D view space is visible and the type of projection mode.

Up to this point, we are still working with Homogeneous coordinates, so the clipping coordinates have four components: x, y, z, and w. The clipping is done by comparing the x, y, and z components against the Homogeneous coordinate, w. If any of them is more than, +w, or less than, -w, then that vertex lies outside the frustum and is discarded.

Perspective Division

Once it has been determined how much of the viewing space will be rendered, the frustum is mapped into the *near plane* in order to produce a 2D image. The near plane is what is going to be rendered on your computer screen.

Different operative systems and displaying devices can have mechanisms to represent 2D information on screen. To provide robustness for all possible cases, WebGL and OpenGL ES provide an intermediate coordinate system that is independent from any specific hardware. This space is known as the **Normalized Device Coordinates (NDC)**.

Normalized device coordinates are obtained by dividing the clipping coordinates by the w component. This is why this step is known as *perspective division*. Also, please remember that when we divide by the Homogeneous coordinate, we go from projective space (4 components) to Euclidean space (3 components), so NDC only has three components. In the NDC space, the x and y coordinates represent the location of your vertices on a normalized 2D screen, while the z-coordinate encodes depth information, which is the relative location of the objects with respect to the near and far planes. Although at this point we are working on a 2D screen, we still keep the depth information. This will allow WebGL to later determine how to display overlapping objects based on their distance from the nearest plane. When using normalized device coordinates, the depth is encoded in the z-component.

The perspective division transforms the viewing frustum into a cube centered in the origin with the minimum coordinates of [-1, -1, -1] and the maximum coordinates of [1, 1, 1]. Also, the direction of the z-axis is inverted, as shown in the following diagram:

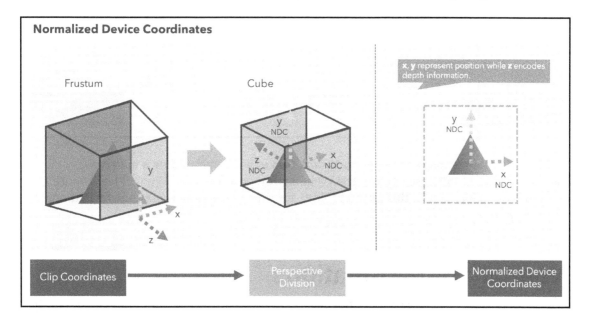

Viewport Transform

Finally, NDCs are mapped to **viewport coordinates**. This step maps these coordinates to the available space in your screen. In WebGL, this space is provided by the HTML5 `canvas`, as shown in the following diagram:

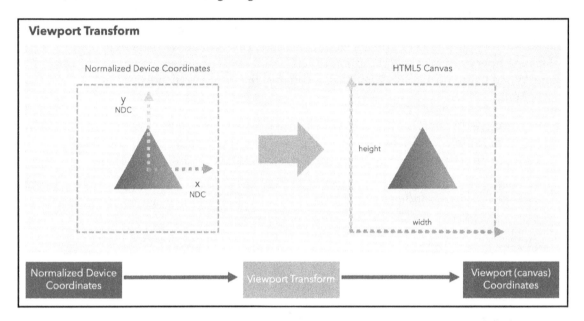

Unlike the previous cases, the viewport transform is not generated by a matrix transformation. In this case, we use the WebGL viewport function. We will learn more about this function later in this chapter. Now, it's time to see how these transformations affect normals.

Normal Transformations

Whenever vertices are transformed, **normal vectors** should also be transformed so that they point in the right direction. We could consider using the Model-View matrix that transforms vertices to do this, but this approach is problematic: the Model-View matrix will not always keep the perpendicularity of normals, as illustrated by the following diagram:

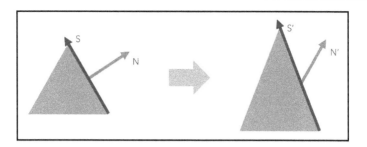

This problem occurs if there is a unidirectional (one axis) scaling transformation or a shearing transformation in the Model-View matrix. In our example, we have a triangle that has undergone a scaling transformation on the y-axis. As you can see, the N' normal is no longer perpendicular after this kind of transformation. How do we solve this?

Calculating the Normal Matrix

If you are not interested in finding out how we calculate the Normal matrix and just want the answer, feel free to jump to the end of this section. Otherwise, stick around to see some linear algebra in action!

Let's start with the mathematical definition of perpendicularity. Two vectors are perpendicular if their dot product is 0. In our example, this will be:

$$N \bullet S = 0$$

Here, S is the surface vector and can be calculated as the difference of two vertices, as shown in the diagram at the beginning of this section.

Let M be the Model-View matrix. We can use M to transform S as follows:

$$S' = M \bullet S$$

This is because S is the difference of two vertices. We use M to transform vertices onto the viewing space.

We want to find a matrix, K, that allows us to transform normals in a similar way. For the N normal, we want the following:

$$N' = K \bullet N$$

For the scene to be consistent after obtaining N' and S', these two need to keep the perpendicularity that the original vectors N and S had. This is as follows:

$$N' \bullet S' = 0$$

Substituting N' and S':

$$(KN) \bullet (MS) = 0$$

A dot product can also be written as a vector multiplication by transposing the first vector so that this still holds:

$$(KN)^T (MS) = 0$$

The transpose of a product is the product of the transposes in the reverse order:

$$N^T K^T MS = 0$$

Grouping the inner terms:

$$N^T (K^T M)S = 0$$

Now, remember that $N \bullet S = 0$ so $N^T S = 0$ (again, a dot product can be written as a vector multiplication). This means that in the previous equation, $(K^T M)$ needs to be the Identity matrix, I, so the original condition of N and S being perpendicular holds:

$$K^T M = I$$

Applying a bit of algebra:

$K^T MM^{-1} = IM^{-1} = M^{-1}$	Multiply by the inverse of M on both sides.
$K^T I = M^{-1}$	Because $MM^{-1} = I$.
$(K^T)^T = (M^{-1})^T$	Transposing on both sides.
$K = (M^{-1})^T$	Double transpose of K is the original matrix K.

Conclusions:

- K is the correct matrix transform that keeps the normal vectors perpendicular to the surface of the object. We call K the **Normal matrix**.
- K is obtained by transposing the inverse of the Model-View matrix (M, in this example).

- We need to use K to multiply the normal vectors so that they keep being perpendicular to the surface when transformed.

WebGL Implementation

Now, let's take a look at how we can implement vertex and normal transformations in WebGL. The following diagram shows the theory we have learned so far, along with the relationships between the steps in the theory and the implementation in WebGL:

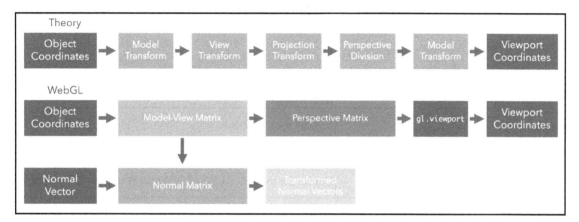

In WebGL, the five transformations that we apply to object coordinates to obtain viewport coordinates are grouped into three matrices and one WebGL method:

- The **Model-View** matrix that groups the *model* and *view* transform in one single matrix. When we multiply our vertices by this matrix, we end up in view coordinates.
- The **Normal matrix** is obtained by inverting and transposing the Model-View matrix. This matrix is applied to normal vectors to ensure that they continue to be perpendicular to the surface. This is very important in cases such as lighting.
- The **Projection matrix** groups the *projection transformation* and *the perspective division*, and as a result, we end up in normalized device coordinates.

Finally, we use the gl.viewport operation to map NDCs to viewport coordinates:

```
gl.viewport(minX, minY, width, height);
```

The viewport coordinates originate in the lower-left corner of the HTML5 canvas.

JavaScript Matrices

The WebGL JavaScript API does not provide its own methods to perform operations on matrices. WebGL simply provides a way to pass matrices to the shaders (as uniforms). So, we need to use a JavaScript library that enables us to manipulate matrices in JavaScript. In this book, we have used **glMatrix** for all matrix operations. However, there are other libraries available online that can do this for you.

glMatrix

We used **glMatrix** for all matrix operations in this book. You can find more information about this library at `https://github.com/toji/gl-matrix`.

Here are some of the operations that you can perform with **glMatrix**:

Operation	Syntax	Description
Creation	`const m = mat4.create();`	Creates the m matrix.
Identity	`mat4.identity(m);`	Sets m as the Identity matrix of rank 4.
Copy	`mat4.copy(target, origin);`	Copies the matrix origin onto the matrix target.
Transpose	`mat4.transpose(target, m);`	Transposes the m matrix onto the matrix target.
Invert	`mat4.invert(target, m);`	Inverts m onto the matrix target.
Rotate	`mat4.rotate(target, m, r, a);`	Rotates the m matrix by r radians around the a axis (this is a three-element array, [x, y, z]) onto the matrix target.

It's important to note that the **glMatrix** provides many more functions to perform other linear algebra operations. To get the full list, visit `http://glmatrix.net/docs/`.

Mapping JavaScript Matrices to ESSL Uniforms

Since the Model-View and Perspective matrices do not change during a single rendering step, they are passed as *uniforms* to the shaders. For example, if we were applying a translation to an object in our scene, we would have to paint the whole object in the new coordinates given by the translation. Painting the whole object in the new position is achieved in exactly one rendering step.

However, before the rendering step is invoked (by calling `drawArrays` or `drawElements`), we need to make sure that the shaders have an updated version of our matrices. We already know how to do that for other uniforms, such as light and color properties. The method to map JavaScript matrices to uniforms is similar to the following:

1. Get a JavaScript reference to the uniform with the following code:

```
const reference = getUniformLocation(program, uniformName);
```

2. Use the reference to pass the matrix to the shader with the following code:

```
// Matrix is the JavaScript matrix variable
gl.uniformMatrix4fv(reference, transpose, matrix);
```

As is the case for other uniforms, ESSL supports two-, three-, and four-dimensional matrices: `uniformMatrix[234]fv(reference, transpose, matrix)`. This will load 2x2, 3x3, or 4x4 matrices (corresponding to 2, 3, or 4 in the command name) of floating points into the uniform referenced by `reference`. The type of `reference` is `WebGLUniformLocation`. For practical purposes, it is an integer number. According to the specification, the transpose value must be set to `false`. The matrix uniforms are always of the floating point type (`f`). The matrices are passed as 4, 9, or 16 element vectors (`v`) and are always specified in a column-major order. The matrix parameter can also be of the `Float32Array` type. This is one of JavaScript's typed arrays. These arrays are included in the language to provide access to and the manipulation of raw binary data, and thus increase efficiency.

Working with Matrices in ESSL

Let's revisit the Phong vertex shader, which was introduced in `Chapter 3`, *Lights*. Please remember that matrices are defined as uniform `mat4`.

In this shader, we have defined three matrices:

- `uModelViewMatrix`: The Model-View matrix
- `uProjectionMatrix`: The Projection matrix
- `uNormalMatrix`: The Normal matrix

```
#version 300 es
precision mediump float;

uniform mat4 uModelViewMatrix;
uniform mat4 uProjectionMatrix;
```

```
uniform mat4 uNormalMatrix;

in vec3 aVertexPosition;
in vec3 aVertexNormal;

out vec3 vVertexNormal;
out vec3 vEyeVector;

void main(void) {
  // Transformed vertex position
  vec4 vertex = uModelViewMatrix * vec4(aVertexPosition, 1.0);

  // Transformed normal position
  vVertexNormal = vec3(uNormalMatrix * vec4(aVertexNormal, 0.0));

  // Eye vector
  vEyeVector = -vec3(vertex.xyz);

  // Final vertex position
  gl_Position = uProjectionMatrix * uModelViewMatrix *
vec4(aVertexPosition, 1.0);
}
```

In ESSL, the multiplication of matrices is straightforward; that is, you do not need to multiply element by element. ESSL knows that you are working with matrices, so it performs the multiplications for you:

```
gl_Position = uProjectionMatrix * uModelViewMatrix * vec4(aVertexPosition,
1.0);
```

The last line of this shader assigns a value to the predefined `gl_Position` variable. This will contain the clipping coordinates for the vertex that is currently being processed by the shader. We need to remember that the shaders work in parallel: each vertex is processed by an instance of the vertex shader.

To obtain the clipping coordinates for a given vertex, we first need to multiply the Model-View matrix by the Projection matrix. To achieve this, we multiply from right to left, because matrix multiplication is not commutative and order matters.

Also, notice that we needed to augment the `aVertexPosition` attribute by including the Homogeneous coordinate. This is because we have defined our geometry in Euclidean space. Luckily, ESSL allows us to do this by simply adding the missing component and creating a `vec4` on the fly. We need to do this because both the Model-View matrix and the Projection matrix are described in Homogeneous coordinates (4 rows by 4 columns).

Now that we've seen how to map JavaScript matrices to ESSL uniforms in our shaders, let's talk about how to operate with the three matrices: the Model-View matrix, the Normal matrix, and the Projection matrix.

The Model-View Matrix

The **Model-View matrix** allows us to perform *affine transformations* in our scene. **Affine** is a mathematical name that describes transformations that do *not* change the structure of the object undergoing such transformations. In our 3D world scene, such transformations are rotation, scaling, reflection shearing, and translation. Fortunately, we do not need to understand how to represent such transformations with matrices. We just need to use one of the many JavaScript matrix libraries that are available online (such as **glMatrix**).

Affine Transformations

You can find more information on how transformation matrices work at https://en.wikipedia.org/wiki/Affine_transformation.

Understanding the structure of the Model-View matrix will not help you if you just want to apply transformations to the scene or to objects in the scene. For that effect, simply use a library, such as **glMatrix**, to do the transformations on your behalf. However, the structure of this matrix could be invaluable information when you are trying to troubleshoot your 3D application. Let's take a look at how the Model-View matrix is constructed.

Spatial Encoding of the World

By default, when you render a scene, you are looking at it from the origin of the world in the negative direction of the z-axis. As shown in the following diagram, the z-axis is coming out of the screen (which means that you're looking at the negative z-axis):

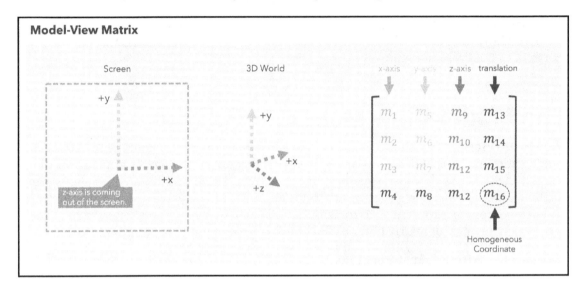

From the center of the screen to the right, you will have the positive x-axis, and from the center of the screen up, you will have the positive y-axis. This is the initial configuration and it is the reference for affine transformations.

In this configuration, the Model-View matrix is the **Identity matrix** of rank four.

The first three rows of the Model-View matrix contain information about rotations and translations that are affecting the world.

Rotation Matrix

The intersection of the first three rows with the first three columns defines the 3x3 Rotation matrix. This matrix contains information about rotations around the standard axis. In the initial configuration, this corresponds to the following:

$$[m1, \ m2, \ m3] = [1, \ 0, \ 0] = \text{x-axis}$$
$$[m5, \ m6, \ m7] = [0, \ 1, \ 0] = \text{y-axis}$$
$$[m9, \ m10, \ m11] = [0, \ 0, \ 1] = \text{z-axis}$$

Translation Vector

The intersection of the first three rows with the last column defines a three-component Translation vector. This vector indicates how much the origin, and the world, have been translated. In the initial configuration, this corresponds to the following:

$$[m13, \ m14, \ m15] = [0, \ 0, \ 0] = \text{origin (no translation)}$$

The Mysterious Fourth Row

The fourth row does not have any special meaning.

- The m4, m8, and m12 elements are always 0.
- The m16 element (the Homogeneous coordinate) will always be 1.

As we described at the beginning of this chapter, there are no cameras in WebGL. However, all the information that we need to operate a camera (mainly rotations and translations) can be extracted from the Model-View matrix itself.

The Camera Matrix

Let's say, for a moment, that we *do* have a camera in WebGL. A camera should be able to rotate and translate to explore this 3D world. As we saw in the previous section, a 4x4 matrix can encode rotations and translations. Therefore, you should use one such matrix to represent our hypothetical camera.

Let's assume that our camera is located at the origin of the world and that it's oriented so that it's looking toward the negative z-axis direction. This is a good starting point; we already know what transformation represents such a configuration in WebGL (Identity matrix of rank four).

For the sake of analysis, let's break the problem down into two subproblems: camera-translation and camera-rotation. We will have a practical demo for each one.

Camera Translation

Let's move the camera to [0, 0, 4] in world coordinates. This means four units from the origin on the positive z-axis. Remember, at this point, we do not know about a matrix that moves the camera. We only know how to move the *world* (with the Model-View matrix). If we applied:

```
mat4.translate(modelViewMatrix, modelViewMatrix, [0, 0, 4]);
```

In such a case, the world would be translated 4 units on the positive z-axis, and since the camera position has not been changed, it would be located at [0, 0, -4], which is exactly the opposite of what we want.

Now, say that we applied the translation in the opposite direction:

```
mat4.translate(modelViewMatrix, modelViewMatrix, [0, 0, -4]);
```

In such a case, the world would be moved 4 units on the negative z-axis and then the camera would be located at [0, 0, 4] in the new world-coordinate system.

In the following section, we will explore translations in both world space and camera space.

Time for Action: Translations in World Space vs Camera Space

Let's cover an example showcasing these differences in action:

1. Open ch04_01_model-view-translation.html in your browser:

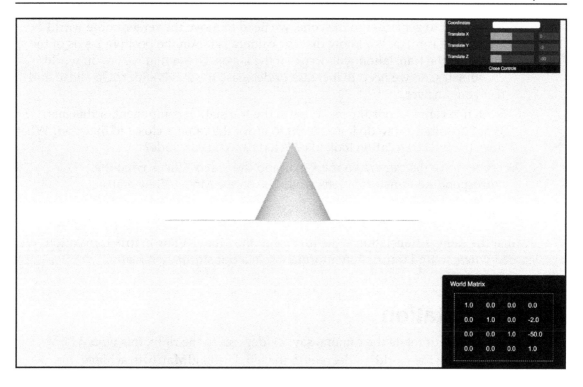

2. From a distance, we are looking at the positive z-axis of a cone located at the origin of the world. There are three sliders that allow you to translate either the world or the camera on the x, y, and z axes, respectively. The world space is activated by default.

3. By looking at the World matrix on the screen, can you tell where the origin of the world is? Is it [0, 0, 0]?

Hint

Check where we define translations in the Model-View matrix.

4. We can think of the `canvas` as the image that our camera sees. If the world's center is at [0, -2, -50], where is the camera?

5. If we want to get closer to the cone, we need to move the center of the world toward the camera. We know that the camera is far on the positive z-axis of the world, so the translation will occur on the z-axis. Given that we are on world coordinates, do we need to increase or decrease the z-axis slider? Go ahead and test your answer.

6. Switch to camera coordinates. What is the translation component of this matrix? What do you need to do if you want to move the camera closer to the cone? What does the final translation look like? What can you conclude?

7. Try to move the camera on the x-axis and the y-axis. Check what the corresponding transformations would be on the Model-View matrix.

What just happened?

We saw that the camera translation is the inverse of the Model-View matrix translation. We also learned where to find translation information in a transformation matrix.

Camera Rotation

Similarly, if we want to rotate the camera, say, 45 degrees to the right, this would be equivalent to rotating the world 45 degrees to the left. Using **glMatrix** to achieve this, we can write the following:

```
mat4.rotate(modelViewMatrix, modelViewMatrix, 45 * Math.PI/180, [0, 1, 0]);
```

Similar to the previous section where we explored translations, in the *Time for Action: Rotations in World Space vs Camera Space* section, we will experiment with rotations in both world and camera spaces. Let's see this behavior in action!

Time for Action: Rotations in World Space vs Camera Space

Let's cover an example showing the different rotations in different spaces:

1. Open ch04_02_model-view-rotation.html in your browser:

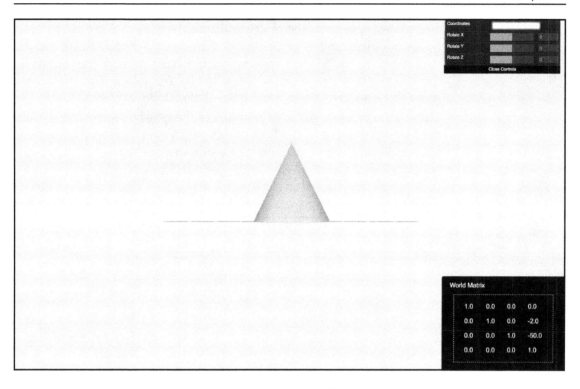

2. As we did in the previous example, we will see the following:
    - A cone at the origin of the world
    - The camera is located at [0, 2, 50] in world coordinates
    - Three sliders that allow us to rotate either the world or the camera
    - A matrix where we can see the result of different rotations

3. Let's see what happens to the axis after we apply a rotation. With the **World** coordinates selected, rotate the world 90 degrees around the x-axis. What does the Model-View matrix look like?

4. Let's see where the axes end up after a 90 degree rotation around the x-axis:
    - By looking at the first column, we can see that the x-axis has not changed. It's still [1, 0, 0]. This makes sense since we are rotating around this axis.

- The second column of the matrix indicates where the y-axis is after the rotation. In this case, we went from [0, 1, 0], which is the original configuration, to [0, 0, 1], which is the axis that is coming out of the screen. This is the z-axis in the initial configuration. This makes sense since we are now looking from above, down at the cone.
- The third column of the matrix indicates the new location of the z-axis. It changed from [0, 0, 1], which as we know, is the z-axis in the standard spatial configuration (without transforms), to [0, -1, 0], which is the negative portion of the y-axis in the original configuration. This makes sense since we rotated around the x-axis:

Interpreting Rotations Using the Model-View Matrix

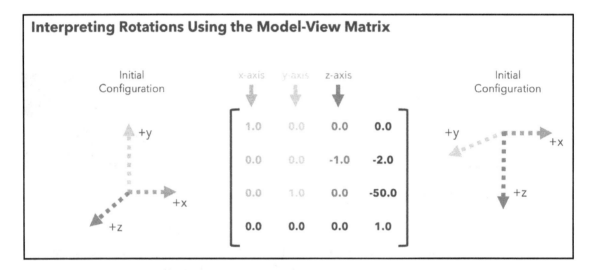

5. As we've just seen, understanding the rotation matrix (the 3x3 upper-left corner of the Model-View matrix) is simple: the first 3 columns always tell us where the axis is.
6. Where are the axes in the following transformation? Take a look at the following diagram:

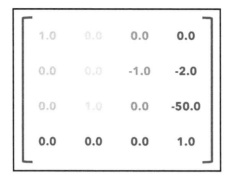

7. Check your answer by using the sliders to achieve the rotation that you believe produces this matrix.
8. Let's see how rotations work in **Camera** space by changing the coordinates, selection.
9. Increase the angle of rotation in the x-axis by incrementing the slider position. What do you notice?
10. Using the sliders, try different rotations in camera space.
11. Are the rotations *commutative*? That is, do you get the same result if you rotate, for example, 5 degrees on the x-axis and 90 degrees on the z-axis, compared to the case where you rotate 90 degrees on the z-axis and then 5 degrees on the x-axis?
12. Return to **World** space. Please remember that when you're in **World** space, you need to reverse the rotations to obtain the same pose, for example, if you were applying 5 degrees on the x-axis and 90 degrees on the z-axis, verify that when you apply –5 degrees on the x-axis and –90 degrees on the z-axis, you obtain the same result.

What just happened?

We've just learned that the Camera matrix rotation is the inverse of the Model-View matrix rotation. We've also learned how to identify the orientation of our world or camera after analyzing the rotation matrix (3x3 upper-left corner of the correspondent transformation matrix).

Have a Go: Combining Rotations and Translations

Let's see how we can combine rotations and translations together:

1. The `ch04_03_model-view.html` file contains the combination of rotations and translations. When you open it your browser, you will see something like this:

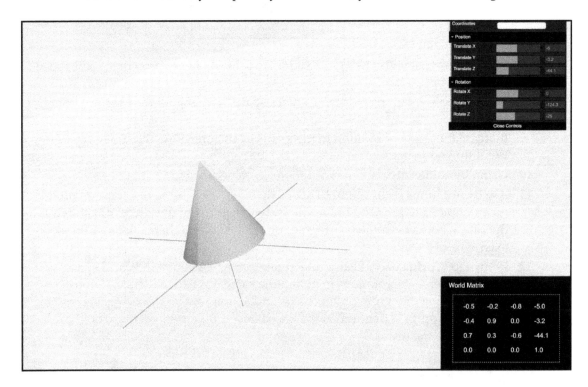

2. Try different configurations of rotations and translations in both the **World** and **Camera** spaces.

Camera Matrix Is the Inverse of the Model-View Matrix

These two scenarios help us appreciate that a Camera matrix is the exact opposite of the Model-View matrix. In linear algebra, this property is known as the **inverse** of a matrix.

The inverse of a matrix is such that when multiplying it by the original matrix, we obtain the Identity matrix. In other words, if M is the Model-View matrix and C is the Camera matrix, we get the following:

$$MC = I$$

$$M^{-1}MC = M^{-1}$$

$$C = M^{-1}$$

We can create the Camera matrix using **glMatrix** by writing something like the following:

```
const cameraMatrix = mat4.create();
mat4.invert(cameraMatrix, modelViewMatrix);
```

Thinking About Matrix Multiplications in WebGL

Before moving forward, we should note that in WebGL, matrix operations are written in the *reverse order* in which they are applied to the vertices. This is an important note that's often confusing for developers new to 3D graphics.

Let's assume, for a moment, that you are writing the code to rotate/move the world; that is, you rotate your vertices around the origin and then you move away. The final transformation would look like this:

$$RTv$$

Here, R is the 4x4 matrix-encoding pure rotation; T is the 4x4 matrix-encoding pure translation, and v corresponds to the vertices present in your scene (in Homogeneous coordinates).

Now, you should have noticed that the first transformation we apply to the vertices is the translation, and then we apply the rotation. Vertices need to be multiplied first by the matrix that is to the left. In this scenario, that matrix is T. Then, the result needs to be multiplied by R.

This fact is reflected in the order of the operations (here, modelViewMatrix is the Model-View matrix):

```
mat4.identity(modelViewMatrix);
mat4.translate(modelViewMatrix, modelViewMatrix, position);
mat4.rotateX(modelViewMatrix, modelViewMatrix, rotation[0] * Math.PI /
180);
```

```
mat4.rotateY(modelViewMatrix, modelViewMatrix, rotation[1] * Math.PI /
180);
mat4.rotateZ(modelViewMatrix, modelViewMatrix, rotation[2] * Math.PI /
180);
```

If we were working in camera coordinates and we wanted to apply the same transformation as before, we need to apply a bit of linear algebra first:

$M = RT$	The Model-View M matrix is the result of multiplying rotation and translation together.
$C = M^{-1}$	We know that the Camera matrix is the inverse of the Model-View matrix.
$C = (RT)^{-1}$	By substitution.
$C = T^{-1}R^{-1}$	The inverse of a matrix product is the reverse product of the inverses.

Fortunately, when we're working in camera coordinates in this chapter's examples, we have the inverse translation and the inverse rotation already calculated in the global variables position and rotation. Therefore, we would write something such as this in the code (here, `cameraMatrix` is the Camera matrix):

```
mat4.identity(cameraMatrix);
mat4.rotateX(cameraMatrix, cameraMatrix, rotation[0] * Math.PI / 180);
mat4.rotateY(cameraMatrix, cameraMatrix, rotation[1] * Math.PI / 180);
mat4.rotateZ(cameraMatrix, cameraMatrix, rotation[2] * Math.PI / 180);
mat4.translate(cameraMatrix, cameraMatrix, position);
```

Basic Camera Types

In this chapter, we will discuss the following two camera types:

- Orbiting camera
- Tracking camera

Orbiting Camera

So far, we've learned how to generate rotations and translations in either world or camera coordinates. In both cases, however, we are always generating the rotations around the center of the world. This may be ideal when we're orbiting around a 3D object, such as our car model. In that example, you put the object at the center of the world, and then examine the object at different angles (rotation); after that, you can move away (translation) to see the result. We will refer to this type of camera as an **orbiting camera**.

Tracking Camera

If we return to the example of the first-person shooting game, we need to have a camera that can look up when we want to check whether there are enemies above us. We should also be able to look left and right (rotations) and then move in the direction in which our camera is pointing (translation). This camera type can be designated as a **first-person** camera. This same type is used when the game follows the main character. Therefore, it is generally known as a **tracking camera**.

To implement first-person cameras, we need to set up the rotations on the camera axis instead of using the world origin.

Rotating the Camera Around Its Location

When multiplying matrices, the order in which we multiply them is relevant. Say, for instance, we have two 4x4 matrices. Let R be the first matrix and let's assume that this matrix encodes pure rotation; let T be the second matrix and let's assume that T encodes pure translation. Now:

$$RT \neq TR$$

In other words, the order of the operations affects the result. It is not the same to rotate around the origin and then translate away from it (orbiting camera), as compared to translating the origin and then rotating around it (tracking camera)! Your success depends on understanding this critical difference.

In order to set the location of the camera as the center for rotations, we need to invert the order in which operations are called. This is equivalent to converting from an orbiting camera to a tracking camera.

Translating the Camera in the Line of Sight

With an orbiting camera, the camera will always look toward the center of the world. Therefore, we will always use the z-axis to move to and from the object we are examining. However, with a tracking camera, since the rotation occurs at the camera location, we can end up looking to any position in the world (which is ideal if you want to move around and explore it). Thus, we need to know the direction in which the camera is pointing in world coordinates (camera axis). We will see how to obtain this next.

The Camera Model

Just like its counterpart, the Model-View matrix, the Camera matrix encodes information about the camera orientation. As we can see in the following diagram, the upper-left 3x3 matrix corresponds to the camera axes:

- The first column corresponds to the x-axis of the camera. We will call it `RightVector`.
- The second column is the y-axis of the camera. This will be `UpVector`.
- The third column determines the vector in which the camera can move back and forth. This is the z-axis of the camera and we will call it `CameraAxis`.

Because the Camera matrix is the inverse of the Model-View matrix, the upper-left 3x3 rotation matrix contained in the Camera matrix gives us the orientation of the camera axes in world space. This is a plus, because it means that we can tell the orientation of our camera in world space just by looking at the columns of this 3x3 rotation matrix (and we now know what each column means):

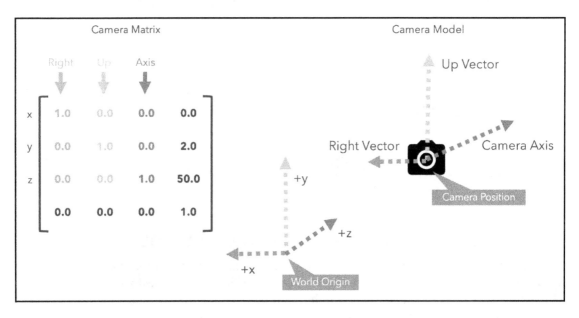

In the following section, we will play with orbiting and tracking cameras to see how we can change the camera position using mouse gestures and sliders. In addition, we will look at a graphical representation of the resulting Model-View matrix. In this exercise, we will integrate both rotations and translations and we will see how they behave under the two basic types of cameras we are studying.

Time for Action: Exploring the Showroom

Let's cover an example covering various camera types:

1. Open the `ch04_04_camera-types.html` file in your browser. You will see something like the following:

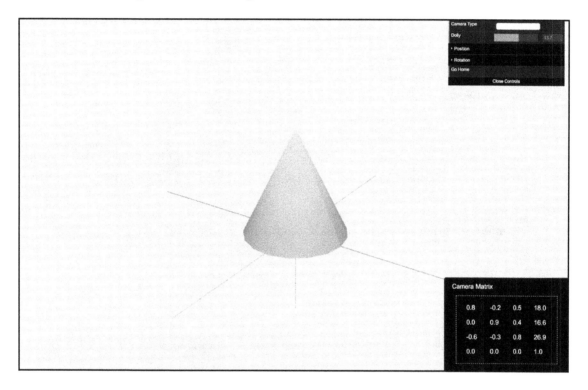

2. Go around the world using the sliders in **Tracking** mode. Cool, huh?
3. Change the camera type to **Orbiting** mode and do the same.
4. Check that besides the slider controls, both in **Tracking** and **Orbiting** mode, you can use your mouse and keyboard to move around the world.
5. In this exercise, we have implemented a camera using two new classes:
   * `Camera`: To manipulate the camera.
   * `Controls`: To connect the camera to the `canvas`. The `canvas` will now receive mouse and keyboard events and pass them along to the camera.

6. If you are curious, you can see the source code of these two classes in the `common/js` directory. We have applied the concepts explained in this chapter to build these two classes.

7. So far, we have seen a cone in the center of the world. As we explore, let's change it to something more interesting. Open the file `ch04_04_camera-types.html` file in your source code editor.

8. Go to the `load` function. Let's add the car to the scene. Rewrite the contents of this function to the following:

```
function load() {
    scene.add(new Floor(2000, 100));
    scene.add(new Axis(2000));
    scene.loadByParts('/common/models/nissan-gtr/part', 178);
}
```

9. You will see that we've increased the size of the axis and the floor so that we can see them. We need to do this because the car model is a much larger object than the original cone.

10. There are a few steps we need to take in order to see the car correctly. We need to make sure that we have a large enough view volume. Go to the `updateTransforms` function and update this line:

```
mat4.perspective(projectionMatrix, 45, canvas.width /
canvas.height, 0.1, 1000);
```

Replace it with this:

```
mat4.perspective(projectionMatrix, 45, canvas.width /
canvas.height, 0.1, 5000);
```

11. Change the type of camera so that when we load the page, we have an orbiting camera by default. In the `configure` function, change this line:

```
camera = new Camera(Camera.TRACKING_TYPE);
```

Replace it with this:

```
camera = new Camera(Camera.ORBITING_TYPE);
```

12. Another thing we must consider is the location of the camera. For a large object such as this car, we need to be farther away from the center of the world. For that purpose, we need to change the home location of `camera.goHome` from `[0, 2, 50]` to `[0, 25, 300]`.

13. Let's modify our scene's lighting so that it better fits into the model we are displaying. In the `configure` function, update the following:

```
gl.uniform3fv(program.uLightPosition, [0, 120, 120]);
gl.uniform4fv(program.uLightAmbient, [0.2, 0.2, 0.2, 1]);
gl.uniform4fv(program.uLightDiffuse, [1, 1, 1, 1]);
```

Replace it with this:

```
gl.uniform4fv(program.uLightAmbient, [0.1, 0.1, 0.1, 1]);
gl.uniform3fv(program.uLightPosition, [0, 0, 2120]);
gl.uniform4fv(program.uLightDiffuse, [0.7, 0.7, 0.7, 1]);
```

14. Save the file with a different name and then load this new file in your browser. You should see something like the following screenshot:

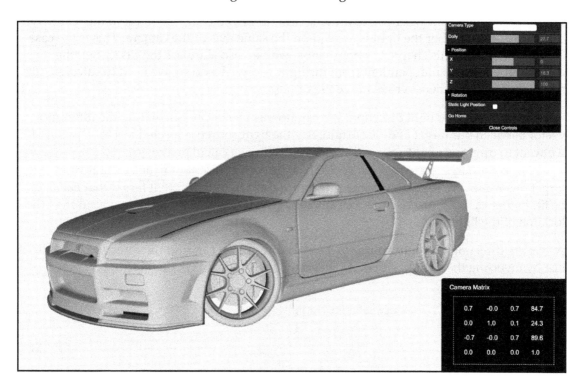

15. Using the mouse, keyboard, and/or the sliders, explore the new scene.
16. Use orbiting mode to explore the car from different angles.
17. See how the Camera matrix is updated when you move around the scene.
18. You can see what the final exercise looks like by opening the ch04_05_car.html file.

What just happened?

We added mouse and keyboard interaction to our scene. We also experimented with the two basic camera types: *tracking* and *orbiting* cameras. Finally, we modified the settings of our scene to visualize a complex model.

Have a Go: Updating Light Positions

As we've seen, by moving the camera, we're applying the inverse transformation to the world. If we do not update the light position, the light source will be located at the same static point, regardless of the final transformation applied to the world.

This is very convenient when we're moving around or exploring an object in the scene. We can always see whether the light is located on the same axis of the camera. This is the case for the exercises in this chapter. Nevertheless, we can also simulate the case when the camera movement is independent from the light source. To do so, we need to calculate the new light position whenever we move the camera.

First, we calculate the light direction. We can do this by simply calculating the difference vector between our target and our origin. Say the light source is located at [0, 2, 50]. If we want to direct our light source toward the origin, we calculate the [0, 0, 0] - [0, 2, 50] vector *(target - origin)*. This vector has the correct orientation of the light when we target the origin. We repeat the same procedure if we have a different target that needs to be lit. In that case, we just use the coordinates of the target and from them, we subtract the location of the light.

As we are directing our light source toward the origin, we can find the direction of the light just by inverting the light position. As you may have noticed, we do this in ESSL in the vertex shader:

```
vec3 L = normalize(-uLightPosition);
```

As `light` is a vector, if we want to update the direction of the light, we need to use the Normal matrix, discussed earlier in this chapter, to update this vector under any world transformation. This step is optional in the vertex shader:

```
if (uFixedLight) {
    L = vec3(uNormalMatrix * vec4(L, 0.0));
}
```

In the previous fragment of code, light is augmented to four components, so we can use the direct multiplication provided by ESSL. (Remember that `uNormalMatrix` is a 4x4 matrix and, as such, the vectors it transforms need to be four-dimensional.) Please bear in mind that, as explained at the beginning of this chapter, the Homogeneous coordinates of vectors are always set to 0, while the Homogeneous coordinates of vertices are set to 1.

1. After the multiplication, we reduce the result to three components before assigning the result back to light.
2. You can test the effects of updating the light position by using the `Static Light Position` button, provided in the `ch04_05_car.html` file.
3. We connect a global variable that keeps track of the state of this button with the `uUpdateLight` uniform.
4. Edit `ch04_05_car.html` and set the light position to a different location. To do this, edit the configure function. Go to the following position:

```
gl.uniform3fv(program.uLightPosition, [0, 0, 2120]);
```

5. Try different light positions:
   - `[2120, 0, 0]`
   - `[0, 2120, 0]`
   - `[100, 100, 100]`

6. For each option, save the file and try it with and without updating the light position (use the `Static Light Position` button):

7. For a better visualization, use an **Orbiting** camera.

The Projection matrix

At the beginning of this chapter, we learned that the **Projection matrix** combines the projection transformation and the perspective division. These two steps take a 3D scene and convert it into a cube, which is then mapped to the 2D `canvas` by the viewport transformation.

In practice, the Projection matrix determines the geometry of the image that is captured by the camera. In a real-world camera, the lens of the camera would determine how distorted the final images are. In a WebGL world, we use the Projection matrix to simulate that effect. Also, unlike in the real world where our images are always affected by perspective, in WebGL, we can pick a different representation (such as the orthographic projection).

Field of View

The Projection matrix determines the **field of view** (**FOV**) of the camera, that is, how much of the 3D space will be captured by the camera. The field of view is a measure given in degrees, and the term is used interchangeably with the term **angle of view**:

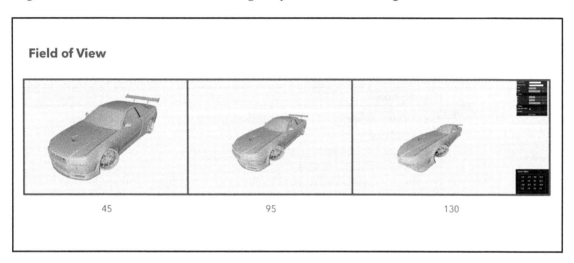

Field of View

45	95	130

Perspective or Orthogonal Projection

A perspective projection assigns more space to details that are closer to the camera than details that are farther away. In other words, the geometry that is close to the camera will appear larger than the geometry that is farther from it. This is the way our eyes see the real world. Perspective projection allows us to assess the distance because it gives our brain a *depth cue*.

In contrast, an orthogonal projection uses parallel lines; this means that lines will appear to be the same size, regardless of their distance to the camera. Therefore, the depth cue is lost when using orthogonal projection.

While perspective projection offers a more realistic view of the scene, orthographic is commonly used in engineering as a means to produce object specifications that communicate dimensions unambiguously. Each line of one unit length (cm, meter) will appear to have the same length everywhere on the drawing. This allows the drafter to dimension only a subset of lines and let the reader know that other lines of that length on the drawing are also that length in reality. Every parallel line in the drawing is also parallel in the object.

If you are looking at a larger scene with buildings, then orthographic rendering gives an exact measure of the distance between the buildings and their relative sizes.

With perspective mode, lines of identical real-world lengths will appear different due to foreshortening. It becomes difficult to judge relative dimensions and object size in the distance.

Using **glMatrix**, we can set up the perspective or the orthogonal projection by calling `mat4.perspective` or `mat4.ortho`, respectively. The signatures for these methods are as follows:

Function	Description

`mat4.perspective(`
    `dest,`
    `fovy,`
    `aspect,`
    `near,`
    `far`
`);`
	Generates a perspective projection matrix with the given bounds.
	Parameters:
	• `dest`: `mat4` frustum the matrix will be written into
	• `fovy`: Vertical field of view
	• `aspect`: Aspect ratio, typically the `width / height` viewport
	• `near, far`: Near and far bounds of the frustum

`mat4.ortho(`
    `dest,`
    `left,`
    `right,`
    `bottom,`
    `top,`
    `near,`
    `far`
`);`
	Generates an orthogonal projection matrix with the given bounds:
	Parameters:
	• `dest`: `mat4` frustum the matrix will be written into
	• `left, right`: Left and right bounds of the frustum
	• `bottom, top`: Bottom and top bounds of the frustum
	• `near, far`: Near and far bounds of the frustum

In the *Time for Action: Orthographic and Perspective Projections* section, we will test how the field of view and the perspective projection affect the image that our camera captures. We will experiment with perspective and orthographic projections for both orbiting and tracking cameras.

Time for Action: Orthographic and Perspective Projections

Let's look at an example covering the different types of projections:

1. Open the `ch04_06_projection-modes.html` file in your browser.

2. This exercise is very similar to the previous one. However, there are two new options under **Projection Mode**: **Perspective** and **Orthogonal Projection**. As you can see, **Perspective** is activated by default.

3. Change the camera type to **Orbiting**.

4. Change the projective mode to **Orthographic**.

5. Explore the scene. Notice the lack of the depth cues characteristic of orthogonal projections:

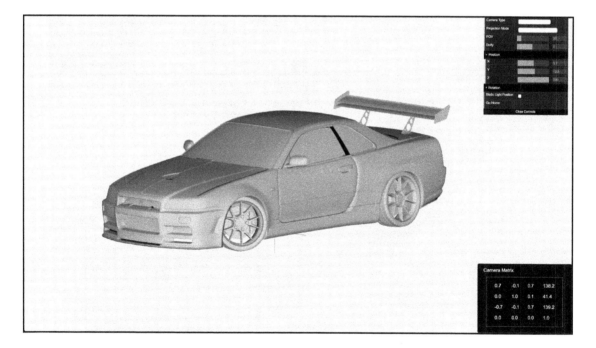

6. Switch to **Perspective** mode:

7. Explore the source code. Go to the `updateTransforms` function:

```
function updateTransforms() {
  const { width, height } = canvas;
  if (projectionMode === PERSPECTIVE_PROJECTION) {
    mat4.perspective(
      projectionMatrix,
      fov,
      width / height,
      10,
      5000
    );
  }
  else {
    mat4.ortho(projectionMatrix,
      -width / fov,
      width / fov,
      -height / fov,
      height / fov,
      -5000,
      5000
    );
  }
}
```

8. Take a look at the parameters we are using to set up the projective view.

9. Notice that as you increase the field of view (fov), your camera will capture more of the 3D space. Think of this as the lens of a real-world camera. With a wide-angle lens, you capture more space with the tradeoff of deforming the objects as they move toward the boundaries of your viewing box.

What just happened?

We experimented with different configurations for the Projection matrix and we saw how these configurations produce different results in the scene.

Have a Go: Integrating the Model-View and the Projective Transform

Recall that once we've applied the Model-View transformation to the vertices, the next step is to transform the view coordinates to NDC coordinates:

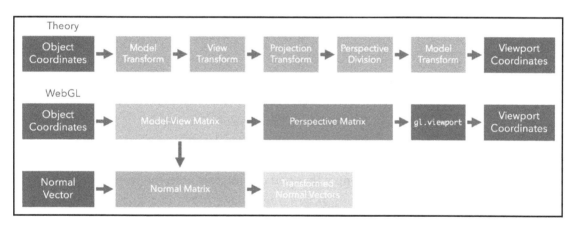

We do this by simple multiplication by using ESSL in the vertex shader:

```
gl_Position = uProjectionMatrix * uModelViewMatrix *
vec4(aVertexPosition,1.0);
```

The predefined variable, gl_Position, stores the NDC coordinates for each vertex of every object defined in the scene.

In the previous multiplication, we augment the shader attribute, aVertexPosition, to a 4-component vertex because our matrices are 4x4. Unlike normals, vertices have a Homogeneous coordinate equal to one (w=1).

After this step, WebGL will convert the computed clipping coordinates to normalized device coordinates and from there to `canvas` coordinates using the WebGL `viewport` function. Let's see what happens when we change this mapping:

1. Open the `ch04_06_projection-modes.html` file in your source code editor.
2. Go to the `draw` function. This is the rendering function that is invoked every time we interact with the scene (by using the mouse, the keyboard, or the widgets on the page).
3. Find the following line:

```
gl.viewport(0, 0, canvas.width, canvas.height);
```

4. Try each of the following three operations:

```
const width = canvas.width,
  height = canvas.height,
  halfWidth = width / 2,
  halfHeight = height / 2;

// First
gl.viewport(0, 0, halfWidth, halfHeight);

// Second
gl.viewport(halfWidth, halfHeight, width, height);

// Third
gl.viewport(50, 50, width - 100, height - 100);
```

5. For each option, save the file and open it on your browser.
6. What do you see? Please note that you can interact with the scene just like before.

Structure of the WebGL Examples

We have improved the structure of the code examples in this chapter. As the complexity of our WebGL applications increases, it is wise to have a good, maintainable, and clear design. We have saved this section until the end of this chapter so that you can use it as a reference when working on the exercises.

Just as in previous exercises, our entry point is the `init` function, which is called when the page is loaded. We have included several `scripts` in the `head` of our document that point to various components to build our 3D application.

Supporting Objects

We have created the following components, each one in its own file inside the `common/js` directory:

- `Program.js`: Creates the program using the shader definitions. Provides the mapping between JavaScript variables (`program.*`) and program attributes and uniforms.
- `Scene.js`: Maintains a list of objects to be rendered. Contains the AJAX/JSON functionality to retrieve remote objects. It also allows us to add local objects to the scene.
- `Floor.js`: Defines a grid on the X-Z plane. This object is added to `scene` to have a reference to the floor and its properties
- `Axis.js`: Represents the axis in world space. When added to `scene`, we will have a reference to the origin.
- `Camera.js`: Creates a camera instance to manipulate the various matrices and operations covered in this chapter with a simple interface.
- `EventEmitter.js`: A simple pub-sub event emitter for decoupling various components in our WebGL application. Instead of passing hard references around between unrelated functionality, we can leverage the pub-sub pattern to emit and listen to actions.
- `Clock.js`: A simple class that abstracts away the `requestAnimationFrame` API to have the entire WebGL application update from a single source of truth (such as `clock`).

  requestAnimationFrame

  The `window.requestAnimationFrame()` method tells the browser that you wish to perform an animation and requests that the browser call a specified function to update an animation before the next repaint. This will request that your animation function be called before the browser performs the next repaint.

- `Controls.js`: Provides the ability to capture various `canvas` DOM events to drive interactions.
- `utils.js`: Utility functions that we covered in earlier chapters.

Although we have enough foundation to understand how each components works, we will cover each component in Chapter 9, *Putting It All Together*. That being said, if you can't wait, feel free to inspect the source code to get an idea of what's to come.

Life Cycle Functions

The following functions define the life cycle of a WebGLApp application.

The configure Function

The configure function sets some parameters of our gl context, such as the color for clearing the canvas. After configuring the necessary states.

The load Function

The load function sets up objects to be added to our scene. For example, the two locally-created objects, floor and axis, are added to scene by calling the add method. After that, a remote object (AJAX call) is loaded using the scene.load method.

The draw Function

The draw function calls updateTransforms to calculate the matrices for the new position (that is, when we move), and then iterates over the objects in scene to render them. Inside this loop, it calls setMatrixUniforms for every object to be rendered.

Matrix-Handling Functions

Open up ch04_02_model-view-rotation.html in your editor. The following are the functions that initialize, update, and pass matrices to the shaders.

initTransforms

As you can see, the Model-View matrix, the Camera matrix, the Projection matrix, and the Normal matrix are set up here:

```
function initTransforms() {
  mat4.identity(modelViewMatrix);
```

```
mat4.translate(modelViewMatrix, modelViewMatrix, home);

mat4.identity(cameraMatrix);
mat4.invert(cameraMatrix, modelViewMatrix);

mat4.identity(projectionMatrix);

mat4.identity(normalMatrix);
mat4.copy(normalMatrix, modelViewMatrix);
mat4.invert(normalMatrix, normalMatrix);
mat4.transpose(normalMatrix, normalMatrix);
}
```

updateTransforms

In `updateTransforms`, we use the contents of the global variables' position and rotation to update the matrices. This is, of course, as follows::

```
function updateTransforms() {
  mat4.perspective(projectionMatrix, 45,canvas.width /gl.canvas.height,
    0.1, 1000);

  if (coordinates === WORLD_COORDINATES) {
    mat4.identity(modelViewMatrix);
    mat4.translate(modelViewMatrix, modelViewMatrix, position);
    mat4.rotateX(modelViewMatrix, modelViewMatrix, rotation[0] * Math.PI /
      180);
    mat4.rotateY(modelViewMatrix, modelViewMatrix, rotation[1] * Math.PI /
      180);
    mat4.rotateZ(modelViewMatrix, modelViewMatrix, rotation[2] * Math.PI /
      180);
  }
  else {
    mat4.identity(cameraMatrix);
    mat4.translate(cameraMatrix, cameraMatrix, position);
    mat4.rotateX(cameraMatrix, cameraMatrix, rotation[0] * Math.PI / 180);
    mat4.rotateY(cameraMatrix, cameraMatrix, rotation[1] * Math.PI / 180);
    mat4.rotateZ(cameraMatrix, cameraMatrix, rotation[2] * Math.PI / 180);
  }
}
```

setMatrixUniforms

This function performs the mapping:

```
function setMatrixUniforms() {
  if (coordinates === WORLD_COORDINATES) {
    mat4.invert(cameraMatrix, modelViewMatrix);
    gl.uniformMatrix4fv(program.uModelViewMatrix, false, modelViewMatrix);
  }
  else {
    mat4.invert(modelViewMatrix, cameraMatrix);
  }

  gl.uniformMatrix4fv(program.uProjectionMatrix, false, projectionMatrix);
  gl.uniformMatrix4fv(program.uModelViewMatrix, false, modelViewMatrix);
  mat4.transpose(normalMatrix, cameraMatrix);
  gl.uniformMatrix4fv(program.uNormalMatrix, false, normalMatrix);
}
```

Summary

Let's summarize what we've learned in this chapter:

- There is no camera object in WebGL. However, we can build one using the Model-View matrix.
- 3D objects undergo several transformations to be displayed on a 2D screen. These transformations are represented as 4x4 matrices.
- Scene transformations are affine. Affine transformations are constituted by a linear transformation followed by a translation. The WebGL groups affine transforms into three matrices: the Model-View matrix, the Projection matrix, and the Normal matrix, and one WebGL operation: gl.viewport().
- Affine transforms are applied in projective space, so they can be represented by 4x4 matrices. To work in projective space, vertices need to be augmented to contain an extra term, namely w, which is called the perspective coordinate. The four-tuple (x, y, z, w) is called Homogeneous coordinates. Homogeneous coordinates allow representation of lines that intersect on infinity by making the perspective coordinate w = 0. Vectors always have a Homogeneous coordinate, w = 0, while points have a Homogeneous coordinate, namely, w = 1 (unless they are at infinity, in which case w = 0).

- By default, a WebGL scene is viewed from the world origin in the negative direction of the z-axis. This can be altered by changing the Model-View matrix.
- The Camera matrix is the inverse of the Model-View matrix. The camera and world operations are opposites. There are two basic types of cameras: *orbiting* and *tracking*.
- Normals receive special treatment whenever the object undergoes an affine transform. Normals are transformed by the Normal matrix, which can be obtained from the Model-View matrix.
- The Projection matrix allows us to determine two basic projective modes: *orthographic* projection and *perspective* projection.

In the next chapter, we will take what we've learned here about transformations to distinguish between global and local transformations. We will look at transformations that are *global*, as we've covered here, and transformations that are *local* to individual objects in our 3D scene.

5
Animations

In the previous chapter, we covered matrices, transformations, and cameras. So far, we have only discussed static scenes, where all interactions are done by moving the camera. With these interactions, a camera transformation is applied to all objects in the 3D scene; we therefore call it a *global* transform. However, objects in 3D scenes can have actions of their own. For instance, in a car-racing game, each car has its own speed and trajectory. In a first-person shooter game, enemies can hide behind barricades, come to fight, or simply run away. In general, each one of these actions is modeled as a matrix transformation that is attached to the corresponding actor in the scene. These are called *local* transforms.

In this chapter, you will:

- Learn the difference between global and local transformations.
- Learn about matrix stacks and how to use them to perform animations.
- Use JavaScript timers to do time-based animations.
- Learn about parametric curves.
- Learn about interpolation.
- Explore various interpolation techniques.

WebGL Matrix Naming Conventions

Before we go any further, let's take a moment to quickly summarize some of the conventions around matrix-naming. As we've seen, WebGL is a simple API with nearly everything – except for a few predefined names, such as `gl_Position` – defined by you, the programmer. That being said, common and semi-common naming conventions do exist. This is especially true for matrices. Here are a few important ones we've already covered, along with a few new ones that we'll cover shortly:

- **World Matrix:** Sometimes referred to as the **Model matrix**, this is a matrix that takes the vertices of a model and moves them to world space.
- **Camera Matrix:** This matrix positions the camera in the world. You can also think of it as the World matrix for the camera.
- **View Matrix:** This matrix moves everything else in the world in front of the camera. As we've seen, this is the inverse of the Camera matrix.
- **Projection Matrix:** This is the matrix that converts a frustum of space into clip space. You can also think of it as the matrix returned by your matrix math library's perspective or orthographic function.
- **Local Matrix:** The matrix is used in scene graphs, where the matrix, at any particular node on the graph, is used before multiplying with any other nodes.

> **Scene graph**
>
>
>
> This is a data structure, commonly used by vector-based graphics-editing applications and modern computer games, that arranges the logical and often spatial representation of a graphical scene. A scene graph is a collection of nodes in a graph or tree structure. For more information, please visit https://en.wikipedia.org/wiki/Scene_graph.

Matrix Stacks

A **matrix stack** provides a way to apply local transforms to individual objects in our scene while preserving global transforms.

The matrix stack works as each rendering cycle (each call to our `render` function) requires calculating the scene matrices to react to camera movements. We first update the Model-View matrix for each object in our scene before passing the matrices to the shading program (as `attributes`). We do this in three steps:

1. Once the global Model-View matrix (such as camera transform) has been calculated, we save (push) it onto a stack. This allows us to recover the original matrix once we've applied local transforms.

2. Calculate an updated Model-View matrix for each object in the scene. This update consists of multiplying the original Model-View matrix by a matrix that represents the rotation, translation, and/or scaling of each object in the scene. The updated Model-View matrix is passed to the program and the respective object then appears in the location indicated by its local transform.

3. Recover the original matrix from the stack, and then repeat steps one to three for the next object that needs to be rendered.

The following diagram shows this three-step procedure for one object:

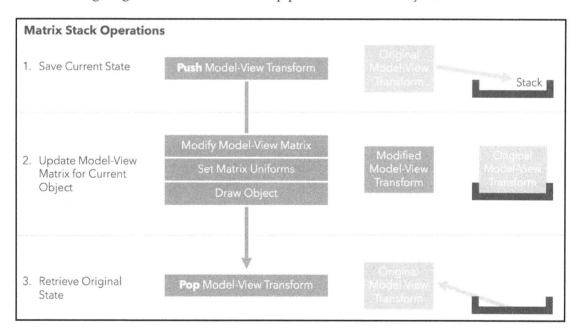

Animating a 3D scene

Animating a scene is nothing more than applying the appropriate local transformations to the objects in the scene. For instance, if we want to move a cone and a sphere, each one of them will have a corresponding local transformation that will describe its location, orientation, and scale. In the previous section, we learned that matrix stacks allow us to preserve the original Model-View transform so that we can apply the correct local transforms to each object.

Now that we know how to move objects with local transforms and matrix stacks, we should address *when* to apply these transforms.

If we calculate the position to apply to the cone and sphere in our example every time we call the `render` function, this would imply that the animation rate would depend on the speed of our rendering cycle. A slow rendering cycle would produce choppy animations and too fast a rendering cycle would create the illusion of objects jumping from one side to the other without smooth transitions.

Therefore, it is important to make the animation independent of the rendering cycle. There are a couple of solutions that we can use to achieve this goal: the `requestAnimationFrame` function and JavaScript timers.

The requestAnimationFrame Function

The `requestAnimationFrame` function is available in all WebGL-enabled browsers. One of the advantages of leveraging this function is that it is designed to call the rendering function (whatever function we indicate) only when the browser/tab window is in focus. Otherwise, there is no call. This saves precious CPU, GPU, and memory resources. By using the `requestAnimationFrame` function, we can obtain a rendering cycle that is in sync with hardware capabilities and one that will automatically suspend itself when the window is out of focus.

requestAnimationFrame

To check out the status of `requestAnimationFrame` in your browser, visit https://caniuse.com/#search=requestanimationframe.

JavaScript Timers

That said, `requestAnimationFrame` is not a magical function that is a complete black box. It's important to remember that we can implement our own in situations where it's not available or if we want a tailored animation experience. To do so, we will use two JavaScript timers to isolate the rendering rate from the animation rate.

Unlike the `requestAnimationFrame` function, JavaScript timers continue running in the background, even when the page is not in focus. This is not optimal performance since computer resources are allocated toward a scene that is not in view. To mimic some of the intelligent behavior of `requestAnimationFrame`, we can use the `onblur` and `onfocus` events of the JavaScript window object.

Let's see what we can do:

Action (What)	Goal (Why)	Method (How)
Pause the rendering	To stop the rendering until the window is in focus.	Clear the timer calling `clearInterval` in the `window.onblur` function.
Slow the rendering	To reduce resource consumption but make sure that the 3D scene keeps evolving, even if we're not looking at it.	We can clear current timer calling `clearInterval` in the `window.onblur` function and create a new timer with a more relaxed interval (higher value).
Resume the rendering	To activate the 3D scene at full speed when the browser window recovers its focus.	We start a new timer with the original render rate in the `window.onfocus` function.

By reducing the JavaScript timer rate or clearing the timer, we can handle hardware resources more efficiently.

Controlling the Render Cycle

An example of this sort of low-level functionality can be seen in the `common/js/Clock.js` file. With this universal clock, you can see how the `onblur` and `onfocus` events have been used to control the clock ticking (the rendering cycle), as we described previously.

Timing Strategies

If you've programmed animations in JavaScript before, you may have used either `setInterval` or `setTimeout` to get your drawing function to be called.

The problem with using these two approaches for drawing is that they have no relation to the browser's render cycle. That is, they aren't synced to when the browser is going to draw a new frame, which can leave the animation out of sync with the user's machine. For example, if you use `setInterval` or `setTimeout` and assume 60 frames a second, and the user's machine is actually running a different frame rate, you'll be out of sync with their machine.

Even though `requestAnimationFrame` is available on all WebGL-enabled browsers, we'll leverage our own animation JavaScript timers for educational purposes. In production, it is recommended that you leverage the browser's optimized version.

In this section, we will create a JavaScript timer that will allow us to control the animation. As we mentioned previously, we will implement a JavaScript timing strategy that provides independence between how fast your computer can render frames and how fast you want the animation to go. We will refer to this property as the **animation rate**.

Before moving forward, we must address a caveat about working with timers: *JavaScript is not a multithreaded language*. This means that if there are several asynchronous events occurring at the same time (blocking events), the browser will queue them for posterior execution. Each browser has a different mechanism to deal with blocking event queues.

There are two blocking event-handling alternatives for the purpose of developing an animation timer.

Animation Strategy

The first alternative is to calculate the elapsed time inside the timer callback. The pseudocode looks like this:

```
const animationRate = 30; // 30 ms

let initialTime, elapsedTime;

function animate(deltaT) {
  // calculate object positions based on deltaT
}

function onFrame() {
  const currentTime = new Date().getTime();
  elapsedTime = currentTime - initialTime;
  if (elapsedTime < animationRate) return; // come back later
  animate(elapsedTime);
  initialTime = currentTime;
}
```

```
function startAnimation() {
  setInterval(onFrame, animationRate / 1000);
}
```

In doing so, we guarantee that the animation time is independent of how often the timer callback is actually executed. If there are big delays (due to other blocking events), this method may result in **dropped frames**. This means that the object's positions in our scene will immediately be moved to the current position that they should be in according to the elapsed time (between consecutive animation timer callbacks), and then the intermediate positions will be ignored. The motion on screen may jump, but often, a dropped animation frame is an acceptable loss in a real-time application. One example is the movement of one object from point A to point B over a given period of time. However, if we used this strategy when shooting a target in a 3D shooting game, we could quickly run into problems. Imagine that you are trying to shoot a target where there is a delay. The next thing you know, the target is no longer there! Since we need to calculate a collision in this case, we cannot afford to miss frames. This is because the collision could occur in any of the frames that we would drop without analyzing. The following strategy solves this problem.

Simulation Strategy

There are several applications, such as the shooting game example, that require all intermediate frames to ensure the integrity of the outcome. These applications include working with collision detection, physics simulations, or artificial intelligence for games. For games, we need to update the object's positions at a constant rate. We do so by directly calculating the next position for the objects inside the timer callback:

```
const animationRate = 30; // 30 ms
const deltaPosition = 0.1;

function animate(deltaP) {
  // Calculate object positions based on deltaP
}

function onFrame() {
  animate(deltaPosition);
}

function startAnimation() {
  setInterval(onFrame, animationRate / 1000);
}
```

This may lead to **frozen frames** that occur when there is a long list of blocking events because the object's positions would not be updated in a timely manner.

Combined Approach: Animation and Simulation

Generally speaking, browsers can efficiently handle blocking events, and in most cases, performance would be similar regardless of the chosen strategy. Deciding to calculate the elapsed time or the next position in timer callbacks will then depend on your particular application.

Nonetheless, there are cases where it is desirable to combine both animation and simulation strategies. We can create a timer callback that calculates the elapsed time and updates the animation as many times as required per frame. The pseudocode looks like the following:

```
const animationRate = 30; // 30 ms
const deltaPosition = 0.1;

let initialTime, elapsedTime;

function animate(delta) {
  // Calculate object positions based on delta
}

function onFrame() {
  const currentTime = new Date().getTime();
  elapsedTime = currentTime - initialTime;
  if (elapsedTime < animationRate) return; // come back later!
  let steps = Math.floor(elapsedTime / animationRate);
  while (steps > 0) {
    animate(deltaPosition);
    steps -= 1;
  }
  initialTime = currentTime;
}

function startAnimation() {
  initialTime = new Date().getTime();
  setInterval(onFrame, animationRate / 1000);
}
```

The preceding code snippet demonstrates that the animation will always update at a fixed rate, regardless of how much time elapses between frames. If the app is running at 60 Hz, the animation will update once every other frame; if the app runs at 30 Hz, the animation will update once per frame; if the app runs at 15 Hz, the animation will update twice per frame. The animation remains far more stable and deterministic if it is always moved forward by a fixed amount.

The following sequence shows the responsibilities of each function in the call stack for the combined approach:

- `render:`
  - Starts the timer
  - Sets the animation rate
  - The timer callback is the `onFrame` function
- `onFrame:`
  - Calculates the elapsed time since the last call.
  - If the elapsed time is less than the animation rate, then it returns without further processing. Otherwise, it calculates the number of frames that the animation needs to be updated.
  - Updates the animation by calling the `animate` function.
- `animate:`
  - Updates the object positions by a fixed increment. In this example, the sphere is updated by `0.1` units every time `animate` is called.
  - It calls `draw` to update the object on screen. This is *optional*, since the rendering loop calls `draw` periodically anyway.
- `draw:`
  - Creates a local transformation using the new position calculated in `animate`, and it applies it to the corresponding object.

The code looks something like this:

```
transforms.calculateModelView();
transforms.push();

if (object.alias === 'sphere') {
  const sphereTransform = transforms.modelViewMatrix;
  mat4.translate(sphereTransform, sphereTransform, [0, 0, spherePosition]);
}
else if (object.alias === 'cone') {
  const coneTransform = transforms.modelViewMatrix;
  mat4.translate(coneTransform, coneTransform, [conePosition, 0, 0]);
```

```
}

transforms.setMatrixUniforms();
transforms.pop();
```

This approach may cause issues if an animation step actually takes longer to compute than the fixed step. If this occurs, you should simplify your animation code or release a recommended minimum system spec for your application.

Web Workers: Multithreading in JavaScript

Though outside the scope of this book, you should consider using **Web Workers** if performance is critical to you. Doing so will ensure that a particular update loop always fires at a consistent rate.

Web Workers is an API that allows web applications to spawn background processes that run scripts in parallel to their main page. This allows for thread-like operation with message-passing as the coordination mechanism.

Web Workers

You can find the Web Workers specification at `http://dev.w3.org/html5/workers/`.

Architectural Updates

Let's review the structure of the examples developed in this book.

App Review

The `init` function defines three function hooks that control the life cycle of the application. As we've covered in previous chapters, we create our application by invoking the `init` function. Then, we call the hooks to the `configure`, `load`, and `render` functions. Also, please note that the `init` function is the entry point for the application and it is automatically invoked using the `onload` event of the web page.

Adding Support for Matrix Stacks

We've also added a new script: `Transforms.js`. This file contains the `Transforms` class that encapsulate the matrix-handling operations, including the `push` and `pop` matrix stack operations. The `Transforms` class replaces the functionality behind the `initTransforms`, `updateTransforms`, and `setMatrixUniforms` functions.

You can find the source code for SceneTransforms in `common/js/Transforms.js`.

Connecting Matrix Stacks and JavaScript Timers

In the following section, we will investigate a simple scene where we've animated a cone and a sphere. We will use matrix stacks to implement local transformations and JavaScript timers to implement the animation sequence.

Time for Action: Simple Animation

Let's look at an example covering a simple animation technique:

1. Open ch05_01_simple-animation.html in your browser:

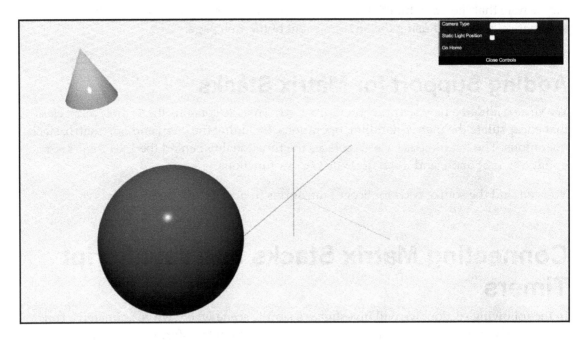

2. Move the camera around (left mouse-click + drag) and see how the objects (sphere and cone) move independently of one another (local transformations) and the camera (global transformation).
3. You can also dolly the camera (left mouse-click + *Alt* + drag).
4. Change the camera type to **Tracking**. If for any reason you lose your bearings, click on **Go Home**.
5. Let's examine the source code to see how we've implemented this example. Open ch05_01_simple-animation.html in a code editor.
6. Take a look at the render, onFrame, and animate functions. Which timing strategy are we using here?

7. The `spherePosition` and `conePosition` global variables contain the position of the sphere and the cone, respectively. Scroll up to the `draw` function. Inside the main loop where each object scene is rendered, a different local transformation is calculated depending on the current object being rendered. The code looks like the following:

```
function draw() {
  gl.viewport(0, 0, gl.canvas.width, gl.canvas.height);
  gl.clear(gl.COLOR_BUFFER_BIT | gl.DEPTH_BUFFER_BIT);

  transforms.updatePerspective();

  try {
    gl.uniform1i(program.uUpdateLight, fixedLight);

    scene.traverse(object => {
      transforms.calculateModelView();
      transforms.push();

      if (object.alias === 'sphere') {
        const sphereTransform = transforms.modelViewMatrix;
        mat4.translate(sphereTransform, sphereTransform, [0, 0,
          spherePosition]);
      }
      else if (object.alias === 'cone') {
        const coneTransform = transforms.modelViewMatrix;
        mat4.translate(coneTransform, coneTransform, [conePosition,
          0, 0]);
      }

      transforms.setMatrixUniforms();
      transforms.pop();

      gl.uniform4fv(program.uMaterialDiffuse, object.diffuse);
      gl.uniform4fv(program.uMaterialSpecular, object.specular);
      gl.uniform4fv(program.uMaterialAmbient, object.ambient);
      gl.uniform1i(program.uWireframe, object.wireframe);

      // Bind VAO
      gl.bindVertexArray(object.vao);

      gl.bindBuffer(gl.ELEMENT_ARRAY_BUFFER, object.ibo);

      if (object.wireframe) {
        gl.drawElements(gl.LINES, object.indices.length,
          gl.UNSIGNED_SHORT, 0);
      }
```

```
    else {
      gl.drawElements(gl.TRIANGLES, object.indices.length,
        gl.UNSIGNED_SHORT, 0);
    }

    // Clean
    gl.bindVertexArray(null);
    gl.bindBuffer(gl.ARRAY_BUFFER, null);
    gl.bindBuffer(gl.ELEMENT_ARRAY_BUFFER, null);
  });
}
catch (error) {
  console.error(error);
}
}
```

8. Using the transforms object (which is an instance of `Transforms`), we obtain the global Model-View matrix by calling `transforms.calculateModelView()`. Push it into a matrix stack by calling the `push` method. We can now apply any transform that we want, knowing that we can retrieve the global transform since it is available for the next object on the list. We do so at the end of the code snippet by calling the `pop` method. Between the `push` and `pop` calls, we determine which object is currently being rendered and use the `spherePosition` or `conePosition` global variable to apply a translation to the current Model-View matrix. By doing so, we create a local transform.

9. Take a second look at the preceding code. As you saw at the beginning of this exercise, the cone is moving in the x-axis while the sphere is moving in the z-axis. What do you need to change to animate the cone in the y-axis? Test your hypothesis by modifying this code, saving the web page, and opening it again in your web browser.

10. Let's return to the `animate` function. What should we modify here to make the objects move faster?

Hint

Take a look at the global variables this function uses.

What just happened?

In this exercise, we saw a simple animation of two objects. We examined the source code to understand the call stack of functions that makes the animation possible.

Have a Go: Simulating Dropped and Frozen Frames

Let's see how we can control the render rate:

1. Open the ch05_02_dropping-frames.html file using your browser. Here, you will see the same scene we analyzed in the previous section. You'll notice that the animation is not smooth because we are simulating dropping frames:

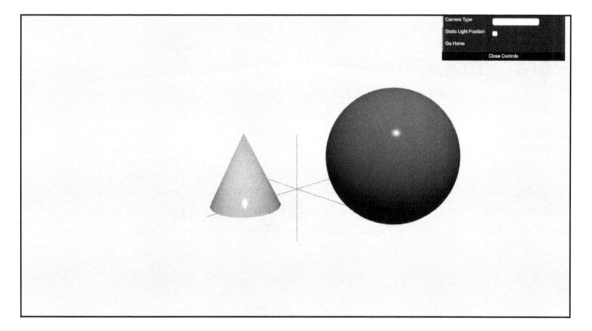

2. Take a look at the source code in your editor.

3. Scroll to the `onFrame` function. You can see that we've included a new variable: `simulationRate`. In the `onFrame` function, this variable calculates how many simulation steps need to be performed when the time elapsed is around 300 ms (`animationRate`). Given that `simulationRate` is 30 ms, this will produce a total of 10 simulation steps. These steps can increase if there are unexpected delays and the elapsed time is considerably higher. This is the behavior that we expect.

4. Experiment with different values for the `animationRate` and `simulationRate` variables to answer the following questions:
   - How do we get rid of the dropping frames issue?
   - How can we simulate frozen frames?
   - What is the relationship between the `animationRate` and `simulationRate` variables when simulating frozen frames?

Parametric Curves

There are many situations where we don't know the exact position of an object at a given time, but we do know an equation that describes its movement. These equations are known as **parametric curves**; they are parametric because the position depends on one parameter—for example, the time.

There are many examples of parametric curves. For example, a projectile shot in a game, a car going downhill, or a bouncing ball. In each case, there are equations that describe the motion of these objects under ideal conditions. The following diagram shows the parametric equation that describes the free-fall motion:

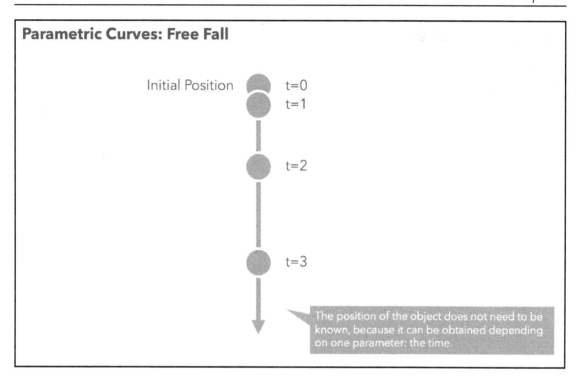

Parametric Curves: Free Fall

Initial Position — t=0
t=1

t=2

t=3

The position of the object does not need to be known, because it can be obtained depending on one parameter: the time.

$$h = H_0 + V_0 t - \frac{1}{2} g t^2$$

Where:

- g: Gravity at $9.8m/s^2$
- V_0: Initial velocity
- H_0: Initial Position
- t: Time
- h: Position

We are going to use parametric curves to animate objects in a WebGL scene. In this example, we will model a set of bouncing balls. The complete source code for this exercise can be found in ch05_03_bouncing-balls.html.

Initialization Steps

We will create a global variable that will store the (simulation) time. We will also create the global variables that regulate the animation:

```
let
    gl, scene, program, camera, transforms,
    elapsedTime, initialTime,
    fixedLight = false,
    balls = [],
    sceneTime = 0,
    animationRate = 15,
    gravity = 9.8,
    ballsCount = 50;
```

The `load` function is updated to load a bunch of balls using the same geometry (same JSON file), but we are adding it several times to the `scene` object. The code looks like this:

```
function load() {
  scene.add(new Floor(80, 2));
  for (let i = 0; i < ballsCount; i++) {
    balls.push(new BouncingBall());
    scene.load('/common/models/geometries/ball.json', `ball${i}`);
  }
}
```

ES6 Template Literals

If you're not familiar with the `ball${i}` syntax, it's equivalent to `'ball' + i`. Instead of concatenating strings, we can leverage template literals in ES6 for dynamic string values. For more information, check out `https://developer.mozilla.org/en-US/docs/Web/JavaScript/Reference/Template_literals`.

Notice that we've also populated an array named `balls[]`. We do this so that we can store the ball positions every time the global time changes. We will talk in depth about the bouncing ball simulation in the next *Time for action* section. For the moment, it's worth mentioning that it is on the `load` function that we load the geometry and initialize the ball array with the initial ball positions.

Setting up the Animation Timer

The `render` and `onFrame` functions look exactly the same as in the previous examples:

```
function onFrame() {
  elapsedTime = (new Date).getTime() - initialTime;
  if (elapsedTime < animationRate) return;

  let steps = Math.floor(elapsedTime / animationRate);
  while (steps > 0) {
    animate();
    steps -= 1;
  }

  initialTime = (new Date).getTime();
}

function render() {
  initialTime = (new Date).getTime();
  setInterval(onFrame, animationRate / 1000);
}
```

Running the Animation

The `animate` function passes the `sceneTime` variable to the `update` method of every ball in the ball array. Then, `sceneTime` updates by a fixed amount. The code looks like this:

```
function animate() {
  balls.forEach(ball => ball.update(sceneTime));
  sceneTime += 33 / 1000;
  draw();
}
```

Again, parametric curves are very helpful because they don't require us to know the location of every object that we want to move beforehand. We just apply a parametric equation that gives us the location based on the current time. This occurs for every ball inside its update method.

Drawing Each Ball in Its Current Position

In the draw function, we use a matrix stack to save the state of the Model-View matrix before applying a local transformation for each one of the balls. The code looks like this:

```
function draw() {
  gl.viewport(0, 0, gl.canvas.width, gl.canvas.height);
  gl.clear(gl.COLOR_BUFFER_BIT | gl.DEPTH_BUFFER_BIT);
  transforms.updatePerspective();

  try {
    gl.uniform1i(program.uUpdateLight, fixedLight);

    scene.traverse(object => {
      transforms.calculateModelView();
  transforms.push();

  if (~object.alias.indexOf('ball')) {
  const index = parseInt(object.alias.substring(4, 8));
  const ballTransform = transforms.modelViewMatrix;
  mat4.translate(ballTransform, ballTransform, balls[index].position);
  object.diffuse = balls[index].color;
  }

  transforms.setMatrixUniforms();
  transforms.pop();

      gl.uniform4fv(program.uMaterialDiffuse, object.diffuse);
      gl.uniform4fv(program.uMaterialSpecular, object.specular);
      gl.uniform4fv(program.uMaterialAmbient, object.ambient);

      gl.uniform1i(program.uWireframe, object.wireframe);
      gl.uniform1i(program.uPerVertexColor, object.perVertexColor);

      // Bind
      gl.bindVertexArray(object.vao);
      gl.bindBuffer(gl.ELEMENT_ARRAY_BUFFER, object.ibo);

      if (object.wireframe) {
        gl.drawElements(gl.LINES, object.indices.length, gl.UNSIGNED_SHORT,
          0);
```

```
      }
      else {
        gl.drawElements(gl.TRIANGLES, object.indices.length,
          gl.UNSIGNED_SHORT, 0);
      }

      // Clean
      gl.bindVertexArray(null);
      gl.bindBuffer(gl.ARRAY_BUFFER, null);
      gl.bindBuffer(gl.ELEMENT_ARRAY_BUFFER, null);
    });
  }
  catch (error) {
    console.error(error);
  }
}
```

The trick here is to use the number that makes up part of the ball alias to look up the respective ball position in the `balls` array. For example, if the ball being rendered has the `ball32` alias, then this code will look for the current position of the ball whose index is 32 in the `balls` array. This one-to-one correspondence between the `ball` alias and its location in the ball array was established in the `load` function.

In the following *Time for Action* section, we will see the bouncing balls animation in action. We will also discuss some of the code detail.

Time for Action: Bouncing Ball

Let's look at an example covering how we'd animate many objects in our scene:

1. Open ch05_03_bouncing-balls.html in your browser:

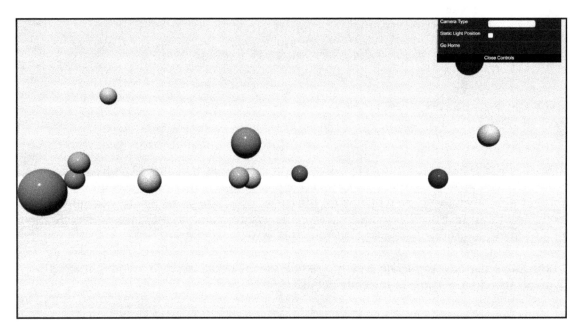

2. The orbiting camera is activated by default. Move the camera and you will see how all the objects adjust to the global transform (camera) and continue bouncing according to their local transforms.

3. Let's explain how we keep track of each ball in more detail.

4. Define the appropriate global variables and constants:

```
let
    gl, scene, program, camera, transforms,
    elapsedTime, initialTime,
    fixedLight = false,
    balls = [],
    sceneTime = 0,
    animationRate = 15,
    gravity = 9.8,
    ballsCount = 50;
```

5. Initialize the `balls` array. We use a `for` loop in the `load` function to achieve this:

```
function load() {
  scene.add(new Floor(80, 2));
  for (let i = 0; i < ballsCount; i++) {
    balls.push(new BouncingBall());
    scene.load('/common/models/geometries/ball.json', `ball${i}`);
  }
}
```

6. The `BouncingBall` class initializes the simulation variables for each ball in the `balls` array. One of these attributes is the position, which we select randomly. You can see how we do this by using the `generatePosition` function:

```
function generatePosition() {
  return [
    Math.floor(Math.random() * 50) - Math.floor(Math.random() *
      50),
    Math.floor(Math.random() * 30) + 50,
    Math.floor(Math.random() * 50)
  ];
}
```

7. After adding a new ball to the `balls` array, we add a new ball object (geometry) to the `scene` instance. Please note that the alias we create includes the current index of the ball object in the `balls` array. For example, if we add the 32nd ball to the array, the alias that the corresponding geometry will have in `scene` will be `ball32`.

8. The only other object that we add to the scene here is `Floor`. We have used this object in previous exercises. You can find the code for the `Floor` class in `common/js/Floor.js`.

9. Let's talk about the `draw` function. Here, we go through the elements of `scene` and retrieve each object's alias. If the alias contains the word `ball`, we know that the alias corresponds to its `index` in the ball array. We could have probably used an associative array here to make it look nicer, but doing so does not really change our goal. The main point here is to make sure that we can associate the simulation variables for each ball with the corresponding object (geometry) in `scene`.

10. Notice that for each object (ball geometry) in `scene`, we extract the current position and the color from the respective `BouncingBall` instance in the `balls` array.

11. Alter the current Model-View matrix for each ball by using a matrix stack to handle local transformations, as described previously. In our case, we want the animation for each ball to be independent from the transformations of the camera and one another.

12. So far, we've described how the bouncing balls are created (`load`) and how they are rendered (`draw`). None of these functions modifies the current position of the balls. We do that by using `BouncingBall.update`. This code uses the animation time (the `sceneTime` global variable) to calculate the position for the bouncing ball. Since each `BouncingBall` has its own simulation parameters, we can calculate the position for each given position when `sceneTime` is provided . In short, the ball position is a function of time and, as such, it falls into the category of motion described by parametric curves.

13. The `BouncingBall.update` method is called inside the `animate` function. As we saw previously, this function is invoked by the animation timer each time the timer is up. Inside this function, you can see how the simulation variables are updated to reflect the current state of that ball in the simulation.

What just happened?

We've learned how to handle several object-local transformations while preserving global transformations by using a matrix stack strategy. In the bouncing ball example, we used an animation timer for the animation that is independent from the rendering timer. Finally, we saw how the bouncing ball `update` method shows how parametric curves work.

Optimization Strategies

If you play around a little bit and increase the value of the `ballsCount` global constant from `50` to `500`, you will start to notice that the frame rate degrades:

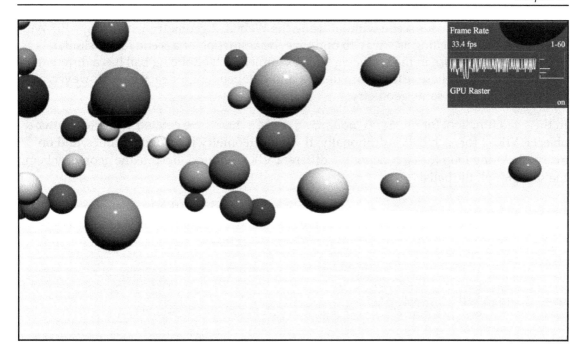

In the preceding screenshot, the rendering hovered roughly around 30 frames per second. Depending on your computer, the average time for the `draw` function can be higher than the frequency at which the animation timer callback is invoked. This will result in dropped frames. To correct this, we need to make the `draw` function faster. Let's see a couple of strategies to do this.

Optimizing Batch Performance

WebGL 2 adds some interesting features, such as **geometry-instancing.** This feature allows us to render the same instance of a single mesh with differing shader attributes using **instancing** and only one `render` call. Though instancing is limited, as it's based on the same mesh only, it's still a great way to improve performance if you have to draw the same meshes multiple times, especially if combined with shaders. While this functionality is provided in WebGL 2, we'll build our own geometry-optimization techniques for educational purposes. We will cover WebGL 2's geometry instancing feature in `Chapter 11`, *WebGL 2 Highlights*.

How do we optimize our scene without using the WebGL 2 geometry-instancing API? We can use geometry-caching as a way to optimize the animation of a scene full of similar objects. This is the case in the bouncing balls example. Each bouncing ball has a different position and color. These features are unique and independent for each ball. However, all of the balls share the same geometry.

In the load function, for ch05_03_bouncing-balls.html, we created 50 vertex buffer objects (VBOs) for each ball. Additionally, the same geometry is loaded 50 times, and on every rendering loop (draw function), a different VBO is bound, despite the geometry being the same for all the balls!

In ch05_04_bouncing-balls-optimized.html, we modified the load and draw functions to handle geometry-caching. In the first place, the geometry is loaded just once (load function):

```
function load() {
  scene.add(new Floor(80, 2));
  scene.add(new Axis(82));
  scene.load('/common/models/geometries/ball.json', 'ball');
}
```

Second, when the object with the 'ball' alias is the current object in the rendering loop (the draw function), the drawBalls delegate function is invoked. This function sets some of the uniforms that are common to all bouncing balls (so that we do not waste time passing them every time to program for every ball). After that, the drawBall function is invoked. This function will set up those elements that are unique for each ball. In our case, we set up the program uniform that corresponds to the ball color and the Model-View matrix, which is unique for each ball because of the local transformation (ball position):

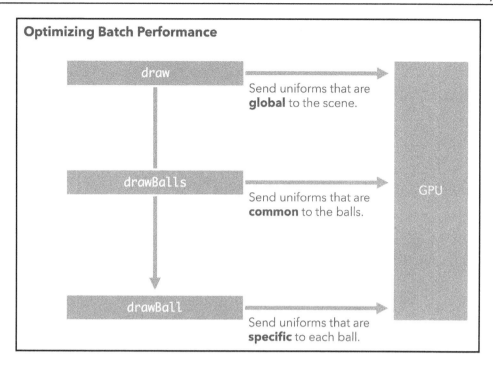

Performing Translations in the Vertex Shader

If you take a look at the code in ch05_04_bouncing-balls-optimized.html, you will see that we have taken an extra step to cache the Model-View matrix.

The basic idea behind this is to transfer the original matrix to the GPU (global) once and then perform the translation for each ball (local) inside the vertex shader. This change significantly improves the performance because of the parallel nature of the vertex shader.

This is what we do, step by step:

1. Create a new uniform that tells the vertex shader whether it should perform a translation (uTranslate).
2. Create a new uniform that contains the ball position for each ball (uTranslation).

3. Map these two new uniforms to JavaScript variables (we do this in the `configure` function):

```
// Create program variable that maps the uniform uTranslation
gl.uniform3fv(program.uTranslation, [0, 0, 0]);

// Create program variable that maps the uniform uTranslate
gl.uniform1i(program.uTranslate, false);
```

4. Perform the translation inside the vertex shader. This part is probably the trickiest part since it requires a little bit of ESSL programming:

```
// Transformed vertex position
vec3 vecPosition = aVertexPosition;
if (uTranslate) {
   vecPosition += uTranslation;
}
```

5. In this code fragment, we are defining `vecPosition`, a variable of the `vec3` type. If the `uTranslate` uniform is `true` (meaning we are trying to render a bouncing ball), then we update `vecPosition` with the translation. This is implemented using vector-addition.

6. Make sure that the transformed vertex carries the translation in case of having one, so the following line looks like this:

```
vec4 vertex = uModelViewMatrix * vec4(vecPosition, 1.0);
```

7. In `drawBall`, pass the current ball position as the content for the `uTranslation` uniform:

```
gl.uniform3fv(program.uTranslation, ball.position);
```

8. In `drawBalls`, set the `uTranslate` uniform to `true`:

```
gl.uniform1i(program.uTranslate, true);
```

9. In `draw`, pass the Model-View matrix once for all balls by using the following line of code:

```
transforms.setMatrixUniforms();
```

10. Increase the `ballsCount` global variable from `50` to `500` and watch how the application continues to perform reasonably well, regardless of the increased scene complexity. The improvement in execution times is shown in the following screenshot:

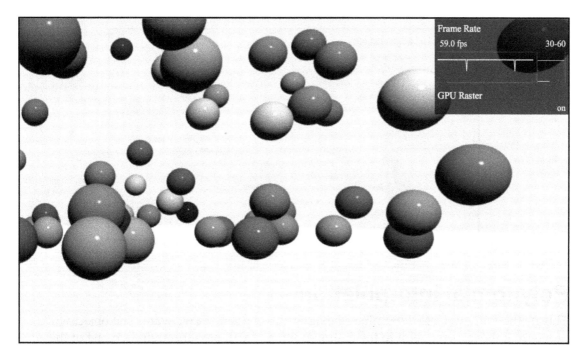

11. After these optimizations, the example runs at a smooth `60` frames per second. The optimized source code is available at `ch05_bouncing-balls-optimized.html`.

Interpolation

Interpolation greatly simplifies a 3D objects' animation. Unlike parametric curves, it is not necessary to define the position of the object as a function of time. When interpolation is used, we only need to define control points or knots. The set of control points describes the path that a particular animate object will follow. There are many interpolation methods; however, it's always a good idea to start with the basics.

Linear Interpolation

This method requires that we define the starting and ending points of the location of our object, along with the number of interpolating steps. The object will move on the line determined by the starting and ending points:

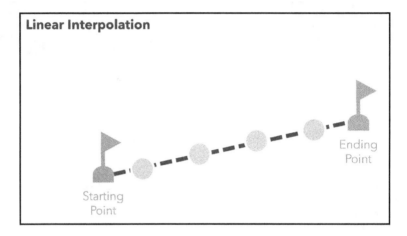

Polynomial Interpolation

This method allows us to determine as many control points as we want. The object will move from the starting point to the ending point and will pass through each one of the control points in between:

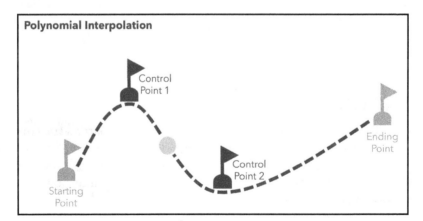

While using polynomials, an increasing number of control points can produce undesired oscillations on the object's path described by this technique. This is known as **Runge's phenomenon**. The following diagram illustrates the result of moving one of the control points of a polynomial described with 11 control points:

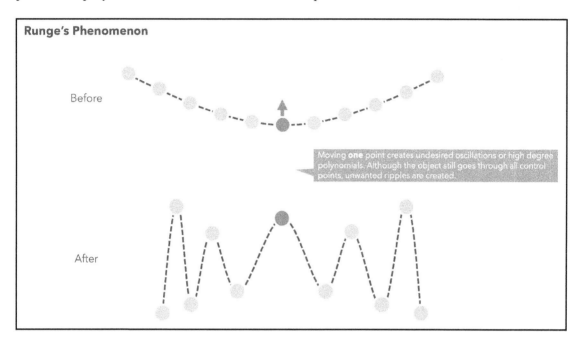

B-Splines

This method is similar to polynomial interpolation with the difference that the control points are outside of the object's path. In other words, the object does not pass through the control points as it moves. In general, this method is common in computer graphics because the knots allow for much smoother path-generation than the polynomial equivalent at the same time that fewer knots are required. B-splines also respond better to Runge's phenomenon:

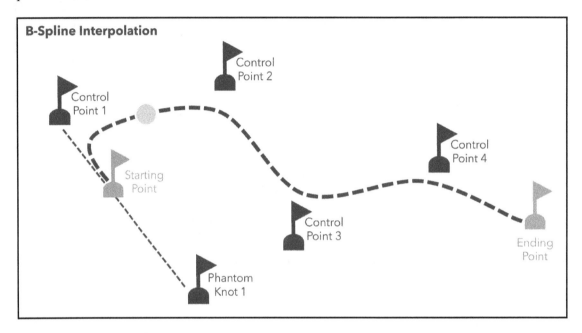

In the following *Time for action* section, we will see in the three different interpolation techniques that have been introduced in practice: **linear**, **polynomial**, and **b-spline**.

Time for Action: Interpolation

Let's cover an example showcasing various interpolation techniques:

1. Open ch05_05_interpolation.html using your browser. You should see something similar to the following:

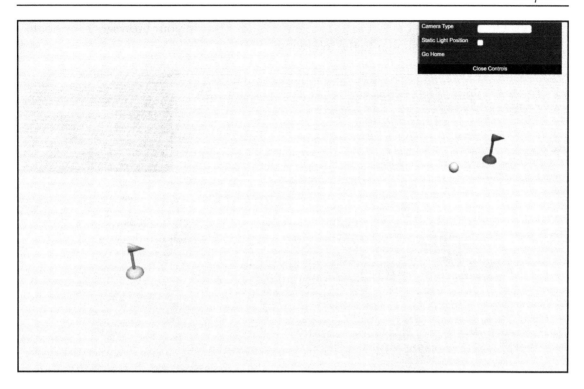

2. Inspect the code in an editor. Nearly all of the functions are the same as before, except for the new function called `interpolate`. This function interpolates the position in a linear fashion:

```
function interpolate() {
  const [X0, Y0, Z0] = initialPosition;
  const [X1, Y1, Z1] = finalPosition;

  const dX = (X1 - X0) / incrementSteps;
  const dY = (Y1 - Y0) / incrementSteps;
  const dZ = (Z1 - Z0) / incrementSteps;

  for (let i = 0; i < incrementSteps; i++) {
    position.push([X0 + (dX * i), Y0 + (dY * i), Z0 + (dZ * i)]);
  }
}
```

3. Open up `ch05_06_interpolation-final.html` in your browser. You should see something similar to the following:

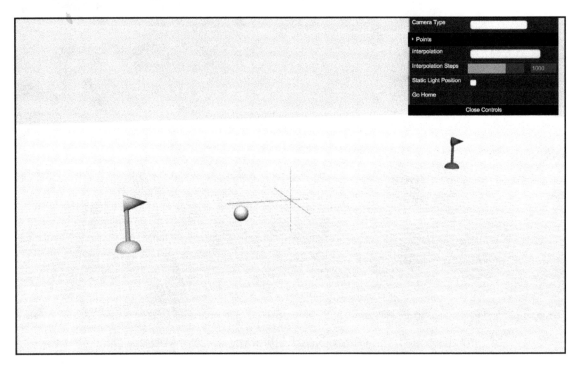

4. Select **Linear** interpolation if it is not already selected.
5. Move the start and end points using the slider provided.
6. Change the number of interpolation steps. What happens to the animation when you decrease the number of steps?
7. The code for the linear interpolation has been implemented in the `doLinearInterpolation` function.
8. Select **Polynomial** interpolation. In this example, we have implemented Lagrange's interpolation method. You can see the source code in the `doLagrangeInterpolation` function.
9. Three new control points (flags) appear on screen. Using the sliders provided on the web page, you can change the location of these control points. You can also change the number of interpolation steps:

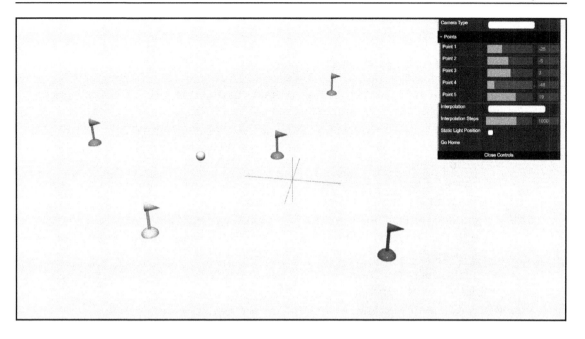

10. You may have also noticed that whenever the ball approaches one of the flags (with the exception of the start and end points), the flag changes color. To do that, we have written the ancillary `close` function. We use this function inside the `draw` routine to determine the color of the flags. If the current position of the ball, determined by `position[sceneTime]`, is close to one of the flag positions, the respective flag changes color. When the ball is far from the flag, the flag changes back to its original color.

11. Modify the source code so that each flag remains *activated*; that is, activated with the new color after the ball passes by until the animation loops back to the beginning. This happens when `sceneTime` is equal to `incrementSteps` (see the `animate` function).

12. Select the **B-Spline** interpolation. Notice how the ball does not reach any of the intermediate flags in the initial configuration. Is there any configuration you can test so that the ball passes through at least two of the flags?

What just happened?

We've learned how to use interpolation to describe the movement of an object in our 3D world. We've also created very simple scripts to detect object proximity and alter our scene accordingly (changing flag colors, in this example). Reaction to proximity is a key element in game design!

Summary

Let's summarize what we learned in this chapter:

- We saw how we can leverage matrix stacks to preserve global transformations while applying local transformations.
- We covered the basic concepts behind object animations in WebGL. More specifically, we learned about the differences between local and global transformations.
- We learned about the `requestAnimationFrame` browser and built our own version with JavaScript timers for animation.
- An animation timer that is not tied up to the rendering cycle provides a lot of flexibility by ensuring that the time in the scene is independent of how fast it can be rendered on screen.
- We distinguished between animation and simulation strategies for various problem-solving approaches.
- We looked at interpolation methods and their various approaches.

In the next chapter, we will play with colors and blending in a WebGL scene. We will study the interaction between objects and light colors, and learn how to create translucent objects.

6
Colors, Depth Testing, and Alpha Blending

In the previous chapter, we covered global versus local transformations, matrix stacks, animation timers, and various interpolation techniques. In this chapter, we start by examining how colors are structured and handled in WebGL and ESSL. We will discuss the use of colors in objects, lights, and scenes. Then, we will see how WebGL leverages the depth buffer for object occlusion when one object is in front of another, blocking it from view. Lastly, we will cover alpha blending, which allows us to combine the colors of objects when one is occluding the other, while also allowing us to create translucent objects.

In this chapter, we will cover the following topics:

- Using colors in objects.
- Assigning colors to light sources.
- Working with several light sources in the ESSL program.
- Learning how to use the depth test and the z-buffer.
- Learning how to blend functions and equations.
- Creating transparent objects with face-culling.

Using Colors in WebGL

WebGL supplies a fourth attribute to the RGB model. This attribute is called the **alpha channel**. The extended model then is known as the **RGBA** model, where A stands for alpha. The alpha channel contains a value between the range of 0.0 to 1.0, just like the other three channels (red, green, and blue). The following diagram shows the RGBA color space. On the horizontal axis, you can see the different colors that can be obtained by combining the R, G, and B channels. The vertical axis corresponds to the alpha channel:

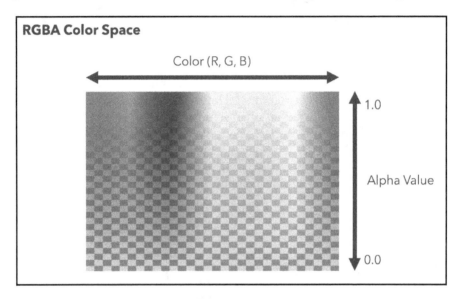

The alpha channel carries extra information about a color. This information affects the way the color is rendered on the screen. In most cases, the alpha value will refer to the amount of opacity that the color contains. A completely opaque color will have an alpha value of 1.0, whereas a completely transparent color will have an alpha value of 0.0. This is the general case, but as we will see, we need to take other factors into account when we obtain translucent colors.

Transparent Versus Translucent

Glass, for example, is transparent to all visible light. Translucent objects allow some light to travel through them. Materials such as frosted glass and some plastics are called translucent. When light strikes translucent materials, only some of the light passes through them.

We use colors everywhere in our WebGL 3D scenes:

- **Objects**: 3D objects can be colored by selecting one color for every pixel (fragment) or by selecting the color that the object will have based on the material's diffuse property.
- **Lights**: Even though we have been using white lights, there is no reason we can't have lights whose ambient or diffuse properties contain other colors.
- **Scene**: The background of our scene has a color that we can change by calling `gl.clearColor`. Also, as we will see later on, there are special operations that need to be performed on objects' colors to achieve translucent effects.

Use of Color in Objects

As earlier chapters have addressed, the final color of a pixel is assigned in the fragment shader by setting an out ESSL variable. If all the fragments in the object have the same color, we can say the object has a constant color. Otherwise, the object is generally understood as having per-vertex color.

Constant Coloring

To obtain a constant color, we store the desired color in a uniform that is passed to the fragment shader. This uniform is usually called the object's **diffuse material property**. We can also combine object normals and light-source information to obtain a Lambert coefficient. We can use the Lambert coefficient to proportionally change the reflecting color depending on the angle on which the light hits the object.

As the following diagram demonstrates, we lose depth perception when we do not use information about the normals to obtain a Lambert coefficient. Please note that we are using a diffusive lighting model:

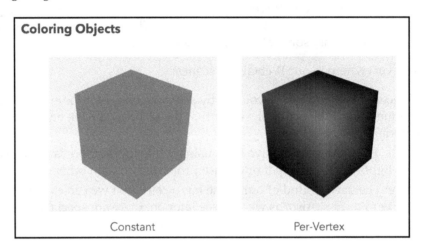

Coloring Objects

Constant   Per-Vertex

Per-Vertex Coloring

In medical and engineering visualization applications, it is common to find color maps that are associated with the vertices of the models we are rendering. These maps assign each vertex a color depending on its scalar value. An example of this idea includes the temperature charts that indicate cold temperatures as blue, and hot temperatures as red overlaid on a map.

To implement per-vertex coloring, we need to define an attribute that stores the color for the vertex in the vertex shader:

```
in vec4 aVertexColor;
```

The next step is to assign the `aVertexColor` attribute to a varying so that it can be passed to the fragment shader. Remember that varyings are automatically interpolated. Therefore, each fragment will have a color that is the weighted result of its contributing vertices.

If we want our color map to be sensitive to lighting conditions, we can multiply each vertex color by the diffuse component of the light. The result is then assigned to the varying that will transfer the result to the fragment shader.

The following diagram demonstrates two different possibilities for this case: on the left, the vertex color is multiplied by the light diffuse term without any weighting from the position of the light; on the right, the Lambert coefficient generates the expected shadows and gives information about the relative location of the light source:

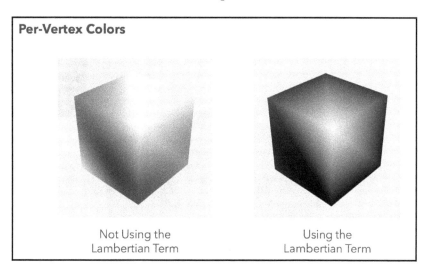

Here, we are using a vertex buffer object that is mapped to the `aVertexColor` vertex shader attribute. We learned how to map VBOs in `Chapter 2`, *Rendering*.

Per-Fragment Coloring

We can also assign a random color to each pixel of the object we are rendering. Although ESSL does not have a pre-built random function, there are algorithms we can use to generate pseudo-random numbers. That being said, the purpose and usefulness of this technique are outside the scope of this book.

Time for Action: Coloring the Cube

Let's cover a simple example of coloring a geometry:

1. Open the ch06_01_cube.html file using your browser. You will see a page similar to the following:

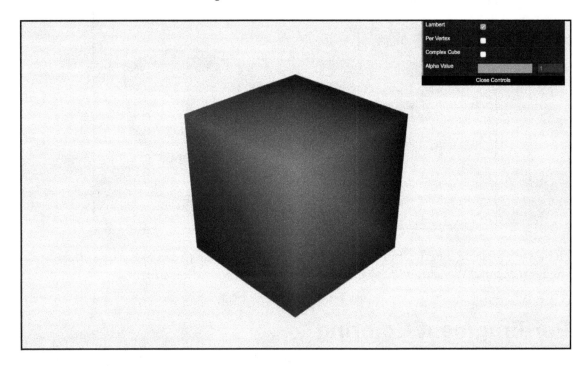

2. In this exercise, we're going to compare constant versus per-vertex coloring. Let's talk about the page's widgets:

   - **Lambert**: When selected, it will include the Lambert coefficient in the calculation of the final color.
   - **Per Vertex**: The two different coloring methods explained before: per-vertex or constant.
   - **Complex Cube**: Loads a JSON object where the vertices are repeated with the goal of obtaining multiple normals and multiple colors per vertex. We will explain how this works later on.
   - **Alpha Value**: This slider is mapped to the uAlpha float uniform in the vertex shader. uAlpha sets the alpha value for the vertex color.

3. Disable the use of the Lambert coefficient by clicking on **Lambert**. Rotate the cube by clicking and dragging. Notice the loss of depth perception when the Lambert coefficient is not included in the final color calculation. The **Lambert** button is mapped to the `uUseLambert` Boolean uniform. The code that calculates the Lambert coefficient can be found in the vertex shader included in the page:

```
float lambertTerm = 1.0;

if (uUseLambert) {
   vec3 normal = vec3(uNormalMatrix * vec4(aVertexNormal, 1.0));
   vec3 lightDirection = normalize(-uLightPosition);
   lambertTerm = max(dot(normal, -lightDirection), 0.20);
}
```

4. If the `uUseLambert` uniform is `false`, then `lambertTerm` remains as `1.0`, not affecting the final diffuse term here:

```
Id = uLightDiffuse * uMaterialDiffuse * lambertTerm;
```

5. Otherwise, `Id` will have the Lambert coefficient factored in.

6. Having **Lambert** disabled, click on the **Per Vertex** button. Rotate the cube to see how ESSL interpolates the vertex colors. The vertex shader key code fragment that allows us to switch from a constant diffuse color to per-vertex colors uses the `uUseVertexColors` Boolean uniform and the `aVertexColor` attribute. This fragment is shown here:

```
if (uUseVertexColor) {
   Id = uLightDiffuse * aVertexColor * lambertTerm;
}
else {
   Id = uLightDiffuse * uMaterialDiffuse * lambertTerm;
}
```

7. Take a look at the `common/models/geometries/cube-simple.json` file. There, the eight vertices of the cube are defined in the vertices array and there is an element in the scalars array for every vertex. As you may expect, each one of these elements corresponds to a respective vertex color, as shown in the following diagram:

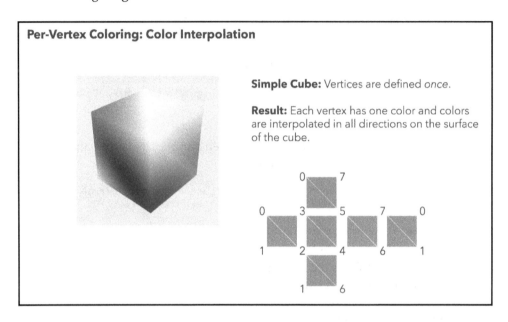

Per-Vertex Coloring: Color Interpolation

Simple Cube: Vertices are defined *once.*

Result: Each vertex has one color and colors are interpolated in all directions on the surface of the cube.

8. Make sure that the **Lambert** button is not active and then click on the **Complex Cube** button. By repeating vertices in the vertex array in the corresponding JSON file, `common/models/geometries/cube-complex.json`, we can achieve independent face-coloring. The following diagram explains how the vertices are organized in `cube-complex.json`. Note that as the definition of colors occurs by vertex (since we are using the shader attribute), we need to repeat each color four times, because each face has four vertices. This idea is depicted in the following diagram:

Per-Vertex Coloring: Color Interpolation

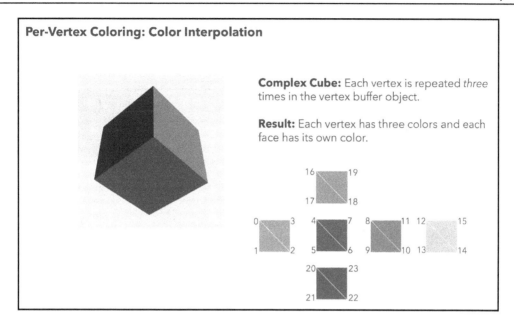

Complex Cube: Each vertex is repeated *three* times in the vertex buffer object.

Result: Each vertex has three colors and each face has its own color.

9. Activate the **Lambert** button to see how the Lambert coefficient affects the color of the object. Try different button configurations to see what happens.

10. Let's quickly explore the effect of changing the alpha channel to a value less than `1.0`. What do you see? Notice that the object does not become transparent but instead starts losing its color. To obtain transparency, we need to activate blending. We will discuss blending in depth later in this chapter. For now, uncomment these lines in the `configure` function, in the source code:

```
// gl.disable(gl.DEPTH_TEST);
// gl.enable(gl.BLEND);
// gl.blendFunc(gl.SRC_ALPHA, gl.ONE_MINUS_SRC_ALPHA);
```

11. Save the page and reload it in your internet browser. If you select **Per-Vertex, Complex Cube** and reduce the alpha value to 0.5, you will see something like the following screenshot:

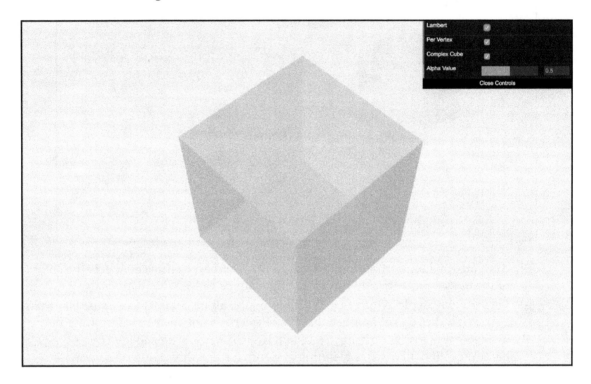

What just happened?

We have studied two different ways of coloring objects: **constant coloring** and **per-vertex coloring**. In both cases, the final color of each fragment is assigned by exporting a color variable via an `out` qualifier in the fragment shader.

We saw that by activating the calculation of the Lambert coefficient, we obtain sensory depth information.

We also saw that repeating vertices in our object allows us to obtain different coloring effects. For instance, we can color an object by faces instead of by vertices.

Use of Color in Lights

Colors are light properties. In Chapter 3, *Lights*, we learned that the number of light properties depends on the lighting-reflection model selected for a scene. For instance, using a Lambertian reflection model, we would only need to model one shader uniform: the light diffuse property/color. In contrast, if the Phong reflection model were selected, each light source would need to have three properties: the ambient, diffuse, and specular colors.

Positional Lights

The light position is usually modeled as a uniform when the shader needs to know the position of the light. Therefore, a Phong model with a positional light would have four uniforms: ambient, diffuse, specular, and position.

For directional lights, the fourth uniform is the light direction. For more information, refer to Chapter 3, *Lights*.

We have seen that each light property is represented by a JavaScript four-element array with mappings to vec4 uniforms in the shaders.

As a quick reminder, which WebGL methods should we use to retrieve and set a uniform? In our case, the two methods we use to pass lights to the shaders are as follows:

- getUniformLocation: Locates the uniform in the program and returns an index we can use to set the value.
- uniform4fv: Since the light components are RGBA, we need to pass a four-element float vector.

Scalability Problem

Given the desire to use more than one light in our scene, we need to define and map the number of appropriate uniforms of the lighting model of choice. If we have four properties per light (ambient, diffuse, specular, and location), we need to define four uniforms for each light. If we want to have three lights, we need to write, use, and map twelve uniforms! We need to resolve this complexity before it gets out of hand.

How Many Uniforms Can We Use?

The OpenGL Shading Language ES specification delineates the number of uniforms that we are allowed to use.

Section 4.3.4 Uniforms

There is an implementation dependent limit on the amount of storage for uniforms that can be used for each type of shader. If this is exceeded, it will cause a compile-time or link-time error.

To find out the limit for your WebGL implementation, you can query WebGL using the `gl.getParameter` function with these constants:

```
gl.MAX_VERTEX_UNIFORM_VECTORS
gl.MAX_FRAGMENT_UNIFORM_VECTORS
```

The implementation limit is given by your browser and heavily depends on your graphics hardware. That said, even though your machine may have enough variable space, it does not necessarily mean that the problem is solved. We still have to define and map each of the uniforms and that can often lead to brittle and verbose code, as we will see in a later exercise.

Simplifying the Problem

In order to simplify the problem, we can assume that the ambient component is the same for all of the lights. This will reduce the number of uniforms—one fewer uniform for each light. However, this is not an extensible solution for more general cases where we cannot assume that the ambient light is constant.

Before we start diving deeper into our scene with multiple lights, let's update our architecture to cover some of the concepts we've addressed.

Architectural Updates

As we progress through this book, we continue to refine our architecture where appropriate to reflect what we've learned. On this occasion, we will improve how we pass uniforms to our program and add support for handling a large number of uniforms to define multiple lights.

Adding Support for Light Objects

Let's cover these changes in detail. We have created a new JavaScript module, `Lights.js`, that has two objects:

- `Light`: Aggregates light properties (position, diffuse, specular, and so on) in a single entity.
- `LightsManager`: Contains the lights in our scene. This allows us to retrieve each light by `index` or `name`.

`LightsManager` also contains the `getArray` method to flatten the arrays of properties by type:

```
getArray(type) {
  return this.list.reduce((result, light) => {
    result = result.concat(light[type]);
    return result;
  }, []);
}
```

This will be useful when we use uniform arrays later on.

Improving How We Pass Uniforms to the Program

We have also improved the way we pass uniforms to the program. In `configure`, we can see how we pass attributes and uniforms to `program.load` rather than manually attaching them to the instance like in the introductory chapters.

The `configure` function is the appropriate place to load the program. We are also going to create a dynamic mapping between JavaScript variables and uniforms. With this in mind, we have updated the `program.load` method to receive two arrays:

- `attributes`: An array containing the names of the attributes that we will map between JavaScript and ESSL.
- `uniforms`: An array containing the names of the uniforms that we will map between JavaScript and ESSL.

The implementation of the function now looks as follows:

```
// Load up the given attributes and uniforms from the given values
load(attributes, uniforms) {
  this.useProgram();
  this.setAttributeLocations(attributes);
```

```
    this.setUniformLocations(uniforms);
  }
```

The last two lines correspond to the two new functions, `setAttributeLocations` and `setUniformLocations`:

```
  // Set references to attributes onto the program instance
  setAttributeLocations(attributes) {
    attributes.forEach(attribute => {
      this[attribute] = this.gl.getAttribLocation(this.program, attribute);
    });
  }

  // Set references to uniforms onto the program instance
  setUniformLocations(uniforms) {
    uniforms.forEach(uniform => {
      this[uniform] = this.gl.getUniformLocation(this.program, uniform);
    });
  }
```

As you can see, these functions look up the attribute and uniform lists, respectively, and then attach the location as a property to the `Program` instance.

In short, if we include the `uLightPosition` uniform name in the `uniforms` list to be passed to `program.load`, we will then have a `program.uLightPosition` property that will contain the location of the respective uniform! Neat!

Once we load the program in the `configure` function, we can initialize the values of the uniforms immediately with the following:

```
  gl.uniform3fv(program.uLightPosition, value);
```

Time for Action: Adding a Blue Light to a Scene

We're ready to take a look at the first example in this chapter. We will work on a scene with **per-fragment** lighting that has three light sources.

Each light has a position and a diffuse color property. This means we have two uniforms per light. Perform the following steps:

1. To keep things simple, we have assumed that the ambient color is the same for all three light sources. We have also removed the specular property. Open the ch06_02_wall_initial.html file in your browser.

2. You will see a scene such as the one displayed in the following screenshot where two lights (red and green) illuminate a black wall:

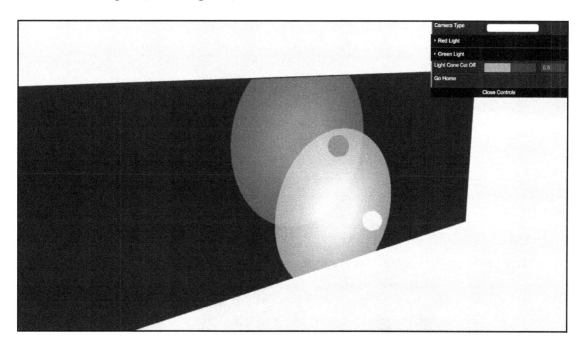

3. Open the ch06_02_wall-initial.html file using your code editor. We will update the vertex shader, the fragment shader, the JavaScript code, and the HTML code to add the blue light.

4. **Updating the vertex shader**: Go to the vertex shader where you can see these two uniforms:

```
uniform vec3 uPositionRedLight;
uniform vec3 uPositionGreenLight;
```

5. Let's add the third uniform here:

```
uniform vec3 uPositionBlueLight;
```

6. We also need to define a varying to carry the interpolated light ray direction to the fragment shader. Remember here that we are using per-fragment lighting. Check where the varyings are defined:

```
out vec3 vRedRay;
out vec3 vGreenRay;
```

7. And, add the third varying there:

```
out vec3 vBlueRay;
```

8. Let's take a look at the body of the vertex shader. We need to update each of the light locations according to our position in the scene. We achieve this by writing the following:

```
vec4 blueLightPosition = uModelViewMatrix *
vec4(uPositionBlueLight, 1.0);
```

9. Notice that the positions for the other two lights are also being calculated.

10. Let's calculate the light ray for the updated position from our blue light to the current vertex. We do that by writing the following code:

```
vBlueRay = vertex.xyz - blueLightPosition.xyz;
```

11. That is all we need to modify in the vertex shader.

12. So far, we've included a new light position and we have calculated the light rays in the vertex shader. These rays will be interpolated by the fragment shader.

13. Let's work out how the colors on the wall will change by including our new blue source of light. Scroll down to the fragment shader and add a new uniform—the blue diffuse property. Look for these uniforms declared right before the main function:

```
uniform vec4 uDiffuseRedLight;
uniform vec4 uDiffuseGreenLight;
```

14. Insert the following line of code:

```
uniform vec4 uDiffuseBlueLight;
```

15. To calculate the contribution of the blue light to the final color, we need to obtain the light ray we defined previously in the vertex shader. This varying is available in the fragment shader. You also need to declare it before the `main` function. Look for the following:

```
in vec3 vRedRay;
in vec3 vGreenRay;
```

16. Insert the following code right under it:

```
in vec3 vBlueRay;
```

17. It is assumed that the ambient component is the same for all the lights. This is reflected in the code by having only one `uLightAmbient` variable. The ambient term, `Ia`, is the product of `uLightAmbient` and the wall's material ambient property:

```
// ambient Term
vec4 Ia = uLightAmbient * uMaterialAmbient;
```

18. If `uLightAmbient` is set to (`1.0, 1.0, 1.0, 1.0`) and `uMaterialAmbient` is set to (`0.1, 0.1, 0.1, 1.0`), then the resulting ambient term, `Ia`, will be really small. This means the contribution of the ambient light will be low in this scene. In contrast, the diffuse component will be different for every light.

19. Let's add the effect of the blue diffuse term. In the fragment shader main function, look for the following code:

```
// diffuse Term
vec4 Id1 = vec4(0.0, 0.0, 0.0, 1.0);
vec4 Id2 = vec4(0.0, 0.0, 0.0, 1.0);
```

20. Add the following line immediately under it:

```
vec4 Id3 = vec4(0.0, 0.0, 0.0, 1.0);
```

21. Scroll down to the following:

```
float lambertTermOne = dot(N, -normalize(vRedRay));
float lambertTermTwo = dot(N, -normalize(vGreenRay));
```

22. Add the following line of code right under it:

```
float lambertTermThree = dot(N, -normalize(vBlueRay));
```

23. Scroll to the following:

```
if (lambertTermOne > uCutOff) {
  Id1 = uDiffuseRedLight * uMaterialDiffuse * lambertTermOne;
}

if (lambertTermTwo > uCutOff) {
  Id2 = uDiffuseGreenLight * uMaterialDiffuse * lambertTermTwo;
}
```

24. Insert the following code after it:

```
if (lambertTermThree > uCutOff) {
  Id3 = uDiffuseBlueLight * uMaterialDiffuse * lambertTermTwo;
}
```

25. Update `fragColor` so that it includes `Id3`:

```
fragColor = vec4(vec3(Ia + Id1 + Id2 + Id3), 1.0);
```

26. That's all we need to do in the fragment shader. Let's move on to our JavaScript code. So far, we have written the code that is needed to handle one more light inside our shaders. Let's see how we create the blue light from the JavaScript side and how we map it to the shaders. Scroll down to the `configure` function and look for the following code:

```
const redLight = new Light('redLight');
redLight.setPosition(redLightPosition);
redLight.setDiffuse([1, 0, 0, 1]);

const greenLight = new Light('greenLight');
greenLight.setPosition(greenLightPosition);
greenLight.setDiffuse([0, 1, 0, 1]);
```

27. Insert the following code:

```
const blue = new Light('blueLight');
blue.setPosition([-2.5, 3, 3]);
blue.setDiffuse([0.0, 0.0, 1.0, 1.0]);
```

28. Scroll to the point where the `uniforms` list is defined. As mentioned earlier, this new mechanism makes it easier to obtain locations for the uniforms. Add the two new uniforms that we are using for the blue light: `uDiffuseBlueLight` and `uPositionBlueLight`. The list should look like the following code:

```
const uniforms = [
    'uProjectionMatrix',
    'uModelViewMatrix',
    'uNormalMatrix',
    'uMaterialDiffuse',
    'uMaterialAmbient',
    'uLightAmbient',
    'uDiffuseRedLight',
    'uDiffuseGreenLight',
    'uDiffuseBlueLight',
    'uPositionRedLight',
    'uPositionGreenLight',
    'uPositionBlueLight',
    'uWireframe',
    'uLightSource',
    'uCutOff'
];
```

29. Let's pass the position and diffuse values of our newly defined light to `program`. Find the following lines, after the line that loads `program`, and make these necessary changes:

```
gl.uniform3fv(program.uPositionRedLight, redLight.position);
gl.uniform3fv(program.uPositionGreenLight, greenLight.position);
gl.uniform3fv(program.uPositionBlueLight, blueLight.position);

gl.uniform4fv(program.uDiffuseRedLight, redLight.diffuse);
gl.uniform4fv(program.uDiffuseGreenLight, greenLight.diffuse);
gl.uniform4fv(program.uDiffuseBlueLight, blueLight.diffuse);
```

Uniform Arrays

Coding one uniform per light makes the code quite verbose. Later on, we will cover how to simplify the code using uniform arrays.

30. Let's update the `load` function. We need a new sphere to represent the blue light, the same way we have two spheres in the scene: one for the red light and the other for the green light. Append the following line:

```
scene.load('/common/models/geometries/sphere3.json', 'blueLight');
```

31. As we saw in the `load` function, we are loading the same geometry (sphere) three times. To differentiate the sphere that represents the light source, we are using local transforms for the sphere (initially centered at the origin). Scroll to the `render` function and find the following lines of code:

```
const modelViewMatrix = transforms.modelViewMatrix;

if (object.alias === 'redLight') {
  mat4.translate(
    modelViewMatrix, modelViewMatrix,
    program.getUniform(program.uPositionRedLight)
  );
  object.diffuse = program.getUniform(program.uDiffuseRedLight);
  gl.uniform1i(program.uLightSource, true);
}

if (object.alias === 'greenLight') {
  mat4.translate(
    modelViewMatrix, modelViewMatrix,
    program.getUniform(program.uPositionGreenLight)
  );
  object.diffuse = program.getUniform(program.uDiffuseGreenLight);
  gl.uniform1i(program.uLightSource, true);
}
```

32. Add the following code:

```
if (object.alias === 'blueLight') {
  mat4.translate(
    modelViewMatrix, modelViewMatrix,
    program.getUniform(program.uPositionBlueLight)
  );
  object.diffuse = program.getUniform(program.uDiffuseBlueLight);
  gl.uniform1i(program.uLightSource, true);
}
```

33. That's it! Save the page with a different name and test it in your browser:

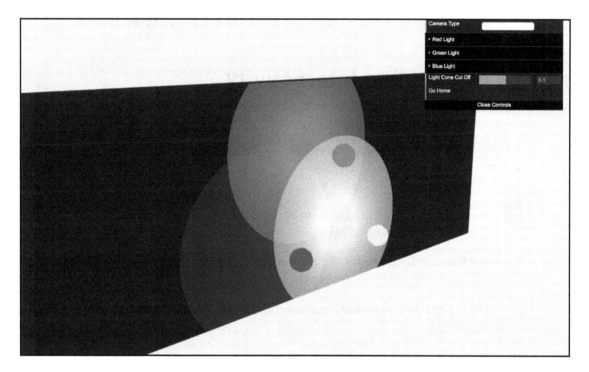

34. If you do not obtain the expected result, please go back and check the steps. You will find the completed exercise in the `ch06_03_wall-final.html` file.

What just happened?

We have modified our sample scene by adding one more light: a blue light. We have updated the following:

- The vertex shader
- The fragment shader
- The `configure` function
- The `load` function
- The `draw` function

As you can see, handling light properties one uniform at a time is not very efficient. Later in this chapter, we will study a more effective way to handle lights in a WebGL scene.

Have a Go: Adding Interactivity

We are going to add an additional slider to our controls widget to interactively change the position of the blue light we just added.

We will use **dat.GUI**, one for each one of the blue light coordinates.

dat.GUI

You can find more information about dat.GUI on GitHub: `https://github.com/dataarts/dat.gui`.

1. Create three sliders: one for the X coordinate, one for the Y coordinate, and a third one for the Z coordinate for the blue light.

2. The final GUI should include the new blue light sliders, which should look like the following:

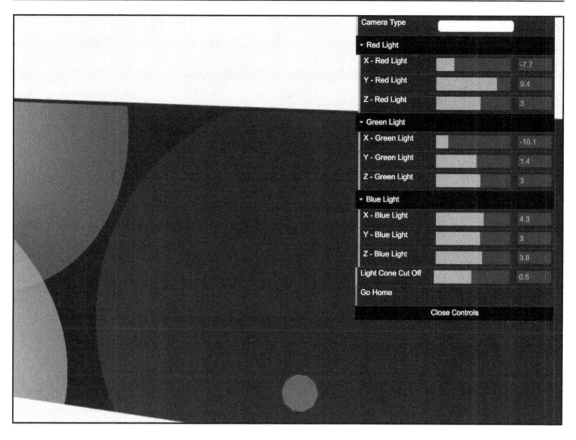

3. Use the sliders present in the page to guide your work.
4. You will find the completed exercise in the `ch06_03_wall-final.html` file.

Using Uniform Arrays to Handle Multiple Lights

As we've seen, handling light properties with individual uniforms makes the code verbose and difficult to maintain. Fortunately, ESSL provides several mechanisms we can use to solve the problem of handling multiple lights. One of them is **uniform arrays**.

This technique allows us to handle multiple lights by introducing enumerable arrays of vectors in the shaders. This allows us to calculate light contributions by iterating through the light arrays in the shaders. We still need to define each light in JavaScript, but the mapping to ESSL becomes simpler since we aren't defining one uniform per light property. Let's see how this technique works. We just need to make two simple changes in our code.

Uniform Array Declaration

First, we need to declare the light uniforms as arrays inside our ESSL shaders. For example, the light position that contains three lights would look like this:

```
uniform vec3 uPositionLight[3];
```

It's important to note that ESSL does not support dynamic initialization of uniform arrays. We could try something such as this:

```
uniform int numLights;
uniform vec3 uPositionLight[numLights]; // will not work
```

If so, the shader will not compile, and you will obtain the following error:

```
ERROR: 0:12 — constant expression required
ERROR: 0:12 — array size must be a constant integer expression
```

However, this construct is valid:

```
const int numLights = 3;
uniform vec3 uPositionLight[numLights]; // will work
```

We declare one uniform array per light property, regardless of how many lights we're going to have. As a result, if we want to pass information about diffuse and specular components of five lights, for example, we need to declare two uniform arrays, as follows:

```
uniform vec4 uDiffuseLight[5];
uniform vec4 uSpecularLight[5];
```

JavaScript Array Mapping

Next, we need to map the JavaScript variables where we have the light property information to the program. For example, we may want to map these three light positions:

```
const lightPosition1 = [0, 7, 3];
const lightPosition2 = [2.5, 3, 3];
const lightPosition3 = [-2.5, 3, 3];
```

If so, we need to retrieve the uniform array location (just like in any other case):

```
const location = gl.getUniformLocation(program, 'uPositionLight');
```

The one difference is that we map these positions as a concatenated flat array:

```
gl.uniform3fv(location, [0, 7, 3, 2.5, 3, 3, -2.5, 3, 3]);
```

There are two important points here:

- The name of the uniform that is passed to `getUniformLocation` is the same as before. The fact that `uPositionLight` is now an array does not change a thing when you locate the uniform with `getUniformLocation`.
- The JavaScript array that we are passing to the uniform is a flat array. If you write something as follows, the mapping will not work:

```
gl.uniform3fv(location, [
  [0, 7, 3],
  [2.5, 3, 3],
  [-2.5, 3, 3]
]);
```

So, if you have one variable per light, you should ensure that you concatenate them before passing them to the shader.

Time for Action: Adding a White Light to a Scene

Let's cover an example of how we'd add a new light to our scene:

1. Open the `ch06_04_wall-light-arrays.html` file in your browser. This scene looks exactly like `ch06_03_wall-final.html`; however, the code is far less complex since we are now using uniform arrays. Let's see how using uniform arrays changes our code.

2. Open the `ch06_04_wall-light-arrays.html` file in your code editor. Let's take a look at the vertex shader. Note the use of the constant integer expression const int, `numLights = 3;`, to declare the number of lights that the shader will handle.

3. There, you can also see that a uniform array is being used to operate on light positions. Note that we are using a varying array to pass the light rays (for each light) to the fragment shader:

```
for(int i = 0; i < numLights; i++) {
  vec4 lightPosition = uModelViewMatrix * vec4(uLightPosition[i],
   1.0);
  vLightRay[i] = vertex.xyz - lightPosition.xyz;
}
```

4. This fragment of code calculates one varying light ray per light. Recall that the same code in the `ch06_03_wall-final.html` file looks like the following code:

```
vec4 redLightPosition = uModelViewMatrix * vec4(uPositionRedLight,
 1.0);
vec4 greenLightPosition = uModelViewMatrix *
 vec4(uPositionGreenLight, 1.0);
vec4 blueLightPosition = uModelViewMatrix *
 vec4(uPositionBlueLight, 1.0);

vRedRay = vertex.xyz - redLightPosition.xyz;
vGreenRay = vertex.xyz - greenLightPosition.xyz;
vBlueRay = vertex.xyz - blueLightPosition.xyz;
```

5. Once you compare these two snippets, the advantage of using uniform arrays (and varying arrays) should be clear.

6. The fragment shader also uses uniform arrays. In this case, the fragment shader iterates through the light diffuse properties to calculate the contribution of each one to the final color on the wall:

```
for(int i = 0; i < numLights; i++) {
  L = normalize(vLightRay[i]);
  lambertTerm = dot(N, -L);
  if (lambertTerm > uCutOff) {
    finalColor += uLightDiffuse[i] * uMaterialDiffuse *
lambertTerm;
  }
}
```

7. For the sake of brevity, we won't cover the verbose version from the `ch06_03_wall-final.html` exercise, but you should check it out for yourself and compare it with this one.

8. In the `configure` function, the size of the JavaScript array containing the uniform names has decreased considerably by omitting the other unnecessary light attributes:

```
const uniforms = [
  'uPerspectiveMatrix',
  'uModelViewMatrix',
  'uNormalMatrix',
  'uMaterialDiffuse',
  'uMaterialAmbient',
  'uLightAmbient',
  'uLightDiffuse',
  'uLightPosition',
  'uWireframe',
  'uLightSource',
  'uCutOff'
];
```

9. The mapping between JavaScript lights and uniform arrays is now simpler because of the `getArray` method from the `LightsManager` class. As we described earlier, the `getArray` method concatenates the lights' data into one flat array.

10. The `load` and `render` functions look exactly the same. If we want to add a new light, we still need to load a new sphere with the `load` function (to represent the light source in our scene), and we still need to translate the sphere to the appropriate location in the `render` function.

11. Let's see how much effort we need to add a new light. Go to the `configure` function and create a new light object, as follows:

```
const whiteLight = new Light('whiteLight');
whiteLight.setPosition([0, 10, 2]);
whiteLight.setDiffuse([1.0, 1.0, 1.0, 1.0]);
```

12. Add `whiteLight` to the `lights` instance:

```
lights.add(whiteLight);
```

13. Move to the `load` function and append this line:

```
scene.load('/common/models/geometries/sphere3.json', 'whiteLight');
```

14. Just like in the previous *Time for Action* section, add this to the `render` function:

```
if (object.alias === 'whiteLight') {
  const whiteLight = lights.get(object.alias);
  mat4.translate(modelViewMatrix, modelViewMatrix,
    whiteLight.position);
  object.diffuse = whiteLight.diffuse;
  gl.uniform1i(program.uLightSource, true);
}
```

15. Save the webpage with a different name and open it using your browser. We have also included the completed exercise in `ch06_05_wall-light-arrays-final.html`, including some minor improvements on keeping the light configuration more declarative. The following diagram shows the final result:

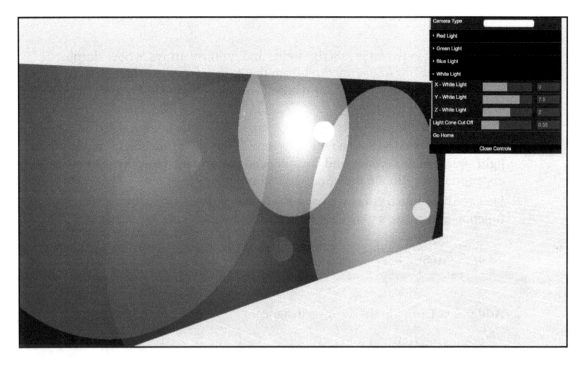

That's all you need to do! If you want to control the white light properties with the controls widget, you would need to write the corresponding code.

Time for Action: Directional Point Lights

In Chapter 3, *Lights*, we compared directional and positional lights:

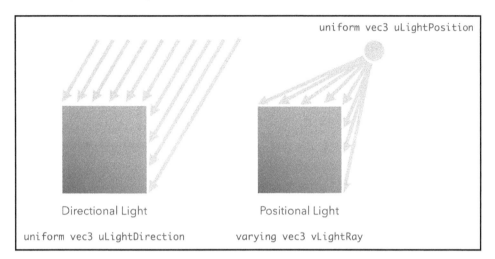

In point lighting, for every point on the surface of our object, we compute the direction from the light to that point on the surface. We then do the same thing we did for directional lighting. Remember that we took the dot product of the surface normal (the direction the surface is facing) and the light direction. This gave us a value of 1 if the two directions matched, which means the fragment should be fully lit, 0 if the two directions were perpendicular, and −1 if they were opposite. We directly used that value to multiply the color of the surface, which gave us lighting.

In this section, we will combine directional and positional lights. We are going to create a third type of light: a **directional point light**, commonly referred to as a **spot light**. This light has both positional and directional properties. We are ready to do this since our shaders can easily handle lights with multiple properties:

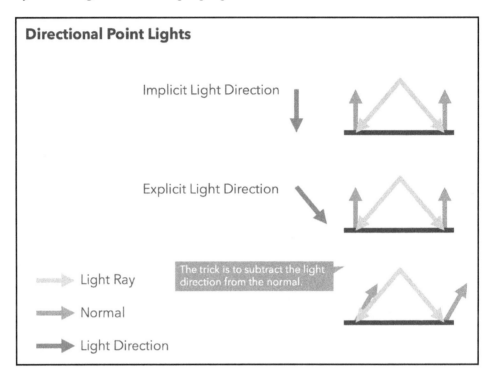

The trick to creating these lights is to subtract the light-direction vector from the normal for each vertex. The resulting vector will create a different Lambert coefficient that will reflect into the cone generated by the light source:

1. Open ch06_06_wall-spot-light.html in your browser. As you can see, the three light sources now have a direction:

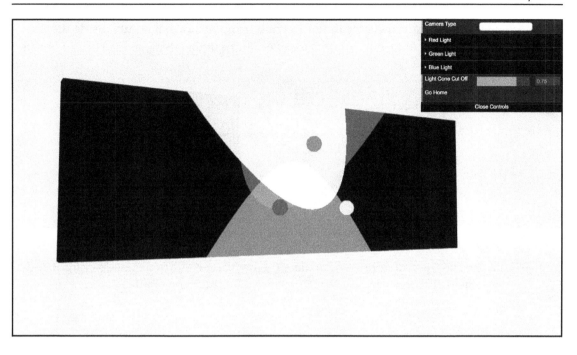

2. Open `ch06_06_wall-spot-light.html` in your source code editor.

3. To create a light cone, we need to obtain one Lambert coefficient per fragment. As we did in previous examples, we obtain these coefficients in the fragment shader by calculating the dot product between the inverted light ray and the normal that has been interpolated. Thus far, we have been using one varying to do this: `vNormal`.

4. So far, one varying has sufficed since we did not need to update the normals, regardless of how many lights we have in the scene. However, to create directional point lights, we do have to update the normals as the direction of each light will create a different normal. Therefore, we replace `vNormal` with a **varying array**:

```
out vec3 vNormal[numLights];
```

5. The line that subtracts the light direction from the normal occurs inside the `for` loop. This is because we do this for every light in the scene, as every light has its own light direction:

```
for(int i = 0; i < numLights; i++) {
  vec4 positionLight = uModelViewMatrix * vec4(uLightPosition[i],
  1.0);
  vec3 directionLight = vec3(uNormalMatrix *
  vec4(uLightDirection[i], 1.0));
  vNormal[i] = normal - directionLight;
  vLightRay[i] = vertex.xyz - positionLight.xyz;
}
```

6. Here, the light direction is transformed by the Normal matrix while the light position is transformed by the Model-View matrix.

7. In the fragment shader, we calculate the Lambert coefficients: one per light and fragment. The key difference is this line in the fragment shader:

```
N = normalize(vNormal[i]);
```

8. Here, we obtain the interpolated updated normal per light.

9. Let's create a cut-off by restricting the allowed Lambert coefficients. There are at least two different ways to obtain a light cone in the fragment shader. The first one consists of restricting the Lambert coefficient to be higher than the `uCutOff` uniform (cut-off value). Let's take a look at the fragment shader:

```
if (lambertTerm > uCutOff) {
  finalColor += uLightDiffuse[i] * uMaterialDiffuse;
}
```

10. The Lambert coefficient is the cosine of the angle between the reflected light and the surface normal. If the light ray is perpendicular to the surface, we obtain the highest Lambert coefficient, and as we move away from the center, the Lambert coefficients change following the cosine function until the light rays are completely parallel to the surface. This creates a cosine of 90 degrees between the normal and the light ray. This produces a Lambert coefficient of zero:

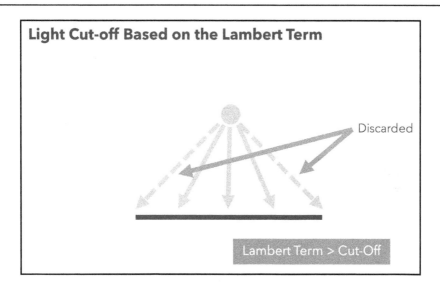

Light Cut-off Based on the Lambert Term

Discarded

Lambert Term > Cut-Off

11. Open `ch06_06_wall-spot-light.html` in your browser if you haven't done so yet. Use the cut-off slider on the page. Notice how this affects the light cone by making it wider or narrower. After playing with the slider, you'll probably notice that these lights don't look very realistic. The reason is that the final color is the same regardless of what Lambert coefficient you obtained: as long as the Lambert coefficient is higher than the set cut-off value, you will obtain the full diffuse contribution from the three light sources.

12. To refine the result, open the web page using your source code editor. Then, go to the fragment shader and multiply the Lambert coefficient in the line that calculates the final color:

```
finalColor += uLightDiffuse[i] * uMaterialDiffuse * lambertTerm;
```

13. Save the web page with a different name (so you can keep the original) and then load it in your web browser. You will notice that the light colors are attenuated as you depart from the center of each light reflection on the wall. This may look better, but there's a simpler way to create more realistic light cut-offs:

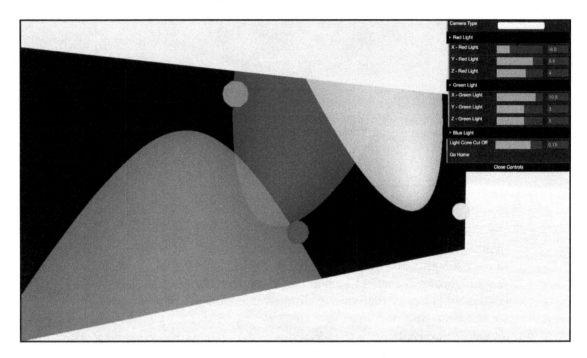

14. Let's create a cut-off by using an **exponential attenuation factor**. In the fragment shader, find the following code:

```
if (lambertTerm > uCutOff) {
    finalColor += uLightDiffuse[i] * uMaterialDiffuse * lambertTerm;
}
```

15. Replace it with the following:

```
finalColor += uLightDiffuse[i] * uMaterialDiffuse *
pow(lambertTerm, 10.0 * uCutOff);
```

16. Notice that we've removed the `if` condition. This time, the attenuation factor is `pow(lambertTerm, 10.0 * uCutOff);`.

17. This modification works as the factor attenuates the final color exponentially. If the Lambert coefficient is close to zero, the final color will be heavily attenuated:

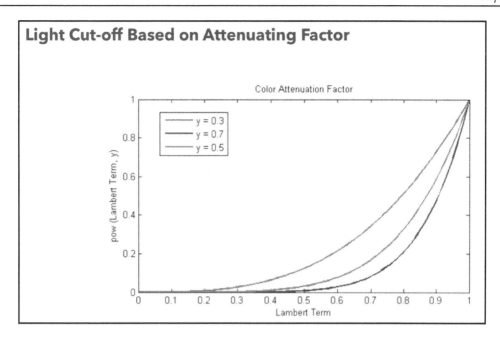

18. Save the web page with a different name and load it in your browser. The improvement is dramatic:

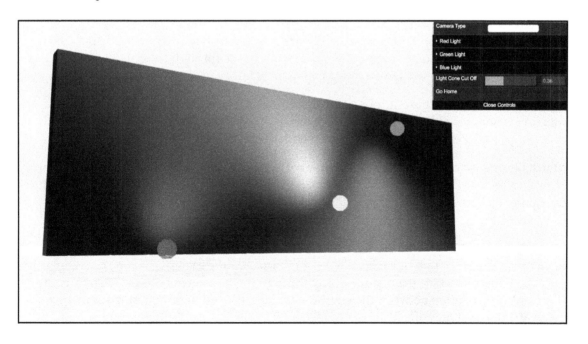

We've included the completed exercises here:

- `ch06_07_wall-spot-light-proportional.html`
- `ch06_08_wall-spot-light-exponential.html`

What just happened?

We've learned how to implement directional point lights. We have also discussed attenuation factors that improve lighting effects.

Use of Color in the Scene

It's time to discuss transparency and alpha blending. As mentioned before, the alpha channel can carry information about the opacity of the object color. However, as we saw in the cube example, it's not possible to obtain a translucent object unless alpha blending is activated. Things get a bit more complicated when we have several objects in the scene. To manage these difficulties, we need to learn what to do in order to have a consistent scene with translucent and opaque objects.

Transparency

The first approach to render transparent objects is to use **polygon stippling**. This technique consists of discarding some fragments so that you can see through the object. Think of this as punching little holes in the surface of your object.

OpenGL supports polygon stippling through the `glPolygonStipple` function. This function is not available in WebGL. You could try to replicate this functionality by dropping some fragments in the fragment shader using the ESSL discard command.

More commonly, we can use the alpha channel information to obtain translucent objects. However, as we've seen in the cube example, modifying the alpha values does not produce transparency automatically.

Creating transparency corresponds to altering the fragments that we've already written to the framebuffer. Think, for instance, of a scene where there is one translucent object in front of an opaque object (from our camera view). In order for the scene to be rendered correctly, we need to be able to see the opaque object through the translucent object. Therefore, the fragments that overlap between the far and near objects need to be combined somehow to create the transparency effect.

The same idea applies when there is only one translucent object in the scene. The only difference is that the far fragments correspond to the back face of the object and the near fragments correspond to the front face of the object. To produce the transparency effect in this case, the far and near fragments need to be combined.

To properly render transparent surfaces, we need to learn about two important WebGL concepts: **depth testing** and **alpha blending**.

Updated Rendering Pipeline

Depth testing and alpha blending are two optional stages for fragments once they've been processed by the fragment shader. If the depth test is not activated, all the fragments are automatically available for alpha blending. If the depth test is enabled, those fragments that fail the test will automatically be discarded by the pipeline and will no longer be available for any other operation. This means that discarded fragments will not be rendered. This behavior is similar to using the ESSL discard command.

The following diagram shows the order in which depth testing and alpha blending are performed:

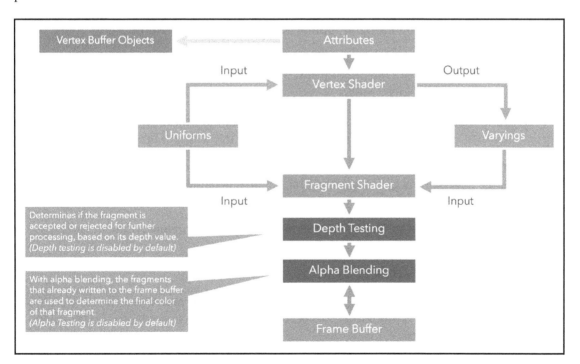

Now, let's see what depth testing is about and why it's relevant to alpha blending.

Depth Testing

Each fragment that has been processed by the fragment shader carries an associated depth value. Though fragments are two-dimensional since they're rendered on the screen, the depth value keeps the information of how far the fragment is from the camera (screen). Depth values are stored in a special WebGL buffer named **depth buffer** or **z-buffer**. The z comes from the fact that x and y values correspond to the screen coordinates of the fragment, while the z value measures distance perpendicular to the screen.

After the fragment has been calculated by the fragment shader, it becomes available for depth testing. This only occurs if the depth test is enabled. Assuming that gl is the JavaScript variable that contains our WebGL context, we can enable depth testing by writing the following:

```
gl.enable(gl.DEPTH_TEST);
```

The depth test takes the depth value of a fragment into consideration and compares it to the depth value for the same fragment coordinates already stored in the depth buffer. The depth test determines whether that fragment is accepted for further processing in the rendering pipeline.

Only the fragments that pass the depth test will be processed. Any fragment that does not pass the depth test will be discarded.

In normal circumstances, when the depth test is enabled, only those fragments with a lower depth value than the corresponding fragments present in the depth buffer will be accepted.

Depth testing is a commutative operation with respect to the rendering order. This means that no matter which object gets rendered first, as long as depth testing is enabled, we will always have a consistent scene.

Let's illustrate this with an example. The following diagram contains a cone and a sphere. The depth test is disabled using the following code:

```
gl.disable(gl.DEPTH_TEST);
```

The sphere is rendered first. As expected, the cone fragments that overlap the cone are not discarded when the cone is rendered. This occurs because there is no depth test between the overlapping fragments:

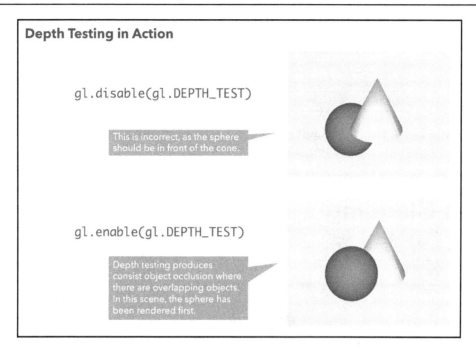

Now, let's enable the depth test and render the same scene. The sphere is rendered first. Since all the cone fragments that overlap the sphere have a higher depth value (they are farther from the camera), these fragments fail the depth test and are discarded, creating a consistent scene.

Depth Function

In some applications, we may be interested in changing the default behavior of depth testing, which discards fragments with a higher depth value than those fragments in the depth buffer. For that purpose, WebGL provides the `gl.depthFunc(function)` method.

This method has only one parameter, the `function` to use:

Parameter	Description
gl.NEVER	The depth test always fails.
gl.LESS	Only fragments with a depth lower than current fragments on the depth buffer will pass the test.
gl.LEQUAL	Fragments with a depth less than or equal to corresponding current fragments in the depth buffer will pass the test.
gl.EQUAL	Only fragments with the same depth as current fragments on the depth buffer will pass the test.

gl.NOTEQUAL	Only fragments that do not have the same depth value as fragments on the depth buffer will pass the test.
gl.GEQUAL	Fragments with greater or equal depth value will pass the test.
gl.GREATER	Only fragments with a greater depth value will pass the test.
gl.ALWAYS	The depth test always passes.

The depth test is disabled by default in WebGL. When enabled, if no depth function is set, the gl.LESS function is selected by default.

Alpha Blending

A fragment is available for alpha blending only if it has passed the depth test. By default, depth testing is disabled and makes all fragments available for alpha blending.

Alpha blending is enabled using the following line of code:

```
gl.enable(gl.BLEND);
```

For each available fragment, the alpha blending operation reads the color from the framebuffer by the appropriate fragment coordinates and creates a new color based on a linear interpolation between the previously calculated color in the fragment shader and the color from the framebuffer.

Alpha Blending

Alpha blending is disabled by default in WebGL.

The Blending Function

With blending enabled, the next step is to define a blending function. This function will determine how fragment colors from the object (source) are combined with the fragment colors present in the framebuffer (destination).

We combine source and destination colors as follows:

```
color = S * sW + D * dW;
```

More precisely:

- `S`: Source color (vec4)
- `D`: Destination color (vec4)
- `sW`: Source scaling factor
- `dW`: Destination scaling factor
- `S.rgb`: RGB components of the source color
- `S.a`: Alpha component of the source color
- `D.rgb`: RGB components of the destination color
- `D.a`: Alpha component of the destination color

It's important to note that the rendering order will determine the source and the destination fragments. Following the example from the previous section, if the sphere is rendered first, it will then become the destination of the blending operation because the sphere fragments are stored in the framebuffer at the time that the cone is rendered. In other words, alpha blending is a non-commutative operation with respect to rendering order:

Rendering Order in Blending Operations

Back to Front Order
The cone is rendered first.
The overlapping sphere fragments pass the depth test are available for blending.

Front to Back Order
The sphere is rendered first.
The overlapping cone fragments do not pass the depth test. Blending is not possible.

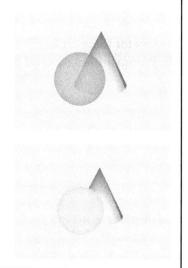

Separate Blending Functions

It is also possible to determine how the RGB channels are going to be combined independently from the alpha channels. For that, we use the `gl.blendFuncSeparate` function.

We define two independent functions this way:

```
color = S.rgb * sW.rgb + D.rgb * dW.rgb;
alpha = S.a * sW.a + D.a * dW.a;
```

More precisely:

- `sW.rgb`: Source scaling factor (only RGB)
- `dW.rgb`: Destination scaling factor (only RGB)
- `sW.a`: Source scaling factor for the source alpha value
- `dW.a`: Destination scaling factor for the destination alpha value

Then, we could have something such as the following:

```
color = S.rgb * S.a + D.rbg * (1.0 - S.a);
alpha = S.a * 1.0 + D.a * 0.0;
```

This would be translated into code as follows:

```
gl.blendFuncSeparate(gl.SRC_ALPHA, gl.ONE_MINUS_SRC_ALPHA, gl.ONE,
gl.ZERO);
```

The parameters for the `gl.blendFuncSeparate` function are the same as `gl.blendFunc`. You can find more information on these functions later in this section.

The Blend Equation

We could have a case where we do not want to interpolate the source and destination fragment colors with scale or add operations. For example, we may want to subtract one from the other. In this case, WebGL provides the `gl.blendEquation` function. This function receives one parameter that determines the operation on the scaled source and destination fragment colors. For example, `gl.blendEquation(gl.FUNC_ADD)` is calculated as such:

```
color = S * sW + D * dW;
```

And, `gl.blendEquation(gl.FUNC_SUBTRACT)` corresponds to the following:

```
color = S * sW - D  * dW;
```

There is a third option, `gl.blendEquation(gl.FUNC_REVERSE_SUBTRACT)`, that corresponds to the following:

```
color = D* dw - S * sW;
```

As expected, you can define the blending equation separately for the RGB channels and for the alpha channel. For that, we use the `gl.blendEquationSeparate` function.

The Blend Color

WebGL provides the `gl.CONSTANT_COLOR` and `gl.ONE_MINUS_CONSTANT_COLOR` scaling factors. These scaling factors can be used with `gl.blendFunc` and `gl.blendFuncSeparate`. However, we need to first establish the blend color. We do so by invoking `gl.blendColor`.

WebGL Alpha-Blending API

The following table summarizes the WebGL functions that are relevant to performing alpha-blending operations:

WebGL function	Description
`gl.enable|disable(gl.BLEND)`	Enable/disable blending.
`gl.blendFunc(sW, dW)`	Specify pixel arithmetic. Accepted values for `sW` and `dW` are as follows: • `ZERO` • `ONE` • `SRC_COLOR` • `DST_COLOR` • `SRC_ALPHA` • `DST_ALPHA` • `CONSTANT_COLOR` • `CONSTANT_ALPHA` • `ONE_MINUS_SRC_ALPHA` • `ONE_MINUS_DST_ALPHA` • `ONE_MINUS_SRC_COLOR` • `ONE_MINUS_DST_COLOR` • `ONE_MINUS_CONSTANT_COLOR` • `ONE_MINUS_CONSTANT_ALPHA` In addition, `sW` can also be `SRC_ALPHA_SATURATE`.
`gl.blendFuncSeparate(sW_rgb, dW_rgb, sW_a, dW_a)`	Specify pixel arithmetic for RGB and alpha components separately.
`gl.blendEquation(mode)`	Specify the equation used for both the RGB blend equation and the alpha blend equation. Accepted values for mode are as follows: • `gl.FUNC_ADD` • `gl.FUNC_SUBTRACT` • `gl.FUNC_REVERSE_SUBTRACT`
`gl.blendEquationSeparate(modeRGB, modeAlpha)`	Set the RGB blend equation and the alpha blend equation separately.
`gl.blendColor(red, green, blue, alpha)`	Set the blend color.

	Just like with other WebGL variables, it is possible to query blending parameters using `gl.getParameter`. Relevant parameters are as follows: • `gl.BLEND` • `gl.BLEND_COLOR` • `gl.BLEND_DST_RGB` • `gl.BLEND_SRC_RGB` • `gl.BLEND_DST_ALPHA` • `gl.BLEND_SRC_ALPHA` • `gl.BLEND_EQUATION_RGB` • `gl.BLEND_EQUATION_ALPHA`
`gl.getParameter(name)`	

Alpha Blending Modes

Depending on the parameter selection for `sW` and `dW`, we can create different blending modes. In this section, we will see how to create additive, subtractive, multiplicative, and interpolative blending modes. All blending modes are derived from the previous formula:

```
color = S * (sW) + D * dW;
```

The Blending Function

Additive blending simply adds the colors of the source and destination fragments, creating a lighter image. We obtain additive blending by writing the following:

```
gl.blendFunc(gl.ONE, gl.ONE);
```

This assigns the weights for source and destination fragments `sW` and `dW` to 1. The color output will be as follows:

```
color = S * 1.0 + D * 1.0;
color = S + D;
```

Since each color channel is in the `[0, 1]` range, blending will clamp all values over 1. When all channels are 1, this results in a white color.

Subtractive Blending

Similarly, we can obtain subtractive blending by writing the following:

```
gl.blendEquation(gl.FUNC_SUBTRACT);
gl.blendFunc(gl.ONE, gl.ONE);
```

This will change the blending equation to the following:

```
color = S * 1.0 - D * 1.0;
color = S - D;
```

All negative values will be set to 0. When all channels are negative, the result is black.

Multiplicative Blending

We obtain multiplicative blending by writing the following:

```
gl.blendFunc(gl.DST_COLOR, gl.ZERO);
```

This will be reflected in the blending equation as the following:

```
color = S * D + D * 0.0;
color = S * D;
```

The result will always be a darker blending.

Interpolative Blending

If we set sW to S.a and dW to $1 - S.a$, then we get the following:

```
color = S * S.a + D *(1 - S.a);
```

This will create a linear interpolation between the source and destination color using the source alpha color, S.a, as the scaling factor. In code, this is translated as the following:

```
gl.blendFunc(gl.SRC_ALPHA, gl.ONE_MINUS_SRC_ALPHA);
```

Interpolative blending allows us to create a transparency effect as long as the destination fragments have passed the depth test. As expected, this requires that the objects be rendered from back to front.

In the next section, we will play with different blending modes on a simple scene composed of a cone and sphere.

Time for Action: Blending Workbench

Let's cover an example of these various blending functions in action:

1. Open the ch06_09_blending.html file in your browser. You will see an interface like the one in the following screenshot:

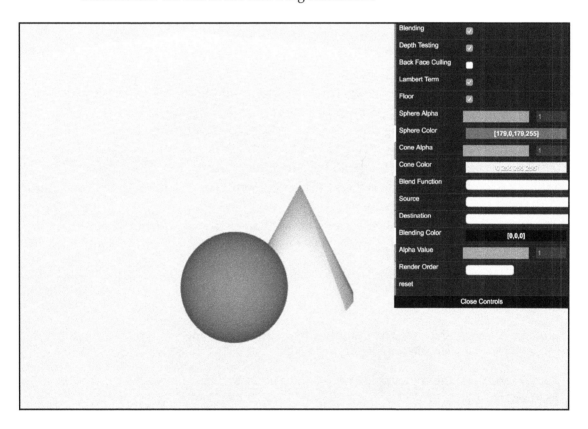

2. This interface has most of the parameters that allow you to configure alpha blending. The default settings are source gl.SRC_ALPHA and destination gl.ONE_MINUS_SRC_ALPHA. These are parameters for interpolative blending. Which slider do you need to use to change the scaling factor for interpolative blending? Why?

3. Change the sphere alpha slider to 0.5. You will see some shadow-like artifacts on the surface of the sphere. This occurs because the sphere back face is now visible. To get rid of the back face, click on **Back Face Culling**.

4. Click on the **Reset** button.

5. Disable the **Lambert Term** and **Floor** buttons.

6. Enable the **Back Face Culling** button.

7. Let's implement multiplicative blending. What values do source and destination need to have?

8. Click and drag the canvas. Check that the multiplicative blending creates dark regions where the objects overlap.

9. Change the blending function to gl.FUNC_SUBTRACT using the provided drop-down menu.

10. Change **Source** to gl.ONE and **Destination** to gl.ONE.

11. What blending mode is this? Click and drag the canvas to check the appearance of the overlapped regions.

12. Try different parameter configurations. Remember you can also change the blending function. If you decide to use a constant color or constant alpha, please use the color widget and the respective slider to modify the values of these parameters.

What just happened?

You have seen how the additive, multiplicative, subtractive, and interpolative blending modes work with a simple exercise.

You have seen that the combination of gl.SRC_ALPHA and gl.ONE_MINUS_SRC_ALPHA produces transparency.

Creating Transparent Objects

We've learned that in order to create transparency, we need to:

- Enable alpha blending and select the interpolative blending function
- Render the faces of objects back to front

How do we create transparent objects when there is nothing to blend them against? In other words, if there's only one object, how can we make it transparent? One solution is to use **face-culling**.

Face-culling allows us to *only* render the back or front face of an object. We used this technique in the previous section when we only rendered the front face by enabling the **Back Face Culling** button.

Let's use the color cube from earlier in this chapter. We are going to make it transparent. For that effect, we will perform the following:

1. Enable alpha blending and use the interpolative blending mode.
2. Enable face-culling.
3. Render the back face (by culling the front face).
4. Render the front face (by culling the back face).

Similar to other options in the pipeline, culling is disabled by default. We enable it by calling the following:

```
gl.enable(gl.FACE_CULLING);
```

To render only the back faces of an object, we call `gl.cullFace(gl.FRONT)` before we call `drawArrays` or `drawElements`.

Similarly, to render only the front face, we use `gl.cullFace(gl.BACK)` before the draw call.

The following diagram summarizes the steps needed to create a transparent object with alpha blending and face-culling:

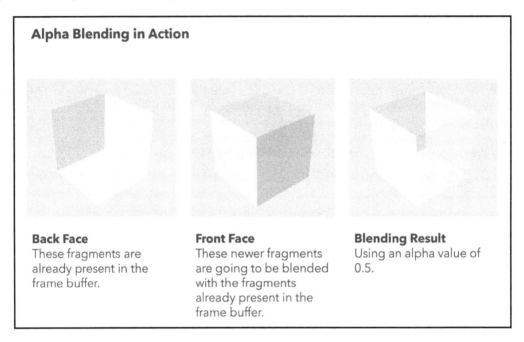

Alpha Blending in Action

Back Face
These fragments are already present in the frame buffer.

Front Face
These newer fragments are going to be blended with the fragments already present in the frame buffer.

Blending Result
Using an alpha value of 0.5.

In the following section, we will see the transparent cube in action and take a look at the code that makes it possible.

Time for Action: Culling

Let's cover an example showcasing culling in action:

1. Open the ch06_10_culling.html file in your browser.
2. You will see that the interface is similar to the blending workbench exercise. However, on the top row, you will see these three options:
   - **Alpha Blending**: Enables or disables alpha blending.
   - **Render Front Face**: If active, renders the front face.
   - **Render Back Face**: If active, renders the back face.

3. Remember that for blending to work, objects need to be rendered back to front. Therefore, the back face of the cube is rendered first. This is reflected in the `draw` function:

```
if (showBackFace) {
  gl.cullFace(gl.FRONT);
  gl.drawElements(gl.TRIANGLES, object.indices.length,
   gl.UNSIGNED_SHORT, 0);
}

if (showFrontFace) {
  gl.cullFace(gl.BACK);
  gl.drawElements(gl.TRIANGLES, object.indices.length,
   gl.UNSIGNED_SHORT, 0);
}
```

4. Going back to the web page, notice how the interpolative blending function produces the expected transparent effect. Move the alpha value slider that appears under the button options to adjust the scaling factor for interpolative blending.

5. Review the interpolative blending function. In this case, the destination is the back face (rendered first) and the source is the front face. If the alpha source equals `1`, what would you obtain according to the function? Test the result by moving the alpha slider to zero.

6. Let's visualize the back face only. For that, disable the **Render Front Face** button. Increase the alpha value using the alpha value slider. Your screen should look like this:

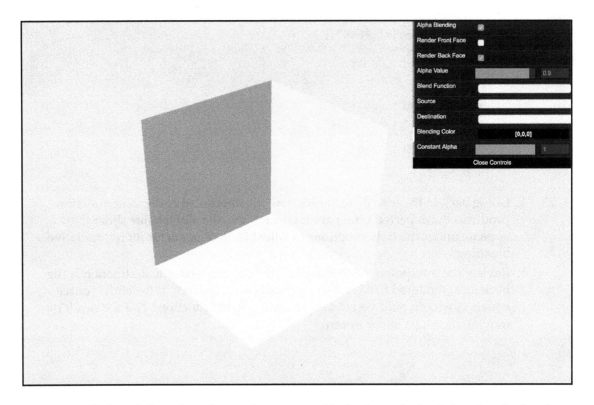

7. Click and drag the cube on the `canvas`. Notice how the back face is calculated every time you move the camera around.
8. Click on the **Render Front Face** again to activate it. Change the blending function so you can obtain subtractive blending.
9. Try different blending configurations using the controls provided in this exercise.

What just happened?

We have seen how face-culling and the alpha-blending interpolative mode can help us properly blend the faces of translucent objects.

Now, let's see how to implement transparency when there are two objects on the screen. In this case, we have a wall that we want to make transparent. Behind it is a cone.

Time for Action: Creating a Transparent Wall

Let's cover an example of how we'd make an object transparent:

1. Open `ch06_11_transparency-initial.html` in your browser. We have two completely opaque objects: a cone behind a wall. Click and drag the `canvas` to move the camera behind the wall and see the cone, as shown in the following screenshot:

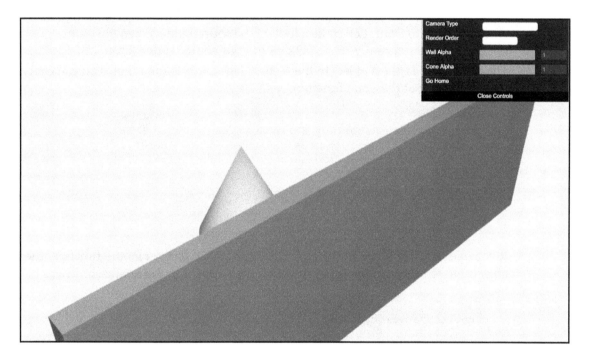

2. Change the wall alpha value by using the provided slider.
3. As you can see, modifying the alpha value does not produce any transparency. The reason for this is that alpha blending is not enabled. Let's edit the source code to include alpha blending. Open the `ch06_11_transparency-initial.html` file in your source code editor. Scroll to the `configure` function and find these lines:

```
gl.enable(gl.DEPTH_TEST);
gl.depthFunc(gl.LESS);
```

4. Below them, append the following lines:

```
gl.enable(gl.BLEND);
gl.blendFunc(gl.SRC_ALPHA, gl.ONE_MINUS_SRC_ALPHA);
```

5. Save your changes as `ch06_12_transparency-final.html` and load this page on your web browser.

6. As expected, the wall changes its transparency as you modify its alpha value using the respective slider.

7. Remember that in order for transparency to be effective, the objects need to be rendered back to front. Let's take a look at the source code. Open `ch06_12_transparency-final.html` in your source code editor.

8. The cone is the farthest object in the scene. Hence, it is loaded first. You can check that by looking at the `load` function:

```
function load() {
  scene.add(new Floor(80, 20));
  scene.load('/common/models/ch6/cone.json', 'cone');
  scene.load('/common/models/ch6/wall.json', 'wall', {
    diffuse: [0.5, 0.5, 0.2, 1.0],
    ambient: [0.2, 0.2, 0.2, 1.0]
  });
}
```

9. It occupies a lower index in the `scene.objects` list. In the `render` function, the objects are rendered in the order in which they appear in the `scene.objects` list:

```
scene.traverse(object => {
  // ...
});
```

10. What happens if we rotate the scene so that the cone is closer to the camera and the wall is farther away?

11. Open `ch06_12_transparency-final.html` in your browser and rotate the scene such that the cone appears in front of the wall. Decrease the alpha value of the cone while the alpha value of the wall remains at `1.0`.

12. As you can see, the blending is inconsistent. This does not have to do with alpha blending because in `ch06_12_transparency-final.html`, the blending is enabled. It has to do with the **rendering order**. Click on the **Wall First** button. The scene should appear consistent now:

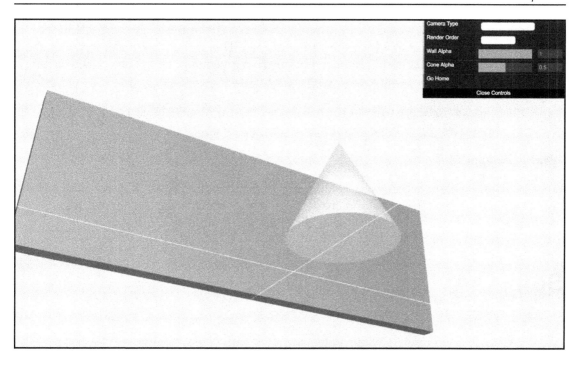

13. The **Cone First** and **Wall First** buttons use a couple of new functions that we have included in the `Scene` class to change the rendering order. These functions are `renderSooner` and `renderFirst`.

14. In total, we have added these functions to the `Scene` object to deal with rendering order:

    - `renderSooner(objectName)`: Moves the `objectName` object one position higher in the `Scene.objects` list.

    - `renderLater(objectName)`: Moves the `objectName` object one position lower in the `Scene.objects` list.

    - `renderFirst(objectName)`: Moves the `objectName` object to the first position of the list (index 0).

    - `renderLast(objectName)`: Moves the `objectName` object to the last position of the list.

- `renderOrder()`: Lists the objects in the `Scene.objects` list in the order in which they are rendered. This is the same order in which they are stored in the list. For any two given objects, the object with the lower index will be rendered first.

15. You can use these functions from the JavaScript console in your browser and see what effect these have on the scene.

What just happened?

We took a simple scene where we implemented alpha blending. After that, we analyzed the importance of the rendering order in creating consistent transparencies. Finally, we presented the new methods of the `Scene` object that control the rendering order.

Summary

Let's summarize what we learned in this chapter:

- We learned how to extensively use colors with objects, lights, and in the scene. Specifically, we've learned that an object can be colored per vertex, per fragment, or can have a constant color.
- We reviewed lights and the various approaches to lighting models.
- We covered how to create lights of different colors and leveraged concepts from directional and point lights to create spot lights. By introducing several light sources in our scene, we updated our architectural patterns and used uniform arrays to reduce the complexity of creating and mapping uniforms between JavaScript and ESSL.
- We learned that proper translucency requires more than just using alpha values in our color vectors. Because of this, we explored various blending behaviors, render sequences, and WebGL functions to create translucent objects.
- We learned how face-culling can help produce better results when there are multiple translucent objects present in the scene.

In the next chapter, we will learn how to leverage textures to help us render images in our scene.

7
Textures

In the previous chapter, we covered colors, multiple lights, and important concepts about depth and alpha testing for various blending techniques. So far, we've added details to our scene with geometry, vertex colors, and lighting; but often, that won't be enough to achieve the results we're looking for. Wouldn't it be great if we could "paint" additional details onto our scene without needing additional geometry? We can! This requires us to use a technique called texture mapping. In this chapter, we'll examine how we can use textures to make our scene more detailed.

In this chapter, you will do the following:

- Learn how to create a texture.
- Learn how to use a texture when rendering.
- Learn about filter and wrapping modes and how they affect the texture's use.
- Learn how to use multi-texturing.
- Learn about cube mapping.

What Is Texture Mapping?

Texture mapping is simply a method for adding detail to a geometry being rendered by displaying an image on the surface. Consider the following screenshot:

Using only the techniques we've learned so far, this relatively simple scene would be very difficult to build. The WebGL logo alone would have to be carefully constructed out of many triangle primitives. Although this is a possible approach, the additional geometry construction would be impractical for a marginally complex scene.

Fortunately, texture mapping makes such requirements incredibly simple. All that's required is an image in an appropriate file format, an additional vertex attribute on the mesh, and a few additions to our shader code.

Creating and Uploading a Texture

Unlike traditional native OpenGL applications, browsers load textures "upside down". As a result, many WebGL applications set textures to be loaded with the Y coordinate flipped. This is done with a single call:

```
gl.pixelStorei(gl.UNPACK_FLIP_Y_WEBGL, true);
```

Inverted Textures

Textures can either be manually flipped or flipped via WebGL. We will programmatically flip them with WebGL.

The process of creating a texture is similar to creating a vertex or an index buffer. We start by creating the texture object, as follows:

```
const texture = gl.createTexture();
```

Textures, like buffers, must be bound before we can manipulate them:

```
gl.bindTexture(gl.TEXTURE_2D, texture);
```

The first parameter indicates the type of texture we're binding, or the texture target. For now, we'll focus on 2D textures, indicated with gl.TEXTURE_2D. More targets will be introduced later in this chapter.

Once we've bound the texture, we can provide it with image data. The simplest way to do that is to pass a DOM image into the texImage2D function, as shown in the following code snippet:

```
const image = document.getElementById('texture-image');
gl.texImage2D(gl.TEXTURE_2D, 0, gl.RGBA, gl.RGBA, gl.UNSIGNED_BYTE, image);
```

In the previous snippet, we selected an image element from our page with the ID of texture-image as the source texture. This is **uploading** the texture, since the image will be stored in the GPU's memory for fast access during rendering. The source can be in any image format that can be displayed on a web page, such as JPEG, PNG, GIF, and BMP files.

The image source for the texture is passed in as the last parameter of the texImage2D call. When texImage2D is called with an image, WebGL will automatically determine the dimensions of the provided texture. The remainder of the parameters instruct WebGL about the type of information the image contains and how to store it. Most of the time, the only values you need to worry about changing are the third and fourth parameters, which can also be gl.RGB, to indicate that your texture has no alpha (transparency) channel.

In addition to the image, we also need to instruct WebGL on how to filter the texture when rendering. We'll get into what filtering means and what the different filtering modes do in a bit. In the meantime, let's use the simplest one to get us started:

```
gl.texParameteri(gl.TEXTURE_2D, gl.TEXTURE_MAG_FILTER, gl.NEAREST);
gl.texParameteri(gl.TEXTURE_2D, gl.TEXTURE_MIN_FILTER, gl.NEAREST);
```

Just as with buffers, it's good practice to unbind a texture when you are finished using it. You can do so by binding `null` as the active texture:

```
gl.bindTexture(gl.TEXTURE_2D, null);
```

Of course, in many cases, you won't want to have all of the textures for your scene embedded in your web page, so it's often more convenient to create the element in JavaScript and load it without adding it to the document. Putting all of this together gives us a simple function that will load any image URL that we provide as a texture:

```
const texture = gl.createTexture();

const image = new Image();

image.src = 'texture-file.png';

image.onload = () => {
  gl.bindTexture(gl.TEXTURE_2D, texture);
  gl.texImage2D(gl.TEXTURE_2D, 0, gl.RGBA, gl.RGBA, gl.UNSIGNED_BYTE,
    image);
  gl.texParameteri(gl.TEXTURE_2D, gl.TEXTURE_MAG_FILTER, gl.NEAREST);
  gl.texParameteri(gl.TEXTURE_2D, gl.TEXTURE_MIN_FILTER, gl.NEAREST);
  gl.bindTexture(gl.TEXTURE_2D, null);
};
```

Asynchronous Loading

There is a slight gotcha when loading images this way. The image loading is **asynchronous**, which means that your program won't stop and wait for the image to finish loading before continuing execution. So what happens if you try to use a texture before it's been populated with image data? Your scene will still render, but any texture values you sample will be black.

In short, creating textures follows the same pattern as using buffers. For every texture we create, we want to do the following:

1. Create a new texture
2. Bind it to make it the current texture
3. Pass the texture contents, typically from an image
4. Set the filter mode or other texture parameters
5. Unbind the texture

If we reach a point where we no longer need a texture, we can remove it and free up the associated memory by using `deleteTexture`:

```
gl.deleteTexture(texture);
```

After this, the texture is no longer valid. Any attempt to use it will react as though `null` has been passed.

Using Texture Coordinates

Before we apply our texture to our surface, we need to figure out which part of the texture maps onto which part of the surface. We do this through another vertex attribute known as **texture coordinates**.

Texture coordinates are two-element float vectors that describe a location on the texture that coincides with that vertex. You may think that it would be most natural to have this vector be an actual pixel location on the image; instead, WebGL forces all of the texture coordinates into a `0` to `1` range, where `(0, 0)` represents the top left-hand side corner of the texture and `(1, 1)` represents the bottom right-hand side corner, as shown in the following image:

This means that, in order to map a vertex to the center of any texture, you would give it a texture coordinate of `(0.5, 0.5)`. This coordinate system holds true even for rectangular textures.

This may seem strange at first; after all, it's easier to determine the pixel coordinates of a particular point than the percentage of an image's height and width of the point's location. That said, there is a benefit to the coordinate system that WebGL uses.

For example, we could build a WebGL application comprised of high resolution textures. Then, at some later point, we will receive feedback that the textures are taking too long to load or the application is causing devices to render slowly. As a result, we may decide to offer a lower resolution texture option for these situations.

If your texture coordinates were defined in terms of pixels, you would now have to modify every mesh used by your application to ensure that the texture coordinates match up to the new, smaller textures correctly. However, when using WebGL's normalized 0 to 1 coordinate range, the smaller textures can use the exact same coordinates as the larger ones and still display correctly.

Figuring out texture coordinates for your mesh is often a tricky part of creating 3D resources, especially with complex meshes.

Polygon Mesh

A polygon **mesh** is a collection of vertices, edges, and faces that defines the shape of a polyhedral object in 3D computer graphics and solid modeling.

Fortunately, most 3D modeling tools come with excellent utilities for laying out textures and generating texture coordinates—this process is called **unwrapping**.

Texture Coordinates

Just as vertex position components are commonly represented with (x, y, z), texture coordinates also have a common symbolic representation. Unfortunately, it's not consistent across all 3D software applications. OpenGL and WebGL refer to these coordinates as s and t for the x and y components, respectively. However, DirectX and many popular modeling packages refer to them as u and v. As a result, you'll often see people referring to texture coordinates as "UVs" and unwrapping as "UV Mapping."

To be consistent with WebGL's usage, we will use st for the remainder of this book.

Using Textures in a Shader

Texture coordinates are exposed to the shader code in the same way that they are with any other vertex attribute. We'll want to include a two-element vector attribute in our vertex shader that will map to our texture coordinates:

```
in vec2 aVertexTextureCoords;
```

Additionally, we will also want to add a new uniform to the fragment shader that uses a type we haven't seen before: `sampler2D`. The `sampler2D` uniform is what allows us to access the texture data in the shader:

```
uniform sampler2D uSampler;
```

In the past, when we've used uniforms, we set them to the value that we want them to be in the shader, such as a light color. **Samplers** work a bit differently. The following code shows how to associate a texture with a specific sampler uniform:

```
gl.activeTexture(gl.TEXTURE0);
gl.bindTexture(gl.TEXTURE_2D, texture);
gl.uniform1i(program.uSampler, 0);
```

So, what's going on here? First off, we are changing the active texture index with `gl.activeTexture`. WebGL supports the use of multiple textures at once (which we'll talk about later in this chapter), so it's good practice to specify which texture index we're working with, even though it won't change for the duration of this program. Next, we bind the texture we wish to use, which associates it with the currently active texture, `TEXTURE0`. Finally, we tell the sampler uniform which texture it should be associated with given the texture unit provided via `gl.uniform1i`. Here, we give it `0` to indicate that the sampler should use `TEXTURE0`.

We are now ready to use our texture in the fragment shader! The simplest way to use a texture is to return its value as the fragment color, as shown here:

```
texture(uSampler, vTextureCoord);
```

`texture` takes in the sampler uniform we wish to query and the coordinates to lookup, and returns the color of the texture image at those coordinates as `vec4`. If the image has no alpha channel, `vec4` will still be returned with the alpha component always set to `1`.

Time for Action: Texturing the Cube

Let's cover an example where we add a texture map to a cube:

1. Open the `ch07_01_textured-cube.html` file in your editor. If you open it in a browser, you should see a scene that looks like the following screenshot:

2. Let's load the texture image. At the top of the script block, add a new variable to hold the texture:

```
let texture;
```

3. At the bottom of the `configure` function, add the following code, which creates the texture object, loads an image, and sets the image as the texture data. In this case, we'll use a PNG image with the WebGL logo as our texture:

```
texture = gl.createTexture();

const image = new Image();

image.src = '/common/images/webgl.png';

image.onload = () => {
  gl.bindTexture(gl.TEXTURE_2D, texture);
  gl.texImage2D(gl.TEXTURE_2D, 0, gl.RGBA, gl.RGBA,
   gl.UNSIGNED_BYTE, image);
  gl.texParameteri(gl.TEXTURE_2D, gl.TEXTURE_MAG_FILTER,
   gl.NEAREST);
  gl.texParameteri(gl.TEXTURE_2D, gl.TEXTURE_MIN_FILTER,
   gl.NEAREST);
  gl.bindTexture(gl.TEXTURE_2D, null);
};
```

4. In the `render` function after the `vertexColors` binding block, add the following code to bind the texture to the shader sampler uniform:

```
if (object.textureCoords) {
  gl.activeTexture(gl.TEXTURE0);
  gl.bindTexture(gl.TEXTURE_2D, texture);
  gl.uniform1i(program.uSampler, 0);
}
```

5. Now we need to add the texture-specific code to the shader. In the vertex shader, add the following attribute and varying to the variable declarations:

```
in vec2 aVertexTextureCoords;
out vec2 vTextureCoords;
```

6. At the end of the vertex shader's `main` function, make sure to copy the texture coordinate attribute into the varying so that the fragment shader can access it:

```
vTextureCoords = aVertexTextureCoords;
```

7. The fragment shader also needs two new variable declarations—the sampler uniform and the varying from the vertex shader:

```
uniform sampler2D uSampler;
in vec2 vTextureCoords;
```

8. We must also remember to add `aVertexTextureCoords` to the `attributes` list and `uSampler` to the `uniforms` list in the `configure` function so that the new variables can be accessed from our JavaScript binding code.

9. To access the texture color, we call `texture` with the sampler and the texture coordinates. Since we want the textured surface to retain the lighting, we'll multiply the lighting color and the texture color together, giving us the following line to calculate the fragment color:

```
fragColor = vColor * texture(uSampler, vTextureCoords);
```

10. Open the file now in browser and you should see a scene like this one:

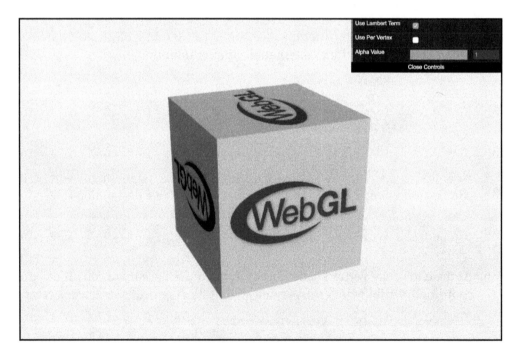

11. If you're having trouble with a particular step and would like a reference, the completed code is available in `ch07_02_textured-cube-final.html`.

What just happened?

We've just loaded a texture from a file, uploaded it to the GPU, rendered it on the cube geometry, and blended it with the lighting information that was already being calculated.

The remaining examples in this chapter will omit the calculation of lighting for simplicity and clarity, but lighting could be applied to all of them if desired.

Have a Go: Try a Different Texture

Try one of your own images to see if you can get it to display as the texture. What happens if you provide a rectangular image rather than a square one?

Texture Filter Modes

So far, we've seen how textures can be used to sample image data in a fragment shader, but we've only used them in a limited context. Some interesting issues arise when you start to investigate textures more closely.

For example, if you were to zoom in on the cube from the previous demo, you would see that the texture begins to alias:

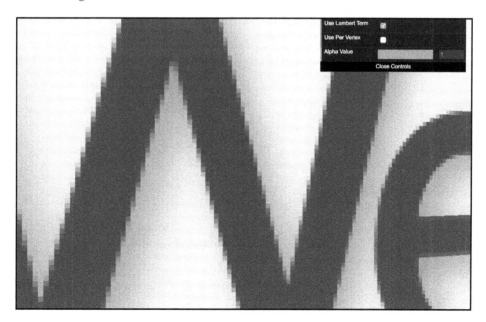

As we zoom in, we can see that jagged edges develop around the WebGL logo. Similar problems become apparent when the texture is very small on the screen. Isolated to a single object, such artifacts are easy to overlook, but they can become very distracting in complex scenes. Why do we see these artifacts in the first place?

From the previous chapter, you should remember how vertex colors are interpolated so that the fragment shader is provided with a smooth gradient of color. Texture coordinates are interpolated in the exact same way, with the resulting coordinates being provided to the fragment shader and used to sample color values from the texture. In a perfect situation, the texture would display at a 1 : 1 ratio on screen, meaning each pixel of the texture (known as **texels**) would take up exactly one pixel on screen. In this scenario, there would be no artifacts:

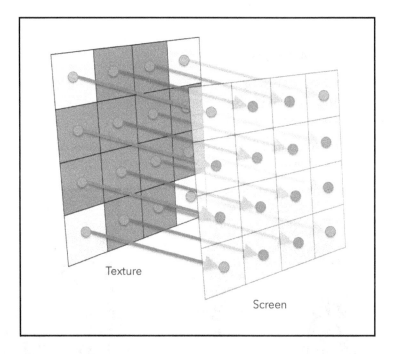

Pixel Versus Texel

Sometimes, the pixels in a texture are called **texels**. Pixel is short for Picture Element. Texel is short for Texture Element.

The reality of 3D applications, however, is that textures are almost never displayed at their native resolution. We refer to these scenarios as **magnification** and **minification**, depending on whether the texture has a lower or higher resolution than the screen space it occupies:

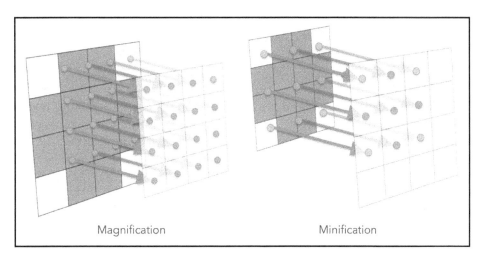

When a texture is magnified or minified, there can be some ambiguity about what color the texture sampler should return. For example, consider the following diagram of sample points against a slightly magnified texture:

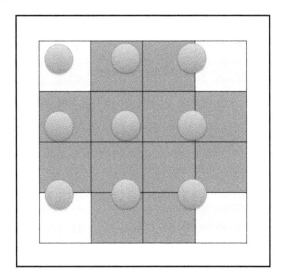

It's pretty obvious what color you would want the top left-hand side or middle sample points to return, but what about those texels in the middle? What color should they return? The answer is determined by your filter mode. Texture filtering allows us to control how textures are sampled and achieve the look we want.

Setting a texture's filter mode is very straightforward, and we already saw an example of how it works when we talked about creating textures:

```
gl.texParameteri(gl.TEXTURE_2D, gl.TEXTURE_MAG_FILTER, gl.NEAREST);
gl.texParameteri(gl.TEXTURE_2D, gl.TEXTURE_MIN_FILTER, gl.NEAREST);
```

As with most WebGL calls, texParameteri operates on the currently bound texture, and must be set for every texture you create. This also means that different textures can have different filters, which can be useful when trying to achieve specific effects.

In this example, we are setting both the magnification filter (TEXTURE_MAG_FILTER) and the minification filter (TEXTURE_MIN_FILTER) to NEAREST. There are several modes that can be passed for the third parameter, and the best way to understand the visual impact they have on a scene is to see the various filter modes in action.

Let's look at a demonstration of the filters in your browser while we discuss different parameters.

Time for Action: Trying Different Filter Modes

Let's cover an example of seeing different filter modes in action:

1. Open the ch07_03_texture-filters.html file using your browser:

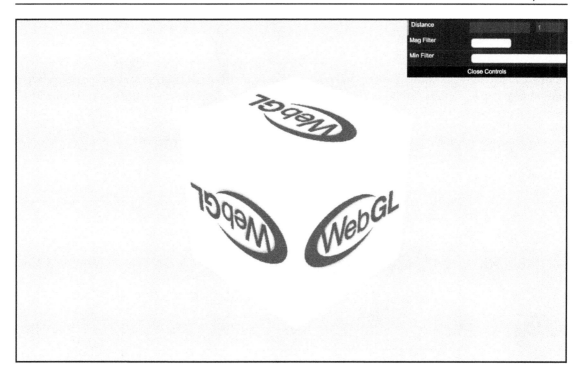

2. The controls include a slider to adjust the distance of the box from the viewer, while the buttons modify the magnification and minification filters.

3. Experiment with different modes to observe the effect they have on the texture. Magnification filters take effect when the cube's textures are being rendered larger than their source image size; minification filters when it is further away. Be sure to rotate the cube as well to observe what the texture looks like when viewed at an angle with each mode.

What just happened?

We learned how to create and load textures into our 3D scene. We also covered various techniques for mapping textures onto objects, along with an interactive example to demonstrate these capabilities.

Let's look at each of the filter modes in depth and discuss how they work.

NEAREST

Textures using the NEAREST filter always return the color of the texel whose center is nearest to the sample point. Using this mode, textures will look blocky and pixilated when viewed up close, which can be useful for creating "retro" graphics. NEAREST can be used for both the MIN and MAG filters:

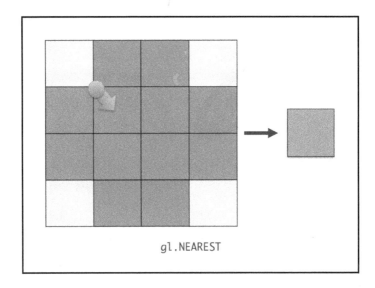

gl.NEAREST

LINEAR

The LINEAR filter returns the weighted average of the four pixels whose centers are nearest to the sample point. This provides a smooth blending of texel colors when looking at textures close up—it's generally the more desirable effect. This does mean that the graphics hardware has to read four times as many pixels per fragment there is, so naturally, it's slower than NEAREST, but modern graphics hardware is so fast that this is almost never an issue. LINEAR can be used for both the MIN and MAG filters. This filtering mode is also known as **bilinear filtering**:

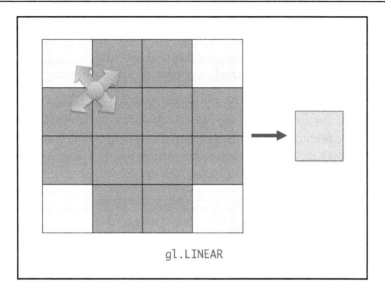

gl.LINEAR

Returning to the close-up example image we showed earlier in this chapter, had we used LINEAR filtering, it would have looked like this:

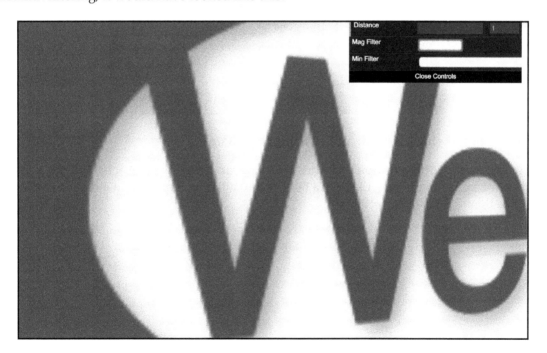

Mipmapping

Before we can discuss the remaining filter modes that are only applicable to TEXTURE_MIN_FILTER, we need to introduce a new concept: **mipmapping**.

A problem arises when sampling minified textures. In cases where we use LINEAR filtering and the sample points are so far apart, we can completely miss some details of the texture. As the view shifts, the texture fragments that we miss change, which results in a shimmering effect. You can see this in action by setting the MIN filter in the demo to NEAREST or LINEAR, zooming out, and rotating the cube:

To avoid this, graphics cards can utilize a **mipmap chain**.

Mipmaps are scaled-down copies of a texture, with each copy being exactly half the size of the previous one. If you were to show a texture and all of its mipmaps in a row, it would look like this:

The advantage is that when rendering, the graphics hardware can choose the copy of the texture that most closely matches the size of the texture on screen and samples from it instead. This reduces the number of skipped texels and the jittery artifacts that accompany them. However, mipmapping is only used if you use the appropriate texture filters.

NEAREST_MIPMAP_NEAREST

This filter will select the mipmap that most closely matches the size of the texture on screen and samples from it using the NEAREST algorithm.

LINEAR_MIPMAP_NEAREST

This filter selects the mipmap that most closely matches the size of the texture on screen and samples from it using the LINEAR algorithm.

NEAREST_MIPMAP_LINEAR

This filter selects two mipmaps that most closely match the size of the texture on screen and samples from both of them by using the NEAREST algorithm. The color returned is a weighted average of those two samples.

LINEAR_MIPMAP_LINEAR

This filter selects two mipmaps that most closely match the size of the texture on screen and samples from both of them using the LINEAR algorithm. The color returned is a weighted average of those two samples. This mode is also known as **trilinear filtering**:

Of the *_MIPMAP_* filter modes, NEAREST_MIPMAP_NEAREST is the fastest and lowest quality while LINEAR_MIPMAP_LINEAR will provide the best quality but the lowest performance. The other two modes sit somewhere in between on the quality/speed scale. In most cases, the performance trade-off will be small enough that it's common to use LINEAR_MIPMAP_LINEAR.

Generating Mipmaps

WebGL doesn't automatically create mipmaps for every texture; so, if we want to use one of the *_MIPMAP_* filter modes, we have to create the mipmaps for the texture first. Fortunately, all this takes is a single function call:

```
gl.generateMipmap(gl.TEXTURE_2D);
```

generateMipmap must be called after the texture has been populated with texImage2D and will automatically create a full mipmap chain for the image.

Alternatively, if you want to provide the mipmaps manually, you can always specify that you are providing a mipmap level rather than the source texture when calling texImage2D by passing a number other than 0 as the second parameter:

```
gl.texImage2D(gl.TEXTURE_2D, 1, gl.RGBA, gl.RGBA, gl.UNSIGNED_BYTE,
mipmapImage);
```

Here, we're manually creating the first mipmap level, which is half the height and width of the normal texture. The second level would be a quarter of the dimensions of the normal texture, and so on.

This can be useful for some advanced effects or when using compressed textures that cannot be used with generateMipmap.

If you are familiar with WebGL 1, you'll remember its limit that textures with dimensions that were not a power of two (**not** 1, 2, 4, 8, 16, 32, 64, 128, 256, 512, and so on) could not use mips and could not repeat. In WebGL 2, these restrictions are gone.

Non Power of Two (NPOT)

In order to use mipmaps with a texture in WebGL 1, mipmaps need to satisfy some dimension restrictions. Namely, the texture width and height must both be **Powers of Two (POT)**. That is, the width and height can be pow(2, n) pixels, where n is any integer. Examples are 16px, 32px, 64px, 128px, 256px, 512px, 1024px, and so on. Also, note that the width and height do not have to be the same as long as both are powers of two. For example, a 512x128 texture can still be mipmapped. NPOT textures can still be used with WebGL 1, but are restricted to only using NEAREST and LINEAR filters.

Why, then, is power restricted for two textures? Recall that the mipmap chain is made up of textures whose sizes are half the previous level. When the dimensions are powers of two, this will always produce integer numbers, which means that the number of pixels never needs to be rounded off, and hence produces clean and fast scaling algorithms.

For all of the texture code samples after this point, we'll be using a simple texture class that cleanly wraps up the texture's download, creation, and setup. Any textures created with the class will automatically have mipmaps generated for them and be set to use LINEAR for the magnification filter and LINEAR_MIPMAP_LINEAR for the minification filter.

Texture Wrapping

In the previous section, we used `texParameteri` to set the filter mode for textures but, as you might expect from the generic function name, that's not all it can do. Another texture behavior that we can manipulate is the **texture wrapping** mode.

Texture wrapping describes the behavior of the sampler when the texture coordinates fall outside the range of 0 and 1.

The wrapping mode can be set independently for both the S and T coordinates, so changing the wrapping mode typically takes two calls:

```
gl.texParameteri(gl.TEXTURE_2D, gl.TEXTURE_WRAP_S, gl.CLAMP_TO_EDGE);
gl.texParameteri(gl.TEXTURE_2D, gl.TEXTURE_WRAP_T, gl.CLAMP_TO_EDGE);
```

Here, we're setting both the S and T wrapping modes for the currently bound texture to `CLAMP_TO_EDGE`, the effects of which we will see in a moment.

As with texture filters, it's easiest to demonstrate the effects of the different wrapping modes via an example and then discuss the results. Please open your browser again for another demonstration.

Time for Action: Trying Different Wrap Modes

Let's cover an example of seeing different wrap modes in action:

1. Open the `ch07_04_texture-wrapping.html` file using your browser:

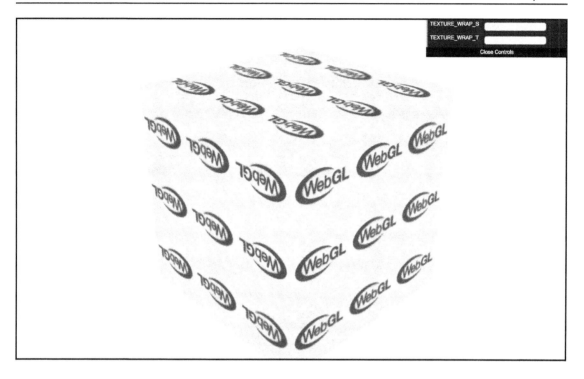

2. The cube shown in the preceding screenshot has texture coordinates that range from -1 to 2, which forces the texture wrapping mode to be used for everything but the center tile of the texture.

3. Experiment with the controls to see the effect that different wrap modes have on the texture.

What just happened?

We experimented with various approaches to texture interpolation and mipmapping techniques, along with interactive examples demonstrating these capabilities.

Now, let's investigate each of the wrap modes and discuss how they function.

CLAMP_TO_EDGE

This wrap mode rounds any texture coordinates greater than 1 down to 1; any coordinates lower than 0 are rounded up to 0, "clamping" the values to the 0-1 range. Visually, this has the effect of repeating the texture's border pixels indefinitely once the coordinates go out of the 0-1 range. Note that this is the only wrapping mode that's compatible with **NPOT** textures:

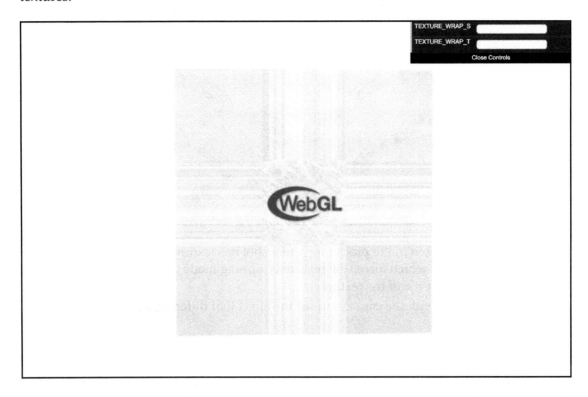

REPEAT

This is the default wrap mode, and the one that you'll probably use most often. In mathematical terms, this wrap mode simply ignores the integer part of the texture coordinate. This creates the visual effect of the texture repeating as you move outside of the 0-1 range. This is a useful effect for displaying surfaces that have a natural repeating pattern to them, such as a tile floor or brick wall:

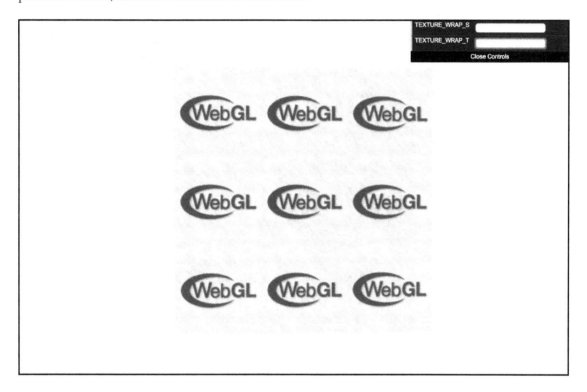

MIRRORED_REPEAT

The algorithm for this mode is a little more complicated. If the coordinate's integer portion is even, the texture coordinates will be the same as they were with REPEAT. If the integer portion of the coordinate is odd, the resulting coordinate is 1 minus the fractional portion of the coordinate. This results in a texture that "flip-flops" as it repeats, with every other repetition being a mirror image:

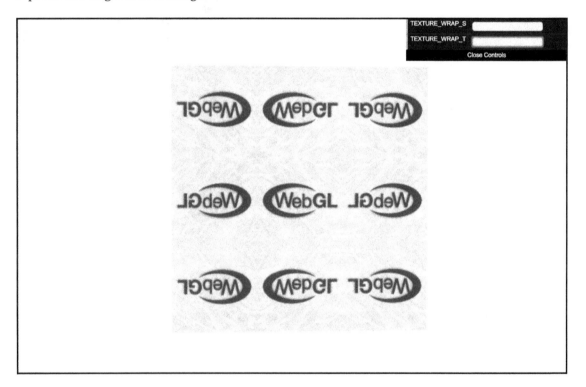

As we mentioned earlier, these modes can be mixed and matched. For example, consider the following code snippet:

```
gl.texParameteri(gl.TEXTURE_2D, gl.TEXTURE_WRAP_S, gl.REPEAT);
gl.texParameteri(gl.TEXTURE_2D, gl.TEXTURE_WRAP_T, gl.CLAMP_TO_EDGE);
```

This would produce the following effect on the texture from the sample:

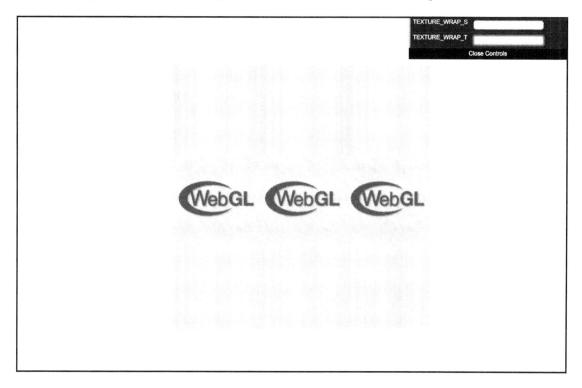

Samplers Versus Textures

Wondering why the shader uniforms are called *samplers* instead of *textures*? A texture is just the image data stored on the GPU, while a sampler contains all of the information about how to look up texture information, including filter and wrap modes.

Using Multiple Textures

So far, we've done all of our rendering by using a single texture. However, there are times when we may want to have multiple textures contribute to a fragment to create more complex effects. In such cases, we can use WebGL's ability to access multiple textures in a single draw call, commonly referred to as **multi-texturing**.

We briefly covered multi-texturing earlier, so let's go back and look at it again. When talking about exposing a texture to a shader as a sampler uniform, we used the following code:

```
gl.activeTexture(gl.TEXTURE0);
gl.bindTexture(gl.TEXTURE_2D, texture);
```

The first line, gl.activeTexture, is the key to utilizing multi-texturing. We use it to tell the WebGL state machine which texture we're going to use in subsequent texture functions. In this case, we passed gl.TEXTURE0, which means that any following texture calls (such as gl.bindTexture) will alter the state of the first texture unit. If we want to attach a different texture to the second texture unit, we would use gl.TEXTURE1 instead.

Different devices will support different numbers of texture units, but WebGL specifies that compatible hardware must always support at least two texture units. We can find out how many texture units the current device supports with the following function call:

```
gl.getParameter(gl.MAX_COMBINED_TEXTURE_IMAGE_UNITS);
```

WebGL provides explicit enumerations for gl.TEXTURE0 through gl.TEXTURE31. It may be more convenient to specify the texture unit programmatically or find a need to refer to a texture unit above 31. In such situations, you can always substitute gl.TEXTURE0 + i for gl.TEXTUREi, as in the following example:

```
gl.TEXTURE0 + 2 === gl.TEXTURE2;
```

Accessing multiple textures in a shader is as simple as declaring multiple samplers:

```
uniform sampler2D uSampler;
uniform sampler2D uOtherSampler;
```

When setting up your draw call, tell the shader which texture is associated with which sampler by providing the texture unit to gl.uniform1i. The code to bind two textures to the samplers above would look something like this:

```
// bind the first texture
gl.activeTexture(gl.TEXTURE0);
gl.bindTexture(gl.TEXTURE_2D, texture);
gl.uniform1i(program.uSampler, 0);

// bind the second texture
gl.activeTexture(gl.TEXTURE1);
gl.bindTexture(gl.TEXTURE_2D, otherTexture);
gl.uniform1i(program.uOtherSampler, 1);
```

We now have two textures available for our fragment shader, but what do we want to do with them?

As an example, we're going to implement a simple multi-texture effect that layers another texture on top of a simple textured cube to simulate static lighting.

Time for Action: Using Multi-Texturing

Let's cover an example of multi-texturing in action:

1. Open the ch07_05_multi-texture.html file with your editor.

2. At the top of the script block, add another texture variable:

```
let texture2;
```

3. At the bottom of the configure function, add the code to load the second texture. We're using a class to make this process easier, so the new code is as follows:

```
texture2 = new Texture();
texture2.setImage('/common/images/light.png');
```

4. The texture we're using is a white radial gradient that simulates a spot light:

5. In the `render` function, directly below the code that binds the first texture, add the following to expose the new texture to the shader:

```
gl.activeTexture(gl.TEXTURE1);
gl.bindTexture(gl.TEXTURE_2D, texture2.tex);
gl.uniform1i(program.uSampler2, 1);
```

6. We need to add the new sampler uniform to the fragment shader:

```
uniform sampler2D uSampler2;
```

7. Don't forget to add the corresponding string to the uniforms list in the `configure` function.

8. We add the code to sample the new texture value and blend it with the first texture. Since we want the second texture to simulate a light, we multiply the two values together as we did with the per-vertex lighting in the first texture example:

```
fragColor = texture(uSampler2, vTextureCoords) * texture(uSampler,
vTextureCoords);
```

9. Note that we're re-using the same texture coordinate for both textures. This is more convenient but, if needed, a second texture coordinate attribute could be provided or we could calculate a new texture coordinate from the vertex position or some other criteria.

10. You should see a scene that looks like this when you open the file in your browser:

11. You can see the completed example in ch07_06_multi-texture-final.html.

What just happened?

We've added a second texture to the `render` call and blended it with the first to create a new effect, which, in this case, simulates a simple static spotlight.

It's important to realize that the colors sampled from a texture are treated like any other color in the shader—that is, as a generic 4-dimensional vector. As a result, we can combine textures just as we would combine vertex and light colors, or any other color manipulation.

Have a Go: Moving Beyond Multiply

Multiplication is one of the most common ways to blend colors in a shader, but there's really no limit to how you can combine color values. Try experimenting with different algorithms in the fragment shader to see what effect it has on the output. What happens when you add values instead of multiply? What if you use the red channel from one texture and the blue and green from the other? Try out the following algorithm and see what the result is:

```
fragColor = vec4(texture(uSampler2, vTextureCoords).rgb - texture(uSampler,
vTextureCoords).rgb, 1.0);
```

The result is as follows:

Have a Go: Using Multi-Dimensional Textures

As you may have noticed, the challenges in maintaining multiple textures resembles the same challenges we faced in Chapter 6, *Colors, Depth Testing, and Alpha Blending*, in managing multiple lights. That being said, does WebGL provide a similar feature as uniform arrays for managing multiple textures? Yes, of course! We can leverage two different solutions that WebGL 2 provides for managing multi-dimensional textures: **3D textures** and **texture arrays**.

Although, we will discuss these features in Chapter 11, *WebGL 2 Highlights*, it may be useful to think about how these features can be useful in reducing complexity, improving code maintainability, and increasing the number of textures that can be used.

Cube Maps

Earlier in this chapter, we mentioned 2D textures and cube maps for creating complex effects using images. We covered textures, but exactly what are cube maps and how do we use them?

A **cube map** is, very much like it sounds, a cube of textures. Six individual textures are created, each assigned to a different face of the cube. The graphics hardware can sample them as a single entity, by using a 3D texture coordinate.

The faces of the cube are identified by the axis they face and whether they are on the positive or negative side of that axis:

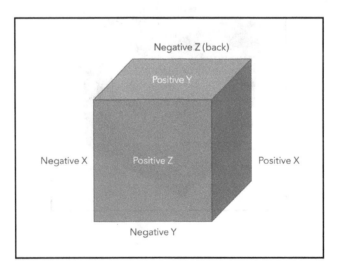

So far, we have manipulated a texture by specifying a texture target of TEXTURE_2D. Cube mapping introduces a few new texture targets that indicate we are working with cube maps. These targets also indicate which face of the cube map we're manipulating:

- TEXTURE_CUBE_MAP
- TEXTURE_CUBE_MAP_POSITIVE_X
- TEXTURE_CUBE_MAP_NEGATIVE_X
- TEXTURE_CUBE_MAP_POSITIVE_Y
- TEXTURE_CUBE_MAP_NEGATIVE_Y
- TEXTURE_CUBE_MAP_POSITIVE_Z
- TEXTURE_CUBE_MAP_NEGATIVE_Z

These targets are collectively known as the gl.TEXTURE_CUBE_MAP_* targets. Which one you need to use depends on the function you're calling.

Cube maps are created like a normal texture, but binding and property manipulation happen with the TEXTURE_CUBE_MAP target, as shown here:

```
const cubeTexture = gl.createTexture();
gl.bindTexture(gl.TEXTURE_CUBE_MAP, cubeTexture);
gl.texParameteri(gl.TEXTURE_CUBE_MAP, gl.TEXTURE_MAG_FILTER, gl.LINEAR);
gl.texParameteri(gl.TEXTURE_CUBE_MAP, gl.TEXTURE_MIN_FILTER, gl.LINEAR);
```

When uploading the image data for the texture, you need to specify the side that you are manipulating, as shown here:

```
gl.texImage2D(gl.TEXTURE_CUBE_MAP_POSITIVE_X, 0, gl.RGBA, gl.RGBA,
gl.UNSIGNED_BYTE, positiveXImage);
gl.texImage2D(gl.TEXTURE_CUBE_MAP_NEGATIVE_X, 0, gl.RGBA, gl.RGBA,
gl.UNSIGNED_BYTE, negativeXImage);
gl.texImage2D(gl.TEXTURE_CUBE_MAP_POSITIVE_Y, 0, gl.RGBA, gl.RGBA,
gl.UNSIGNED_BYTE, positiveYImage);
// ...
```

Exposing the cube map texture to the shader is done in the same way as a normal texture, just with the cube map target:

```
gl.activeTexture(gl.TEXTURE0);
gl.bindTexture(gl.TEXTURE_CUBE_MAP, cubeTexture);
gl.uniform1i(program.uCubeSampler, 0);
```

However, the uniform type within the shader is specific to cube maps:

```
uniform samplerCube uCubeSampler;
```

When sampling from the cube map, you also use a cube map-specific function:

```
texture(uCubeSampler, vCubeTextureCoords);
```

The 3D coordinates you provide are normalized by the graphics hardware into a unit vector, which specifies a direction from the center of the "cube." A ray is traced along that vector, and where it intersects the cube face is where the texture is sampled:

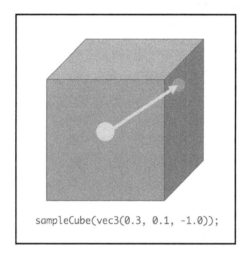

```
sampleCube(vec3(0.3, 0.1, -1.0));
```

Time for Action: Trying out Cube Maps

Let's cover an example of seeing cube maps in action:

1. Open the ch07_07_cubemap.html file in your browser. Once again, this contains a simple textured cube example on top of which we'll build the cube map example. We want to use the cube map to create a reflective-looking surface.

2. Creating the cube map is a bit more complicated than the textures we've loaded in the past, so this time, we'll use a function to simplify the asynchronous loading of individual cube faces. It's called loadCubemapFace and has already been to the file. Inside of the configure function, at the bottom, add the following code, which creates and loads the cube map faces:

```
cubeTexture = gl.createTexture();

gl.bindTexture(gl.TEXTURE_CUBE_MAP, cubeTexture);
gl.texParameteri(gl.TEXTURE_CUBE_MAP, gl.TEXTURE_MAG_FILTER,
gl.LINEAR);
gl.texParameteri(gl.TEXTURE_CUBE_MAP, gl.TEXTURE_MIN_FILTER,
```

```
gl.LINEAR);

loadCubemapFace(gl, gl.TEXTURE_CUBE_MAP_POSITIVE_X, cubeTexture,
'/common/images/cubemap/positive_x.png');

loadCubemapFace(gl, gl.TEXTURE_CUBE_MAP_NEGATIVE_X, cubeTexture,
'/common/images/cubemap/negative_x.png');

loadCubemapFace(gl, gl.TEXTURE_CUBE_MAP_POSITIVE_Y, cubeTexture,
'/common/images/cubemap/positive_y.png');

loadCubemapFace(gl, gl.TEXTURE_CUBE_MAP_NEGATIVE_Y, cubeTexture,
'/common/images/cubemap/negative_y.png');

loadCubemapFace(gl, gl.TEXTURE_CUBE_MAP_POSITIVE_Z, cubeTexture,
'/common/images/cubemap/positive_z.png');

loadCubemapFace(gl, gl.TEXTURE_CUBE_MAP_NEGATIVE_Z, cubeTexture,
'/common/images/cubemap/negative_z.png');
```

3. In the `render` function, add the code to bind the cube map to the appropriate sampler:

```
gl.activeTexture(gl.TEXTURE1);
gl.bindTexture(gl.TEXTURE_CUBE_MAP, cubeTexture);
gl.uniform1i(program.uCubeSampler, 1);
```

4. Turning to the shader now, we want to add a new varying to the vertex shader:

```
out vec3 vVertexNormal;
```

5. We'll be using the vertex normals instead of a dedicated texture coordinate to do the cube map sampling, which will give us the mirror effect we're looking for. Unfortunately, the actual normals of each face on the cube point straight out. If we were to use them, we would only get a single color per face from the cube map. In this case, we can "cheat" and use the vertex position as the normal instead (for most models, using the normals would be appropriate):

```
vVertexNormal = (uNormalMatrix * vec4(-aVertexPosition, 1.0)).xyz;
```

6. We need to define the following varying inside of the fragment shader:

```
in vec3 vVertexNormal;
```

7. We also need to add the new sampler uniform inside of the fragment shader. Be sure to also include this in the `uniforms` list inside of the `configure` function:

```
uniform samplerCube uCubeSampler;
```

8. And then, in the fragment shader's `main` function, add the code to actually sample the cube map and blend it with the base texture:

```
fragColor = texture(uSampler, vTextureCoords) *
texture(uCubeSampler, vVertexNormal);
```

9. We should now be able to reload the file in a browser and see the scene shown in the following screenshot:

10. The completed example is available in `ch07_08_cubemap-final.html`.

What just happened?

As you rotate the cube, you'll notice that the scene displayed on the cube map does not rotate along, creating a "mirror" effect on the cube faces. This is due to multiplication of the normals by the Normal matrix when assigning the `vVertexNormal` varying, which puts the normals in world space.

Using cube maps for reflective surfaces is a common technique, but it's not the only use for cube maps. Other common uses include skyboxes and advanced lighting models.

Skybox

A skybox is a method that's used for creating backgrounds to make computer and video game levels look bigger than they really are. When a skybox is used, the level is enclosed in a cuboid. The sky, distant mountains, distant buildings, and other unreachable objects are projected onto the cube's faces (using a technique called cube mapping), hence creating the illusion of distant, three-dimensional surroundings. A skydome employs the same concept but uses either a sphere or a hemisphere instead of a cube. For more information, check out the following URL: `https://en.wikipedia.org/wiki/Skybox_(video_games)`.

Have a Go: Shiny Logo

In this example, we've created a reflective "mirrored" cube. But what if we only wanted the logo to be reflective? How could we constrain the cube map to only be displayed within the red portion of the texture?

Summary

Let's summarize what we've learned in this chapter:

- How to use textures to add a new level of detail to our scenes.
- How to create and manage texture objects and use HTML images as textures.
- We covered texture coordinates and the ability to mipmap for various rendering techniques.
- We examined the various filter modes and how they affect the texture's appearance and usage, as well as the available texture wrapping modes and how they alter the way texture coordinates are interpreted.
- We learned how to use multiple textures in a single draw call, and how to combine them in a shader.
- We learned how to create and render cube maps and saw how they can be used to simulate reflective surfaces.

In the next chapter, we will look at selecting and interacting with objects in our WebGL scene by using a clever technique known as picking.

8
Picking

In the previous chapter, we covered how to use textures to add more detail to our 3D application. In this chapter, we'll learn how to interact with our WebGL application through a technique called **picking**. Picking refers to the ability to select objects in a 3D scene. The most common device used for picking is a computer mouse. However, picking can also be performed using other human computer interfaces, such as tactile screens and haptic devices. In this chapter, we will learn how picking can be implemented in WebGL.

In this chapter, you will:

- Learn how to select objects in a WebGL scene using the mouse.
- Create and use offscreen framebuffers.
- Learn what renderbuffers are and how they are used by framebuffers.
- Read pixels from framebuffers.
- Use color labels to perform object selection based on color.

Picking

Virtually any 3D computer-graphics application needs to provide mechanisms for the user to interact with the scene. For instance, in a game, you may want to point at your target and perform an action upon it. Or in a CAD system, you may want to be able to select an object in your scene and modify its properties. In this chapter, we'll learn the basics of implementing these kinds of interactions in WebGL.

To start, we should point out that we can select objects by casting a ray (vector) from the camera position (also known as the eye position) into the scene and calculate the objects that lie along its path. This is known as **ray-casting** and involves detecting intersections between the ray and object surfaces in the scene.

Ray-Casting

Ray-casting is the use of ray–surface intersection tests to solve a variety of problems in computer graphics and computational geometry. The term was first used in computer graphics in a 1982 paper by Scott Roth to describe a method for rendering constructive solid geometry models. If you're interested in learning more, check out https://en.wikipedia.org/wiki/Ray_casting.

That being said, in this chapter, we'll implement picking based on object colors in an offscreen framebuffer, as it is a simpler and more foundational technique to help you understand how to interact with objects in a 3D application. If you're interested in ray-casting, you'll find a section dedicated to this technique in Chapter 10, *Advanced Techniques*.

The basic idea behind picking is to assign a different identifier to every object in the scene and render the scene to an offscreen framebuffer. We will start by identifying objects with a unique color. When the user clicks on canvas, we go to the offscreen framebuffer and read the color of the pixel at the location of the click action. Since we assigned a unique color to each object in the offscreen buffer, we can use this color to identify the object that has been selected and perform an action upon it. The following diagram illustrates this concept:

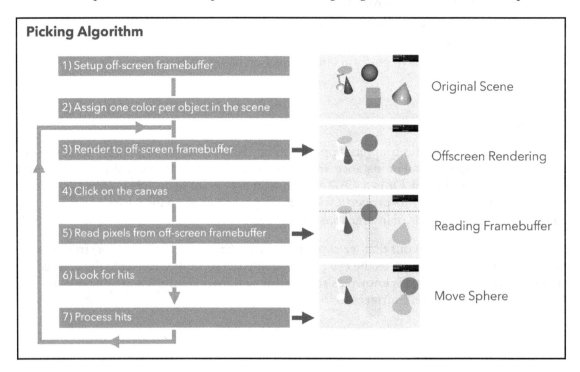

An interesting example that may help explain picking is Duck Hunt, the popular Nintendo game from the 90s, where players used a physical plastic gun controller to hunt ducks:

Can you guess how the game determined whether the player hit a duck? That's right, picking! When the player points at a duck and pulls the trigger, the computer in the NES blacks out the screen and the Zapper diode in the gun begins reception. Then, the computer flashes a solid white block around the targets you're supposed to be shooting at. The photodiode in the Zapper detects the change in light intensity and tells the computer that it's pointed at a lit target block—in other words, you should receive a point because you hit the target. Of course, when you're playing the game, you don't notice the blackout and the targets flashing because it all happens in a fraction of a second. Pretty clever, right?

Let's break down the steps for implementing our own form of picking in WebGL.

Setting up an Offscreen Framebuffer

As shown in Chapter 2, *Rendering*, the framebuffer is the final rendering destination in WebGL. The results of the rendering on your screen are the contents of the framebuffer. Assuming that gl is our WebGL context, every call
to gl.drawArrays, gl.drawElements, and gl.clear will change the contents of the framebuffer.

Instead of rendering to the default framebuffer, we can also render to a scene that is offscreen – we call this the offscreen framebuffer. This is the first step in implementing picking. To do so, we need to set up a new framebuffer and tell WebGL that we want to use it instead of the default one. Let's see how we can do that.

To set up a framebuffer, we need to create storage for at least two things: colors and depth information. We need to store the color for every fragment that is rendered in the framebuffer so we can create an image. Additionally, we need depth information to make sure that we have a scene where overlapping objects look consistent. If we do not have depth information, then we would not be able to tell, in the case of two overlapping objects, which object is at front and which one is at the back.

To store colors, we will use a WebGL texture; to store depth information, we will use a renderbuffer.

Creating a Texture to Store Colors

The code to create a texture should be pretty straightforward after reading Chapter 7, *Textures*:

```
const canvas = document.getElementById('webgl-canvas');
const { width, height } = canvas;

const texture = gl.createTexture();
gl.bindTexture(gl.TEXTURE_2D, texture);
gl.texImage2D(gl.TEXTURE_2D, 0, gl.RGBA, width, height, 0, gl.RGBA,
gl.UNSIGNED_BYTE, null);
```

The only difference is that we do not have an image to bind to the texture, so when we call `gl.texImage2D`, the last argument is `null`. This is because we are allocating space to store colors for the offscreen framebuffer.

It's important to note that the `width` and `height` of the texture are set to the `canvas` size. This is because we want to ensure that the offscreen framebuffer resembles the dimensions of our 3D scene.

Creating a Renderbuffer to Store Depth Information

Renderbuffers are used to provide storage for the individual buffers used in a framebuffer. The depth buffer (z-buffer) is an example of a renderbuffer. It is always attached to the screen framebuffer, which is the default rendering destination in WebGL.

The code to create a renderbuffer looks like the following code:

```
const renderbuffer = gl.createRenderbuffer();
gl.bindRenderbuffer(gl.RENDERBUFFER, renderbuffer);
gl.renderbufferStorage(gl.RENDERBUFFER, gl.DEPTH_COMPONENT16, width,
height);
```

The first line of code creates the renderbuffer. Similar to other WebGL buffers, the renderbuffer needs to be bound before we can operate on it. The third line of code determines the storage size of the renderbuffer.

Please note that the size of the storage is the same as with the texture. Similar to before, we need to ensure that for every fragment (pixel) in the framebuffer, we have a color (stored in the texture) and a depth value (stored in the renderbuffer).

Creating a Framebuffer for Offscreen Rendering

We need to create a framebuffer and attach the texture and the renderbuffer that we created in the previous example. Let's see how this works in code.

First, we need to create a new framebuffer:

```
const framebuffer = gl.createFramebuffer();
```

Similar to the VBO manipulation, we tell WebGL that we're going to operate on this framebuffer by making it the currently bound framebuffer. We do so with the following instruction:

```
gl.bindFramebuffer(gl.FRAMEBUFFER, framebuffer);
```

With the framebuffer bound, the texture is attached by calling the following method:

```
gl.framebufferTexture2D(gl.FRAMEBUFFER, gl.COLOR_ATTACHMENT0,
gl.TEXTURE_2D, texture, 0);
```

Then, the renderbuffer is attached to the bound framebuffer using the following:

```
gl.framebufferRenderbuffer(gl.FRAMEBUFFER, gl.DEPTH_ATTACHMENT,
gl.RENDERBUFFER, renderbuffer);
```

Finally, we clean up the bound buffers as usual with the following code:

```
gl.bindTexture(gl.TEXTURE_2D, null);
gl.bindRenderbuffer(gl.RENDERBUFFER, null);
gl.bindFramebuffer(gl.FRAMEBUFFER, null);
```

When the previously created framebuffer is unbound, the WebGL state machine goes back to rendering into the default screen framebuffer.

Assigning One Color per Object in the Scene

To keep things simple, we will pick an object based on its primitive color. That is, we discard the shiny reflections or shadows, and render the object with its uniform color. This is important, because to pick an object based on a color, we need to make sure that the color is constant per object and that each object has a different unique color.

We achieve constant coloring by telling the fragment shader to use only the material diffuse property to set the ESSL output color variable. We are assuming that each object has a unique diffuse property.

In situations where objects may share the same diffuse color, we can create a new ESSL uniform to store the picking color and make it unique for every object that's rendered into the offscreen framebuffer. This way, the objects will look the same when they are rendered on the screen, but their colors will be unique every time they are rendered into the offscreen framebuffer. Later in this chapter, we will implement this strategy along with other approaches for uniquely identifying objects.

For now, let's assume that the objects in our scene have unique diffuse colors, as shown in the following diagram:

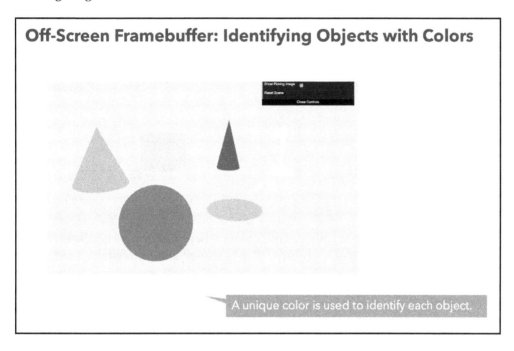

Let's see how to render the scene offscreen by using the framebuffer we just set up.

Rendering to an Offscreen Framebuffer

In order to perform object selection using the offscreen framebuffer, we need to ensure that both framebuffers are synchronized. If the onscreen framebuffer and the offscreen framebuffer are not synchronized, we could miss crucial data, which may make our picking strategy inconsistent.

A lack of consistency will limit the ability to read colors from the offscreen framebuffer and use them to identify objects in the scene.

To ensure that the buffers are synchronized, we will create a custom `render` function. This function calls the `draw` function twice. First, when the offscreen buffer is bound, and a second time when the onscreen default framebuffer is bound. The code looks like this:

```
function render() {
  // off-screen rendering
  gl.bindFramebuffer(gl.FRAMEBUFFER, framebuffer);
  // we set the uniform to true because of an offscreen render
  gl.uniform1i(program.uOffscreen, true);
  draw();

  // on-screen rendering
  gl.bindFramebuffer(gl.FRAMEBUFFER, null);
  // we set the uniform to false because of the default render
  gl.uniform1i(program.uOffscreen, false);
  draw();
}
```

We tell our ESSL program to use only diffuse colors when rendering into the offscreen framebuffer using the `uOffscreen` uniform. The fragment shader contains the following code:

```
void main(void) {

  if (uOffscreen) {
    fragColor = uMaterialDiffuse;
    return;
  }

  // ...
}
```

The following diagram shows the behavior of the `render` function:

Rendering Cycle

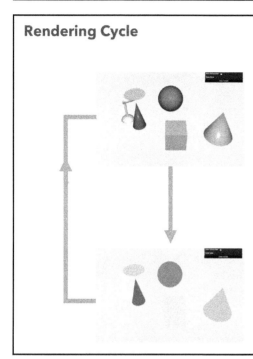

Off-Screen Framebuffer
Constant colors are used.
Lights are disabled.
The material diffuse property can be used as long as it is unique for every object in the scene. Otherwise, a unique color/label needs to be assigned to each object.

On-Screen Framebuffer
Textures are enabled.
Light and material properties are enabled (i.e. specular, diffuse, specular, etc.).

Therefore, every time the scene updates, the `render` function is called instead of calling the `draw` function.

We change this in the `init` function:

```
function init() {
  configure();
  load();

  // instead of calling 'draw', we are now calling 'render'
  clock.on('tick', render);
}
```

This way, the `scene` will be periodically updated using the `render` function instead of the original `draw` function.

Clicking on the Canvas

The next step is to capture and read the mouse coordinates of a user click from the offscreen framebuffer. We can use the standard onmouseup event from the canvas element in our webpage:

```
const canvas = document.getElementById('webgl-canvas');

canvas.onmouseup = event => {
  // capture coordinates from the `event`
};
```

Since the given event returns the mouse coordinates (clientX and clientY) from the top-left rather than the coordinates with respect to the canvas, we need to leverage the DOM hierarchy to know the total offset that we have around the canvas element.

We can do this with a code fragment inside the canvas.onmouseup function:

```
let top = 0,
  left = 0;

while (canvas && canvas.tagName !== 'BODY') {
  top += canvas.offsetTop;
  left += canvas.offsetLeft;
  canvas = canvas.offsetParent;
}
```

The following diagram shows how we use the offset calculation to obtain the clicked canvas coordinates:

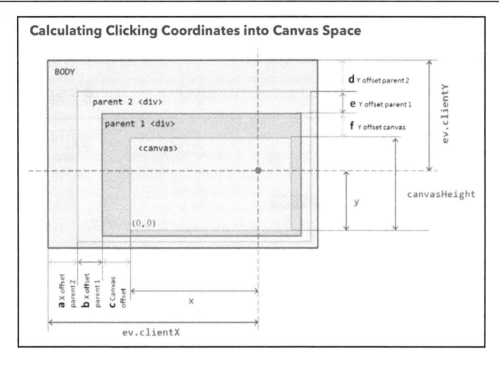

```
const x = ev.clientX - (a + b + c);
const y = canvasHeight - (ev.clientY - (d + e + f));
```

Also, we should take any possible page offset into account. The page offset is the result of scrolling, which affects the calculation of the coordinates. We want to obtain the same coordinates for the canvas every time, regardless of any scrolling. To do so, we add the following two lines of code just before calculating the clicked canvas coordinates:

```
left += window.pageXOffset;
top -= window.pageYOffset;
```

Then, we calculate the canvas coordinates:

```
x = ev.clientX - left;
y = canvas.height - (ev.clientY - top);
```

Remember that unlike the browser window, the canvas coordinates (and also the framebuffer coordinates for this purpose) start in the lower-left corner.

Reading Pixels from the Offscreen Framebuffer

We can now go to the offscreen buffer and read the color from the appropriate coordinates:

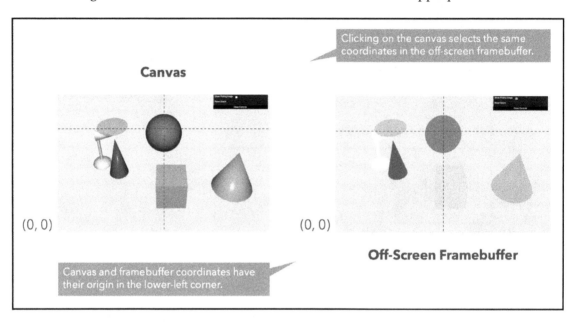

WebGL allows us to read back from a framebuffer using the `readPixels` function. As usual, having `gl` as the WebGL context variable within our context:

Function	Description
`gl.readPixels(x, y, width, height, format, type, pixels)`	• x and y: Starting coordinates. • `width` and `height`: The extent of pixels to read from the framebuffer. In our example, we are just reading one pixel (where the user clicks), so this will be 1, 1. • `format`: Supports the `gl.RGBA` format. • `type`:: Supports the `gl.UNSIGNED_BYTE` type. • `pixels`: A typed array that will contain the results of querying the framebuffer. It needs to have sufficient space to store the results depending on the extent of the query (x, y, `width`, `height`). It supports the `Uint8Array` type.

Remember that WebGL works as a state machine; thus, many operations depend on the validity of its state. In this case, we need to ensure that the offscreen framebuffer that we want to read from is the currently bound one. To do so, we bind it by using `bindFramebuffer`. Putting everything together, the code looks like this:

```
// read one pixel
const readout = new Uint8Array(1 * 1 * 4);
gl.bindFramebuffer(gl.FRAMEBUFFER, framebuffer);
gl.readPixels(coords.x, coords.y, 1, 1, gl.RGBA, gl.UNSIGNED_BYTE,
readout);
gl.bindFramebuffer(gl.FRAMEBUFFER, null);
```

Here, the size of the readout array is `1 * 1 * 4`. This means that it has one pixel of width times one pixel height times four channels, since the format is RGBA. You do not need to specify the size this way; this was done to demonstrate why the size is `4` when we are just retrieving one pixel.

Looking for Hits

Now, we will check whether the color obtained from the offscreen framebuffer matches any of the objects in our scene. Remember here that we are using colors as object labels. If the color matches one of the objects, then we call it a **hit**. If it does not, we call it a **miss**.

When looking for hits, we compare each object's diffuse color with the label obtained from the offscreen framebuffer. There is, however, an additional step to consider: each color channel comes back in a `[0, 255]` range while the object diffuse colors are in a `[0, 1]` range. We need to update this before we check for any possible hits. We can do so with a compare function:

```
function compare(readout, color) {
  return (
    Math.abs(Math.round(color[0] * 255) - readout[0]) <= 1 &&
    Math.abs(Math.round(color[1] * 255) - readout[1]) <= 1 &&
    Math.abs(Math.round(color[2] * 255) - readout[2]) <= 1
  );
}
```

In the preceding code, we scale the diffuse property to a `[0, 255]` range and then compare each channel individually. We do not need to compare the alpha channel. If we had two objects with the same color but a different alpha channel, we could use the alpha channel in the comparison, but this is not the case in our example.

Also, it's important to note that the comparison is not precise, as we are dealing with decimal values in the [0, 1] range. Because of that, we introduce a fudge factor by assuming that we have a hit after rescaling the colors and subtract the readout (object label) – the difference is less than one.

Then, we just iterate through the object list in our scene and check whether we have a hit or miss with the following code:

```
let pickedObject;

scene.traverse(object => {
  if (compare(readout, object.diffuse)) {
    // Returning any value from the 'scene.traverse' method breaks the loop
    return pickedObject = object;
  }
});
```

This code iterates through every object in our scene and assigns pickedObject to the matching object if we have a hit.

Processing Hits

Processing a hit is a large concept that heavily depends on the type of application you're using. For instance, if your application is a CAD system, you may want to retrieve the properties of the selected object so that you can edit or delete it. In contrast, if you're developing a game, selecting an object may involve setting it as a target your character should fight next. As you would expect, this part needs to be adaptable to a variety of uses. That being said, we will soon cover a practical example where you can drag and drop objects in our scene. But first, we need to review some of the architectural updates of our application.

Architectural Updates

We have replaced the draw function with the render function, as described earlier in this chapter.

There is now a new class: **Picker**. The source code for this class can be obtained from common/js/Picker.js. This class encapsulates the offscreen framebuffer and the code necessary to create, configure, and read from it. We've also updated the Controls class to notify the picker when the user clicks on the canvas.

Now, let's see picking in action!

Time for Action: Picking

Let's cover an example of this technique in action:

1. Open the ch08_01_picking.html file using your browser. You will see a screen similar to this:

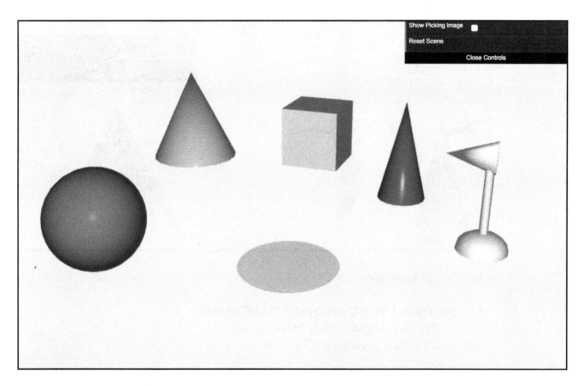

2. Here, you have a set of objects, each one of which has a unique diffuse color property. As was the case in previous examples, you can move the camera around the scene. Also, note that the cube has a texture and that the flat disk is translucent. As you may expect, the code in the draw function handles textures, coordinates, and also transparencies, so it looks a bit more complex than before (you can check it out in the source code). This is a more realistic draw function. In a real application, you will have to handle these cases.

3. Click on the sphere and drag it around the scene. Notice that the object becomes translucent. Also, note that the displacement occurs along the axis of the camera. To make this evident, please go to your web browser's `console` and type in the following:

```
camera.setElevation(0);
```

4. Once you resume the clock by clicking inside of the scene, you will see that the camera updates its position to an elevation of zero degrees, as shown in the following screenshot:

JavaScript Console

Firefox: **Tools | WebDeveloper | WebConsole**
Safari: **Develop | Show Web Inspector**
Chrome: **Tools | Javascript Console**

5. When you click and drag objects in the scene from this perspective, you will see that they change their position according to the camera's axis. In this case, the up axis of the camera is aligned with the scene's y-axis. If you move an object up and down, you will see that they change their position in the y coordinate. If you change the camera position (by clicking on the background and dragging the mouse around), and then move a different object, you will see that the object moves according to the camera's new y-axis.

6. Try different camera angles and see what happens.

7. Let's see what the offscreen framebuffer looks like. Click on the **Show Picking Image** button. Here, we are instructing the fragment shader to use each of the object diffuse properties to color the fragments. You can also rotate the scene and pick objects in this mode. If you want to go back to the original shading method, click on **Show Picking Image** again to deactivate it.

8. To reset the scene, click on **Reset Scene**.

What just happened?

We have seen an example of picking in action. The source code uses the `Picker` class that we previously described in the *Architectural Updates* section. Let's examine it a bit closer.

Picker Architecture

As you may have noticed, every picker state has a callback function associated with it. The following process outlines what happens in the `Picker` class when the user clicks the mouse on the `canvas`, drags it, and releases it:

State	Callback
`Picker` searches for a hit	`hitPropertyCallback(object)`: This callback informs the picker about which object property to use to make the comparison with the retrieved color from the offscreen framebuffer.
User drags mouse in picking mode	`moveCallback(dx, dy)`: When the picking mode is activated (by having picked at least one object), this callback allows us to move the objects in the picking list (hits). This list is maintained internally by the `Picker` class.
Remove hit from picking list	`addHitCallback(object)`: If we click on an object and this object is not in the picking list, the picker notifies the application by triggering this callback.
Add hit to picking list	`removeHitCallback(object)`: If we click on an object and this object is already in the picking list, the picker will remove it from the list and then it will inform the application by triggering this callback.
End Picking Mode	`processHitsCallback(hits)`: If the user releases the mouse button while the *Shift* key is not pressed, the picking mode finishes and the application is notified by triggering this callback. If the *Shift* key is pressed, then the picking mode continues, and the picker waits for a new click to continue looking for hits.

Implementing Unique Object Labels

We previously mentioned that picking based on the diffuse property could be difficult if two or more objects in the scene share the same diffuse color. If that were the case and you selected one of them, how could you determine which one is picked based on its color? In the following *Time for Action* section, we will implement unique object labels. The objects will be rendered in the offscreen framebuffer using these color labels instead of the diffuse colors. The scene will still be rendered on the screen using the non-unique diffuse colors.

Time for Action: Unique Object Labels

This section is divided into two parts. In the first part, you will develop code to generate a random scene with cones and cylinders. Each object will be assigned a unique object label that will be used for coloring the object in the offscreen renderbuffer. In the second part, we will configure the picker to work with unique labels. Let's get started:

1. Open the `ch08_02_picking-initial.html` file in your browser. This is a scene that is only showing the floor object. We are going to create a scene that contains multiple objects that can be either balls or cylinders.

2. Open `ch08_02_picking-initial.html` in a source code editor.

3. We will write code so that each object in the scene can have the following:
    - A position assigned randomly
    - A unique object label color
    - A non-unique diffuse color
    - A scale factor that will determine the size of the object

4. We have provided empty functions that you will implement in this section.

5. Let's write the `positionGenerator` function. Scroll down to it and add the following code:

```
function positionGenerator() {
  const
    flagX = Math.floor(Math.random() * 10),
    flagZ = Math.floor(Math.random() * 10);

  let x = Math.floor(Math.random() * 60),
    z = Math.floor(Math.random() * 60);

  if (flagX >= 5) {
    x = -x;
  }
```

```
    if (flagZ >= 5) {
        z = -z;
    }

    return [x, 0, z];
}
```

6. Here, we are using the `Math.random` function to generate the `x` and `z` coordinates for an object in the scene. Since `Math.random` always returns a positive number, we use the `flagX` and `flagZ` variables to randomly distribute the objects on the x-z plane (floor). Also, because we want all of the objects to be on the x-z plane, the `y` component is always set to `0` in the `return` statement.

7. Let's write a unique object label generator function. Scroll to the empty `objectLabelGenerator` function and add the following code:

```
const colorset = {};

function objectLabelGenerator() {
    const
        color = [Math.random(), Math.random(), Math.random(), 1],
        key = color.toString();

    if (key in colorset) {
        return objectLabelGenerator();
    }
    else {
        colorset[key] = true;
        return color;
    }
}
```

8. We create a random color using the `Math.random` function. If the `key` variable is already a property of the `colorset` object, then we call the `objectLabelGenerator` function recursively to get a new value; otherwise, we make `key` a property of `colorset` and then `return` the respective color. Notice how well the handling of JavaScript objects as sets allows us to resolve any possible key collision.

9. Write the `diffuseColorGenerator` function. We will use this function to assign diffuse properties to the objects:

```
function diffuseColorGenerator(index) {
    const color = (index % 30 / 60) + 0.2;
    return [color, color, color, 1];
}
```

10. This function represents the case where we want to generate colors that are not unique. The index parameter represents the index of the object in the `scene.objects` list to which we are assigning the diffuse color. In this function, we are creating a gray-level color since the `r`, `g`, and `b` components in the `return` statement all have the same `color` value.

11. The `diffuseColorGenerator` function will create collisions every 30 indices. The remainder of the division of the index by 30 will create a loop in the sequence:

```
 0 % 30 = 0
 1 % 30 = 1
. . .
29 % 30 = 29
30 % 30 = 0
31 % 30 = 1
. . .
```

12. Since this result is being divided by 60, the result will be a number in the [0, 0.5] range. Then, we add 0.2 to make sure that the minimum value that `color` has is 0.2. This way, the objects will not look too dark during the onscreen rendering (they would be black if the calculated diffuse color were 0).

13. The last auxiliary function we will write is the `scaleGenerator` function:

```
function scaleGenerator() {
  const scale = Math.random() + 0.3;
  return [scale, scale, scale];
}
```

14. This function will allow us to have objects of different sizes. 0.3 is added to control the minimum scaling factor that any object will have in the scene.

15. Let's load 100 objects to our scene. By the end of this section, you will be able to test picking on any of them!

16. Go to the `load` function and edit it so that it looks like this:

```
function load() {
  scene.add(new Floor(80, 20));

  for (let i = 0; i < 100; i++) {
    const objectType = Math.floor(Math.random() * 2);

    const options = {
      position: positionGenerator(),
      scale: scaleGenerator(),
```

```
    diffuse: diffuseColorGenerator(i),
    pcolor: objectLabelGenerator()
  };

  switch (objectType) {
    case 1:
      return scene.load('/common/models/ch8/sphere.json',
        `ball_${i}`, options);
    case 0:
      return scene.load('/common/models/ch8/cylinder.json',
        `cylinder_${i}`, options);
  }
  }
}
```

17. The picking color is represented by the `pcolor` attribute. This attribute is passed in a list of attributes to the `scene.load` function. Once the object is loaded (using **JSON/Ajax**), `load` uses this list of attributes and adds them as object properties.

18. The shaders in this exercise have already been set up for you.
    The `pcolor` property that corresponds to the unique object label is mapped to the `uPickingColor` uniform, and the `uOffscreen` uniform determines whether it is used in the fragment shader:

```
uniform vec4 uPickingColor;

void main(void) {

  if (uOffscreen) {
    fragColor = uPickingColor;
    return;
  }
  else {
    // on-screen rendering
  }

}
```

19. As described previously, we keep the offscreen and onscreen buffers in sync by using the `render` function as follows:

```
function render() {
  // Off-screen rendering
  gl.bindFramebuffer(gl.FRAMEBUFFER, picker.framebuffer);
  gl.uniform1i(program.uOffscreen, true);
```

```
      draw();

      // On-screen rendering
      gl.uniform1i(program.uOffscreen, showPickingImage);
      gl.bindFramebuffer(gl.FRAMEBUFFER, null);
      draw();
   }
```

20. Save your work as ch08_03_picking-no-picker.html.
21. Open ch08_03_picking-no-picker.html in your browser.
22. Click on **Show Picking Image**. What happens?
23. The scene is being rendered to both the offscreen and default onscreen framebuffer. However, we have not configured the Picker callbacks yet.
24. Open ch08_03_picking-no-picker.html in your source code editor.
25. Scroll down to the configure function. The picker is already set up for you:

```
      picker = new Picker(canvas, {
         hitPropertyCallback: hitProperty,
         addHitCallback: addHit,
         removeHitCallback: removeHit,
         processHitsCallback: processHits,
         moveCallback: movePickedObjects
      });
```

26. This code fragment maps functions in the web page to picker callback hooks. These callbacks are invoked according to the picking state.
27. We will now implement the necessary callbacks. Again, we have provided empty functions that you will need to code.
28. Let's create the hitProperty function. Scroll down to the empty hitProperty function and add the following code:

```
      function hitProperty(obj) {
         return obj.pcolor;
      }
```

29. We are returning the pcolor property to make the comparison with the color that will be read from the offscreen framebuffer. If these colors match, then we have a hit.

30. Write the `addHit` and `removeHit` functions. We want to create the effect where the diffuse color is changed to the picking color during picking. We need an extra property to temporarily save the original diffuse color so that we can restore it later:

```
function addHit(obj) {
  obj.previous = obj.diffuse.slice(0);
  obj.diffuse = obj.pcolor;
}
```

31. The `addHit` function stores the current diffuse color in an auxiliary property named `previous`. Then, it changes the diffuse color to `pcolor`, the object-picking label:

```
function removeHit(obj) {
  obj.diffuse = obj.previous.slice(0);
}
```

32. The `removeHit` function restores the diffuse color.

33. Now, let's write the code for `processHits`:

```
function processHits(hits) {
  hits.forEach(hit => hit.diffuse = hit.previous);
}
```

34. Remember that `processHits` is called upon exiting picking mode. This function will receive one parameter: the `hits` that the `picker` detected. Each element of the `hits` list is an object in `scene`. In this case, we want to give the hits their diffuse color back. For that, we use the previous property that we set in the `addHit` function.

35. The last picker callback we need to implement is the `movePickedObjects` function:

```
function movePickedObjects(dx, dy) {
  const hits = picker.getHits();

  if (!hits) return;

  const factor = Math.max(
    Math.max(camera.position[0], camera.position[1]),
     camera.position[2]
  ) / 2000;
```

```
hits.forEach(hit => {
  const scaleX = vec3.create();
  const scaleY = vec3.create();

  if (controls.alt) {
    vec3.scale(scaleY, camera.normal, dy * factor);
  }
  else {
    vec3.scale(scaleY, camera.up, -dy * factor);
    vec3.scale(scaleX, camera.right, dx * factor);
  }

  vec3.add(hit.position, hit.position, scaleY);
  vec3.add(hit.position, hit.position, scaleX);
});
}
```

36. This function allows us to move the objects in the hits list interactively. The parameters that this callback function receives are as follows:
    - dx: Displacement in the horizontal direction obtained from the mouse when it is dragged on `canvas`
    - dy: Displacement in the vertical direction obtained from the mouse when it is dragged on `canvas`

37. Let's analyze the code. First, we retrieve all of the hits from the picker instance:

```
const hits = picker.getHits();
```

38. If there are no hits, the function `returns` immediately:

```
if (!hits) return;
```

39. We calculate a weighing factor that we will use later (the fudge factor):

```
const factor = Math.max(
  Math.max(camera.position[0], camera.position[1]),
camera.position[2]
) / 2000;
```

40. We create a loop to go through the hits list so that we can update each object's position:

```
hits.forEach(hit => {
  const scaleX = vec3.create();
  const scaleY = vec3.create();

  // ...
});
```

41. The `scaleX` and `scaleY` variables are initialized for every hit.

42. The *Alt* key is being used to perform dollying (moving the camera along its normal path). In this case, we want to move the objects that are in the picking list along the camera's normal direction when the user is pressing the *Alt* key to provide a consistent user experience.

43. To move the hits along the camera normal, we use the `dy` (up-down) displacement, as follows:

```
if (controls.alt) {
  vec3.scale(scaleY, camera.normal, dy * factor);
}
```

44. This creates a scaled version of `camera.normal` and stores it into the `scaleY` variable. Notice that `vec3.scale` is an operation that's available in the **glMatrix** library.

45. If the user is not pressing the *Alt* key, then we use `dx` (left-right) and `dy` (up-down) to move the hits in the camera plane. Here, we use the camera's up and right vectors to calculate the `scaleX` and `scaleY` parameters:

```
else {
  vec3.scale(scaleY, camera.up, -dy * factor);
  vec3.scale(scaleX, camera.right, dx * factor);
}
```

46. We update the position of the hit:

```
vec3.add(hit.position, hit.position, scaleY);
vec3.add(hit.position, hit.position, scaleX);
```

47. Save the page as `ch08_04_picking-final.html` and open it using your browser.

48. You will see a scene like the one shown in the following screenshot:

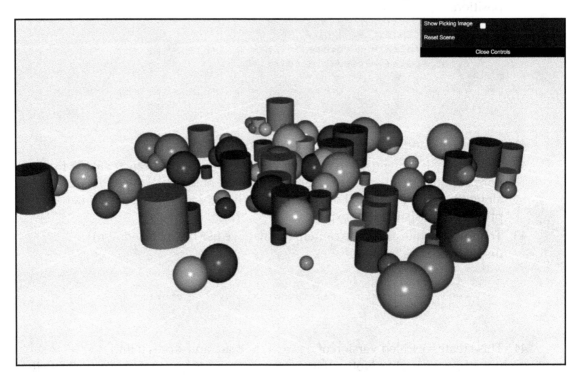

49. Click on **Reset Scene** several times and verify that you get a new scene every time.

50. In this scene, all of the objects have very similar colors. However, each one has a unique picking color. To verify this, click on the **Show Picking Image** button. You will see on the screen what is being rendered in the offscreen buffer:

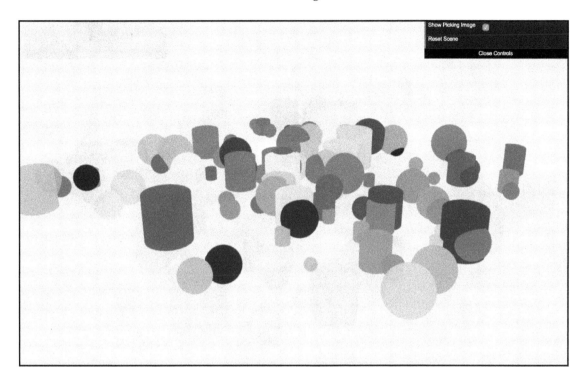

51. Let's validate the changes that we made to the picker callbacks. Let's start by picking one object. As you can see, the object diffuse color becomes its picking color (this was the change you implemented in the addHit function):

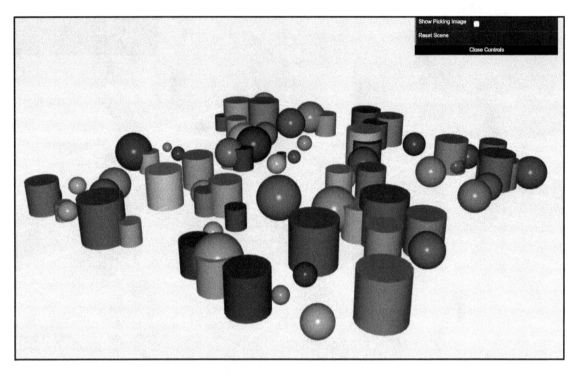

52. When the mouse is released, the object goes back to the original color. This is the change that was implemented in the processHits function.

53. While the mouse button is held down over an object, you can drag it around. When this is done, movePickedObjects is being invoked.

54. Pressing the *Shift* key while objects are being selected will tell the picker not to exit **picking mode**. This way, you can select and move more than one object at once:

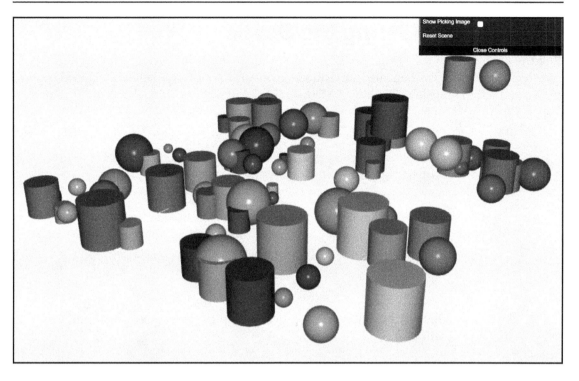

55. You will exit picking mode if you select an object and the *Shift* key is no longer pressed or if your next click does not produce any hits (in other words, clicking anywhere else).

56. If you have any problems with this exercise or missed one of the steps, we have included the complete exercise in the `ch08_03_picking-no-picker.html` and `ch08_04_picking-final.html` files.

What just happened?

We have done the following:

- Created the property-picking color. This property is unique for every object in the scene and allows us to implement picking based on it.
- Modified the fragment shader to use the picking color property by including a new uniform, `uPickingColor`, and mapping this uniform to the `pcolor` object property.
- Learned about the different picking states. We have also learned how to modify the `Picker` callbacks to perform specific application logic such as removing picked objects from the scene.

Have a Go: Clearing the Scene

Rewrite the `processHits` function to remove the balls in the hit list from the scene. If the user has removed all of the balls from the scene, display a message with the elapsed time for accomplishing this task.

Hint

Use `scene.remove(objectName)` in the `processHits` function if the alias starts with `ball_`.

Hint

Once the hits are removed from the scene, revisit the `scene.objects` list and make sure that there are no objects whose alias starts with `ball_`.

Hint

Use a JavaScript timer to measure and display the elapsed time until task completion.

Have a Go: Using Alternative Identifiers for Picking

How would you uniquely identify objects without using colors? Since we are leveraging an offscreen framebuffer, we could identify each object with a unique ID rather than a color since the visuals of our offscreen render do not matter. Go ahead and implement an ID-based strategy for identifying each object.

Packing Indices into RGBA Channels

You can think of object 1 as being the index (or color) `[0, 0, 0, 1]`, object 2 as `[0, 0, 0, 2]`, all the way up to where object `1020` (that is, `255 * 4`) would be `[255, 255, 255, 255]`.

Since our RGBA channel is bound to a range of `[0-255]`, how could we pack more IDs into our four-based vector?

Different Base Numeral System

 You may first think of leveraging decimals instead of whole numbers. This is a viable solution, especially after you account for the accuracy of floating points in ESSL. Another viable solution would be to use a 255 based numeral system rather than our traditional base 10. With this approach, you could uniquely identify 4+ billions objects without decimals.

Have a Go: Decoupling WebGL Components

Although we can implement `Controls` and `Picker` by decoupling them with a more scalable architecture, we opted for a simpler implementation for educational purposes.

That being said, how would you rebuild the examples in this chapter with the goal of decoupling classes from one another to minimize component interdependence?

Hint

 One approach would be to leverage the pub/sub pattern discussed earlier for our `Clock`. That is, each component can extend the `EventEmitter` class – similar to `Clock` – to publish events that other components may subscribe to.

Summary

Let's summarize what we learned in this chapter:

- We studied the difference between a framebuffer and a renderbuffer. A renderbuffer is a special buffer that is attached to a framebuffer.
- We learned that WebGL provides mechanisms to create offscreen framebuffers that differ from the default onscreen framebuffer.
- We covered how a framebuffer needs to have at least one texture to store colors and a renderbuffer to store depth information.
- We discussed how to convert user click coordinates to `canvas` coordinates so that we can map them to values in the offscreen framebuffer.

- We discussed the `Picker` architecture. Picking can have different states, and each state is associated with a callback function. Picker callbacks allow custom application logic to determine what happens when picking is in progress.
- We learned how to implement color-based picking in WebGL. Picking purely based on a diffuse color is limited, because there could be scenarios where several objects have the same diffuse color.
- We learned that it's better to assign a new color property that is unique for every object to perform picking. This property is known as picking the color/object label.
- We discussed encoding unique IDs rather than unique colors into the four-based vector, RGBA.

In the next chapter, we will bring all of the concepts we've covered in the previous chapters together and build a 3D virtual car showroom. Additionally, we will see how to import car models from Blender, a 3D editing tool, into a WebGL application.

Putting It All Together

9

In the previous chapter, we covered framebuffers, renderbuffers, and the steps required to interact with a 3D application using picking. In this chapter, we will bring together all of the concepts we've learned so far to build a 3D virtual car showroom. In the development of this demo application, we will use models, lights, cameras, animation, colors, textures, and more. We will also learn how to integrate these elements with a simple yet effective graphical user interface.

In this chapter, you will learn to do the following:

- Put together all of the architecture we've developed throughout this book
- Create a 3D virtual car showroom application using our architecture
- Import car models from Blender into a WebGL scene
- Set up several light sources
- Create robust shaders to handle multiple materials
- Learn about the OBJ and MTL file formats
- Program the camera to fly through the scene

Creating a WebGL Application

At this point, we've covered the basic topics required to create a WebGL application. These topics have been implemented in the framework that we've iteratively built throughout this book.

In Chapter 1, *Getting Started*, we introduced WebGL and learned how to use it in our browser. We learned that the WebGL context behaves as a state machine. As a result, we can query the different state variables using gl.getParameter.

Then, we studied how objects in a WebGL scene are defined by vertices. We saw how we can use indices to label vertices so that the WebGL rendering pipeline can quickly rasterize to render an object. We studied the functions that manipulate buffers and the two main functions to render primitives: `drawArrays` (no indices) and `drawElements` (with indices). We learned about using JSON to represent geometries and how we can download models from a web server.

Next, we studied how to illuminate our 3D scene. We learned about normal vectors, the physics of light reflection, and the 3D math required to implement illumination. We also learned how to implement different lighting models using shaders in ESSL.

Then, we implemented our own custom cameras since WebGL does not have cameras. We studied the Camera matrix and demonstrated how it's actually the inverse of the Model-View matrix. In other words, rotation, translation, and scaling in world space produces the inverse operations in camera space.

Following cameras and matrices, we covered the basics of animation. We discussed useful techniques for animations, such as the matrix stack with `push` and `pop` operations to represent local and global transformations, and we analyzed how to establish an animation cycle that is independent of the rendering cycle. Our animations covered different types of interpolation techniques, with examples showcasing various animation styles.

Then, we investigated color representation with WebGL and how we can use colors in objects, lights, and the overall scene. In doing so, we also studied blending and the creation of translucent and transparent effects. After colors and blending, we covered textures for adding more detail to our scene. Then, we saw how users can interact with our 3D application with picking.

In this chapter, we will leverage all of these concepts to create an impressive 3D application. Reasonably enough, we will use all of the components we have developed so far. Let's quickly review them.

Architectural Review

The following components are present in the architecture that has been built throughout this book:

- `Axis.js`: Auxiliary object that represents the center of the scene with visual helpers.
- `Camera.js`: Contains a camera representation from the two types of camera we have developed: orbiting and tracking.

- `Clock.js`: A requestAnimationFrame-based timer to synchronize our entire application from a single source of truth.
- `Controls.js`: Listens for mouse and keyboard events on the HTML5 `canvas`. It interprets these events and then transforms them into camera actions.
- `EventEmitter.js`: A simple class that provides a pub-sub approach for managing interactions between components in our application.
- `Floor.js`: Auxiliary object that appears like a rectangular mesh and provides the floor reference for the scene.
- `Light.js`: Simplifies the creation and managing of lights in the scene.
- `Picker.js`: Provides color-based object picking.
- `Program.js`: Composes the functions that handle programs, shaders, and the mapping between JavaScript values and ESSL uniforms.
- `Scene.js`: Contains a list of objects to be rendered by WebGL.
- `Texture.js`: A class for the creation and managing of WebGL textures.
- `Transforms.js`: Contains the matrices discussed in this book, that is, the Model-View matrix, the Camera matrix, the uProjectionMatrix, and the Normal matrix. It implements the matrix stack with the `push` and `pop` operations.
- `utils.js`: Contains auxiliary functions, such as `getGLContext`, which helps create a WebGL context for a given HTML5 `canvas`.
- Application hook functions, which are as follows:
    - `init`: This function initializes the application and is only called when the document has loaded via `window.onload = init;`.
    - `configure`: This function creates and configures dependencies, such as the program, cameras, lights, and so on.
    - `load`: This function requests objects from the web server by calling `scene.load`. We can also add locally generated geometry (such as the `Floor`) by calling `scene.add`.
    - `draw`: This function is called when the rendering timer goes off. Here, we retrieve objects from the `scene` and render them appropriately by ensuring their location (for example, applying local transforms using the matrix stack) and their properties (for example, passing the respective uniforms to the `program`).

Now, let's bring all of these concepts together and create a 3D virtual car showroom.

Time for Action: 3D Virtual Car Showroom

Leveraging the WebGL skills and infrastructure code we have developed thus far, we will create an application that visualizes different 3D car models. The final result will look like this:

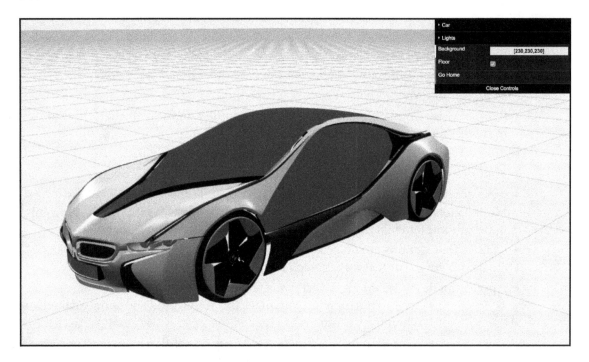

First, we'll start by defining the **graphical user interface (GUI)** of our application. Then, we'll add WebGL support by creating a `canvas` element and obtaining a WebGL context. After obtaining a valid WebGL context, we will define and implement the vertex and fragment shader using ESSL. Then, we will implement the three functions that hook into the life cycle of our application: `configure`, `load`, and `draw`.

Before we get started, let's consider some of the fundamentals of our virtual showroom application.

Complexity of the Models

Real-world applications are, generally, much more complex than PoC (proof of concept) demos. This is especially true with 3D applications, since 3D assets, such as models, are much more complex than simple spheres, cones, and other primitive geometric figures. Models in large 3D applications tend to have lots of vertices with complicated configurations that provide the level of detail and realism users expect. Apart from the pure geometrical representation of these models, they often come with several textures. As expected, creating geometries and textures *manually* with JSON files is nothing short of daunting.

Fortunately, we can use various industry proved 3D design software to create and import models into a WebGL scene. For our 3D virtual car showroom, we will use models that have been created with **Blender**, a widely used, open source 3D tool.

Blender

 Blender is an open source 3D computer graphics software that allows you to create animations, games, and other interactive applications. Blender provides numerous features so that you can create complex models. You can check out the official Blender website for more information: `https://www.blender.org`.

We will use Blender to import car models into our WebGL scene. First, we will export the models to an intermediary file format called **OBJ** and then parse them into consumable JSON files. We will cover more on these concepts later.

Shader Quality

Since we will be using complex models, such as cars, we'll need to develop shaders that can render the different materials of our models. This should be relatively simple, since the shaders we've developed already handle diffuse, specular, and ambient components for materials. In Blender, we will select the option to export materials when generating the OBJ files. Blender will then generate a second file known as the **Material Template Library** (**MTL**). For the best results, our shaders will use Phong shading and Phong lighting, with support for multiple lights.

Network Delays and Bandwidth Consumption

When it comes to WebGL applications with large 3D assets, we generally download geometries and textures from a web server. As expected, this can take some time depending on the quality of the network connection and the amount of data that needs to be transferred. There are, however, several strategies for optimizing this process, such as compression and 3D asset optimizations, which will be covered in a later chapter. We will use AJAX to provide users with a great user experience by downloading these large assets in the background.

With these considerations in mind, let's get started.

Designing Our GUI

We will define a very simple layout for our application. First, we will define our HTML document and include all of the necessary dependencies:

```html
<html>
<head>
  <title>Real-Time 3D Graphics with WebGL 2</title>
  <link rel="shortcut icon" type="image/png"
   href="/common/images/favicon.png" />

  <!-- libraries -->
  <link rel="stylesheet" href="/common/lib/normalize.css">
  <script type="text/javascript" src="/common/lib/dat.gui.js"></script>
  <script type="text/javascript" src="/common/lib/gl-matrix.js"></script>

  <!-- modules -->
  <script type="text/javascript" src="/common/js/utils.js"></script>
  <script type="text/javascript" src="/common/js/EventEmitter.js"></script>
  <script type="text/javascript" src="/common/js/Camera.js"></script>
  <script type="text/javascript" src="/common/js/Clock.js"></script>
  <script type="text/javascript" src="/common/js/Controls.js"></script>
  <script type="text/javascript" src="/common/js/Floor.js"></script>
  <script type="text/javascript" src="/common/js/Light.js"></script>
  <script type="text/javascript" src="/common/js/Program.js"></script>
  <script type="text/javascript" src="/common/js/Scene.js"></script>
  <script type="text/javascript" src="/common/js/Texture.js"></script>
  <script type="text/javascript" src="/common/js/Transforms.js"></script>
</head>
<body>
</body>
</html>
```

As you can see, we've included the following libraries that are required for our application:

- `normalize.css`: A set of styles that makes browsers render all elements more consistently
- `dat.gui.js`: A lightweight graphical user interface for changing variables in JavaScript
- `gl-matrix.js`: A JavaScript matrix and vector library for high performance applications

Now that we've included the required libraries, we will include the various components we've covered throughout this book.

Adding canvas Support

Now that we have the shell for our application, let's add the `canvas` that's required for our WebGL application:

```
<canvas id="webgl-canvas">
  Your browser does not support the HTML5 canvas element.
</canvas>
```

The `canvas` element with the `webgl-canvas` ID goes between the `body` of our HTML document.

Adding Shader Scripts

Next, let's include the two shaders that we'll need for our application by using the following code:

```
<script id="vertex-shader" type="x-shader/x-vertex">
  #version 300 es
  precision mediump float;

  void main(void) {}
</script>

<script id="fragment-shader" type="x-shader/x-fragment">
  #version 300 es
  precision mediump float;

  void main(void) {}
</script>
```

These `scripts` are placed inside the `head` of our document.

Adding WebGL Support

Now that we have the basic boilerplate for our application, let's initialize our WebGL application:

```
<script type="text/javascript">
  'use strict';

  let gl, program, scene, clock;

  function configure() {
    const canvas = utils.getCanvas('webgl-canvas');
    utils.autoResizeCanvas(canvas);

    gl = utils.getGLContext(canvas);
    gl.clearColor(0.9, 0.9, 0.9, 1);
    gl.clearDepth(1);
    gl.enable(gl.DEPTH_TEST);
    gl.depthFunc(gl.LESS);
    gl.blendFunc(gl.SRC_ALPHA, gl.ONE_MINUS_SRC_ALPHA);

    program = new Program(gl, 'vertex-shader', 'fragment-shader');

    scene = new Scene(gl, program);

    clock = new Clock();
  }

  function draw() {
    gl.viewport(0, 0, gl.canvas.width, gl.canvas.height);
    gl.clear(gl.COLOR_BUFFER_BIT | gl.DEPTH_BUFFER_BIT);
  }

  function init() {
    configure();
    clock.on('tick', draw);
  }

  window.onload = init;
</script>
```

This `script` tag goes after the shader scripts to ensure that we can reference them as needed.

Let's cover this code in detail:

```
let gl, program, scene, clock;
```

We need to define the various global variables that we'll be setting and using throughout the application. As in all of our previous exercises, we need to define the entry point for the application. We do this with the following code:

```
function init() {
  configure();
  clock.on('tick', draw);
}

window.onload = init;
```

The `init` function is called once our document has loaded via `window.onload`. In the `init` function, we set up our application by calling `configure` and using the `clock` instance to call `draw` on every `tick`—that is, every `requestAnimationFrame` call:

```
function configure() {
  const canvas = utils.getCanvas('webgl-canvas');
  utils.autoResizeCanvas(canvas);

  gl = utils.getGLContext(canvas);
  gl.clearColor(0.9, 0.9, 0.9, 1);
  gl.clearDepth(1);
  gl.enable(gl.DEPTH_TEST);
  gl.depthFunc(gl.LESS);
  gl.blendFunc(gl.SRC_ALPHA, gl.ONE_MINUS_SRC_ALPHA);

  program = new Program(gl, 'vertex-shader', 'fragment-shader');

  scene = new Scene(gl, program);

  clock = new Clock();
}
```

We initialize and set our `canvas` with the ID of `webgl-canvas`. Then, we pass the `canvas` instance to our utility function for full screen and auto resizing capabilities. This function is useful because it automatically updates the size of the `canvas` to the available window space without hardcoding the size of the `canvas`. Then, we initialize `gl`, `scene`, `clock`, and `program` using the provided shaders. Finally, we set the `gl` context with the basic configurations, such as a clear color, depth testing, and blending functions:

```
function draw() {
    gl.viewport(0, 0, gl.canvas.width, gl.canvas.height);
    gl.clear(gl.COLOR_BUFFER_BIT | gl.DEPTH_BUFFER_BIT);
}
```

The `draw` function is simple, as it simply sets the viewport and clears the `canvas`. You can find this source code inside the `ch09_scaffolding.html` file for this book.

Now, if you run `ch09_scaffolding.html` in your browser, you will see that the `canvas` resizes according to the size of the browser, as follows:

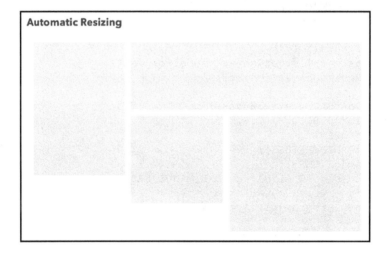

Implementing the Shaders

With our shaders, we will implement **Phong shading** and the **Phong reflection** model. Remember that Phong shading interpolates vertex normals and creates a normal for every fragment–the processing happens in the fragment shader. The Phong reflection model describes illumination as the addition of ambient, diffuse, and specular interaction of the object with the light sources.

To be consistent with the Material Template Library (MTL) format, we'll follow some typical conventions to set out uniform names that refer to material properties:

Material Uniform	Description
uKa	Ambient property.
uKd	Diffuse property.
uKs	Specular property.
uNi	Optical density. We will not use this feature, but you will see it in the MTL file.
uNs	Specular exponent. A high exponent results in a tight, concentrated highlight. Ns values normally range from 0 to 1000.
uD	Transparency (alpha channel).
uIllum	Determines the illumination model for the object being rendered. Unlike previous chapters where we had one model for all objects, we let objects describe their reflective properties. According to the MTL file format specification, **illum** can be any of the following: • Color on and Ambient off. • Color on and Ambient on. • Highlight on. • Reflection on and Ray trace on. • Transparency: Glass on, Reflection: Ray trace on. • Reflection: Fresnel on and Ray trace on. • Transparency: Refraction on, Reflection: Fresnel off and Ray trace on. • Transparency: Refraction on, Reflection: Fresnel on and Ray trace on. • Reflection on and Ray trace off. • Transparency: Glass on, Reflection: Ray trace off. • Casts shadows onto invisible surfaces.

The Wavefront .obj file

For more information on OBJ and MTL file specifications, please refer to the following link: https://en.wikipedia.org/wiki/Wavefront_.obj_file.

Our shaders will also support multiple lights by using uniform arrays, as described in earlier chapters. The number of lights is defined by a constant in both the vertex and fragment shaders:

```
const int numLights = 4;
```

We will use the following uniform arrays to work with lights:

Light Uniform Array	Description
uLa[numLights]	Ambient property.
uLd[numLights]	Diffuse property.
uLs[numLights]	Specular property.

Source code

You can refer to ch09_02_showroom.html if you wish to explore the source code for the shaders in this chapter.

Here's the vertex shader:

```
<script id="vertex-shader" type="x-shader/x-vertex">
  #version 300 es
  precision mediump float;

  const int numLights = 4;

  uniform mat4 uModelViewMatrix;
  uniform mat4 uProjectionMatrix;
  uniform mat4 uNormalMatrix;
  uniform vec3 uLightPosition[numLights];

  in vec3 aVertexPosition;
  in vec3 aVertexNormal;

  out vec3 vNormal;
  out vec3 vLightRay[numLights];
  out vec3 vEye[numLights];

  void main(void) {
    vec4 vertex = uModelViewMatrix * vec4(aVertexPosition, 1.0);
    vec4 lightPosition = vec4(0.0);

    for(int i= 0; i < numLights; i++) {
      lightPosition = vec4(uLightPosition[i], 1.0);
      vLightRay[i] = vertex.xyz - lightPosition.xyz;
      vEye[i] = -vec3(vertex.xyz);
```

```
    }

    vNormal = vec3(uNormalMatrix * vec4(aVertexNormal, 1.0));
    gl_Position = uProjectionMatrix * uModelViewMatrix *
vec4(aVertexPosition, 1.0);
  }
</script>
```

Along with the corresponding fragment shader:

```
<script id="fragment-shader" type="x-shader/x-fragment">
  #version 300 es
  precision mediump float;

  const int numLights = 4;

  uniform vec3 uLd[numLights];
  uniform vec3 uLs[numLights];
  uniform vec3 uLightPosition[numLights];
  uniform vec3 uKa;
  uniform vec3 uKd;
  uniform vec3 uKs;
  uniform float uNs;
  uniform float uD;
  uniform int uIllum;
  uniform bool uWireframe;

  in vec3 vNormal;
  in vec3 vLightRay[numLights];
  in vec3 vEye[numLights];

  out vec4 fragColor;

  void main(void) {
    if (uWireframe || uIllum == 0) {
      fragColor = vec4(uKd, uD);
      return;
    }

    vec3 color = vec3(0.0);
    vec3 light = vec3(0.0);
    vec3 eye = vec3(0.0);
    vec3 reflection = vec3(0.0);
    vec3 normal = normalize(vNormal);

    if (uIllum == 1) {
      for (int i = 0; i < numLights; i++) {
        light = normalize(vLightRay[i]);
```

```
        normal = normalize(vNormal);
        color += (uLd[i] * uKd * clamp(dot(normal, -light), 0.0, 1.0));
      }
    }

    if (uIllum == 2) {
      for (int i = 0; i < numLights; i++) {
        eye = normalize(vEye[i]);
        light = normalize(vLightRay[i]);
        reflection = reflect(light, normal);
        color += (uLd[i] * uKd * clamp(dot(normal, -light), 0.0, 1.0));
        color += (uLs[i] * uKs * pow(max(dot(reflection, eye), 0.0), uNs) *
          4.0);
      }
    }

    fragColor =  vec4(color, uD);
  }
</script>
```

As expected, the vertex and fragment shaders borrow concepts from earlier chapters covered in this book, except for `uIllum`. As described earlier, the `illum` property determines the illumination model for the object being rendered. We could default to a simpler fragment shader (such as `uIllum == 2`), but a simple example has been provided for educational purposes.

Next, we will configure the three main functions that hook into the life cycle of our WebGL application. These are the `configure`, `load`, and `render` functions.

Setting up the Scene

We can set up the scene by defining some global variables for our application and writing the code for the `configure` function. Let's analyze this line by line:

```
let gl, program, scene, clock, camera, transforms, lights,
  floor, selectedCar, lightPositions, carModelData,
  clearColor = [0.9, 0.9, 0.9, 1];

function configure() {
  // ...
}
```

At this stage, we want to set some of the WebGL properties, such as the clear color and the depth test. Then, we need to create a camera and set its initial position and orientation. We also need to create a camera controls instance so that we can update the position of the camera during scene interactions. Finally, we need to define the JavaScript variables that will be mapped to the shaders.

To accomplish these tasks, we will use `Camera.js`, `Controls.js`, `Program.js`, and `Transforms.js` from our architecture.

Configuring WebGL Properties

We need to initialize and configure our `canvas` and `gl` instances:

```
function configure() {
  canvas = utils.getCanvas('webgl-canvas');
  utils.autoResizeCanvas(canvas);
  gl = utils.getGLContext(canvas);

  // ...
}
```

Then, we need to initialize `scene`, `clock`, and `program`:

```
clock = new Clock();
program = new Program(gl, 'vertex-shader', 'fragment-shader');
scene = new Scene(gl, program);
```

These core components are defined globally so that we can reference them throughout our application.

Finally, we need to set the background color and the depth test properties, as follows:

```
gl.clearColor(...clearColor);
gl.clearDepth(1);
gl.enable(gl.DEPTH_TEST);
gl.depthFunc(gl.LESS);
gl.blendFunc(gl.SRC_ALPHA, gl.ONE_MINUS_SRC_ALPHA);
```

Setting up the Camera

To keep things simple, the `camera` variable will be global so that we can access it from the GUI controls:

```
camera = new Camera(Camera.ORBITING_TYPE);
```

Creating the Camera Controls

We need to instantiate a `Controls` instance that will bind mouse gestures to `camera` actions. The first argument is the `camera` we are controlling, and the second argument is a reference to our `canvas`:

```
new Controls(camera, canvas);
```

Scene Transforms

Once we have a `camera`, we can use it to create a new `Tranforms` instance, as follows:

```
transforms = new Transforms(gl, program, camera, canvas);
```

The `transforms` variable is also declared globally, so we can use it in the `draw` function to retrieve the current matrix transformations and pass them to the shaders.

Creating the Lights

We will create four lights by using the `Light` class from our framework with the following configurations:

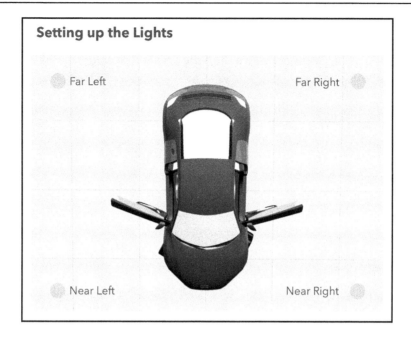

Setting up the Lights

Far Left

Far Right

Near Left

Near Right

First, we instantiate a `LightsManager` instance to manage our lights:

```
lights = new LightsManager();
```

Then, we create four light positions for each light and iterate over each position to uniquely position each light:

```
lightPositions = {
  farLeft: [-1000, 1000, -1000],
  farRight: [1000, 1000, -1000],
  nearLeft: [-1000, 1000, 1000],
  nearRight: [1000, 1000, 1000]
};

Object.keys(lightPositions).forEach(key => {
  const light = new Light(key);
  light.setPosition(lightPositions[key]);
  light.setDiffuse([0.4, 0.4, 0.4]);
  light.setSpecular([0.8, 0.8, 0.8]);
  lights.add(light)
});
```

Since every light has the same diffuse, ambient, and specular properties, we only set a dynamic position by using the `lightPositions` data.

Mapping Program Attributes and Uniforms

Next, inside the `configure` function, we map the JavaScript values to the attributes and uniforms inside of our shaders.

Using the program `instance` from earlier, we will set up the values to map attributes and uniforms to the shaders. The code looks like this:

```
const attributes = [
  'aVertexPosition',
  'aVertexNormal',
  'aVertexColor'
];

const uniforms = [
  'uProjectionMatrix',
  'uModelViewMatrix',
  'uNormalMatrix',
  'uLightPosition',
  'uWireframe',
  'uLd',
  'uLs',
  'uKa',
  'uKd',
  'uKs',
  'uNs',
  'uD',
  'uIllum'
];

program.load(attributes, uniforms);
```

When creating shaders, make sure that the shader attributes and uniforms are properly mapped to JavaScript values. This mapping step allows us to refer to attributes and uniforms effortlessly. Check out the `setAttributeLocations` and `setUniformLocations` methods inside of `Program.js`, which are called by `program.load`.

Uniform Initialization

After mapping the variables, we can initialize shader uniforms, such as lights:

```
gl.uniform3fv(program.uLightPosition, lights.getArray('position'));
gl.uniform3fv(program.uLd, lights.getArray('diffuse'));
gl.uniform3fv(program.uLs, lights.getArray('specular'));
```

The default material properties are as follows:

```
gl.uniform3fv(program.uKa, [1, 1, 1]);
gl.uniform3fv(program.uKd, [1, 1, 1]);
gl.uniform3fv(program.uKs, [1, 1, 1]);
gl.uniform1f(program.uNs, 1);
```

Lastly, we will create a `floor` instance that we will use later. We will also structure the data that describes the car model that we'll be loading later:

```
floor = new Floor(200, 2);

carModelData = {
  'BMW i8': {
    paintAlias: 'BMW',
    partsCount: 25,
    path: '/common/models/bmw-i8/part'
  }
};
```

Although we have only described one car model here, we'll leverage this data format so that we can add other car models later in this chapter.

Here's the final `configure` function, which you can find in the `ch09_02_showroom.html` source code:

```
function configure() {
  const canvas = utils.getCanvas('webgl-canvas');
  utils.autoResizeCanvas(canvas);

  gl = utils.getGLContext(canvas);
  gl.clearColor(...clearColor);
  gl.clearDepth(1);
  gl.enable(gl.DEPTH_TEST);
  gl.depthFunc(gl.LESS);
  gl.blendFunc(gl.SRC_ALPHA, gl.ONE_MINUS_SRC_ALPHA);

  program = new Program(gl, 'vertex-shader', 'fragment-shader');

  const attributes = [
    'aVertexPosition',
    'aVertexNormal',
    'aVertexColor'
  ];

  const uniforms = [
    'uProjectionMatrix',
    'uModelViewMatrix',
```

```
        'uNormalMatrix',
        'uLightPosition',
        'uWireframe',
        'uLd',
        'uLs',
        'uKa',
        'uKd',
        'uKs',
        'uNs',
        'uD',
        'uIllum'
    ];

    program.load(attributes, uniforms);

    scene = new Scene(gl, program);
    clock = new Clock();

    camera = new Camera(Camera.ORBITING_TYPE);
    new Controls(camera, canvas);

    transforms = new Transforms(gl, program, camera, canvas);

    lights = new LightsManager();

    lightPositions = {
      farLeft: [-1000, 1000, -1000],
      farRight: [1000, 1000, -1000],
      nearLeft: [-1000, 1000, 1000],
      nearRight: [1000, 1000, 1000]
    };

    Object.keys(lightPositions).forEach(key => {
      const light = new Light(key);
      light.setPosition(lightPositions[key]);
      light.setDiffuse([0.4, 0.4, 0.4]);
      light.setSpecular([0.8, 0.8, 0.8]);
      lights.add(light)
    });

    gl.uniform3fv(program.uLightPosition, lights.getArray('position'));
    gl.uniform3fv(program.uLd, lights.getArray('diffuse'));
    gl.uniform3fv(program.uLs, lights.getArray('specular'));

    gl.uniform3fv(program.uKa, [1, 1, 1]);
    gl.uniform3fv(program.uKd, [1, 1, 1]);
    gl.uniform3fv(program.uKs, [1, 1, 1]);
    gl.uniform1f(program.uNs, 1);
```

```
floor = new Floor(200, 2);

carModelData = {
  'BMW i8': {
    paintAlias: 'BMW',
    partsCount: 25,
    path: '/common/models/bmw-i8/part'
  }
};
}
```

We have finished setting up the scene. Next, we'll implement the `load` function.

Loading the Cars

Inside of the `load` function, we will download some assets in the background that we can load into our application.

When the JSON files that describe the cars are available, we just use the `scene` instance to load these files. Keep in mind that it's uncommon to have ready-to-use JSON files. In such situations, there are specialized design tools, such as Blender, which can significantly help create and convert consumable models.

That said, we will use the pre-built models that are available on `blendswap.org`. All of these models are publicly available, and are free of charge to use and distribute. Before we can use these models, we need to export them to an intermediate file format from where we can extract the geometry and material properties to create the appropriate JSON files. The file format we are going to use is **Wavefront OBJ**.

Exporting the Blender Models

All of the assets for this exercise are provided in this book's source code. However, if you want to go through the steps of converting the models, here are the steps. For this exercise, we will be using Blender (v2.6).

Blender

If you do not have Blender, you can download it for your operating system from `https://www.blender.org/download/`.

Once you have loaded the car into Blender, you need to export it as an OBJ file. To do so, go to **File** | **Export** | **Wavefront (.obj)**, as shown in the following screenshot:

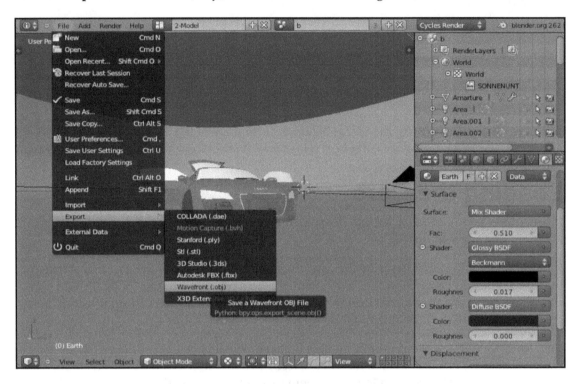

In the **Export OBJ** panel, make sure that the following options are active:

- **Apply Modifiers**: This will write the vertices in the scene that are the result of a mathematical operation instead of direct modeling. If you do not check this option, the model may appear incomplete in the WebGL scene.
- **Write Materials**: Blender will create the matching Material Template Library (MTL) file. We'll cover more on this in the following section.
- **Triangulate Faces**: Blender will write the indices as triangles. This is ideal for WebGL rendering.
- **Entity as OBJ Objects**: This configuration will identify every object in the Blender scene as an object in the OBJ file.
- **Material Groups**: If an object in the Blender scene has several materials, for example, a car tire that can be made of aluminum and rubber, then the object will be subdivided into groups, one per material in the OBJ file.

OBJ file. Then, click on **Export**. Once you have checked these export parameters, select the directory and name for your

Understanding the OBJ Format

There are several types of definitions in an OBJ file. Let's cover them line-by-line with a simple example. We are going to dissect a sample `square.obj` file that we will export from the Blender file called `square.blend`. This file represents a square divided into two parts, one painted red and the other painted blue, as shown in the following diagram:

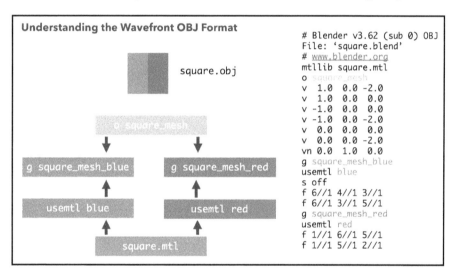

When we export Blender models to an OBJ format, the resulting file normally starts with a comment:

```
# Blender v2.62 (sub 0) OBJ
File: 'squares.blend'
# www.blender.org
```

These are comments, and they are denoted with a hash # symbol at the beginning of the line.

Next, we will usually find a line referring to the Material Template Library that this OBJ file is using. This line will begin with the keyword `mtllib`, followed by the name of the material's file:

```
mtllib square.mtl
```

There are several ways that geometries can be grouped into entities in an OBJ file. We can find lines starting with the prefix o, followed by the object name, or by the prefix g, followed by the group name:

```
o squares_mesh
```

After object declaration, the following lines will refer to vertices, v, optionally to vertex normals, vn, and texture coordinates, vt. It's important to note that vertices are shared by all groups in an object in the OBJ format. That is, you will not find lines referring to vertices when defining a group, because it's assumed that all vertex data was defined when the object was defined:

```
v   1.0   0.0  -2.0
v   1.0   0.0   0.0
v  -1.0   0.0   0.0
v  -1.0   0.0  -2.0
v   0.0   0.0   0.0
v   0.0   0.0  -2.0
vn  0.0   1.0   0.0
```

In our case, we have instructed Blender to export group materials. This means that each part of the object that has a different set of material properties will appear in the OBJ file as a group. In this example, we are defining an object with two groups (`squares_mesh_blue` and `squares_mesh_red`) and two corresponding materials (blue and red):

```
g squares_mesh_blue
```

If materials are being used, the line after the group declaration will be the material that's being used for that group. In this case, only the name of the material is required. It's assumed that the material properties for this material are defined in the MTL file that was declared at the beginning of the OBJ file:

```
usemtl blue
```

The lines that begin with the prefix s refer to smooth shading across polygons. Although mentioned here, we will not be using this definition when parsing the OBJ files into JSON files:

```
s off
```

The lines that start with f refer to faces. There are different ways to represent faces. Let's see them.

Vertex

```
f i1 i2 i3...
```

In this configuration, every face element corresponds to a vertex index. Depending on the number of indices per face, you could have triangular, rectangular, or polygonal faces. However, we have instructed Blender to use triangular faces to create the OBJ file. Otherwise, we would need to decompose the polygons into triangles before we could call `drawElements`.

Vertex/Texture Coordinate

```
f i1/t1 i2/t2 i3/t3...
```

In this combination, every vertex index appears to be followed by a forward slash and texture coordinate index. You will normally find this combination when texture coordinates are defined at the object level with `vt`.

Vertex/Texture Coordinate/Normal

```
f i1/t1/n1 i2/t2/n2 i3/t3/n3...
```

Here is a normal index that has been added as the third element in the configuration. If both texture coordinates and vertex normals are defined at the object level, you will most likely see this configuration at the group level.

Vertex//Normal

There can also be cases where normals are defined but texture coordinates are not. In this case, the second part of the face configuration is missing:

```
f i1//n1 i2//n2 i3//n3...
```

This is the case for `square.obj`, which looks like this:

```
f 6//1 4//1 3//1
f 6//1 3//1 5//1
```

Note that faces are defined using indices. In our example, we have defined a square divided into two parts. Here, we can see that all of the vertices share the same normal, which has been identified with index `1`.

The remaining lines in this file represent the red group:

```
g squares_mesh_red
usemtl red
f 1//1 6//1 5//1
f 1//1 5//1 2//1
```

As we mentioned previously, groups belonging to the same object share indices.

Parsing the OBJ Files

After exporting our cars into OBJ format, the next step is to parse the OBJ files to create JSON files that we can load into our scene. We have included the parser that we developed for this step in `common/models/obj-parser.py`. This parser has the following features:

- It's written in Python (quite common for OBJ parsers) and can be called in the command line with the following format:

  ```
  obj-parser.py arg1 arg2
  ```

- Where `arg1` is the name of the OBJ file to parse and `arg2` is the name of the MTL. The file extension is needed in both cases. For example:

  ```
  obj-parser.py square.obj square.mtl
  ```

- It creates one JSON file per OBJ group.
- It searches into the Material Template Library (if defined) for the material properties for each group and adds them to the corresponding JSON file.
- It will calculate the appropriate indices for each group. Remember that OBJ groups share indices. Since we are creating one independent WebGL object per group, each object needs to have indices starting with 0. The parser takes care of this for you.

Python

If you do not have Python installed in your system, you can get it from http://www.python.org/ or https://anaconda.org/anaconda/python.

The following diagram summarizes the procedure needed to create JSON files from Blender scenes:

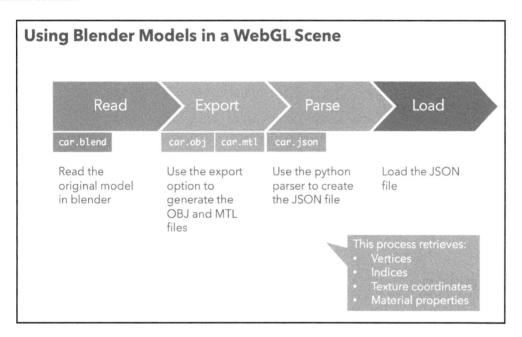

Loading Cars into Our WebGL Scene

Now that we have cars stored as JSON files, they are ready to be used in our WebGL scene. First, we have to let the user choose which car to visualize. That said, it's still a good idea to load one by default. To do so, we will write the following code inside the `load` function:

```
function goHome() {
  camera.goHome([0, 0.5, 10]);
  camera.setFocus([0, 0, 0]);
  camera.setAzimuth(25);
  camera.setElevation(-11);
}

function load() {
  goHome();
  loadCar('BMW i8');
}
```

We call `goHome`, a helper function, that sets the `camera` position to a particular point in our scene. This is defined as a function, since we'll later use it as a way to reset our `camera` location, as needed. Then, we call `loadCar`, which is where we supply the `key` of the car (for example, `BMW i8`) we want to load from the `carModelData` that we defined inside of `configure`. Let's see what `loadCar` looks like:

```
function loadCar(model) {
    scene.objects = [];
    scene.add(floor);
    const { path, partsCount } = carModelData[model];
    scene.loadByParts(path, partsCount);
    selectedCar = model;
}
```

This function clears all of the objects in our `scene`, adds the already created `floor` instance, and extracts the necessary data from the `carModelData` object, such as the `path` to the model and the number of parts to load.

Rendering

Let's take a step back and assess the big picture. We previously mentioned that, in our architecture, we have defined three main functions that define the life cycle of our WebGL application. These functions are `configure`, `load`, and `draw`.

Thus far, we've set up the scene by writing the code for the `configure` function. After that, we created our JSON cars and loaded them by writing the code for the `load` function. Now, we will implement the code for the third function: the `draw` function.

The code is pretty standard and almost identical to the `draw` functions that we've written in previous chapters. As the following code demonstrates, we set and clear the area that we are going to draw. Then, we check the camera's perspective and process every object in `scene`.

One important consideration is that we need to ensure that we are correctly mapping the material properties defined in our JSON objects to the appropriate shader uniforms.

Let's start implementing the `draw` function:

```
function draw() {
  gl.viewport(0, 0, gl.canvas.width, gl.canvas.height);
  gl.clear(gl.COLOR_BUFFER_BIT | gl.DEPTH_BUFFER_BIT);
  transforms.updatePerspective();

  // ...
}
```

First, we set our viewport and clear the scene, followed by applying the perspective update by using the `transforms` instance we initialized inside of `configure`.

Then, we move to the objects in our scene:

```
try {
  scene.traverse(object => {
    if (!object.visible) return;

    transforms.calculateModelView();
    transforms.push();
    transforms.setMatrixUniforms();
    transforms.pop();

    gl.uniform3fv(program.uKa, object.Ka);
    gl.uniform3fv(program.uKd, object.Kd);
    gl.uniform3fv(program.uKs, object.Ks);
    gl.uniform1f(program.uNs, object.Ns);
    gl.uniform1f(program.uD, object.d);
    gl.uniform1i(program.uIllum, object.illum);

    // Bind
    gl.bindVertexArray(object.vao);
    gl.bindBuffer(gl.ELEMENT_ARRAY_BUFFER, object.ibo);

    if (object.wireframe) {
      gl.uniform1i(program.uWireframe, 1);
      gl.drawElements(gl.LINES, object.indices.length, gl.UNSIGNED_SHORT,
        0);
    }
    else {
      gl.uniform1i(program.uWireframe, 0);
      gl.drawElements(gl.TRIANGLES, object.indices.length,
       gl.UNSIGNED_SHORT, 0);
    }

    // Clean
    gl.bindVertexArray(null);
```

```
        gl.bindBuffer(gl.ARRAY_BUFFER, null);
        gl.bindBuffer(gl.ELEMENT_ARRAY_BUFFER, null);
    });
}
catch (error) {
    console.error(error);
}
```

It may be helpful to take a look at the list of uniforms that was defined in the earlier section on shaders. We need to make sure that all of the shader uniforms are paired with object attributes.

The following diagram shows the process that occurs inside the `draw` function:

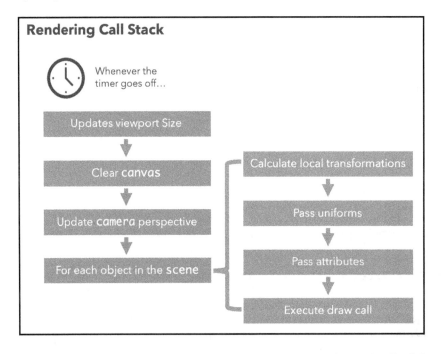

Each car part is a different JSON file. The `draw` function iterates through all of these parts inside the `scene`. For each part, the material properties are passed as uniforms to the shaders and the geometry is passed as attributes (reading data from the respective VBOs). Finally, the draw call (`drawElements`) is executed. The result looks something like this:

Here's the final JavaScript source code that can be found in `ch09_02_showroom.html`:

```html
<html>
<head>
  <title>Real-Time 3D Graphics with WebGL2</title>
  <link rel="shortcut icon" type="image/png"
   href="/common/images/favicon.png" />

  <!-- libraries -->
  <link rel="stylesheet" href="/common/lib/normalize.css">
  <script type="text/javascript" src="/common/lib/dat.gui.js"></script>
  <script type="text/javascript" src="/common/lib/gl-matrix.js"></script>

  <!-- modules -->
  <script type="text/javascript" src="/common/js/utils.js"></script>
  <script type="text/javascript" src="/common/js/EventEmitter.js"></script>
  <script type="text/javascript" src="/common/js/Camera.js"></script>
  <script type="text/javascript" src="/common/js/Clock.js"></script>
  <script type="text/javascript" src="/common/js/Controls.js"></script>
  <script type="text/javascript" src="/common/js/Floor.js"></script>
  <script type="text/javascript" src="/common/js/Light.js"></script>
  <script type="text/javascript" src="/common/js/Program.js"></script>
  <script type="text/javascript" src="/common/js/Scene.js"></script>
  <script type="text/javascript" src="/common/js/Texture.js"></script>
  <script type="text/javascript" src="/common/js/Transforms.js"></script>
```

The following code is for the vertex shader:

```html
<script id="vertex-shader" type="x-shader/x-vertex">
  #version 300 es
  precision mediump float;

  const int numLights = 4;

  uniform mat4 uModelViewMatrix;
  uniform mat4 uProjectionMatrix;
  uniform mat4 uNormalMatrix;
  uniform vec3 uLightPosition[numLights];

  in vec3 aVertexPosition;
  in vec3 aVertexNormal;

  out vec3 vNormal;
  out vec3 vLightRay[numLights];
  out vec3 vEye[numLights];

  void main(void) {
    vec4 vertex = uModelViewMatrix * vec4(aVertexPosition, 1.0);
    vec4 lightPosition = vec4(0.0);

    for(int i= 0; i < numLights; i++) {
      lightPosition = vec4(uLightPosition[i], 1.0);
      vLightRay[i] = vertex.xyz - lightPosition.xyz;
      vEye[i] = -vec3(vertex.xyz);
    }

    vNormal = vec3(uNormalMatrix * vec4(aVertexNormal, 1.0));
    gl_Position = uProjectionMatrix * uModelViewMatrix *
      vec4(aVertexPosition, 1.0);
  }
</script>
```

The following code is for the fragment shader:

```html
<script id="fragment-shader" type="x-shader/x-fragment">
  #version 300 es
  precision mediump float;

  const int numLights = 4;

  uniform vec3 uLd[numLights];
  uniform vec3 uLs[numLights];
  uniform vec3 uLightPosition[numLights];
  uniform vec3 uKa;
```

```
    uniform vec3 uKd;
    uniform vec3 uKs;
    uniform float uNs;
    uniform float uD;
    uniform int uIllum;
    uniform bool uWireframe;

    in vec3 vNormal;
    in vec3 vLightRay[numLights];
    in vec3 vEye[numLights];

    out vec4 fragColor;

    void main(void) {
      if (uWireframe || uIllum == 0) {
        fragColor = vec4(uKd, uD);
        return;
      }

      vec3 color = vec3(0.0);
      vec3 light = vec3(0.0);
      vec3 eye = vec3(0.0);
      vec3 reflection = vec3(0.0);
      vec3 normal = normalize(vNormal);

      if (uIllum == 1) {
        for (int i = 0; i < numLights; i++) {
          light = normalize(vLightRay[i]);
          normal = normalize(vNormal);
          color += (uLd[i] * uKd * clamp(dot(normal, -light), 0.0, 1.0));
        }
      }

      if (uIllum == 2) {
        for (int i = 0; i < numLights; i++) {
          eye = normalize(vEye[i]);
          light = normalize(vLightRay[i]);
          reflection = reflect(light, normal);
          color += (uLd[i] * uKd * clamp(dot(normal, -light), 0.0, 1.0));
          color += (uLs[i] * uKs * pow(max(dot(reflection, eye), 0.0), uNs)
            * 4.0);
        }
      }

      fragColor =  vec4(color, uD);
    }
</script>
```

The following is the application code with the appropriate global variable definitions:

```
<script type="text/javascript">
  'use strict';

  let gl, program, scene, clock, camera, transforms, lights,
    floor, selectedCar, lightPositions, carModelData,
    clearColor = [0.9, 0.9, 0.9, 1];
```

The following is the configuration step:

```
function configure() {
  const canvas = utils.getCanvas('webgl-canvas');
  utils.autoResizeCanvas(canvas);

  gl = utils.getGLContext(canvas);
  gl.clearColor(...clearColor);
  gl.clearDepth(1);
  gl.enable(gl.DEPTH_TEST);
  gl.depthFunc(gl.LESS);
  gl.blendFunc(gl.SRC_ALPHA, gl.ONE_MINUS_SRC_ALPHA);

  program = new Program(gl, 'vertex-shader', 'fragment-shader');

  const attributes = [
    'aVertexPosition',
    'aVertexNormal',
    'aVertexColor'
  ];

  const uniforms = [
    'uProjectionMatrix',
    'uModelViewMatrix',
    'uNormalMatrix',
    'uLightPosition',
    'uWireframe',
    'uLd',
    'uLs',
    'uKa',
    'uKd',
    'uKs',
    'uNs',
    'uD',
    'uIllum'
  ];

  program.load(attributes, uniforms);
```

```
    scene = new Scene(gl, program);
    clock = new Clock();

    camera = new Camera(Camera.ORBITING_TYPE);
    new Controls(camera, canvas);

    transforms = new Transforms(gl, program, camera, canvas);

    lights = new LightsManager();

    lightPositions = {
      farLeft: [-1000, 1000, -1000],
      farRight: [1000, 1000, -1000],
      nearLeft: [-1000, 1000, 1000],
      nearRight: [1000, 1000, 1000]
    };

    Object.keys(lightPositions).forEach(key => {
      const light = new Light(key);
      light.setPosition(lightPositions[key]);
      light.setDiffuse([0.4, 0.4, 0.4]);
      light.setSpecular([0.8, 0.8, 0.8]);
      lights.add(light)
    });

    gl.uniform3fv(program.uLightPosition, lights.getArray('position'));
    gl.uniform3fv(program.uLd, lights.getArray('diffuse'));
    gl.uniform3fv(program.uLs, lights.getArray('specular'));

    gl.uniform3fv(program.uKa, [1, 1, 1]);
    gl.uniform3fv(program.uKd, [1, 1, 1]);
    gl.uniform3fv(program.uKs, [1, 1, 1]);
    gl.uniform1f(program.uNs, 1);

    floor = new Floor(200, 2);

    carModelData = {
      'BMW i8': {
        paintAlias: 'BMW',
        partsCount: 25,
        path: '/common/models/bmw-i8/part'
      }
    };
}

function goHome() {
  camera.goHome([0, 0.5, 5]);
  camera.setFocus([0, 0, 0]);
```

```
      camera.setAzimuth(25);
      camera.setElevation(-10);
    }
```

The following code is for loading the required assets:

```
function loadCar(model) {
    scene.objects = [];
    scene.add(floor);
    const { path, partsCount } = carModelData[model];
    scene.loadByParts(path, partsCount);
    selectedCar = model;
}

function load() {
    goHome();
    loadCar('BMW i8');
}
```

The following code states where we draw our scene:

```
function draw() {
    gl.viewport(0, 0, gl.canvas.width, gl.canvas.height);
    gl.clear(gl.COLOR_BUFFER_BIT | gl.DEPTH_BUFFER_BIT);
    transforms.updatePerspective();

    try {
      scene.traverse(object => {
        if (!object.visible) return;

        transforms.calculateModelView();
        transforms.push();
        transforms.setMatrixUniforms();
        transforms.pop();

        gl.uniform3fv(program.uKa, object.Ka);
        gl.uniform3fv(program.uKd, object.Kd);
        gl.uniform3fv(program.uKs, object.Ks);
        gl.uniform1f(program.uNs, object.Ns);
        gl.uniform1f(program.uD, object.d);
        gl.uniform1i(program.uIllum, object.illum);

        // Bind
        gl.bindVertexArray(object.vao);
        gl.bindBuffer(gl.ELEMENT_ARRAY_BUFFER, object.ibo);

        if (object.wireframe) {
          gl.uniform1i(program.uWireframe, 1);
```

```
        gl.drawElements(gl.LINES, object.indices.length,
          gl.UNSIGNED_SHORT, 0);
      }
      else {
        gl.uniform1i(program.uWireframe, 0);
        gl.drawElements(gl.TRIANGLES, object.indices.length,
          gl.UNSIGNED_SHORT, 0);
      }

      // Clean
      gl.bindVertexArray(null);
      gl.bindBuffer(gl.ARRAY_BUFFER, null);
      gl.bindBuffer(gl.ELEMENT_ARRAY_BUFFER, null);
    });
  }
  catch (error) {
    console.error(error);
  }
}
```

The initialization of our application after the document has loaded is performed with the following code:

```
    function init() {
      configure();
      load();
      clock.on('tick', draw);
    }

    window.onload = init;

  </script>
</head>

<body>

  <canvas id="webgl-canvas">
    Your browser does not support the HTML5 canvas element.
  </canvas>

</body>
</html>
```

What just happened?

We have covered a demo that uses many of the elements we've discussed throughout this book. We used the infrastructure code that we developed throughout the previous chapters and implemented the three main functions: `configure`, `load`, and `draw`. As we've seen, these functions define the life cycle of our application.

Have a Go: Interactive Controls

Let's leverage **dat.GUI** to add more interactivity and customization to our application. Go ahead and try and add the following functionality:

1. Create a dropdown so that you can select from the following car models provided in the `common/models/` directory: `bmw-i8`, `audi-r8`, `ford-mustang`, and `lamborghini-gallardo`.

Hint

You can leverage `carModelData` to declaratively describe the car models and use the already created `loadCar` function with the appropriate information.

2. Create a color picker to change the color of the loaded car.

Hint

By inspecting the car data files, you will find various indicators that signify which parts are body panels. These are described as `paintAlias` in `carModelData`, which can be used to change the `Kd` property of each individual item in the scene.

3. Create a slider to change the shininess of the selected car.

Hint

You can use `paintAlias` once again and update the `Ks` property of each individual item in the scene.

The following functionality has been implemented in ch09_03_showroom-controls.html, along with controls for each individual light, the background color, floor visibility, and so forth:

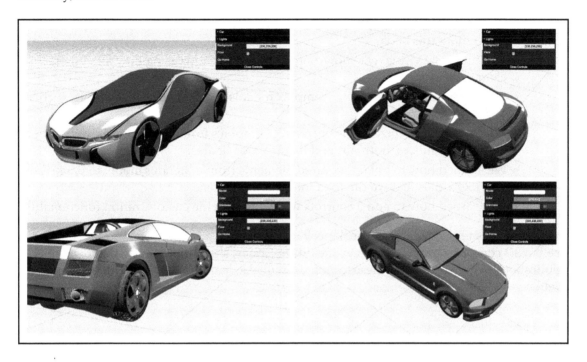

utils.configureControls

The utils.configureControls method is a simple abstraction on top of the dat.GUI interface to remove repetition and provide a more declarative way for describing our controls widget. You can use dat.GUI directly or build upon this simple helper function.

Bonus

You made it! How awesome is that?! As a bonus, a few additional examples have been provided for you in the source code under the ch10 directory. The bonus examples use the virtual car showroom as a base to showcase a few more advanced features for you to leverage in your future ventures in building compelling 3D experiences. Enjoy!

Summary

Let's summarize what we've learned in this chapter:

- We've reviewed concepts, architecture, and code that has been developed throughout this book.
- We built a 3D virtual car showroom application showcasing how all of these elements fit together.
- We've learned that designing complex models requires specialized tools, such as Blender.
- We covered how most of the current 3D graphics formats require the definition of vertices, indices, normals, and texture coordinates.
- We studied how to obtain required elements from a Blender model to parse them into JSON files that we can load into a WebGL scene.
- We learned how to add a controls widget to provide customization functionality.

In the next chapter, we will get a sneak peek at some of the advanced techniques commonly used in 3D computer graphic systems, including games, simulations, and other 3D applications. After addressing these topics, we will also learn how to implement them in WebGL.

10
Advanced Techniques

In the previous chapters of this book, we covered many foundational computer graphics concepts that, ultimately, gave us the knowledge and skills to build a 3D virtual car showroom. This means that at this point, you have all of the information you need to create rich 3D applications with WebGL. However, we've only just scratched the surface of what's possible with WebGL! Creative use of shaders, textures, and vertex attributes can yield fantastic results. In these final chapters, we'll cover a few advanced WebGL concepts that should leave you eager to explore more.

In this chapter, we will cover the following:

- Learn various post-processing effects
- Implementing a particle system using point sprites
- Understand how to use normal mapping
- Implement how to use ray tracing

Post-Processing

Post-processing is the process of adding effects by re-rendering the image of the scene with a shader that alters the final image. You can think of this as the process of taking a screenshot of your scene (ideally at 60+ frames per second), opening it up in your favorite image editor, and applying various filters. The difference is, of course, that we can do so in real time!

Some examples of simple post-processing effects include the following:

- Grayscale
- Sepia tone
- Inverted colors
- Film grain
- Blur
- Wavy/dizzy effect

The basic technique for creating these effects is relatively simple: create a framebuffer with the same dimensions as the `canvas` and have the entire scene rendered to it at the beginning of the `draw` cycle. Then, a quad is rendered to the default framebuffer using the texture that makes up the framebuffer's color attachment. The shader used during the rendering of the quad is what contains the post-process effect. That shader can transform the color values of the rendered scene as they get written to the quad to produce the desired visuals.

Let's investigate the individual steps of this process more closely.

Creating the Framebuffer

The code we will use to create the framebuffer is nearly the same as what we created earlier in Chapter 8, *Picking*. There are, however, a few key differences worth noting:

```
const { width, height } = canvas;

// 1. Init Color Texture
const texture = gl.createTexture();
gl.bindTexture(gl.TEXTURE_2D, texture);
gl.texParameteri(gl.TEXTURE_2D, gl.TEXTURE_MAG_FILTER, gl.NEAREST);
gl.texParameteri(gl.TEXTURE_2D, gl.TEXTURE_MIN_FILTER, gl.NEAREST);
gl.texParameteri(gl.TEXTURE_2D, gl.TEXTURE_WRAP_S, gl.CLAMP_TO_EDGE);
gl.texParameteri(gl.TEXTURE_2D, gl.TEXTURE_WRAP_T, gl.CLAMP_TO_EDGE);
gl.texImage2D(gl.TEXTURE_2D, 0, gl.RGBA, width, height, 0, gl.RGBA,
gl.UNSIGNED_BYTE, null);

// 2. Init Renderbuffer
const renderbuffer = gl.createRenderbuffer();
gl.bindRenderbuffer(gl.RENDERBUFFER, renderbuffer);
gl.renderbufferStorage(gl.RENDERBUFFER, gl.DEPTH_COMPONENT16, width,
height);

// 3. Init Framebuffer
```

```
const framebuffer = gl.createFramebuffer();
gl.bindFramebuffer(gl.FRAMEBUFFER, framebuffer);
gl.framebufferTexture2D(gl.FRAMEBUFFER, gl.COLOR_ATTACHMENT0,
gl.TEXTURE_2D, texture, 0);
gl.framebufferRenderbuffer(gl.FRAMEBUFFER, gl.DEPTH_ATTACHMENT,
gl.RENDERBUFFER, renderbuffer);

// 4. Clean up
gl.bindTexture(gl.TEXTURE_2D, null);
gl.bindRenderbuffer(gl.RENDERBUFFER, null);
gl.bindFramebuffer(gl.FRAMEBUFFER, null);
```

We use the `width` and `height` of the `canvas` to determine our buffer size, instead of using the arbitrary values that were used for the picker. Because the content of the picker buffer is not for rendering to the screen, we don't need to worry about resolution as much. For the post-process buffer, however, we'll get the best results if the output matches the dimensions of the `canvas`.

Since the texture will be exactly the same size as the `canvas`, and since we're rendering it as a full-screen quad, we've created a situation where the texture will be displayed at exactly a `1:1` ratio on the screen. This means that no filters need to be applied and that we can use `NEAREST` filtering with no visual artifacts. Also, in post-processing cases where we want to warp the texture coordinates (such as the wavy effect), we would benefit from using `LINEAR` filtering. We also need to use a wrap mode of `CLAMP_TO_EDGE`. That being said, the code is nearly identical to the `Picker` we used for framebuffer creation.

Creating the Geometry

Although we could load the quad from a file, the geometry is simple enough that we can include it directly in the code. All that's needed are the vertex positions and texture coordinates:

```
// 1. Define the geometry for the full-screen quad
const vertices = [
  -1, -1,
   1, -1,
  -1,  1,

  -1,  1,
   1, -1,
   1,  1
];

const textureCoords = [
```

```
    0, 0,
    1, 0,
    0, 1,

    0, 1,
    1, 0,
    1, 1
];

// 2. Create and bind VAO
const vao = gl.createVertexArray();
gl.bindVertexArray(vao);

// 3. Init the buffers
const vertexBuffer = gl.createBuffer();
gl.bindBuffer(gl.ARRAY_BUFFER, vertexBuffer);
gl.bufferData(gl.ARRAY_BUFFER, new Float32Array(vertices),
// Configure instructions for VAO
gl.STATIC_DRAW);gl.enableVertexAttribArray(program.aVertexPosition);
gl.vertexAttribPointer(program.aVertexPosition, 3, gl.FLOAT, false, 0, 0);

const textureBuffer = gl.createBuffer();
gl.bindBuffer(gl.ARRAY_BUFFER, textureBuffer);
gl.bufferData(gl.ARRAY_BUFFER, new Float32Array(textureCoords),
gl.STATIC_DRAW);
// Configure instructions for VAO
gl.enableVertexAttribArray(program.aVertexTextureCoords);
gl.vertexAttribPointer(program.aVertexTextureCoords, 2, gl.FLOAT, false, 0,
0);

// 4. Clean up
gl.bindVertexArray(null);
gl.bindBuffer(gl.ARRAY_BUFFER, null);
```

Setting up the Shader

The vertex shader for the post-process draw is quite simple:

```
#version 300 es
precision mediump float;

in vec2 aVertexPosition;
in vec2 aVertexTextureCoords;

out vec2 vTextureCoords;
```

```
void main(void) {
  vTextureCoords = aVertexTextureCoords;
  gl_Position = vec4(aVertexPosition, 0.0, 1.0);
}
```

Notice that unlike the other vertex shaders we've worked with so far, this one doesn't use any matrices. That's because the vertices we declared in the previous step are **pre-transformed**.

Recall from `Chapter 4, *Cameras*`, that we retrieved normalized device coordinates by multiplying the vertex position by the Projection matrix. Here, the coordinates mapped all positions to a `[-1, 1]` range on each axis, which represents the full viewport. In this case, however, our vertex positions are already mapped to a `[-1, 1]` range; therefore, no transformation is needed because they will map perfectly to the viewport bounds when we render.

The fragment shader is where most of the interesting operations happen. The fragment shader will be different for every post-process effect. Let's look at a simple **grayscale effect** as an example:

```
#version 300 es
precision mediump float;

uniform sampler2D uSampler;

in vec2 vTextureCoords;

out vec4 fragColor;

void main(void) {
  vec4 frameColor = texture(uSampler, vTextureCoords);
  float luminance = frameColor.r * 0.3 + frameColor.g * 0.59 + frameColor.b
    * 0.11;
  fragColor = vec4(luminance, luminance, luminance, frameColor.a);
}
```

In the preceding code, we sample the original color rendered by the scene (available through uSampler) and output a color that is a weighted average of the red, green, and blue channels. The result is a simple grayscale version of the original scene:

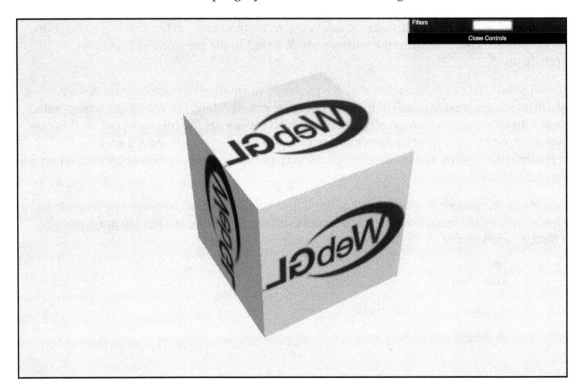

Architectural Updates

We've added a new class, PostProcess, to assist with the post-processing effects. This code can be found in the common/js/PostProcess.js file. This class will create the appropriate framebuffer and quad geometry, compile the post-process shader, and set up the render needed to draw the scene out to the quad.

Let's see how this component works with an example!

Time for Action: Post-Process Effects

Let's see a few post-processing effects in action:

1. Open the `ch10_01_post-process.html` file in your browser, like so:

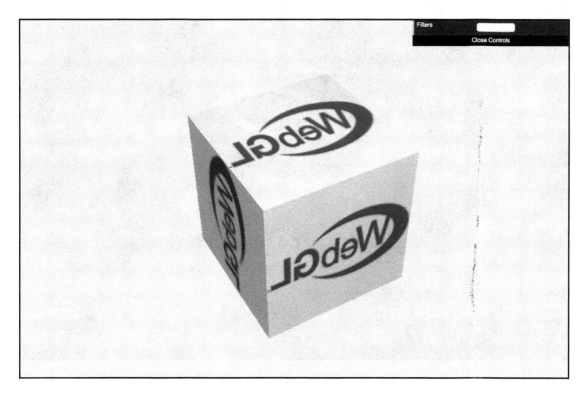

2. The controls dropdown allows you to switch between different sample effects. Try them out to get a feel for the effects they have on the scene. We've already looked at grayscale, so let's examine the rest of the filters individually.

3. The **invert effect**, similar to grayscale in that it only modifies the color output, inverts each color channel:

```
#version 300 es
precision mediump float;

uniform sampler2D uSampler;

in vec2 vTextureCoords;

out vec4 fragColor;
```

```
void main(void) {
  vec4 frameColor = texture(uSampler, vTextureCoords);
  fragColor = vec4(vec3(1.0) - frameColor.rgb, frameColor.a);
}
```

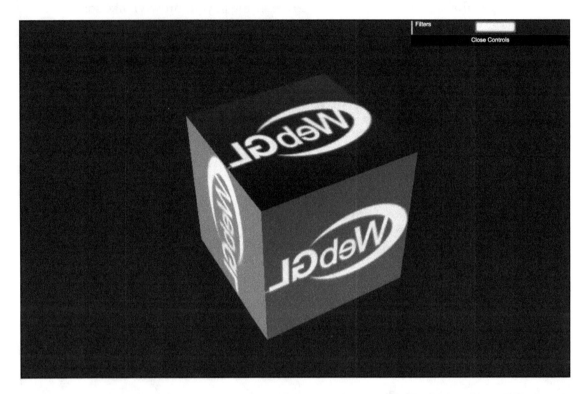

4. The **wavy effect** manipulates the texture coordinates to make the scene swirl and sway. In this effect, we also provide the current time to allow the distortion to change as time progresses:

```
#version 300 es
precision mediump float;

const float speed = 15.0;
const float magnitude = 0.015;

uniform sampler2D uSampler;
uniform float uTime;

in vec2 vTextureCoords;

out vec4 fragColor;
```

```
void main(void) {
  vec2 wavyCoord;
  wavyCoord.s = vTextureCoords.s + sin(uTime + vTextureCoords.t *
   speed) * magnitude;
  wavyCoord.t = vTextureCoords.t + cos(uTime + vTextureCoords.s *
   speed) * magnitude;
  fragColor = texture(uSampler, wavyCoord);
}
```

5. The **blur effect** samples several pixels around the current pixel and uses a weighted blend to produce a fragment output that is the average of its neighbors. This gives a blurry feel to the scene. A new uniform, uInverseTextureSize, provides values that are 1 over the width and height of the viewport. We use these values to accurately target individual pixels within the texture. For example, vTextureCoords.x + 2 * uInverseTextureSize.x will be exactly 2 pixels to the left of the original texture coordinate:

```glsl
#version 300 es
precision mediump float;

uniform sampler2D uSampler;
uniform vec2 uInverseTextureSize;

in vec2 vTextureCoords;

out vec4 fragColor;

vec4 offsetLookup(float xOff, float yOff) {
  return texture(
    uSampler,
    vec2(
      vTextureCoords.x + xOff * uInverseTextureSize.x,
      vTextureCoords.y + yOff * uInverseTextureSize.y
    )
  );
}

void main(void) {
  vec4 frameColor = offsetLookup(-4.0, 0.0) * 0.05;
  frameColor += offsetLookup(-3.0, 0.0) * 0.09;
  frameColor += offsetLookup(-2.0, 0.0) * 0.12;
  frameColor += offsetLookup(-1.0, 0.0) * 0.15;
  frameColor += offsetLookup(0.0, 0.0) * 0.16;
  frameColor += offsetLookup(1.0, 0.0) * 0.15;
  frameColor += offsetLookup(2.0, 0.0) * 0.12;
  frameColor += offsetLookup(3.0, 0.0) * 0.09;
  frameColor += offsetLookup(4.0, 0.0) * 0.05;
  fragColor = frameColor;
}
```

6. Our final example is a **film grain** effect. This uses a noisy texture to create a grainy scene, which simulates the use of an old camera. This example is significant because it demonstrates the use of a second texture besides the framebuffer when rendering:

```
#version 300 es
precision mediump float;

const float grainIntensity = 0.1;
const float scrollSpeed = 4000.0;

uniform sampler2D uSampler;
uniform sampler2D uNoiseSampler;
uniform vec2 uInverseTextureSize;
uniform float uTime;

in vec2 vTextureCoords;

out vec4 fragColor;

void main(void) {
```

```
    vec4 frameColor = texture(uSampler, vTextureCoords);
    vec4 grain = texture(
      uNoiseSampler,
      vTextureCoords * 2.0 + uTime * scrollSpeed *
      uInverseTextureSize
    );
    fragColor = frameColor - (grain * grainIntensity);
  }
```

What just happened?

All of these effects are achieved by manipulating the rendered image before it is outputted to the screen. Since the amount of geometry processed for these effects is small, they are efficient, regardless of the scene's complexity. That being said, performance may be affected as the size of the `canvas` or the complexity of the post-process shader increases.

Have a Go: Funhouse Mirror Effect

What would it take to create a post-process effect that stretches the image near the center of the viewport and squashes it toward the edges?

Point Sprites

Particle effects is a common technique used in many 3D applications and games. A particle effect is a generic term for any special effect created by rendering groups of **particles** (displayed as points, textured quads, or repeated geometry), typically with some simple physics simulation acting on the individual particles. They can be used for simulating smoke, fire, bullets, explosions, water, sparks, and many other effects that are difficult to represent by a single geometric model.

One very efficient way of rendering particles is to use **point sprites**. Throughout this book, we've been rendering triangle primitives, but if you render vertices with the POINTS primitive type, then each vertex will be rendered as a single pixel on the screen. A point sprite is an extension of the POINTS primitive rendering, where each point is provided a size and is textured in the shader.

A point sprite is created by setting the gl_PointSize value in the vertex shader. It can be set to either a constant value or a value calculated from shader inputs. If it's set to a number greater than one, the point is rendered as a quad that always faces the screen (also known as a **billboard**). The quad is centered on the original point and has a width and height equal to the gl_PointSize in pixels:

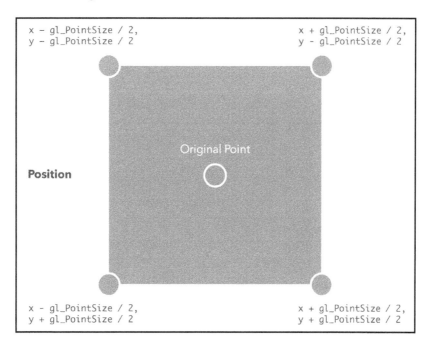

When the point sprite is rendered, it also generates texture coordinates for the quad, covering a simple 0–1 range from the upper left to the lower right:

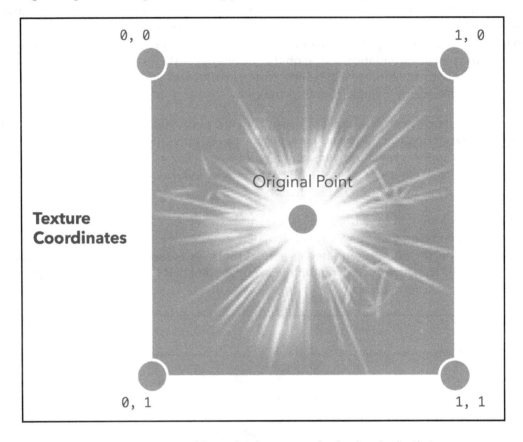

The texture coordinates are accessible in the fragment shader by the built-in vec2 gl_PointCoord. Combining these properties gives us a simple point sprite vertex shader that looks like this:

```
#version 300 es
precision mediump float;

uniform mat4 uModelViewMatrix;
uniform mat4 uProjectionMatrix;
uniform float uPointSize;

in vec4 aParticle;

out float vLifespan;
```

```
void main(void) {
  gl_Position = uProjectionMatrix * uModelViewMatrix * vec4(aParticle.xyz,
    1.0);
  vLifespan = aParticle.w;
  gl_PointSize = uPointSize * vLifespan;
}
```

The corresponding fragment shader looks like this:

```
#version 300 es
precision mediump float;

uniform sampler2D uSampler;

in float vLifespan;

out vec4 fragColor;

void main(void) {
  vec4 texColor = texture(uSampler, gl_PointCoord);
  fragColor = vec4(texColor.rgb, texColor.a * vLifespan);
}
```

The following is an example of the appropriate draw command:

```
gl.drawArrays(gl.POINTS, 0, vertexCount);
```

This renders each point in the vertex buffer as a 16x16 texture.

Time for Action: Fountain of Sparks

Let's see how we can use point sprites to create a fountain of sparks:

1. Open the `ch10_02_point-sprites.html` file in your browser:

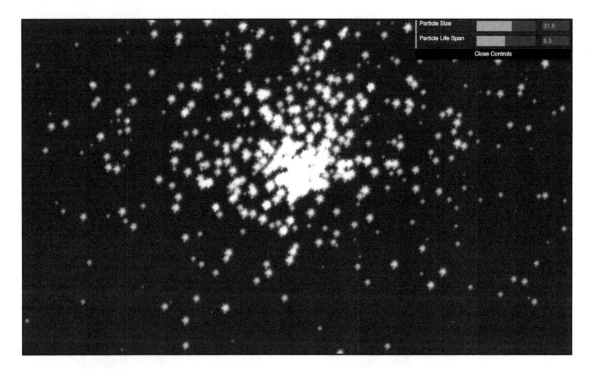

2. This example showcases a simple *fountain of sparks* effect with point sprites. You can adjust the size and lifetime of the particles by using the sliders.

3. The particle simulation is performed by maintaining a list of particles that are comprised of position, velocity, and lifespan. In every frame, we iterate through the list and move the particles according to the velocity; we also apply gravity and reduce the remaining lifespan. Once a particle's lifespan has reached 0, it's reset to the origin with a random velocity and updated lifespan.

4. With every iteration of the particle's simulation, the particle positions and lifespans are copied to an array that is then used to update a vertex buffer. This vertex buffer is what is rendered to produce the onscreen sprites.

5. Let's experiment with some of the other values that control the simulation and see how they affect the scene. Open up `ch10_02_point-sprites.html` in your editor.

6. First, locate the call to `configureParticles` at the bottom of the `configure` function. The number passed as an argument, initially set to `1024`, determines how many particles are created. Try changing it to a lower or higher value to see the effect it has on the particle system. Be careful, though, since extremely high values (for example, in the millions) may cause performance issues.

7. Next, find the `resetParticle` function. This function is called any time a particle is created or reset. There are several values here that can have a significant effect on how the scene renders:

```
function resetParticle(particle) {
  particle.position = [0, 0, 0];

  particle.velocity = [
    Math.random() * 20 - 10,
    Math.random() * 20,
    Math.random() * 20 - 10,
  ];

  particle.lifespan = Math.random() * particleLifespan;
  particle.remainingLife = particle.lifespan;
}
```

8. The `particle.position` is the x, y, z starting coordinates for the particle. Initially, all points start at the world origin (`0, 0, 0`), but this could be set to anything. It's often desirable to have the particles originate from the location of another object so as to give the impression that the object is producing the particles. You can also randomize the position to make the particles appear within a given area.

9. `particle.velocity` is the initial velocity of the particle. Here, you can see that it has been randomized so that particles spread out as they move away from the origin. Particles that move in random directions tend to look more like explosions or sprays, while those that move in the same direction give the appearance of a steady stream. In this case, the y value is designed to always be positive, while the x and z values may either be positive or negative. Experiment with what happens when you increase or decrease these velocity values or remove the random element from one of the components.

10. Finally, `particle.lifespan` determines how long a particle is displayed before being reset. This uses the value from the controls while being randomized to provide visual variety. If you remove the random element from the particle lifespan, all of the particles will expire and reset at the same time, resulting in fireworks-like *bursts* of particles.

11. Next, find the `updateParticles` function. This function is called once per frame to update the position and velocity of all particles before pushing the new values to the vertex buffer. It's interesting to note that in terms of manipulating the simulation behavior, gravity is applied mid-way through the function:

```
function updateParticles(elapsed) {
  // Loop through all the particles in the array
  particles.forEach((particle, i) => {
    // Track the particles lifespan
    particle.remainingLife -= elapsed;
    if (particle.remainingLife <= 0) {
      // Once the particle expires, reset it to the origin with a
      // new velocity
      resetParticle(particle);
    }

    // Update the particle position
    particle.position[0] += particle.velocity[0] * elapsed;
    particle.position[1] += particle.velocity[1] * elapsed;
    particle.position[2] += particle.velocity[2] * elapsed;

    // Apply gravity to the velocity
    particle.velocity[1] -= 9.8 * elapsed;
    if (particle.position[1] < 0) {
      // Allow particles to bounce off the floor
      particle.velocity[1] *= -0.75;
      particle.position[1] = 0;
    }

    // Update the corresponding values in the array
    const index = i * 4;
    particleArray[index] = particle.position[0];
    particleArray[index + 1] = particle.position[1];
    particleArray[index + 2] = particle.position[2];
    particleArray[index + 3] = particle.remainingLife /
      particle.lifespan;
  });

  // Once we are done looping through all the particles, update the
  // buffer once
  gl.bindBuffer(gl.ARRAY_BUFFER, particleBuffer);
  gl.bufferData(gl.ARRAY_BUFFER, particleArray, gl.STATIC_DRAW);
  gl.bindBuffer(gl.ARRAY_BUFFER, null);
}
```

12. The 9.8 here is the acceleration applied to the y component over time. In other words, this is the gravity. We can remove this calculation entirely to create an environment where the particles float indefinitely along their original trajectories. We can increase the value to make the particles fall very quickly (giving them a *heavy* appearance), or we can change the component that the deceleration is applied to so that we can change the direction of gravity. For example, subtracting from `velocity[0]` makes the particles *fall* sideways.

13. This is also where we apply a simple collision response with the *floor*. Any particles with a y position less than 0 (below the floor) have their velocities reversed and reduced. This gives us a realistic bouncing motion. We can make the particles less bouncy by reducing the multiplier (that is, `0.25` instead of `0.75`) or even eliminate bouncing altogether by simply setting the y velocity to 0. Additionally, we can remove the floor by taking away the check for y < 0, which will allow the particles to fall indefinitely.

14. It's also worth seeing the different effects we can achieve with different textures. Try changing the path for the `spriteTexture` in the `configure` function to see what it looks like when you use different images.

What just happened?

We've seen how point sprites can be used to efficiently render particle effects. We've also seen the different ways that we can manipulate a particle simulation to achieve various effects.

Have a Go: Bubbles!

The particle system in place here could be used to simulate bubbles or smoke floating upward just as easily as bouncing sparks. How would you change the simulation to make the particles float rather than fall?

Normal Mapping

A very powerful and popular technique among real-time 3D applications is **normal mapping**. Normal mapping creates the illusion of highly detailed geometry on a low-poly model by storing surface normals in a texture map that can then be used to calculate the lighting of the objects. This method is especially popular in modern games, since this allows developers to strike a balance between high performance and scene detail.

Typically, lighting is calculated by using the surface normals of the triangles being rendered, meaning that the entire polygon will be lit as a continuous, smooth surface:

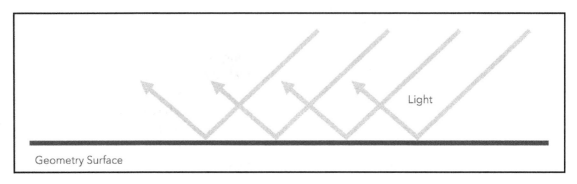

With normal mapping, the surface normals are replaced by normals that are encoded in a texture that give the appearance of a rough or bumpy surface. Note that the actual geometry is not changed when using a normal map – only how it's lit changes. If you look at a normal mapped polygon from the side, it will still appear to be perfectly flat:

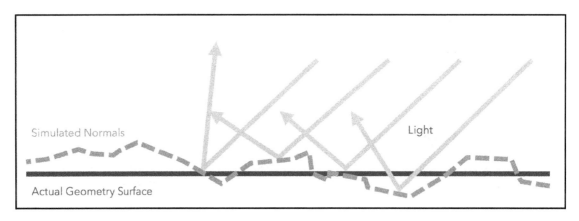

The texture used to store the normals is called a **normal map**, and it's typically paired with a specific diffuse texture that complements the surface that the normal map is trying to simulate. For example, here is a diffuse texture of some flagstones and the corresponding normal map:

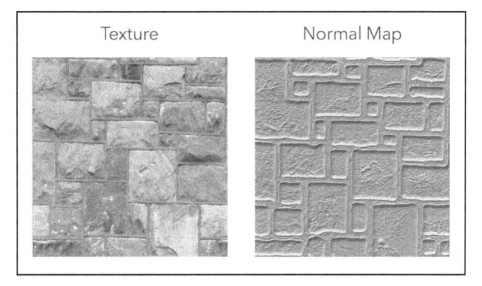

You can see that the normal map contains a similar pattern to the diffuse texture. Together, the two textures give the appearance that the stones are raised with a rough finish, while the grout is sunken in.

Mapping Techniques

Although normal mapping is a powerful technique for efficiently adding more detail to assets, there are many other mapping techniques that follow the same line of reasoning. You can read about some of the other techniques that are available for use here: `https://en.wikipedia.org/wiki/Category:Texture_mapping`.

The normal map contains custom-formatted color information that can be interpreted by the shader at runtime as a fragment normal. A fragment normal is essentially the same as a vertex normal: it is a three-component vector that points away from the surface. The normal texture encodes the three components of the normal vector into the three channels of the texture's texel color. Red represents the `x-axis`, green represents the `y-axis`, and blue represents the `z-axis`.

The normals that have been encoded are typically stored in **tangent space**, as opposed to world or object space. Tangent space is the coordinate system for the texture coordinates of a face. Normal maps are commonly blue, since the normals they represent generally point away from the surface and thus have larger `z` components.

Time for Action: Normal Mapping in Action

Let's cover an example showcasing normal mapping in action:

1. Open the `ch10_03_normal-map.html` file in a browser:

2. Rotate the cube to see the effect that the normal map has on the lit cube. Keep in mind that the profile of the cube has not changed. Let's examine how this effect is achieved.

3. First, we need to add a new attribute to our vertex buffers. There are three vectors needed to calculate the tangent space coordinates for lighting: the **normal**, the **tangent**, and the **bitangent**:

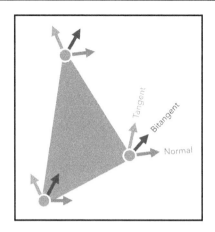

4. We have already covered normals, so let's investigate the other two vectors. The tangent represents the *up* (positive y) vector for the texture relative to the polygon surface. The bitangent represents the *left* (positive x) vector for the texture relative to the polygon surface.

5. We only need to provide two of the three vectors as vertex attributes. Traditionally, the normal and tangent suffice, as the third vector is calculated as the cross-product of the other two in the vertex shader.

6. It is common for 3D modeling packages to generate tangents for you. However, if they aren't provided, they can be calculated from the vertex positions and texture coordinates, similar to calculating vertex normals:

Tangent Generation Algorithm
We won't cover this algorithm here, but for reference, it has been implemented in common/js/utils.js as calculateTangents and used in scene.add.

```
const tangentBufferObject = gl.createBuffer();

gl.bindBuffer(gl.ARRAY_BUFFER, tangentBufferObject);

gl.bufferData(
  gl.ARRAY_BUFFER,
  new Float32Array(utils.calculateTangents(
    object.vertices,
    object.textureCoords,
    object.indices
  )),
  gl.STATIC_DRAW
);
```

7. In the vertex shader, at the top of `ch10_03_normal-map.html`, the tangent needs to be transformed by the Normal matrix. The two transformed vectors can be used to calculate the third:

```
// Transformed normal position
vec3 normal = vec3(uNormalMatrix * vec4(aVertexNormal, 1.0));
vec3 tangent = vec3(uNormalMatrix * vec4(aVertexTangent, 1.0));
vec3 bitangent = cross(normal, tangent);
```

8. The three vectors can then be used to create a matrix that transforms vectors into tangent space:

```
mat3 tbnMatrix = mat3(
    tangent.x, bitangent.x, normal.x,
    tangent.y, bitangent.y, normal.y,
    tangent.z, bitangent.z, normal.z
);
```

9. Unlike before, where we applied lighting in the vertex shader, the bulk of the lighting calculations needs to happen in the fragment shader so that we can incorporate normals from the texture. That being said, we do transform the light direction into tangent space in the vertex shader before passing it to the fragment shader as a varying:

```
// Light direction, from light position to vertex
vec3 lightDirection = uLightPosition - vertex.xyz;

vTangentEyeDir = eyeDirection * tbnMatrix;
```

10. In the fragment shader, we start by extracting the tangent space normal from the normal map texture. Since texture texels don't store negative values, the normal components must be encoded to map from a $[-1, 1]$ to a $[0, 1]$ range. Therefore, they must be *unpacked* into the correct range before being used in the shader. The algorithm to perform this operation can be easily expressed in ESSL:

```
// Unpack tangent-space normal from texture
vec3 normal = normalize(2.0 * (texture(uNormalSampler,
vTextureCoords).rgb - 0.5));
```

11. Lighting is calculated nearly the same as the vertex-lit model, which is done by using the texture normal and tangent space light direction:

```
// Normalize the light direction and determine how much light is
hitting this point
vec3 lightDirection = normalize(vTangentLightDir);
float lambertTerm = max(dot(normal, lightDirection), 0.20);

// Calculate Specular level
vec3 eyeDirection = normalize(vTangentEyeDir);
vec3 reflectDir = reflect(-lightDirection, normal);
float Is = pow(clamp(dot(reflectDir, eyeDirection), 0.0, 1.0),
8.0);

// Combine lighting and material colors
vec4 Ia = uLightAmbient * uMaterialAmbient;
vec4 Id = uLightDiffuse * uMaterialDiffuse * texture(uSampler,
vTextureCoords) * lambertTerm;

fragColor = Ia + Id + Is;
```

12. To help accentuate the normal mapping effect, the code sample also includes the calculation of a specular term.

What just happened?

We've seen how we can use normal information that's been encoded into a texture to add a new level of complexity to our lit models without additional geometry.

Ray Tracing in Fragment Shaders

A common (if somewhat impractical) technique used to demonstrate how powerful shaders can be is to use them to **ray trace** a scene. Thus far, all of our rendering has been done with **polygon rasterization**, which is the technical term for the triangle-based rendering that WebGL incorporates. Ray tracing is an alternate rendering technique that traces the path of light through a scene as it interacts with mathematically defined geometry.

Ray tracing has several advantages compared to traditional polygonal rendering. Primarily, this includes creating more realistic scenes due to a more accurate lighting model that can easily account for things like reflection and reflected lighting. That said, ray tracing tends to be considerably slower than polygonal rendering, which is the reason it's not often used for real-time applications.

Ray tracing a scene is achieved by creating a series of rays (represented by an origin and direction) that start at the camera's location and pass through each pixel in the viewport. These rays are then tested against every object in the scene to determine whether there are any intersections. If an intersection occurs, the closest intersection to the ray origin is returned, determining the color of the rendered pixel:

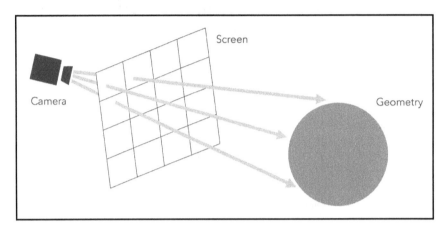

Although there are many algorithms that can be used to determine the color of the intersection point – ranging from simple diffuse lighting to multiple bounces of rays coming off other objects to simulate reflection – we'll keep our example simple. It's important to note that the rendered scene will entirely be the product of the shader code.

Time for Action: Examining the Ray Traced Scene

Let's cover an example showcasing the power of ray tracing:

1. Open the ch10_04_ray-tracing.html file in your browser. You should see a scene with a simple lit, bobbing sphere like the one shown in the following screenshot:

2. In order to trigger the shader, we need a way to draw a full-screen quad. Fortunately, we have a class from our post-processing examples earlier in this chapter to help us do just that. Since we don't have a scene to process, we can omit a large part of the rendering code and simplify JavaScript's draw function:

```
function draw() {
    gl.viewport(0, 0, gl.canvas.width, gl.canvas.height);
    gl.clear(gl.COLOR_BUFFER_BIT | gl.DEPTH_BUFFER_BIT);

    // Checks to see if the framebuffer needs to be re-sized to match
    // the canvas
    post.validateSize();
    post.bind();

    // Render the fullscreen quad
    post.draw();
}
```

3. That's it. The remainder of our scene will be built in to the fragment shader.

4. There are two functions at the core of our shader: one that determines if a ray is intersecting a sphere and one that determines the normal of a point on the sphere. We're using spheres because they're typically the easiest type of geometry to raycast, and they also happen to be a type of geometry that is difficult to represent accurately with polygons:

```
// ro is the ray origin.
// rd is the ray direction.
// s is the sphere
float sphereIntersection(vec3 ro, vec3 rd, vec4 s) {
  // Transform the ray into object space
  vec3 oro = ro - s.xyz;

  float a = dot(rd, rd);
  float b = 2.0 * dot(oro, rd);
  // w is the sphere radius
  float c = dot(oro, oro) - s.w * s.w;

  float d = b * b - 4.0 * a * c;

  // No intersection
  if (d < 0.0) return d;

  return (-b - sqrt(d)) / 2.0;
}

vec3 sphereNormaml(vec3 pt, vec4 s) {
  return (pt - s.xyz) / s.w;
}
```

5. Next, we will use these two functions to determine where the ray is intersecting with a sphere (if at all), along with what the normal and color of the sphere are at that point. To keep things simple, the sphere information is hardcoded as global variables, but they could just as easily be provided as uniforms from JavaScript:

```
vec4 sphere = vec4(1.0);
vec3 sphereColor = vec3(0.9, 0.8, 0.6);
float maxDistance = 1024.0;

float intersect(vec3 ro, vec3 rd, out vec3 norm, out vec3 color) {
  float distance = maxDistance;

  // If we wanted multiple objects in the scene you would loop
  // through them here and return the normal and color with the
  // closest intersection point (lowest distance).
```

```
float intersectionDistance = sphereIntersection(ro, rd, sphere);

if (intersectionDistance > 0.0 && intersectionDistance <
  distance) {
  distance = intersectionDistance;
  // Point of intersection
  vec3 pt = ro + distance * rd;
  // Get normal for that point
  norm = sphereNormaml(pt, sphere);
  // Get color for the sphere
  color = sphereColor;
}

return distance;
}
```

6. Now that we can determine the normal and color of a point with a ray, we need to generate the rays for casting. We can do this by determining the pixel that the current fragment represents and then creating a ray that points from the camera position through that pixel. To do so, we will utilize the `uInverseTextureSize` uniform that the `PostProcess` class provides to the shader:

```
// Pixel coordinate of the fragment being rendered
vec2 uv = gl_FragCoord.xy * uInverseTextureSize;
float aspectRatio = uInverseTextureSize.y / uInverseTextureSize.x;

// Cast a ray out from the eye position into the scene
vec3 ro = eyePos;

// The ray we cast is tilted slightly downward to give a better
// view of the scene
vec3 rd = normalize(vec3(-0.5 + uv * vec2(aspectRatio, 1.0),
-1.0));
```

7. Using the ray we just generated, we call the `intersect` function to get the information about the sphere's intersection. Then, we apply the same diffuse lighting calculations we've been using all along! To keep things simple, we're using directional lighting here, but it would be easy enough to update the lighting model to point or spot lights:

```
// Default color if we don't intersect with anything
vec3 rayColor = backgroundColor;

// See if the ray intersects with any objects.
// Provides the normal of the nearest intersection point and color
vec3 objectNormal, objectColor;
```

```
float t = intersect(ro, rd, objectNormal, objectColor);

if (t < maxDistance) {
  // Diffuse factor
  float diffuse = clamp(dot(objectNormal, lightDirection), 0.0,
    1.0);
  rayColor = objectColor * diffuse + ambient;
}

fragColor = vec4(rayColor, 1.0);
```

8. Thus far, our example is a static lit sphere. How do we add a bit of motion to the scene to give us a better sense of how fast the scene renders and how the lighting interacts with the sphere? We do so by adding a simple looping circular motion to the sphere by using the uTime uniform to modify the x and z coordinates at the beginning of the shader:

```
// Wiggle the sphere back and forth a bit
sphere.x = 1.5 * sin(uTime);
sphere.z = 0.5 * cos(uTime * 3.0);
```

What just happened?

We covered how we can construct a 3D scene, lighting and all, entirely in a fragment shader. It's a simple scene, of course, but also one that would be nearly impossible to render using polygon-based rendering. That's because perfect spheres can only be approximated with triangles.

Shader Toy

Now that you've seen how to construct 3D scenes entirely in fragment shaders, you will find the demos on ShaderToy.com both beautiful and inspiring.

Have a Go: Multiple Spheres

In our example, we've kept things simple by rendering only one single sphere. That being said, all of the pieces needed to render several spheres are in place! How would you render a scene of multiple spheres with different colors and motion?

Hint
The main shader function that needs editing is `intersect`.

Summary

Let's summarize what we've learned in this chapter:

- We covered a variety of advanced techniques to create more visually complex and compelling scenes.
- We learned how to apply post-processing effects by leveraging a framebuffer.
- We rendered particle effects using point sprites.
- We created the illusion of complex geometry by using normal maps.
- Finally, we rendered a scene entirely in a fragment shader using ray casting.

These advanced effects are only a glimpse into the vast landscape of effects possible with WebGL. Given the power and flexibility of shaders, the possibilities are endless!

In the next chapter, we will cover the major differences between WebGL 1 (OpenGL ES 2.0) and WebGL 2 (OpenGL ES 3.0), along with a migration plan to WebGL 2.

11
WebGL 2 Highlights

In this book, we have covered the foundations of computer graphics with WebGL 2, the web-based 3D Graphics API that ships with all modern browsers. We learned that WebGL 1 is based on OpenGL ES 2.0, while WebGL 2 is based on OpenGL ES 3.0, which guarantees many features that are offered in WebGL 1 as *optional* extensions, along with many other powerful methods. Although we've used WebGL 2 to learn a wide range of computer graphics topics, almost all that knowledge and all of those skills translate to other graphics APIs. That being said, let's take a moment to cover the key features that WebGL 2 provides over WebGL 1, along with a strategy for migration from WebGL 1 to WebGL 2.

In this chapter, we will cover the following:

- A more extensive look at the WebGL 2 API
- New additions to the WebGL 2 core specification
- A strategy for migrating 3D applications from WebGL 1 to WebGL 2

What's New in WebGL 2?

As of January 27, 2016, WebGL 2 is available by default in Firefox and Chrome. This means that you will automatically have access to WebGL 2 without any additional dependencies, as long as you use one of the following browsers:

- Firefox 51 or above
- Google Chrome 56 or above
- Chrome for Android 64 or above

WebGL 2 Support

For an updated list of the browsers that support WebGL 2, please visit the Khronos Group web page by following this link: `http://www.khronos.org/WebGL/wiki/Getting_a_WebGL_Implementation`. Or, you can visit the well-known **CanIUse.com** resource at: `https://caniuse.com/#search=WebGL 2`.

As described in `Chapter 1`, *Getting Started*, WebGL 1 is based on OpenGL ES 2.0; therefore, it doesn't expose features like query timers, compute shaders, uniform buffers, and so on. That being said, with WebGL 2 (based on OpenGL ES 3.0), we are getting access to more GPU features like instancing and multiple render targets. Since WebGL 2 is a considerable upgrade from WebGL 1, let's highlight some of its important features.

Vertex Array Objects

As described in `Chapter 2`, *Rendering*, we can implement **vertex array objects** in WebGL 1 by using the `OES_vertex_array_object` extension. That being said, they are available by default in WebGL 2. This is an important feature that should always be used, since it significantly reduces rendering times. When not using vertex array objects, all attributes data is in a global WebGL state, which means that calling functions such as `gl.vertexAttribPointer`, `gl.enableVertexAttribArray`, and `gl.bindBuffer(gl.ELEMENT_ARRAY_BUFFER, buffer)` manipulates the global state. This leads to performance loss, because before any draw call, we would need to set up all vertex attributes and set the `ELEMENT_ARRAY_BUFFER` where indexed data is being used. On the other hand, with vertex array objects, we would set up all attributes during our application's initialization and simply bind the data during rendering, yielding much better performance.

This is very similar to the `IDirect3DVertexDeclaration9`/`ID3D11InputLayout` interfaces in DirectX land.

WebGL 1 with Extension	WebGL 2
`createVertexArrayOES`	`createVertexArray`
`deleteVertexArrayOES`	`deleteVertexArray`
`isVertexArrayOES`	`isVertexArray`
`bindVertexArrayOES`	`bindVertexArray`

An example of this is as follows:

```
// Create a VAO instance
var vertexArray = gl.createVertexArray();

// Bind the VAO
gl.bindVertexArray(vertexArray);

// Set vertex array states

// Set with GLSL layout qualifier
const vertexPositionLocation = 0;
// Enable the attribute
gl.enableVertexAttribArray(vertexPositionLocation);
// Bind Buffer
gl.bindBuffer(gl.ARRAY_BUFFER, vertexPositionBuffer);
// ...
// Configure instructions for VAO
gl.vertexAttribPointer(vertexPositionLocation, 2, gl.FLOAT, false, 0, 0);

// Clean
gl.bindVertexArray(null);
gl.bindBuffer(gl.ARRAY_BUFFER, null);

// ...

// Render
gl.bindVertexArray(vertexArray);
gl.drawArrays(gl.TRIANGLES, 0, 6);
```

Wider Range of Texture Formats

While WebGL 1 had a limited set of texture formats, WebGL 2 provides a much larger set, some of which are listed here:

RGBA32I	RG8	RGB16UI
RGBA32UI	RG8I	RGB8_SNORM
RGBA16I	RG8UI	RGB8I
RGBA16UI	R32I	RGB8UI
RGBA8	R32UI	SRGB8

RGBA8I	R16I	R11F_G11F_B10F
RGBA8UI	R16UI	RGB9_E5
SRGB8_ALPHA8	R8	RG32F
RGB10_A2	R8I	RG16F
RGB10_A2UI	R8UI	RG8_SNORM
RGBA4	RGBA32F	R32F
RGB5_A1	RGBA16F	R16F
RGB8	RGBA8_SNORM	R8_SNORM
RGB565	RGB32F	DEPTH_COMPONENT32F
RG32I	RGB32I	DEPTH_COMPONENT24
RG32UI	RGB32UI	DEPTH_COMPONENT16
RG16I	RGB16F	
RG16UI	RGB16I	

3D Textures

A **3D texture** is a texture in which each mipmap level contains a single three-dimensional image. A 3D texture is essentially just a stack of 2D textures that can be sampled with x, y, and z coordinates in the shader. This functionality allows us to have multiple 2D textures in a single object so that shaders can seamlessly select which image to use for each object.

This is useful for visualizing volumetric data (like medical scans), 3D effects like smoke, storing lookup tables, and so on.

Texture Arrays

Texture arrays, similar to 3D textures, are a great feature for reducing complexity, improving code maintainability, and increasing the number of textures that can be used. By ensuring that all texture slices in a texture array are the same size, shaders can have access to many textures with a smaller footprint.

Instanced Rendering

In WebGL 2, **instancing** or **instanced rendering** is available by default. Instance rendering is a way to execute the same drawing commands many times in a row, with each producing a slightly different result. This can be a very efficient method for rendering a large amount of geometry with very few API calls.

Instancing is a great performance booster for certain types of geometry, especially objects with many instances but without many vertices. Good examples are grass and fur. Instancing avoids the overhead of an individual API call per object, while minimizing memory costs by avoiding storing geometric data for each separate instance.

Here's a quick example:

```
gl.drawArraysInstanced(gl.TRIANGLES, 0, 3, 2);
```

Non-Power of 2 Texture Support

As we saw in `Chapter 7`, *Textures*, mipmaps are a powerful feature in which pre-calculated, optimized sequences of images, each of which is a progressively lower-resolution representation of the same image, allow for more optimized rendering. While in WebGL 1 the height and width of each image, or level, in the mipmap is a power of two smaller than the previous level, in WebGL 2, that limit is removed. That is, **non-power of 2 textures** work the same as power of 2 textures.

Fragment Depth

In WebGL 2, we can manually set our own custom values to the depth buffer (z-buffer). This feature allows you to manipulate the depth of a fragment from the fragment shader. This can be expensive, because it forces the GPU to bypass a lot of it's normal fragment discard behavior, but can also allow for some interesting effects that would be difficult to accomplish without having incredibly high poly geometry.

Texture Size in Shaders

In WebGL 2, you can look up the size of any texture within ESSL shaders using `textureSize`. With WebGL 1, you'd need to create a uniform and pass the data into the shader manually.

For example:

```
vec2 size = textureSize(sampler, lod);
```

Sync Objects

With WebGL 1, the path from Javascript to GPU to screen is fairly opaque to developers. That is, you dispatch draw commands and at some undefined point in the future, the results show up on the screen. In WebGL 2, **sync objects** allow the developer to gain a little more insight into when the GPU has completed it's work. Using `gl.fenceSync`, you can place a marker at some point in the GPU command stream and then later call `gl.clientWaitSync` to pause Javascript execution until the GPU has completed all commands up to the fence. Obviously blocking execution isn't desirable for applications that want to render fast, but this can be very beneficial for getting accurate benchmarks. It may also possibly be used in the future for synchronizing between workers.

Direct Texel Lookup

It's often convenient to store large arrays of data in a texture. This is possible in WebGL 1, but you can only address textures with texture coordinates inside a range spanning from `0.0` to `1.0`. In WebGL 2, accessing this sort of data is considerably easier, as you can easily look up values from a texture with pixel/texel coordinates.

For example:

```
vec4 values = texelFetch(sampler, ivec2Position, lod);
```

Flexible Shader Loops

In WebGL 1, loops in the shader had to use a constant integer expression. However, since WebGL 2 is based on OpenGL ES 3.0, this limit no longer exists.

Shader Matrix Functions

Given that WebGL 2's shading language is much more feature-rich than WebGL 1's, we now have many more matrix math operations at our fingertips. For example, if an `inverse` or `transpose` of a matrix is needed, we would need to pass it in as a uniform. However, in WebGL 2, functions such as `inverse` and `transpose` are functions directly built into shaders.

Common Compressed Textures

In WebGL 1, there are various compressed texture formats that are hardware-dependent. For example, formats such as `S3TC` and `PVTC` are desktop and iOS only, respectively. However, in WebGL 2, the following formats are much more flexible by being hardware independent:

- `COMPRESSED_R11_EAC RED`
- `COMPRESSED_SIGNED_R11_EAC RED`
- `COMPRESSED_RG11_EAC RG`
- `COMPRESSED_SIGNED_RG11_EAC RG`
- `COMPRESSED_RGB8_ETC2 RGB`
- `COMPRESSED_SRGB8_ETC2 RGB`
- `COMPRESSED_RGB8_PUNCHTHROUGH_ALPHA1_ETC2 RGBA`
- `COMPRESSED_SRGB8_PUNCHTHROUGH_ALPHA1_ETC2 RGBA`
- `COMPRESSED_RGBA8_ETC2_EAC RGBA`
- `COMPRESSED_SRGB8_ALPHA8_ETC2_EAC`

Uniform Buffer Objects

Setting shader program uniforms is a huge part of almost any WebGL/OpenGL draw loop. This can make your draw calls fairly chatty as they make hundreds or thousands of `gl.uniform` calls.

In WebGL 1, if we have n number of uniforms that need to be updated, then it would require n number of calls with the appropriate uniform method—this can be quite slow. However, with WebGL 2, we can use **uniform buffer objects,** which allow us to specify a large number of uniforms from a single buffer. This is a major boost in performance, since we can manipulate uniforms in the buffer outside of WebGL by using JavaScript-typed arrays and updating a set of uniforms with a single call. Additionally, uniform buffers can be bound to multiple programs at the same time, so it's possible to update global data (like projection or view matrices) once and all programs that use them will automatically see the changed values.

Heterogeneous Uniform Buffer Objects

It's important to note that, in a given application, you can leverage a diverse set of uniform buffer objects to fit your application's needs.

Integer Textures and Attributes

While in WebGL 1 textures and attributes are represented as floating-point values, regardless of their original type, in WebGL 2, textures and attributes are provided integer representation.

Transform Feedback

A powerful technique offered in WebGL 2 is that vertex shaders can write their results back into a buffer. This can be very useful in situations where we want to leverage the GPU's computational power to perform complex computations so that we are able to read them within our application.

Sampler Objects

While in WebGL 1 all texture parameters are *per texture*, in WebGL 2, we can optionally use **sampler objects**. By using samplers, we can move all texture parameters to a sampler, allowing a single texture to be sampled in different ways.

In WebGL 1, texture image data and sampling information (which tells GPU how to read the image data) are both stored in texture objects. It can be painful when we want to read from the same texture twice but with a different method (say, linear filtering vs nearest filtering) because we need to have two texture objects. With sampler objects, we can separate these two concepts. We can have one texture object and two different sampler objects. This will result in a change in how our engine organize textures.

Here's an example:

```
const samplerA = gl.createSampler();
gl.samplerParameteri(samplerA, gl.TEXTURE_MIN_FILTER,
gl.NEAREST_MIPMAP_NEAREST);
gl.samplerParameteri(samplerA, gl.TEXTURE_MAG_FILTER, gl.NEAREST);
gl.samplerParameteri(samplerA, gl.TEXTURE_WRAP_S, gl.CLAMP_TO_EDGE);
gl.samplerParameteri(samplerA, gl.TEXTURE_WRAP_T, gl.CLAMP_TO_EDGE);

const samplerB = gl.createSampler();
gl.samplerParameteri(samplerB, gl.TEXTURE_MIN_FILTER,
gl.LINEAR_MIPMAP_LINEAR);
gl.samplerParameteri(samplerB, gl.TEXTURE_MAG_FILTER, gl.LINEAR);
gl.samplerParameteri(samplerB, gl.TEXTURE_WRAP_S, gl.MIRRORED_REPEAT);
gl.samplerParameteri(samplerB, gl.TEXTURE_WRAP_T, gl.MIRRORED_REPEAT);

// ...

gl.activeTexture(gl.TEXTURE0);
gl.bindTexture(gl.TEXTURE_2D, texture);
gl.bindSampler(0, samplerA);

gl.activeTexture(gl.TEXTURE1);
gl.bindTexture(gl.TEXTURE_2D, texture);
gl.bindSampler(1, samplerB);
```

Depth Textures

A major drawback to WebGL 1 is the lack of support for **depth textures**. In WebGL 2, they are available by default.

Standard Derivatives

While in WebGL 1 you'd need to compute normal and pass them to shaders, in WebGL 2, you can compute them within shaders by using a larger set of mathematical operations that are available by default.

UNSIGNED_INT Indices

In WebGL 2, there isn't a practical size limit for indexed geometries since we can use 32-bit `int` for indices.

Blend Equation MIN / MAX

In WebGL, you can easily take the `MIN` or `MAX` of two colors when blending using these added functions.

Multiple Render Targets (MRT)

In WebGL 2, you can draw to multiple buffers at once from a shader. This can be quite powerful for various deferred rendering techniques. This is "the big one" for many developers, because it makes many of the modern deferred rendering techniques that have become such a core part of modern realtime 3D practical for WebGL.

Texture Access in Vertex Shaders

While accessing textures within vertex shaders is possible in WebGL 1, you would need to count how many textures you could access, and that could equal zero. In WebGL 2, texture access is much more streamlined, and the texture access count is required to be at least `16`.

Multi-Sampled Renderbuffers

While in WebGL 1 we could only use the GPU's built in multi-sample system to anti-alias our `canvas`, in WebGL 2, there is support to perform our own custom multi-sampling.

Query Objects

Query objects give developers another, more explicit way to peek at the inner workings of the GPU. A query wraps a set of GL commands for the GPU to asynchronously report some sort of statistic about. For example, occlusion queries are done in the following way: performing a `gl.ANY_SAMPLES_PASSED` query around a set of draw calls will let you detect if any of the geometry passed the depth test. If not, you know that the object wasn't visible and may choose not to draw that geometry in future frames until something happens (object moved, camera moved, and so on) that indicates that the geometry might have become visible again.

It should be noted that these queries are asynchronous, which means that a queries' results may not be ready for many frames after the query was originally issued! This makes them tricky to use, but it can be worth it in the right circumstances.

Here's an example:

```
gl.beginQuery(gl.ANY_SAMPLES_PASSED, query);
gl.drawArraysInstanced(gl.TRIANGLES, 0, 3, 2);
gl.endQuery(gl.ANY_SAMPLES_PASSED);

//...

(function tick() {
  if (!gl.getQueryParameter(query, gl.QUERY_RESULT_AVAILABLE)) {
    // A query's result is never available in the same frame
    // the query was issued.  Try in the next frame.
    requestAnimationFrame(tick);
    return;
  }

  var samplesPassed = gl.getQueryParameter(query, gl.QUERY_RESULT);
  gl.deleteQuery(query);
})();
```

Texture LOD

The **texture LOD** parameter is used to determine which mipmap to fetch from. This allows for mipmap streaming, that is, loading only the mipmap levels currently needed. This is very useful for a WebGL environment, where textures are downloaded via a network.

```
gl.texParameterf(gl.TEXTURE_2D, gl.TEXTURE_MIN_LOD, 0.0);
gl.texParameterf(gl.TEXTURE_2D, gl.TEXTURE_MAX_LOD, 10.0);
```

Shader Texture LOD

The **Shader Texture LOD** bias control makes mipmap level control simpler for glossy environment effects in physically-based rendering. Now as part of the WebGL 2 core, the `lodBias` can be passed as an optional parameter to texture.

Floating Point Textures Always Available

While in WebGL 1, floating point textures are optional, but in WebGL 2, they are available by default.

Migrating to WebGL 2

As we described previously, WebGL 2 is nearly 100 percent backward compatible with WebGL 1.

Backward Compatibility

All exceptions to backward compatibility are recorded at the following link: `https://www.khronos.org/registry/WebGL/specs/latest/2.0/#BACKWARDS_INCOMPATIBILITY`.

That being said, let's cover some key components of migrating a WebGL 1 application to WebGL 2.

Attaining context

In WebGL 1, you'd attain a WebGL context with something that looks like the following:

```
const names = ['WebGL', 'experimental-WebGL', 'webkit-3d', 'moz-WebGL'];

for (let i = 0; i < names.length; ++i) {
  try {
    const context = canvas.getContext(names[i]);
    // work with context
  } catch (e) {
    console.log('Error attaining WebGL context', e);
  }
}
```

In WebGL 2, you'd simply attain the context with a single line, as follows:

```
const context = canvas.getContext('WebGL 2');
```

Extensions

While in WebGL many optional extensions were *required* for more advanced functionality, in WebGL 2 you can remove most of those extensions, because they are available by *default*. Some of these include the following:

- Depth textures: https://www.khronos.org/registry/WebGL/extensions/WebGL_depth_texture
- Floating point textures:
    - https://www.khronos.org/registry/WebGL/extensions/OES_texture_float
    - https://www.khronos.org/registry/WebGL/extensions/OES_texture_float_linear
- Vertex array objects: https://www.khronos.org/registry/WebGL/extensions/OES_vertex_array_object
- Standard derivatives: https://www.khronos.org/registry/WebGL/extensions/OES_standard_derivatives
- Instanced drawing: https://www.khronos.org/registry/WebGL/extensions/ANGLE_instanced_arrays
- UNSIGNED_INT indices: https://www.khronos.org/registry/WebGL/extensions/OES_element_index_uint
- Setting gl_FragDepth: https://www.khronos.org/registry/WebGL/extensions/EXT_frag_depth
- Blend equation MIN/MAX: https://www.khronos.org/registry/WebGL/extensions/EXT_blend_minmax
- Direct texture LOD access: https://www.khronos.org/registry/WebGL/extensions/EXT_shader_texture_lod
- Multiple draw buffers: https://www.khronos.org/registry/WebGL/extensions/WebGL_draw_buffers
- Texture access in vertex shaders

Shader Updates

While WebGL 2's shader language, based on GLSL 300, is backward compatible with WebGL 1's shader language, we need to make a few changes to ensure that our shaders compile. Let's cover them now.

Shader Definitions

With WebGL 2's shaders, we have to prepend all shaders with the following line of code: `#version 300 es`. It's important to note that this *must* be the very first line in the shader, otherwise the shader will not compile.

Attribute Definitions

Given that attributes are *provided as inputs* to shaders, in GLSL 300 ES, the `attribute` qualifier is removed. For example, with WebGL's GLSL 100, you might have the following:

```
attribute vec3 aVertexNormal;
attribute vec4 aVertexPosition;
```

In GLSL 300 ES, this would be as follows:

```
in vec3 aVertexNormal;
in vec4 aVertexPosition;
```

Varying Definitions

While in GLSL 100, varyings are often defined in both the vertex and fragment shaders, the `varying` qualifier has been removed in GLSL 300 ES. That is, varying qualifiers are updated with their appropriate `in` and `out` qualifiers, depending on whether the values are provided as *inputs* or returned as *outputs*. For example, consider the following from GLSL 100:

```
// inside of the vertex shader
varying vec2 vTexcoord;
varying vec3 vNormal;

// inside of the fragment shader
varying vec2 vTexcoord;
varying vec3 vNormal;
```

This would be changed to the following in GLSL 300 ES:

```
// inside of the vertex shader
out vec2 vTexcoord;
out vec3 vNormal;

// inside of the fragment shader
in vec2 vTexcoord;
in vec3 vNormal;
```

No More gl_FragColor

While in GLSL 100 you'd ultimately render the color of the pixel by setting the gl_FragColor inside of the fragment shader, in GLSL 300 ES, you simply expose a value from your fragment shader. Consider, for example, the following in GLSL 100:

```
void main(void) {
   gl_FragColor = vec4(1.0, 0.2, 0.3, 1.0);
}
```

This would be updated by setting a defined custom output variable, as follows:

```
out vec4 fragColor;

void main(void) {
   fragColor = vec4(1.0, 0.2, 0.3, 1.0);
}
```

It's important to note that even though we declared a variable called fragColor, you can choose any name not starting with the prefix gl_, due to ambiguity. Throughout this book, we have defined this custom variable as fragColor.

Automatic Texture Type Detection

While in GLSL 100 you'd get a color from a texture by using the appropriate methods, such as texture2D, in GLSL 300 ES, shaders automatically detect the type based on the sampler type in use. For example, consider the following in GLSL 100:

```
uniform sampler2D uSome2DTexture;
uniform samplerCube uSomeCubeTexture;

void main(void) {
   vec4 color1 = texture2D(uSome2DTexture, ...);
   vec4 color2 = textureCube(uSomeCubeTexture, ...);
}
```

This would be updated to the following in GLSL 300 ES:

```
uniform sampler2D uSome2DTexture;
uniform samplerCube uSomeCubeTexture;

void main(void) {
  vec4 color1 = texture(uSome2DTexture, ...);
  vec4 color2 = texture(uSomeCubeTexture, ...);
}
```

Non-Power of 2 Texture Support

As demonstrated in Chapter 7, *Textures*, in WebGL 1, mipmaps don't exist for textures that don't conform to the *power of 2* restriction. In WebGL 2, however, non-power of 2 textures work exactly the same as power of 2 textures.

Floating Point Framebuffer Attachments

While in WebGL 1 a strange hack is required to check whether there is support for rendering to a floating point texture, in WebGL 2, this involves a simple check via standard methods.

Vertex Array Objects

While using vertex array objects is not a *necessary* requirement, it's a highly *recommended* feature to use in your migration. By using vertex array objects, you can improve both the overall structure of your code and the performance of your application.

Summary

Let's summarize what we've learned in this chapter:

- We covered many of the core methods available only in the WebGL 2 specification.
- We learned some of the key differences between WebGL 1 and WebGL 2.
- We discussed migration strategies for converting a WebGL 1 application to WebGL 2.

We're nearly done! Can you believe it? Up next, in the final chapter, *Journey Ahead*, we will conclude this book by laying out a roadmap of concepts, resources, and other useful pieces of information that are both inspiring and empowering, to help you continue down the path of mastering real-time computer graphics.

12
Journey Ahead

In this book, we have covered the foundational concepts, techniques, and resources required to build interactive 3D web applications with WebGL 2. Now that you're on your way to becoming a computer graphics expert, the resources in this final chapter are dedicated to helping you on that journey.

In this concluding chapter, you will do the following:

- Cover WebGL libraries of various sizes and capabilities.
- Investigate strategies for testing WebGL applications.
- Learn about 3D reconstruction.
- Explore the power of physically-based rendering.
- Meet various graphics communities.

WebGL Libraries

Before we dive into various WebGL libraries, we should first define what a software library is. Although **library** and **framework** are often used interchangeably, they refer to *different* concepts in computer science. A software library comprises defined code, configuration, documentation, classes, scripts, and more, so that developers may include them in their programs to enhance their products. For example, in developing a program requiring extensive mathematical operations, a developer may include a suitable software library (for example, glMatrix) to reduce the need for writing those operations themselves.

That being said, as you may have noticed, we've built our 3D application in such a way that the classes, utilities, and overall architecture could, eventually, be turned into a library. This process was done intentionally so that we could learn concepts in isolation and also write code that could eventually comprise a feature-rich WebGL library that can be used by other applications.

That being said, it's important to know when and where to use libraries, so let's cover a few WebGL libraries of various sizes.

Small Libraries

Here are a few examples of small, non-prescriptive WebGL libraries that provide many helpers, utilities, and abstraction layers over WebGL's low-level API.

TWGL

TWGL (`https://github.com/greggman/twgl.js`) is an open-source WebGL library that serves to "*make using the WebGL API less verbose*". For example, here's a simple TWGL demo that shows its intelligible, yet low-level, API on top of WebGL:

```
const
  canvas = document.getElementById('webgl-canvas'),
  gl = canvas.getContext('webgl'),
  program = twgl.createProgramInfo(gl, ['vertex-shader', 'fragment-
shader']),
  arrays = {
    position: [
      -1, -1, 0,
       1, -1, 0,
      -1,  1, 0,
      -1,  1, 0,
       1, -1, 0,
       1,  1, 0
    ],
  },
  bufferInfo = twgl.createBufferInfoFromArrays(gl, arrays);

function draw(time) {
  const { width, height } = gl.canvas;

  twgl.resizeCanvasToDisplaySize(gl.canvas);
  gl.viewport(0, 0, width, height);

  const uniforms = {
    time: time * 0.001,
    resolution: [width, height],
  };

  gl.useProgram(program.program);
```

```
twgl.setBuffersAndAttributes(gl, program, bufferInfo);
twgl.setUniforms(program, uniforms);
twgl.drawBufferInfo(gl, bufferInfo);

requestAnimationFrame(draw);
}

requestAnimationFrame(draw);
```

You can see the live demo on their GitHub page, which resembles the following:

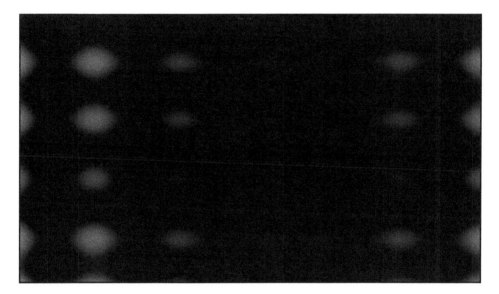

Regl

Regl (`https://github.com/regl-project/regl`) is an open-source WebGL library with a functional flavor. As its documentation explains, Regl "*simplifies WebGL programming by removing as much shared state as it can get away with. To do this, it replaces the WebGL API with two fundamental abstractions, **resources** and **commands***". Here's the snippet of code that illustrates the functional Regl API:

```
const regl = require('regl')();

const vertexShader = `
  precision mediump float;

  attribute vec2 position;
  void main(void) {
```

```
      gl_Position = vec4(position, 0, 1);
  }
`;

const fragmentShader = `
  precision mediump float;

  uniform vec4 color;

  void main(void) {
    gl_FragColor = color;
  }
`;

const drawTriangle = regl({
  vert: vertexShader,
  frag: fragmentShader,
  attributes: {
    position: regl.buffer([
      [-2, -2],
      [4, -2],
      [4, 4]
    ])
  },
  uniforms: {
    color: regl.prop('color')
  },
  count: 3
});

regl.frame(({ time }) => {
  regl.clear({
    color: [1, 1, 1, 1],
    depth: 1
  });

  drawTriangle({
    color: [
      Math.cos(time * 0.001),
      Math.sin(time * 0.0008),
      Math.cos(time * 0.003),
      1
    ]
  });
});
```

You can see the live demo on their GitHub page, which resembles the following:

StackGL

StackGL (`http://stack.gl`) is an open source WebGL project with an interesting approach to building WebGL applications. Instead of being bundled as a single library, it's an ecosystem, comprised of many small, lean modules, inspired by the Unix philosophy.

Unix philosophy

 The Unix mindset is a philosophical approach to writing minimalist, modular software, often expressed with the mantra "do one thing, and do it well!". For more information, please visit the following URL: `https://en.wikipedia.org/wiki/Unix_philosophy`.

Unlike many 3D engines, StackGL emphasizes lean, modular code that is focused on writing shader code. That being said, be sure to visit their website, as it includes extensive documentation and demos that will help you master this approach.

Feature-Rich Libraries

While small, lean, and modular WebGL libraries are useful, they may not be enough for complex applications. Here are several feature-rich WebGL libraries that offer an extensive list of features and capabilities.

Three.js

Three.js (`https://github.com/mrdoob/three.js`) is an open source library that powers many of the WebGL applications on the web. It aims to create an easy to use, lightweight, 3D library, with multiple renderers that target 2D `canvas`, WebGL, SVG, and CSS3D. Here's a neat demo of a rotating cube, showcasing the simplicity of the Three.js API:

```
let
  renderer,
  scene,
  camera,
  mesh,
  width = window.innerWidth,
  height = window.innerHeight;

function init() {
  camera = new THREE.PerspectiveCamera(70, width / height, 0.01, 10);
  camera.position.z = 1;

  scene = new THREE.Scene();

  const mesh = new THREE.Mesh(
    // geometry
    new THREE.BoxGeometry(0.2, 0.2, 0.2),
    // material
    new THREE.MeshNormalMaterial()
  );
  scene.add(mesh);

  renderer = new THREE.WebGLRenderer({ antialias: true });
  renderer.setSize(width, height);
  document.body.appendChild(renderer.domElement);
}

function render() {
  requestAnimationFrame(render);
  mesh.rotation.x += 0.01;
  mesh.rotation.y += 0.02;
```

```
    renderer.render(scene, camera);
}

init();
render();
```

You can see the live demo on their GitHub page, which resembles the following:

Babylon.js

Babylon.js (`https://github.com/mrdoob/three.js`) is an open source WebGL library that came to fruition inside of Microsoft. It is a powerful library that was recently rewritten entirely in TypeScript.

TypeScript

TypeScript is an open source language developed by Microsoft. It is a powerful language that is a strict syntactical superset of JavaScript and adds optional static typing to JavaScript. For more information, visit `https://github.com/Microsoft/TypeScript`.

Although choosing Babylon.js doesn't require using TypeScript, it can be a major advantage over other libraries if you or your team prefer the features that TypeScript provides. Here's an interesting JavaScript demo, showcasing the simple Babylon.js API:

```
const canvas = document.getElementById('webgl-canvas');

const engine = new BABYLON.Engine(
  canvas,
  true,
  {
    preserveDrawingBuffer: true,
    stencil: true
  }
);

function initScene() {
  const scene = new BABYLON.Scene(engine);

  const camera = new BABYLON.FreeCamera('camera', new BABYLON.Vector3(0, 5,
    -10), scene);
  camera.setTarget(BABYLON.Vector3.Zero());
  camera.attachControl(canvas, false);

  const ground = BABYLON.Mesh.CreateGround('ground', 6, 6, 2, scene,
    false);

  const sphere = BABYLON.Mesh.CreateSphere('sphere', 16, 2, scene, false,
    BABYLON.Mesh.FRONTSIDE);
  sphere.position.y = 1;

  const light = new BABYLON.HemisphericLight('light', new
    BABYLON.Vector3(0, 1, 0), scene);

  return scene;
}

const scene = initScene();
engine.runRenderLoop(() => scene.render());
```

You can see the live demo on their GitHub page, which resembles the following:

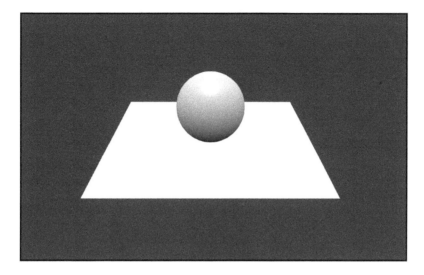

A-Frame

A-Frame (`https://github.com/aframevr/aframe`) is an open-source web framework for building virtual reality (VR) experiences. It is primarily maintained by Mozilla and the WebVR community. Although other WebGL libraries, such as Three.js and Babylon.js, offer VR support, A-Frame was designed entirely for building VR applications for the web.

A-Frame Core

Although A-Frame is an entirely new project, it is built on top of the Three.js game engine.

Here's a demo showcasing the A-Frame's declarative API:

```
<!DOCTYPE html>
<html>
<head>
  <title>Hello, WebVR! - A-Frame</title>
  <meta name="description" content="Hello, WebVR! - A-Frame">
  <script src="https://aframe.io/releases/0.8.2/aframe.min.js"></script>
</head>
<body>
<a-scene>
  <a-box position="-1 0.5 -3" rotation="0 45 0" color="#4CC3D9" shadow>
  </a-box>
```

```
      <a-sphere position="0 1.25 -5" radius="1.25" color="#EF2D5E" shadow>
      </a-sphere>
      <a-cylinder position="1 0.75 -3" radius="0.5" height="1.5"
       color="#FFC65D" shadow></a-cylinder>
      <a-plane position="0 0 -4" rotation="-90 0 0" width="4" height="4"
       color="#7BC8A4" shadow></a-plane>
      <a-sky color="#ECECEC"></a-sky>
    </a-scene>
  </body>
</html>
```

You can see the live demo on their GitHub page, which resembles the following:

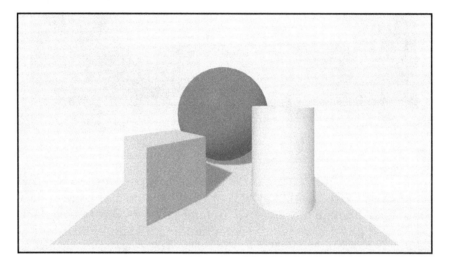

Game Engines

Another approach to building complex 3D applications is to use an established game engine. A game engine is a software development environment designed so that people can build complex 3D applications. Although developers use 3D engines to create games for consoles, mobile devices, and personal computers, they can also be used to build interactive web applications. Two powerful game engines that you can use in building complex WebGL applications are Unity and PlayCanvas.

Unity

Unity (`https://unity3D.com`) is a portable game engine developed by Unity Technologies that offers cross-platform capabilities. It was first announced and released in June 2005 at the Apple Inc. Worldwide Developers Conference as an OS X-exclusive game engine. Over the years, it has become the leading game engine for delivering some of the most well-known games across diverse platforms. Although Unity prioritizes native over web-based outputs, it does offer WebGL support:

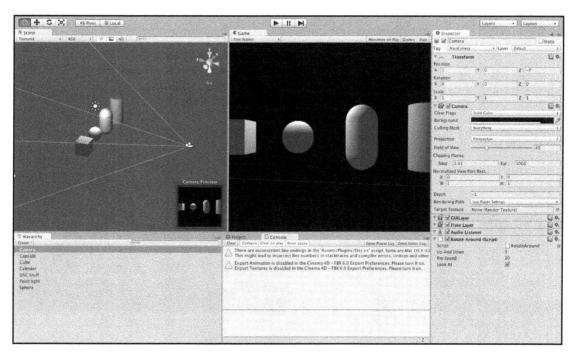

PlayCanvas

PlayCanvas (https://playcanvas.com) is an open source 3D game engine that also offers a proprietary cloud-hosted creation platform. Although other game engines, such as Unity, offer WebGL support, PlayCanvas was built from the ground-up for the web. Additionally, PlayCanvas offers a wonderful development experience since it has many powerful features, such as a visual workspace, full WebGL 2 support, simultaneous editing from multiple computers, and more:

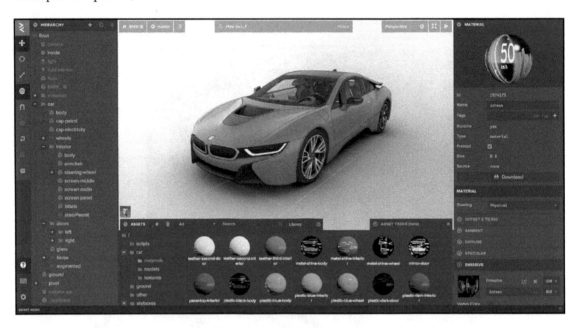

Testing WebGL 2 Applications

If you happened to open your browser's debugger tools throughout this book, you may have noticed that the `canvas` you saw was a complete "black box". That is, you cannot inspect any of its elements as you could with the DOM elements on a web page. If you come from a traditional web-development background, this may seem like a big problem, since we're used to leveraging the DOM to help us query elements to test our application. So, how can we ensure the quality and stability of our WebGL applications?

Visual Regression Testing

Image comparisons of various application states throughout the development cycle is a common approach for testing WebGL applications. This technique, often referred to as **visual regression testing**, performs front-end or user-interface regression testing by capturing the screenshots of web pages/UI and comparing them with the original images (either historical baseline screenshots or reference images from a live website):

Article Title	Article Title	Article Title
Lorem ipsum dolor sit amet, consectetur adipiscing elit. Morbi eleifend sollicitudin varius. Mauris urna nibh, bibendum non nunc id, mollis lacinia leo. Nam egestas auctor feugiat.	Lorem ipsum dolor sit amet, consectetur adipiscing elit. Morbi eleifend sollicitudin varius. Mauris urna nibh, bibendum non nunc id, mollis lacinia leo. Nam egestas auctor feugiat.	Lorem ipsum dolor sit amet, consectetur adipiscing elit. Morbi eleifend sollicitudin varius. Mauris urna nibh, bibendum non nunc id, mollis lacinia leo. Nam egestas auctor feugiat.
Baseline	Change	Diff

In the previous screenshot, you can see how the **Baseline** and **Change** are different via the final **Diff** output. This technique can be an effective approach for ensuring that your WebGL application continues to behave as expected.

Visual Regression Testing Tools

Given your language of choice, you can find many open source visual regression testing tools that fit your technology stack on GitHub (`https:/ /github.com/search?q=visual+regression`).

Application Introspection Testing

Another approach is to mimic the DOM API by exposing your WebGL elements via a custom API. For example, if we want to query a DOM element by its ID, we would do so via `document.getElementById('element-id')`. We could do the same with jQuery's simpler API via `$('#element-id')`.

jQuery

 jQuery is a JavaScript library designed to simplify many of the common client-side scripting operations that are available. It is a free, open source software that uses the permissive MIT License. For more information, please visit `https://jquery.com`.

To see an implementation of this approach, please refer to **Three Musketeers** (`https://github.com/webgl/three-musketeer`), an open source library, which can be included in *any* Three.js application with a single line of code. By including `three-musketeers`, we can run a variety of queries on elements in our scene, similar to DOM elements in a web page. Here are some sample queries for further illustration:

```
$$$.debug();
```

`$$$` is an alias for a `three-musketeers` instance. The `debug` method enables visual debugging mode:

```
$$$
.find('Cube_1')
.exists();
// returns true
```

The `find` method searches the scene for an item with the ID of `Cube_1`. By calling `exists`, it returns a Boolean on whether it exists:

```
$$$
.findAll((node) => node.geometry.type === 'BoxGeometry');
```

Similar to `find`, `findAll` returns an array of items. In this case, instead of searching for a unique ID, we're looking for all of the geometries that match the `BoxGeometry` type:

```
$$$
.find('Cube_1')
.click();
```

We find the geometry with the unique ID, `Cube_1`, and trigger a mouse click event on the *appropriate* coordinates:

```
window.addEventListener('click', (event) => {
  const intersectedItems = $$$.pickFromEvent(event);
  console.log(intersectedItems);
});
```

This is a simple technique that's very helpful for debugging. Every time we click in our web page, we log all intersected geometries, given the mouse click's 2D coordinates mapped onto our 3D scene.

For more information, be sure to check out `three-musketeers` on GitHub (`https://github.com/webgl/three-musketeers`) or its documentation (`https://webgl.github.io/three-musketeers`).

3D Reconstruction

Throughout this book, we either constructed our own geometries or imported models that have been created in 3D modeling tools, such as Maya or Blender. Although these are common approaches for building 3D assets, they require manual labor to create them. Are there other techniques for getting geometries? Yes, of course! **3D reconstruction** is the process of creating 3D models from images. It is the reverse process of obtaining 2D images from 3D scenes. Here's an example of a 3D model that has been generated purely from aerial photographs by a technique called Photogrammetry:

Photogrammetry

Photogrammetry is the science of making spatial measuring from photographs. This is a powerful technique for recovering the exact positions of surface points. For more information, please visit `https://en.wikipedia.org/wiki/Photogrammetry`.

Physically-Based Rendering

In `Chapter 3`, *Lights*, we learned how to illuminate our scene by mimicking light. We did so by leveraging various shading and light reflection techniques that use two main components: specular and diffuse. Although we've been modeling materials with specular and diffuse in computer graphics for a long time, these techniques produce results that are not very realistic. For example, changing the specularity of a material doesn't change the diffuse:

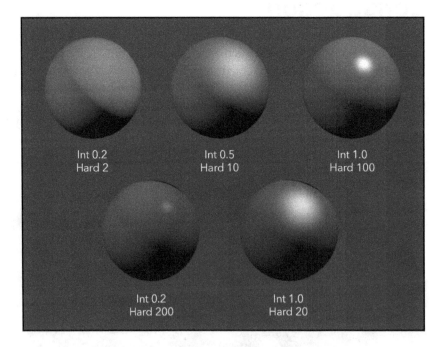

The preceding screenshot demonstrates that changing the two parameters of specular intensity and specular hardness only changes the whitish part of the reflection. The blue diffuse reflection doesn't change at all—that's not how our physical world works! So, in applications aiming for more realistic effects, an artist would be tasked with manually tuning these values for each material until it "looked right", which is an inefficient method at best. There has to be a better way!

Enter **Physically-Based Rendering** (PBR), an approach to validate our material descriptions in the more objective, measurable, and scientific properties of real surfaces. One of the most apparent properties is the conservation of energy: a rougher surface will scatter light diffusely, while a smoother/more metallic surface will reflect light more directly, even though it's the same pool of light they are both drawn from. So, with all things being equal, the rule follows that as materials become shinier, the diffuse component should darken:

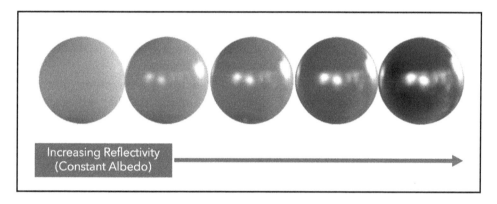

Of course, there's more to physically-based rendering than energy conservation; however, this is a clear example that demonstrates the properties of a physically-based system. By keeping the reflection models similar to the way materials work in real life, we reduce the need for subjective manual tuning and produce real-world materials that look realistic under a variety of light conditions.

Communities

Computer graphics is a vast landscape of complex, beautiful, and inspiring concepts. One of the best ways to learn, share, and inspire others is to involve yourself in communities dedicated to this discipline. Here is a non-exhaustive list of some of the most popular communities:

- **Chrome Experiments** (`https://experiments.withgoogle.com`) is an online showroom of web browser-based experiments, interactive programs, and artistic projects.
- **WebGL.com** (`https://WebGL.com`) is the leading community for WebGL developers and comprises demos, tutorials, news, and more.
- **SketchFab** (`https://sketchfab.com`) is a platform to publish, share, discover, buy, and sell 3D, VR, and AR content. It provides a viewer based on the WebGL and WebVR technologies that allows users to display 3D models on the web.
- **ShaderToy** (`https://www.shadertoy.com`) is a cross-browser online community and tool for creating and sharing shaders through WebGL, used both for learning and teaching 3D computer graphics in a web browser.
- **CGTrader** (`https://www.cgtrader.com/3D-models`) is an online platform that allows designers and modeling studios to upload and either sell or share their 3D models with their community.
- **TurboSquid** (`https://www.turbosquid.com`) is a digital media company that sells stock 3D models used in 3D graphics to a variety of industries, including computer games, architecture, and interactive training.
- **Poly** (`https://poly.google.com`) is a website that was created by Google for users to browse, distribute, and download 3D objects. It features a free library containing thousands of 3D objects that can be used in virtual reality and augmented reality applications.

Summary

Thank you for taking the time to read this book. By covering a wide range of topics—such as rendering, shaders, 3D math, lighting, cameras, textures, and many more—and guiding you in building compelling 3D applications, we hope that it has accomplished its goal of helping you learn interactive 3D computer graphics with WebGL 2.

> *"Stories don't end," he says. "They just turn into new beginnings."*
>
> *– Lindsay Eagar, Hour of the Bees*

With that in mind, please be sure to stay in touch and share your work—we look forward to seeing what you build! If you have any questions or feedback, please refer to the preface of this book for contact details.

Other Books You May Enjoy

If you enjoyed this book, you may be interested in these other books by Packt:

Mastering SVG
Rob Larsen

ISBN: 9781788626743

- Deliver the elements that make up an SVG image
- Replace your old CSS sprites with SVG
- Understand animation and data visualization with SVG are explained in pure JavaScript and using common libraries
- Use SVG to scale images across multiple devices easily
- Harness the power of CSS animations and transformations to manipulate your SVG images in a replicable, remixable way
- Interface SVG with common libraries and frameworks, such as jQuery, React, and Angular

Learn Three.js - Third Edition
Jos Dirksen

ISBN: 9781788833288

- Work with the different types of materials in Three.js and see how they interact with your 3D objects and the rest of the environment
- Implement the different camera controls provided by Three.js to effortlessly navigate around your 3D scene
- Work with vertices directly to create snow, rain, and galaxy-like effects
- Import and animate models from external formats, such as OBJ, STL, and COLLADA
- Create and run animations using morph targets and bones animations
- Explore advanced textures on materials to create realistic looking 3D objects by using bump maps, normal maps, specular maps, and light maps
- Interact directly with WebGL by creating custom vertex and fragment shaders

Leave a Review - Let Other Readers Know What You Think

Please share your thoughts on this book with others by leaving a review on the site that you bought it from. If you purchased the book from Amazon, please leave us an honest review on this book's Amazon page. This is vital so that other potential readers can see and use your unbiased opinion to make purchasing decisions, we can understand what our customers think about our products, and our authors can see your feedback on the title that they have worked with Packt to create. It will only take a few minutes of your time, but is valuable to other potential customers, our authors, and Packt. Thank you!

Index

www.ingramcontent.com/pod-product-compliance
Lightning Source LLC
Chambersburg PA
CBHW060641060326
40690CB00020B/4477